The Courts and the Charter

This is Volume 58 in the series of studies commissioned as part of the research program of the Royal Commission on the Economic Union and Development Prospects for Canada.

The studies contained in this volume reflect the views of their authors and do not imply endorsement by the Chairman or Commissioners.

The Courts
and the Charter

CLARE F. BECKTON
AND
A. WAYNE MACKAY
Research Coordinators

Published by the University of Toronto Press in cooperation with the Royal Commission on the Economic Union and Development Prospects for Canada and the Canadian Government Publishing Centre, Supply and Services Canada

University of Toronto Press
Toronto   Buffalo   London

Grateful acknowledgment is made to the following for permission to reprint previously published and unpublished material: Rt. Hon. Brian Dickson, P.C.; Schultheiss Polygraphischer Verlag, Zurich; Economica, Paris.

6003374632

Printed in Canada
ISBN 0-8020-7305-0
ISSN 0829-2396
Cat. No. Z1-1983/1-41-58E

CANADIAN CATALOGUING IN PUBLICATION DATA

Main entry under title:
The Courts and the Charter

(*The Collected research studies / Royal Commission on the Economic Union and Development Prospects for Canada*,
ISSN 0829-2396 ; 58)
Includes bibliographical references.
ISBN 0-8020-7305-0

1. Canada. Canadian Charter of Rights and Freedoms — Addresses, essays, lectures. 2. Canada — Constitutional law — Amendments — Addresses, essays, lectures. 3. Civil rights — Canada — Addresses, essays, lectures. 4. Canada — Constitutional law — Interpretation and construction — Addresses, essays, lectures. 5. Courts — Canada — Addresses, essays, lectures. I. Beckton, C. F. II. MacKay, A. Wayne, 1949–   III. Royal Commission on the Economic Union and Development Prospects for Canada. IV. Series: The Collected research studies (Royal Commission on the Economic Union and Development Prospects for Canada) ; 58.

KE4381.5.Z85C68 1985 342.71'085 C85-099486-1

PUBLISHING COORDINATION: Ampersand Communications Services Inc.
COVER DESIGN: Will Rueter
INTERIOR DESIGN: Brant Cowie/Artplus Limited

CONTENTS

When the members of the Rowell-Sirois Commission began their collective task in 1937, very little was known about the evolution of the Canadian economy. What was known, moreover, had not been extensively analyzed by the slender cadre of social scientists of the day.

When we set out upon our task nearly 50 years later, we enjoyed a substantial advantage over our predecessors; we had a wealth of information. We inherited the work of scholars at universities across Canada and we had the benefit of the work of experts from private research institutes and publicly sponsored organizations such as the Ontario Economic Council and the Economic Council of Canada. Although there were still important gaps, our problem was not a shortage of information; it was to interrelate and integrate — to synthesize — the results of much of the information we already had.

The mandate of this Commission is unusually broad. It encompasses many of the fundamental policy issues expected to confront the people of Canada and their governments for the next several decades. The nature of the mandate also identified, in advance, the subject matter for much of the research and suggested the scope of enquiry and the need for vigorous efforts to interrelate and integrate the research disciplines. The resulting research program, therefore, is particularly noteworthy in three respects: along with original research studies, it includes survey papers which synthesize work already done in specialized fields; it avoids duplication of work which, in the judgment of the Canadian research community, has already been well done; and, considered as a whole, it is the most thorough examination of the Canadian economic, political and legal systems ever undertaken by an independent agency.

The Commission's Research Program was carried out under the joint direction of three prominent and highly respected Canadian scholars: Dr. Ivan Bernier (*Law and Constitutional Issues*), Dr. Alan Cairns (*Politics and Institutions of Government*) and Dr. David C. Smith (*Economics*).

Dr. Ivan Bernier is Dean of the Faculty of Law at Laval University. Dr. Alan Cairns is former Head of the Department of Political Science at the University of British Columbia and, prior to joining the Commission, was William Lyon Mackenzie King Visiting Professor of Canadian Studies at Harvard University. Dr. David C. Smith, former Head of the Department of Economics at Queen's University in Kingston, is now Principal of that University. When Dr. Smith assumed his new responsibilities at Queen's in September, 1984, he was succeeded by Dr. Kenneth Norrie of the University of Alberta and John Sargent of the federal Department of Finance, who together acted as co-directors of Research for the concluding phase of the Economics research program.

I am confident that the efforts of the Research Directors, research coordinators and authors whose work appears in this and other volumes, have provided the community of Canadian scholars and policy makers with a series of publications that will continue to be of value for many years to come. And I hope that the value of the research program to Canadian scholarship will be enhanced by the fact that Commission research is being made available to interested readers in both English and French.

I extend my personal thanks, and that of my fellow Commissioners, to the Research Directors and those immediately associated with them in the Commission's research program. I also want to thank the members of the many research advisory groups whose counsel contributed so substantially to this undertaking.

DONALD S. MACDONALD

At its most general level, the Royal Commission's research program has examined how the Canadian political economy can better adapt to change. As a basis of enquiry, this question reflects our belief that the future will always take us partly by surprise. Our political, legal and economic institutions should therefore be flexible enough to accommodate surprises and yet solid enough to ensure that they help us meet our future goals. This theme of an adaptive political economy led us to explore the interdependencies between political, legal and economic systems and drew our research efforts in an interdisciplinary direction.

The sheer magnitude of the research output (over 280 separate studies in 72 volumes) as well as its disciplinary and ideological diversity have, however, made complete integration impossible and, we have concluded, undesirable. The research output as a whole brings varying perspectives and methodologies to the study of common problems and we therefore urge readers to look beyond their particular field of interest and to explore topics across disciplines.

The three research areas, *Law and Constitutional Issues*, under Ivan Bernier, *Politics and Institutions of Government* under Alan Cairns, and *Economics* under David C. Smith (co-directed with Kenneth Norrie and John Sargent for the concluding phase of the research program) — were further divided into 19 sections headed by research coordinators.

The area *Law and Constitutional Issues* has been organized into five major sections headed by the research coordinators identified below.

- Law, Society and the Economy — *Ivan Bernier and Andrée Lajoie*
- The International Legal Environment — *John J. Quinn*

- The Canadian Economic Union — *Mark Krasnick*
- Harmonization of Laws in Canada — *Ronald C.C. Cuming*
- Institutional and Constitutional Arrangements — *Clare F. Beckton and A. Wayne MacKay*

Since law in its numerous manifestations is the most fundamental means of implementing state policy, it was necessary to investigate how and when law could be mobilized most effectively to address the problems raised by the Commission's mandate. Adopting a broad perspective, researchers examined Canada's legal system from the standpoint of how law evolves as a result of social, economic and political changes and how, in turn, law brings about changes in our social, economic and political conduct.

Within *Politics and Institutions of Government*, research has been organized into seven major sections.

- Canada and the International Political Economy — *Denis Stairs and Gilbert Winham*
- State and Society in the Modern Era — *Keith Banting*
- Constitutionalism, Citizenship and Society — *Alan Cairns and Cynthia Williams*
- The Politics of Canadian Federalism — *Richard Simeon*
- Representative Institutions — *Peter Aucoin*
- The Politics of Economic Policy — *G. Bruce Doern*
- Industrial Policy — *André Blais*

This area examines a number of developments which have led Canadians to question their ability to govern themselves wisely and effectively. Many of these developments are not unique to Canada and a number of comparative studies canvass and assess how others have coped with similar problems. Within the context of the Canadian heritage of parliamentary government, federalism, a mixed economy, and a bilingual and multicultural society, the research also explores ways of rearranging the relationships of power and influence among institutions to restore and enhance the fundamental democratic principles of representativeness, responsiveness and accountability.

Economics research was organized into seven major sections.

- Macroeconomics — *John Sargent*
- Federalism and the Economic Union — *Kenneth Norrie*
- Industrial Structure — *Donald G. McFetridge*
- International Trade — *John Whalley*
- Income Distribution and Economic Security — *François Vaillancourt*
- Labour Markets and Labour Relations — *Craig Riddell*
- Economic Ideas and Social Issues — *David Laidler*

Economics research examines the allocation of Canada's human and other resources, how institutions and policies affect this allocation, and the distribution of the gains from their use. It also considers the nature of economic development, the forces that shape our regional and industrial structure, and our economic interdependence with other countries. The thrust of the research in economics is to increase our comprehension of what determines our economic potential and how instruments of economic policy may move us closer to our future goals.

One section from each of the three research areas — The Canadian Economic Union, The Politics of Canadian Federalism, and Federalism and the Economic Union — have been blended into one unified research effort. Consequently, the volumes on Federalism and the Economic Union as well as the volume on The North are the results of an interdisciplinary research effort.

We owe a special debt to the research coordinators. Not only did they organize, assemble and analyze the many research studies and combine their major findings in overviews, but they also made substantial contributions to the Final Report. We wish to thank them for their performance, often under heavy pressure.

Unfortunately, space does not permit us to thank all members of the Commission staff individually. However, we are particularly grateful to the Chairman, The Hon. Donald S. Macdonald, the Commission's Executive Director, Gerald Godsoe, and the Director of Policy, Alan Nymark, all of whom were closely involved with the Research Program and played key roles in the contribution of Research to the Final Report. We wish to express our appreciation to the Commission's Administrative Advisor, Harry Stewart, for his guidance and advice, and to the Director of Publishing, Ed Matheson, who managed the research publication process. A special thanks to Jamie Benidickson, Policy Coordinator and Special Assistant to the Chairman, who played a valuable liaison role between Research and the Chairman and Commissioners. We are also grateful to our office administrator, Donna Stebbing, and to our secretarial staff, Monique Carpentier, Barbara Cowtan, Tina DeLuca, Françoise Guilbault and Marilyn Sheldon.

Finally, a well deserved thank you to our closest assistants, Jacques J.M. Shore, *Law and Constitutional Issues*; Cynthia Williams and her successor Karen Jackson, *Politics and Institutions of Government*; and I. Lilla Connidis, *Economics*. We appreciate not only their individual contribution to each research area, but also their cooperative contribution to the research program and the Commission.

IVAN BERNIER
ALAN CAIRNS
DAVID C. SMITH

Courts have in the past played a significant role in the shaping of Canadian economic and social policy, but they have done so in a very low-profile way. In recent years the role of the courts as a distinct political institution has grown in both dimension and profile. This growth will be accentuated by the arrival on the Canadian scene of the Charter of Rights and Freedoms on April 17, 1982. In the overview for this research section, found in the companion volume (Volume 57 of the Commission's Collected Research Studies), the courts are referred to as an emerging national institution.

The present volume contains a unique collection of articles about the past, present and future role of courts in Canadian society and the likely impact of the Charter of Rights and Freedoms. Professor Henri Brun makes a scholarly analysis of how the Charter has modified some of Canada's basic constitutional principles. Supremacy of Parliament has been blunted but not broken, and rather than embrace U.S.- style judicial supremacy, Canada has adopted a middle position between that of the United Kingdom and that of the United States. Professor Brun labels the new judicial status as judicial primacy.

Mary Eberts brings her expertise as a student of equality and her experience as a litigator to the difficult task of assessing the impact of the Charter's equality provisions, which came into effect on April 17, 1985. In a thorough and scholarly fashion Ms. Eberts examines first the kind of government institutions that will be swept into the Charter net; then she makes a close analysis of the section 15 equality provisions and speculates on their broad impact. While Ms. Eberts argues that the Charter should be used as a tool of social reform, Professor Brun in his paper cautions that the Charter not be used to impede legislative efforts at social reform.

Even as the volume moves to the more institutional evaluation of courts it cannot escape the ghost of the Charter. Professors Wayne MacKay and Richard Bauman argue that the policy-making role of the Supreme Court of Canada will be greatly extended by the Charter. Their focus is reform of an emerging national institution — the Supreme Court of Canada. After a thorough and well documented examination of previous reform proposals, MacKay and Bauman reject most of them and call for a constitutionally entrenched court to be appointed by a new Appointing Council. Rejecting regional representation as a sacred principle for appointments to Canada's highest court, the authors call for diversity and pluralism as the best foundation for post-Charter interpretation.

The Supreme Court of Canada is not the only court in the judicial constellation, and Professor Gilles Pépin suggests that there be significant change in the broader judicial structure. Drawing upon his extensive writing and research on section 96 of the *Constitution Act, 1867*, Professor Pépin argues that the Constitution not be used to block provincial iniatives in dispute resolution, whether at the inferior court or administrative tribunal level. What is needed is fresh thinking about how modern disputes should be resolved, not historical dissection of how things were done in 1867.

These rich judicial patches go together to form an interesting coat of many colours. The authors themselves are an example of the diversity which they applaud. Quebec, Ontario, the Maritimes and the West are the regional origins of the authors who also reflect a range of experiences and perspectives: academic, practising lawyer, anglophone, francophone, female, male and varying political views.

This volume will provide an excellent jumping off point for what will undoubtedly become the popular sport of court watching.

A. WAYNE MACKAY

ACKNOWLEDGMENTS

The authors would like to acknowledge the leadership and assistance of Dean Ivan Bernier, Director of Research (Constitutional/Legal), who demonstrated the twin virtues of patience and understanding. We would also like to thank Jacques J.M. Shore, Executive Assistant and Research Program Administrator, who added vital doses of enthusiasm, encouragement and contagious good cheer.

A.W.M.

The Canadian Charter of Rights and Freedoms as an Instrument of Social Development

HENRI BRUN

Introduction

The Canadian Charter of Rights and Freedoms came into focus on April 17, 1982,[1] but its impact is still difficult to assess. Until the Supreme Court of Canada has handed down a considerable number of decisions on the Charter, anything that is said about it will be largely conjecture.[2]

Since April 1982, there has been a wealth of legal writing pertaining to the Charter. The courts have handed down well over one thousand decisions on the Charter, fifty or more by courts of appeal one level below the Supreme Court of Canada. The literature includes fifteen books and at least forty journal articles, a number that may appear excessive in so short a time.[3] Is there any point in adding to this body of literature? In most of their decisions, the courts have merely answered the questions put to them, which is quite proper. When they have commented more generally on the role of the Charter, they have usually done so in a reserved and cautious fashion.

The authors of the legal literature, on the other hand, have usually been more willing to deal with general principles and in doing so have been notably unanimous and repetitive. With very few exceptions, they have not diverged from the classic libertarian position so common among Anglo-Saxon jurists.

Since April 1982, the message from Canadian authors has been in the form of an invitation to judges not to hesitate to invoke the rights of the Charter to oppose acts of legislatures or governments. The Charter is a formal constitutional document and thus has supremacy over the laws of Parliament; judges must therefore apply it in a spirit of liberalism. Therefore, the Charter should receive a broad and generous interpretation; the linguistic version most favourable to the individual should be used. When called upon, the onus is on Parliament to prove that its laws are reasonable or necessary, and it should not rely on the principle of presumption of constitutionality. This is the dominant theme, which amounts to an obsession with some authors, judging from the number of pages they devote to it.

Such a doctrinal approach was predictable; indeed, it was inevitable in light of the experience of the Canadian Bill of Rights,[4] which received a very cautious judicial interpretation. It is, however, a one-sided approach and could be harmful if it succeeded in exerting significant moral or social pressure on judges.

Since the decision has already been made to entrench a charter of fundamental human rights in the Constitution, it necessarily follows that a portion of the state's power has been transferred from the legislature to the judiciary.[5] We must now determine how and under what conditions the Charter can best serve Canadian society. Thus, while it may be useful to remind judges that they have a new power, it is more useful to reflect upon the real nature of this new instrument and on the context in which it should be used.

This reflection requires that certain distinctions be made about how a constitutional charter should be handled in Canada. My fundamental thesis is that it is important to make a clear distinction between the *interpretation* and the *application* of this new legal instrument. In other words, it is as important to apply the Charter generously as it is to interpret the rights contained in it with circumspection.

Any contrary approach would be liable to cause much dissatisfaction. A narrow application of the Charter, entangled in a technical definition of the scope of its application and its rights, would produce immediate frustration. However, an absolutist interpretation of the Charter's rights, even when accompanied by generous intentions, would run the risk of simply delaying the frustration. A generous interpretation of human rights, which at the time seems benevolent to the individual, may very well at a later time become an argument against using the law to assist the social classes who need it most.

In more general terms, a *broad application* and a *cautious interpretation* of the Canadian Charter can be expected to help it play its proper role of watchdog. This will enable the Charter to respond to the basic issues it is asked to resolve without preventing the rest of the law from choosing practical means of advancing that social development, whose objectives after all are those of the Charter: liberty, justice and equality.

In itself, the Charter is not an instrument of social development. Rather, it is the statement of the general objectives of sound development; consequently, it is natural that it would not thwart the concrete means by which such development takes place. Therefore, the Charter will be faithful to its proper mission if its field of application is as broad as possible, provided that the rights contained in it are interpreted as inclusively as possible; in other words, on condition that its interpreters realize that the development of Canadian society takes place in other ways.

The Real Nature of the Charter

Fundamental human rights, as found in the Charter as a whole, are the laws that govern laws. They formulate material standards within which the law must be confined.

Fundamental rights constitute a specific field of law that deals with the law itself. They relate to precise situations but only to the extent that the law helps them to come into being or to be maintained. Such situations are generally considered to be the most unjust legal situations for individuals, that is, those in which the law prevents free expression, those in which a legal rule is applied in defiance of certain substantive and procedural principles, and finally, those in which a legal rule makes undue distinctions between individuals. The Charter addresses these three situations by proclaiming the right to freedom of expression, the right to due process of law and the right to equality.

Injustice does not, of course, flow only from the law. In principle, the law exists in order to reduce injustice. The ultimate purpose of the law is to counterbalance the power of some against the weakness of others through corrective and distributive justice.[6] Thus, it would be pointless to claim that fundamental human rights are intended to cover the various factual situations that are sources of injustice and frustration for individuals. To do so would be to claim that fundamental rights and the law are one and the same thing, and thus to deprive the field of fundamental human rights of any specificity and therefore, any purpose.

Human rights, as a specific field of law, deal only with the law. They require that laws and everything that flows from them (regulations, contracts, judgments, and so on) should obey certain principles that are considered to be fundamental. The juridical role of fundamental rights is of the greatest importance, so that its focus must be precise and clearly defined.[7]

It has been argued that the Charter is drafted in overly general terms but in my opinion, this criticism is unfounded. In their capacity as standards, fundamental rights can be expressed only in very general terms. But one criticism that can be made of the authors of the Charter is that they took the opportunity to regulate certain factual situations that do not really fall within the field of fundamental rights.[8] As an instrument of fundamental human rights, a charter should not contain minor details and endless explanations; it should be the direct opposite of, for example, fiscal legislation.

The above comments demonstrate both the importance and the limitations of fundamental rights. Their importance lies in the fact that they deal with essential matters, the matters that are vital to society; in other words, to the individual. Their limitations result from the fact that they are only a framework for the law and are, consequently, unable to make a positive contribution to the development of society.[9] Fundamental rights and the charters in which they are proclaimed are in one sense preventive measures and, in another, a last line of defence.[10]

The concept of fundamental rights can, of course, serve nonjudicial purposes. For example, it can serve to promote certain values: in this respect its field is virtually unlimited. Even charters of positive rights sometimes contain provisions that suggest or claim that the law is obliged to deal with particular factual situations. However, these efforts to predetermine the areas where the law should intervene fail to provide truly effective sanctions when they do more than simply refer to the state of current law.[11]

Basically, charters of rights delineate the areas in which the law may intervene. This is essentially what the Canadian Charter does. Its use of any particular situation should depend on the real nature of the Charter.

Constitutional Context of the Charter

The context of the Charter calls into question two principles of constitutional law in particular: first, the principle of the supremacy of Parliament as the primary principle governing the operations of the Canadian state; and second, the federal principle as the primary principle governing the organization of this state.

Since the adoption of the Charter was not accompanied by constitutional amendments relating to the principles by which the Canadian state should operate, Canadian law continues to exist and evolve in step with the work of the eleven governments and legislatures. And, although the courts have a new means of intervention, it is still very much within the traditional role played by the courts, which is to control and sanction. If used indiscriminately, the Charter could weaken the social fabric of the country.

Nor was the Charter accompanied by any modification in the federal character of Canada's Constitution. In some fields, the law must continue to develop independently in the various provinces just as, in other fields, it develops in the federation as a whole. An ill-considered application of the Charter could have dangerous centralizing effects upon the diversity and duality of the country.

Parliamentary, Collective or Judicial Sovereignty?

Some authors have claimed that the Charter put an end to the supremacy of Parliament. Others, more subtle or politically minded, have said that the Charter marked the arrival of collective sovereignty.

Parliamentary and Collective Sovereignty

It should be stated from the outset that the existence of collective sovereignty has very little to do with the Charter. What matters is to know where the ultimate power resides in the state. However, it has long been recognized that the power of the Canadian state rests with the collectivity, even though the principle has not been explicitly proclaimed as it has in the constitutions of some other countries.[12] It may even be said that, at the present time, all states expressly or tacitly base their authority on the collective sovereignty. The real question then, is whether this collective supremacy is a reality in law and in fact.

As noted above, the supremacy of Parliament is an operating principle of the state. It means that, in Canada, as in various other countries, parliaments (both federal and provincial) gradually formulate the state's ultimate judicial standards. The supremacy of Parliament in no way means that Parliament and the legislatures have supreme authority in the Canadian state.[13] The supremacy of Parliament is an operating principle for the state, but it does not contradict the idea that the collectivity is sovereign in the state. On the contrary, to the extent that it establishes a genuine representative democracy, the supremacy of Parliament contributes to the realization of a collective sovereignty.

That situation has not been changed substantially by the Charter, since collective sovereignty was already firmly established in Canada, above and beyond the letter of the Constitution. By formally introducing freedom of expression and the right to vote into the Constitution, the Charter confirms and protects that reality. However, by transferring the powers of elected parliaments to appointed judges, it does diminish their scope. Are we, then, justified in suggesting that we have passed from a regime of parliamentary sovereignty to one of judicial sovereignty?

Parliamentary and Judicial Sovereignty

Since the adoption of the Charter, most authors have suggested that judges may behave as if the supremacy of Parliament no longer existed. This advice may not be based on an entirely accurate evaluation of the Constitution. If it is simply a matter of making judges aware that they have acquired a new power, that of invalidating laws for reasons other than the federal division of powers, the point is self-evident and does not need to be stressed. Since the Charter is part of the country's formal Constitution, it has supra-legislative force and is binding on Parliament and the legislatures; thus, the courts may, by invoking the Charter, declare laws invalid. While it is true that the actual experience with the Bill of Rights may explain why so much is made of the courts' new power,[14] other reasons must also be considered.

The supremacy of Parliament has been weakened in the sense that the laws of Parliament may now be challenged in the courts by virtue of specific criteria set forth in the Charter.[15] It remains unweakened, however, in the sense that the parliaments are still the bodies authorized to express the ultimate standards of the state in accordance with the Constitution. And dynamic law, the body of law that a society gradually creates for itself as its needs evolve, continues to flow, at the very highest level, from parliamentary legislation.

The Charter has changed nothing in the field of constitutional law relating to the functioning of the state. The laws can be challenged in the courts, but only parliaments can make laws. The Charter permits no one, not even the courts, to replace parliaments.

Although this new role for the courts is important, it is essentially passive, since, like a fire extinguisher, it operates only in an emergency. It can prevent the worst, but it is powerless to nourish the living law that a society needs.

The Charter of Rights has in no sense deprived the legislative bodies of their responsibility to act as the primary agents in the continuous evolution and reform of the law. The Charter's purpose is quite different — to guard against extreme situations. If its interpretation draws it too rapidly outside its proper domain, the law will inevitably lose its flexibility.

A charter of rights is a particularly conservative judicial instrument: it sets and establishes certain values, for a considerable time. Our respect for established values leads us to erect monuments to them and write them in stone, as the Babylonians did with their Code of Hammurabi some 2,000 years before Christ. On the other hand, not everyone is in fact completely able to enjoy these established values. It is those in high places who are best situated to benefit to the full.

The Canadian Charter as a whole does sanction truly fundamental rights: freedom of expression, due process of law and equality. Therefore, there can be no objection to the entrenchment of these rights simply because they might occasionally be of service to those who need them least. In the case of fundamental values, a little is better than nothing.

On the other hand, precisely because they deal only with the legal aspects of fundamental rights as described at the beginning of this paper, the rights in the Charter must be given an interpretation that does not prevent parliaments from adopting social, cultural and economic legislation likely to encourage access to fundamental rights. This proposition calls for a cautious interpretation of the rights of the Charter, in other words, an inclusive interpretation that takes into consideration the actual weight of the values contained in the laws that are challenged.

It must be remembered that, in itself, the Charter is utterly powerless to improve the lot of native people, women, and linguistic minorities, including the French-speaking minority throughout Canada. For the poor, its effect is even more cosmetic. In fact, if the Charter did not contain a few loopholes, it would confirm the deplorable lot of these Canadians.[16]

The only means of improving the position of these most vulnerable Canadians is through ordinary legislation. However, such action should not always be hampered by a blind interpretation of the rights contained in the Charter. The *Income Tax Act*,[17] which enables the state to take the taxpayer's money in spite of the right to equality and in spite of the right to enjoyment of property, is perhaps the legislation most likely to improve the situation of those who are the most dispossessed,[18] just as the *Criminal Code*[19] is perhaps the most precious of laws for those who are weakest.

Even though the Charter proclaims equality for men and women, if such equality does not in fact exist in real social, economic and cultural terms, its proclamation merely accentuates the insecurity of the weakest: a woman living in a state of equality will have no right to support payments even if her unemployment is a result of the years she has spent away from the labour market to raise children.[20] Conversely, any measure that promotes a different division of social functions between the two sexes might appear contrary to the abstract ideal of equality if it were not for the loophole in section 15(2).[21]

A charter of rights is a shield that can guard against serious attacks but it should not be allowed to obscure the horizon. It should receive a cautious and circumstantial interpretation, not because it does not provide bread and butter, not because it gives additional powers to appointed judges rather than to elected representatives, but because a blind and unbridled interpretation of its rights will only reduce juridical dynamism and curb social development.

With respect to this first aspect of the Charter, there should be very serious and profound reasons for condemning any law in the name of fundamental rights. Mere appearances must, of necessity, be set aside, for if they are not, there is a danger that these fundamental rights will serve goals diametrically opposed to their purpose, namely, the protection and well-being of those who are most vulnerable.[22] Thus, before condemning a legislative measure in the name of human rights, it could be important simply to realize that we may be dealing with a professional corporation clinging to its financial assets despite a serious financial crisis.[23] Similarly, the expropriation of a mining company may, depending upon the circumstances, be seen either as an attack on property rights or as a job creation measure. The extremely general nature of fundamental rights in a charter calls for interpretations that are as concrete as possible.[24]

The Charter is a mechanism for safeguarding the vital functions of society. This is its major role. Any careless application of its provisions could cause some segment of society to reject it. It may save a life, but its very nature is not such as to improve the quality of that life. For this reason, we must still rely on parliaments and governments.

Union, Standardization or Centralization?

Moreover, the Charter exists in a federal context: Canadian constitutional law is federal in organizational terms just as the supremacy of Parliament is federal in terms of the functioning of the state.

In 1867, the founding provinces of the federation decided to transfer some of their power to common authorities. The criteria governing this division of powers were not gratuitous: the provinces intended to maintain under their exclusive jurisdiction the matters that they considered essential for preserving their identities. This objective was, of course, more important for some provinces than for others.

In 1982, the Charter subjected the entire body of Canadian law, both provincial and federal, whether it was passed before or after that year, to certain uniform material standards. Setting aside the conditions under which these standards were created (which are not the subject of this paper), this context alone supports the suggestion that the rights of the Charter ought to be interpreted cautiously.

There is no doubt that the objectives of those who promoted the Charter included a more unified Canada and even a uniformity of its laws.[25] The objective of centralization, on the other hand, is less obvious because people are less willing to admit it. In any case, we are interested not so much in intentions as in the reality of the Charter's impact.

Section 31 of the Charter is clearly misleading. Yet, it has been used widely for the purposes for which it was designed. This section says in essence that the Charter does not increase the legislative powers of anyone in Canada, which is a truism. The section does, however, serve to mask a real transfer of power from Parliament and the legislatures to the judiciary under conditions that can only increase the centralization of the country. The simple fact that it contains national standards is, in our opinion, evidence of a measure of centralization. Although these standards are not only the fruit of federal institutions, they are, nevertheless, the product of a centralized power base.

On the other hand, certain provisions of the Charter do not fall within the usual domain of fundamental rights. Their presence in the Charter can only be explained by the federal character of the Constitution, and their terms demonstrate an obvious desire to regulate, at the central level, certain issues that were previously considered too decentralized. This holds particularly true for the provisions dealing with mobility rights and with language rights in education.[26]

Some rights in the Charter are defined using standards that refer primarily to federal law or to that of the majority of the provinces or to both. That is the case, for example, when determining what is cruel, unreasonable or unusual, as in sections 8, 11a and 12 of the Charter, and also in deciding what is reasonable and justified in a free and democratic society as in section 1. The courts have already had occasion to interpret these various concepts by referring to what is taking place in the country as a whole.[27]

It is, however, the living Charter that is avowedly centralist, a constant source of specific and detailed standards designed to meet the needs of real situations. This detailing of the principles of the Charter, which are by their nature very general, is intended to be used more often than not in certain places in central Canada where the population is larger, where certain activities take place, and according to perceptions particular to such milieus. It is very interesting to note that approximately 40 percent of the decisions by Canadian courts of appeal, including the Federal Court of Appeal, reported up to March 1, 1984, have been rendered by the Ontario Court of Appeal sitting in Toronto.[28]

However, the courts cannot be asked to interpret the Charter differently in different parts of Canada, or to act differently according to whether they are dealing with federal or provincial law. Indeed, the courts have quite rightly defended the principle of a standard interpretation.[29] It is thus inevitable that the dominant attitudes should become even more dominant. The rule of *stare decisis* exerts a strong influence on Canadian courts to follow the jurisprudence of higher courts in other Canadian jurisdictions.[30]

Lastly, we should not lose sight of the fact that there is an extreme centralization in the Canadian judicial hierarchy, to which the Charter has transferred a substantial slice of national power. Let us not forget that all the judges of superior courts are appointed by the federal government and that the Supreme Court of Canada, an institution that is exclusively federal in every respect, is in all areas, and particularly with respect to the constitutional Charter, the court of last resort.[31]

If the federal character of the Constitution is to remain a living reality, then the Charter must be interpreted in a cautious and circumstantial manner. Further, given the much more political role that the constitutional judge is expected to play as a result of the Charter, it also gives some urgency to the reform of our judicial institutions. Under the Charter, the political role of the judge is much more important, both quantitatively and qualitatively, than it was when we had simply the division of powers between Ottawa and the provinces. It is no longer the form or vehicle that is in question here; what we are now dealing with, directly and immediately, are the substantive values of a society.[32]

The main reply to this moderating approach is, of course, the universal character of fundamental human rights. How could a charter threaten a federation if the rights it proclaims are common to all peoples?

First, as we have already noted, the Canadian Charter contains exceptions to this notion of universality.[33] However, the real answer to this argument is that human rights are universal only when expressed in a theoretical and abstract way, which implies very general concepts. In their practical interpretation, which must necessarily be factual and closely integrated with the actual experiences of individuals, this universality is considerably blunted. When human rights penetrate the particular milieu of individual peoples and groups, they must take into consideration the cultural characteristics and specific needs of those groups. It is here that a charter of rights may possibly play a role.[34]

Given its context, the Canadian Charter should be interpreted carefully and circumspectly rather than aggressively, since the latter type of interpretation would tend to minimize Canada's diversity. It would, after all, be paradoxical if this instrument of justice, made necessary in part by the depersonalizing tendency of the law, should eventually serve to deny individuals and groups the right to their own identity.

Section 27 of the Charter recognizes this imperative in requiring that it be interpreted in a manner consistent with promoting, preserving and enhancing the multicultural heritage of Canadians. Such a clause should carry a great deal of weight when, for example, a Charter right is applied to Quebec civil law or native civil law.[35] The Charter must leave room for recourse to a law, in the name of the right to be different, which, in the final analysis, is perhaps the only truly universal right.[36]

The constitutional judge must make sure that the judicial acculturation flowing from the Charter is limited to what is ineluctably imposed by the intrinsically centralizing influence of such an instrument in a federal country. The strongest proponents of the argument that interpretations of the Charter should draw upon the American Bill of Rights never fail to add that this should not, however, occur to the detriment of the Canadian cultural identity, a fragile identity characterized by, among other things, a greater trust in the state than in individual laissez-faire.[37] What, then, holds true for the cultural relationship between Canada and the United States should even more so hold true for the cultural relationship between Quebec and Canada.

The organizational framework of the Canadian state plays a role similar to that of its functional framework: it suggests that the rights of the Charter should receive a serious and careful interpretation and one that attempts to get to the heart of the matter on the basis of concrete realities. An overly enthusiastic interpretation, or one that simply seeks attention, would reduce the dynamism and diversity of Canadian society. By contrast, however, the *application* of the Charter should be as broad as possible. As an instrument of last resort, designed to deal with essentials, its field of application should not be defined artificially or capriciously.

Interpretation of the Rights of the Charter

Because of its constitutional status and the mobility of its objectives, the Charter should be guaranteed as broad an application as possible. Nevertheless, the day-to-day interpretation of the rights contained in it should, for the reasons given above, take two factors into consideration: the essentially passive and conservative role of a Charter; and the standardizing and centralizing impact of such a charter in a federal country. Otherwise, the Charter may betray its objectives.

The drafters of the Charter were conscious of this danger. The first section invites the constitutional judge not to interpret its rights in an absolute or abstract fashion. Therefore, it provides interpretation guidelines whose meaning and functioning are worthy of consideration.

Section 1 of the Charter: An Interpretation Clause

In essence, section 1 of the Charter requires that reasonable rules of law should not be found incompatible with the rights of the Charter. This criterion of reasonableness is, in our opinion, a guideline for interpreting the various rights of the Charter; that is to say, a standard by which they should be judged and not a means to avoid or derogate these rights. This is a justifiable position that has certain consequences.

It is often said that section 1 is a clause of exception or derogation of the rights guaranteed by the Charter. This argument seems faithful neither to the letter nor to the context of this provision. As we shall see, however, our understanding of section 1 conditions its use and function; similarly, it conditions, to a great extent, the way in which the Charter is applied.

The terms used in the Charter, in this regard, are "restreints" in the French version and "limits" in the English version. The restrictions or limitations to which these two words refer can easily be an integral part of the definition of the rights protected by the Charter. This is clearly not the case with respect to exceptions or derogations to these rights. There is a difference in kind between these two groups of ideas: the former may apply only to constitutional judges in order to guide them in their work of interpretation, whereas the latter necessarily applies to legislators because it implies, as do amendments, abrogations or restrictions, an active reversal of something that already exists.[38] However, the context of section 1 gives credence to the idea that that section should be evaluated and dealt with as an interpretation clause that provides a full understanding of the rights to be protected by the Charter, and not as a clause that allows us to avoid, derogate from, or make an exception to, rights that are in other respects fully defined.

As is appropriate, the Charter sets forth in very general terms the principal rights it seeks to protect. As formulated, these rights clearly cannot be taken to be absolute. They must necessarily be interpreted and defined using external guidelines.

One might go so far as to say that if section 1 did not exist, judges would have to provide themselves with an equivalent as they did for the Canadian Bill of Rights and for the American Bill of Rights, which contain no such interpretation clause. We may also assume that the drafters of the Charter formulated section 1 in order to ensure that Canadian courts would not apply to the Charter the implicit interpretation clause that they created for the Bill of Rights.[39]

A number of authorities have criticized the courts for using section 1 of the Charter too often. However, this criticism seems unjustified. The principal rights of the Charter are expressed in such general terms that, by themselves, they have no functional meaning. It is essential that they be transformed from abstract absolutes to situations that are relatively concrete. In order to bring them down to earth, they have to be given an interpretation, something that the Charter itself suggests should be done by reference to section 1. Any interpretation of a right that is limited to the words in which it is expressed remains an abstraction that does not correspond to the requirements of the Charter.

However, to a certain extent, the same is not true of the rights in the Charter that are not really fundamental human rights.[40] These rights have been elaborated in such detail that they are, in themselves, sufficient[41] to hold the courts' attention.

Furthermore, in a general way, it is understandable that the courts would at first do no more than articulate the fundamental right in question, even if only to verify at the outset the existence of a minimal connection between this right and the state of the disputed law.[42] Yet the first phase in this two-step process will not amount to very much in the case of true human rights such as freedom of expression, equality and due process of law. Since judges are not justified in leaving it at that point, except in the absence of any cause of action, basically what they have to do is to ask themselves whether the state of the disputed law is reasonable.

As far as the more explicit provisions of section 6 and sections 16 to 23 are concerned, as noted above, one could alternatively say that section 1 does not have to enter the picture. On the one hand, the textual basis for this is not clear, and on the other hand, we doubt that these rights could in any case be formulated in sufficient detail that any challenge to them would be unconstitutional.[43] This interpretative role of section 1 also flows from the terms of the Charter and from its position in the Constitution Act, 1982.

It should be emphasized that the primary function of section 1 is to guarantee the rights and freedoms set out in the Charter.

Since it is part of the Constitution, the Charter renders inoperative any incompatible provisions of any other legal rule.[44] However, incompatibility is itself a relative concept. According to Canadian constitutional law, only operational or absolute incompatibility produces inoperability, a fact that clearly authorizes the limitation or amendment of rights.[45] By guaranteeing the rights and freedoms of the Charter, the first part of section 1 modifies this situation in the case of the Charter. Everything that negatively affects the rights guaranteed by the Charter is incompatible, but the rights thus guaranteed by the Charter are precisely the rights restricted and limited by reasonable laws and are not absolute rights. The

English version of section 1 is particularly eloquent in this regard.

Whatever approach is used, section 1 clearly seems to be the means by which the rights guaranteed by the Charter are correctly interpreted and understood and not a means of avoiding or derogating these rights or of amending or circumventing them. There are concrete consequences which derive from this. In a general sense it requires the constitutional judge to reason in the actual context of the conflict between values contained by the Charter and the rest of the law rather than speculate on the semantics of the words used by the Charter in formulating various rights.[46] The real question is what this rule of interpretation means.

The Meaning of Section 1

The basic problem, then, is to decide what is meant by reasonable, which is no mean feat, even in a specific context. In this context, reasonableness may be viewed in absolute or relative terms. The first notion refers to an intrinsic evaluation of the point at issue, the second to an evaluation that establishes the relationship between the point at issue and some value expressed in the Charter.

If one follows the absolutist approach, the only rules of law that would be contrary to the Charter would be those which, in the eyes of the constitutional judge, were unreasonable, irrational, absurd, arbitrary, gratuitous or whimsical. In other words, the constitutional judge would have only to question the pertinence of the rule by examining whether it pursued its purpose using means that bear a relationship to that purpose. This approach and its vocabulary are derived from a principle of administrative law relating to the exercise of regulatory power.[47]

Despite the jurisprudence deriving from the Bill of Rights, it would seem clear that this interpretation of section 1 must be rejected,[48] essentially because such an interpretation leads to the same type of excess, but at the opposite extreme, that results from the notion of an equally absolutist interpretation of the rights set forth in the Charter. With an absolutist approach, as we have seen, it would be possible to interpret the rights of the Charter without clarification of the values transmitted by the various legal rules being challenged, whereas according to the notion under consideration here, these legal rules could be considered without referring to the specific values guaranteed by the Charter. An absolutist interpretation of the criterion of reasonableness means, in fact, that section 1 is itself sufficient and that it summarizes the entire Charter, an argument that would seem difficult to support.

Relative reasonableness opens two doors: that of necessity and that of proportionality. If understood in this manner, the reasonableness of a legal rule suggests that a choice has to be made between the values defended by the Charter and those pursued by the rule in question. The essential point is to know whether the constitutional judges are thereby substituting their choice for that of Parliament or whether they are reserving their intervention for a certain type of case. Can they require that any legislation affecting Charter rights should flow from strict necessity, or should they simply condemn only that which affects the Charter in an exaggerated, inadequate, excessive, unbalanced, disproportionate or abusive manner vis-à-vis the goal being pursued?

For the reasons stated above, it would seem that the choice should be made in favour of the proportionality test: only those measures affecting a Charter right in a manner disproportionate to their aim would be contrary to the Charter.[49] The choice of the necessity test would, on the other hand, suggest a radical change in the organizational and operational rules of the state, a change that was not made by the constitutional reform of 1982.

Necessity, as a criterion of control, differs markedly from the test of reasonableness. Moreover, it would appear completely inappropriate as a principle of judicial control. It is far too broad: it enables the judiciary to substitute itself entirely for the legislature in assessing what is in the public interest. It creates an obstacle that may render legislative activity impractical, given the very broad and general character of the principal rights of the Charter.

The European Human Rights Convention speaks of necessity,[50] as do some national constitutions.[51] However, even in these instances, jurisprudence has been obliged to develop a less rigorous test.[52] The concept of reasonableness as a criterion for interpreting the rights of the Charter seems to be a clear invitation to the constitutional judges to prefer their own perception of the needs of society only in the case of excess or disproportion.

The reference to the notion of a free and democratic society in section 1 also suggests minimal respect for the decisions of elected parliaments.[53] This is not to suggest that the Charter consequently has no supremacy over parliamentary legislation. The section makes it clear that justification must be shown to exist, but it would seem that this reference could allow the constitutional judge to exercise a greater or lesser degree of proportionality, depending upon the level of state intervention in question. The terms of the Charter do not allow such distinctions on the basis of the various fundamental rights in the Charter.[54] On the other hand, there is nothing to prevent a distinction of degree being made between the test applicable to the elected legislators and that applicable to others: governments, judges, school boards, individuals, and so on.[55]

The Functioning of Section 1

ABSTRACT OR CASE-BY-CASE INTERPRETATION?

Section 1 is the general interpretation clause of the rights and freedoms in the Charter. Since it requires that a test of reasonableness be applied to the various measures challenged under the Charter, this interpretation clause requires that the rights of the Charter be interpreted on a case-by-case basis. This means that the general principle of interpretation, which provides that the Constitution shall be interpreted strictly on the basis of the needs of each case, applies to the constitutional Charter.[56]

Such case-by-case interpretations will eventually produce a general interpretation of the rights of the Charter, as was the case with categories of legislative power allocated by the *Constitution Act, 1867*.[57] However, the actual interpretation of Charter rights must be carried out in the context of concretely challenged values.[58]

BROAD OR DYNAMIC INTERPRETATION?

Under the heading of interpretation of Charter rights, it is not particularly useful to state that the Charter should receive a broad and generous interpretation. Since it is basically a matter of choosing between two values, both of which often appear in the Charter, it is very difficult to say how far generosity should go.

It is even more important to guarantee the Charter a dynamic and evolving form of interpretation capable of adapting gracefully over the years.[59] However, there are some provisions in the Constitution, such as section 93 (1) of the *Constitution Act, 1867* relating to denominational education, whose minimal adaptation is guaranteed by the strictest possible interpretation.[60]

Under the same heading of the interpretation of rights, it would also seem inappropriate in this context of conflicting values to proclaim that the linguistic version of the Charter offering the greater latitude should systematically be preferred. Rather it would seem that the version should be preferred that best represents the intentions of the drafter.[61] However, this intention was, in general terms, to formally constitutionalize certain rights and not to change the material meaning of these rights other than through recourse to section 1.

THE ONUS OF PROOF

If, as seems certain, section 1 is indeed an interpretation clause that enables the true sense of the rights of the Charter to be understood, it follows that the legislature has no obligation to prove the reasonableness of its legislation. On the contrary, if the contested measure is reasonable in the circumstances, it forms an integral part of the asserted right. Therefore, it is incumbent on the party who claims that the law is unconstitutional for reasons based on the Charter to show that the law is not reasonable within the meaning of section 1.[62]

This first aspect of the principle of presumption of constitutionality[63] does not appear to have been overturned by the adoption of the Charter. Once again, the rights of the Charter are, as is appropriate, expressed in such general terms that they are not, in themselves, functional. In order for them to become so, it is necessary to complete their definition by recourse to section 1. Consequently, it would be illogical to require that a party contesting a law demonstrate only the limitation of a right as provided for in the Charter. Contestation on the basis of the Charter would then become so easy that practical application of the law might be paralyzed.

It is not suggested, however, that the person who invokes the Charter bear the entire burden of proof beyond all reasonable doubt. It simply means that this individual should go a little further and not just provide evidence of violation, curtailment or restriction of notions as general as freedom of expression, the right to security or the right to equality, for example.

All of these Charter rights have, of course, a certain general meaning, but the particular meaning given them by the Charter is the one imposed by section 1: they are rights whose functional significance is to render any incompatible law inoperative if it is not reasonable within the meaning of section 1. Thus, the person invoking one of these rights must, to a great extent, move into the realm of the unreasonable.

If the government considers it necessary, it will respond to these arguments. Then, if required, it will demonstrate that the legislation under attack may be justified in a free and democratic society. In the end, the constitutional judges will rule in favour of the challenge if they are convinced by argument that the legislation in question is infringing upon a right contained in the Charter in a manner disproportionate to the objectives being pursued. If there is uncertainty or doubt about the existence of such disproportion or imbalance between the values in question, in the end they will give precedence to the evaluation of the legislature over that of the individual.

This way of interpreting the rights of the Charter does not flow from a technical and literal examination of section 1.[64] It is, rather, because of the very nature of fundamental rights and because of the constitutional context of the Charter that the interpretation based on the principle of presumption of constitutionality must be retained. It is difficult to understand why the jurisprudence of the Supreme Court relating to the Bill of Rights would not be considered applicable in this regard.[65]

The secondary aspects of the principle of presumption of constitutionality recognized in Canadian constitutional law should also be applicable to the Charter. Thus, to the fullest extent possible, a law should be interpreted in such a way that its impact on the rights of the Charter is not excessive under the circumstances.[66] If such an interpretation is not possible, the law should be declared inoperative, since the judge can in no way act as a substitute for the legislature; however, such a declaration should apply only to defective provisions of the law, if that is possible without betraying the legislature's intention.[67]

Similarly, the procurement of a preventive judicial remedy before a final decision about the existence of the alleged right should be subject to rigorous conditions. An interlocutory injunction whose effect is to prevent the application of a law should require that the applicant show proof of serious or irreparable harm and demonstrate the existence of a fairly clear right. The mere appearance of a right as a criterion for issuing this type of judicial order would allow the Charter to be used too easily for improper ends.[68]

PROOF OF WHAT?

What should be the focus of this proof, the burden of which is primarily on the person challenging a legal rule in the name of the Charter?

Traditionally, Canadian constitutional law relating to the division of powers between the federal government and the provinces has made a distinction in this regard between intrinsic and extrinsic proof. Since the criterion of constitutionality with regard to the division of powers is the very object of the legislation in question, extrinsic proof seems, a priori, to be irrelevant. It becomes relevant only if the intention is to demonstrate that the law in question does not truly have the purpose claimed by its authors. In this respect, jurisprudence has reached a point where it can conceive of the admissibility of virtually any type of relevant proof in order to demonstrate the existence or non-existence of a rational link between a piece of legislation and constitutional competence.[69]

In the case of the Charter, this problem does not arise, since the constitutionality of legislation is to be judged not by its purpose, but by its real impact. Thus, any pertinent proof is admissible, not to demonstrate that the law in question has or has not any rational relationship with the constitutional purpose, but to show that it has a proportionate or disproportionate impact upon the rights of the Charter.

There can be various types of extrinsic proof. Since it is once again a question of evaluating the real impact of the law rather than understanding the intention of the legislature, any statement, even from a minister in the House, may be pertinent and admissible. It is the responsibility of the constitutional judge to assess its relative weight.

However, one thing is certain: such extrinsic proof must pertain to the laws challenged under the Charter and not to the Charter itself. As noted above, the rights of the Charter must be considered and understood on a case-by-case basis with respect to reasonableness pursuant to section 1 and not in light of statements made by authors or promoters of the Charter at some particular time. The fundamental objective of dynamic, evolving and flexible interpretation, which is even more important in the case of fundamental rights than in the case of legislative jurisdiction, is entirely irreconcilable with the admissibility of extrinsic proof relative to the Charter.[70]

For that reason, the various rights guaranteed by the Charter must be interpreted cautiously. With the exception of certain specific rights, which are not truly fundamental human rights and whose limits are, in any case, defined in the manner of statutory rights,[71] the rights in the Charter should not be able to render a law unconstitutional unless that law is first deemed unreasonable within the meaning of section 1. The following question must then be asked: does this law restrict or limit the Charter right in question in an abusive, exaggerated or disproportionate manner as compared to its concrete and precise aims?

In my view this is the way to understand the rights in the Charter; it is based both on the terms of the Charter and on its constitutional context. The Charter itself states that the rights that it guarantees are rights limited or restricted by reasonable law, and it is appropriate to assume that parliamentary law, especially that of decentralized parliaments, pursues the general objectives of liberty, justice and equality established by the Charter.

Scope of the Charter

The corollary of a circumspect, cautious and prudent *interpretation* of rights under the Charter is a broad and generous definition of its fields of *application*. That is because the interpretation of rights goes to the heart of the issue when rights and values that are equally fundamental must be reconciled, whereas the definition of fields of application is a matter of implementation. It is socially necessary to interpret rights in the context of other rights. On the other hand, it is difficult to justify refusing to permit these truly fundamental rights to apply in certain areas on the basis of a legal technique that produces answers unrelated to concrete situations.

This theme can be illustrated by considering several questions relating to the general scope of the Charter and to more specific areas of application of the most fundamental rights entrenched in it.[72]

General Scope of the Charter

The Charter states expressly that it applies to the federal Parliament and to the legislature of each province.[73] This statement may be considered redundant given the formal constitutional status of the Charter.[74] Indeed, there is no longer any doubt about the supra-legal authority of the Charter, and the discussions that surrounded the application of the Canadian Bill of Rights in the legislative field will not be repeated with the Charter.[75]

The Charter also affirms that it applies to the federal government and to the government of each province.[76] For the same reason, this second statement was, a fortiori, superfluous: a constitutional Charter, which binds parliaments, must of necessity bind governments. The prerogatives of common law and the statutory immunities enjoyed by governments cannot prevent the application of the Constitution.[77]

If one acknowledges that this reference to governments is required in order for them to be bound by the Charter, it would then be necessary to give the word "government," used in this context, the restrictive meaning of a central body of public administration, i.e., the hierarchy of civil servants headed by the Governor General or Lieutenant-Governor in Council.[78] However, since the reference has its own raison d'être, it should not be interpreted as limiting the scope of the Charter.

If, the reference to government must be considered superfluous as far as binding governments is concerned, then in principle it is necessary to find another justification, which can only be to help define the field of application of the Charter. This hypothesis does not, however, require that the word "government" be given an organic rather than a functional meaning.

By referring to governments as they have done, the drafters of the Charter may have sought to focus on specific bodies or on certain functions of the state. In the first instance, a reference defining the scope of the Charter would allow it to apply only to the central organs of the federal and provincial public administrations, whereas in the second case it would extend the application of the Charter to functions of a governmental nature exercised both by governments and by decentralized para-governmental institutions.

Certain authors have dealt with the first of these two hypotheses, either on the basis of the decision in *Blaikie no. 2* or on the basis of concepts used in administrative law to identify government agents.[79] In my opinion, the first hypothesis should be rejected because it would tend to restrict the scope of the Charter.

In the *Blaikie no. 2* decision, the Supreme Court favoured the organic position with respect to section 133 of the *Constitution Act, 1867*, but the case was quite unusual.[80] The Supreme Court was asked to decide in what cases the Quebec public administration could circumvent the rule of legislative bilingualism by using regulatory power. The Province of Quebec, which was the appellant in the case, argued that such circumvention could only be the act of a government that is part of and, in many ways, has authority over the legislature. The Court replied that section 133 should apply to government regulations and also to regulations of para-governmental organizations, with the exception of municipal and educational bodies, whose regulations must be approved by the government.

Regardless of the logic of the decision, what must be noted here is that the Supreme Court ruling was based on the mechanism and not the tasks of the administrative body. Section 133 of the *Constitution Act, 1867* refers to "Acts of Parliament." Swayed by the eloquence of the lower court judgment, the court had at first ruled that this expression should be interpreted broadly to cover all regulatory power.[81] Since this statement was meaningless, given the obligation it implied, it became necessary, at a later stage, to distinguish between the various categories of bodies endowed with regulatory powers. There is no functional difference between government regulations and municipal regulations.

The present case is not the same. What is at issue is the application of the Charter in its entirety and thus, the application of the fundamental rights that mark the ultimate boundaries of law. There is nothing standing in the way of this application being as broad as possible. It might, of course, be quite a different story for some Charter rights that are not of this nature and which, like section 133, impose obligations rather than restrictions on the state. However, this is not the case in determining the general scope of the Charter.

It would not appear that the criteria of administrative law concerning the identification of government agents are of any further use in determining the general scope of the Charter. These criteria seek to identify para-governmental institutions that must, in order to perform their duties properly, enjoy the same prerogatives, privileges and immunities as the government. It is difficult to see how these criteria could be used to formulate a restrictive definition of the scope of the Charter. Their objective would appear to be quite the opposite.

The hypothesis that a concept of government has a functional meaning that would define the scope of the Charter is more acceptable because it is less restrictive. The Charter would apply every time the public administration exercised its power to coerce or restrain individuals. Such a definition would include both regulatory and administrative powers, whether of a legal or administrative nature. However, the fact remains that it could be very disillusioning for a citizen if the constitutional Charter of human rights did not apply to the public administration which buys, investigates, employs, manages, compiles, reports and so on.

If a specific meaning absolutely must be given to the Charter's reference to governments, it could only be a functional rather than an organic meaning. The scope of the Charter would then extend to the area covered by the traditional concept of the executive function.

But in any case, it does not seem necessary to attribute a specific role to the Charter's reference to governments. It is not unusual for legislative texts to contain references that cannot and should not be given a distinct role. The simple rule of interpretation which states that a legislator does not speak without a purpose does not constitute sufficient grounds to restrict, in the absence of other reasons, the scope of the *Constitution Act* of which the Charter is a part.[82] The text of the Charter does not demand such a restriction. It may be that those who drafted the Constitution expressly mentioned parliaments and governments as a safety measure.

A definition of the scope of the Charter should not provide its interpreters with ready-made answers. On the contrary, the Charter must be ready for use in any case where a legal rule would have a disproportionate impact on any of the rights it guarantees. Only explicit and very clear provisions should establish the principle that the constitutional Charter of Rights, an integral part of the *Constitution Act*, cannot, for example, apply to courts of law or to individuals who are not otherwise mentioned in the Charter.[83]

Freedom of Expression

The Charter contains a section concerning freedom of expression. This section affirms the general principle of freedom of expression as well as certain corollaries of this right. It is not my intention here to endeavour to predict how these rights will be interpreted, but only to illustrate how their scope may be broadly or narrowly construed.

The Charter guarantees freedom of expression to "everyone" (in French "chacun"). Therefore, under the Charter, there is no a priori reason to limit freedom of expression exclusively to individuals in an artificial or doctrinaire manner. One can easily imagine cases where there would be an interest in extending this right to corporations.

Does freedom of expression under the Charter mean political and religious expression only, or should it also apply to the arts, literature and advertising? American case law has shown great hesitation in dealing with this issue, but we believe that the wording of section 2 of the Charter does not, in principle, require that any doors be closed so long as the test of whether it is reasonable is applied in the specific and concrete context of each case.

It is one thing to say that freedom of expression under the Charter does not apply to pornography, but it is quite another to say that the actual consequences of this form of expression must be taken into consideration in deciding a case.[84] It is a question of the approach: in the first case, an absolute rule is laid down that leads to a mechanical response; in the second case, the question asked is whether a certain measure to suppress pornography unduly restricts the right to freedom of expression, taking into account the impact of pornography on the right of women to equality.

In the same way, we should avoid laying down "in vacuum" the principle that freedom of expression under the Charter does not apply to symbolic language, or that it applies in a general way only to the content of messages and not to the way in which they are expressed. Expression by means of a certain style of dress, by means of certain language or through a certain intermediary might be so significant under certain circumstances that restrictive measures could readily be perceived as abusive.[85] Protection of content often implies protection of the medium of communication.

A response to the question of the scope of freedom of expression based on a distinction between rights and freedoms would also be unduly technical. Following this approach, freedom of expression under the

Charter would not apply to a right that tended to favour institutional rather than individual expression.[86] Here again, although we must obviously take into consideration the intended aim of a disputed electoral law, this does not mean that we must accept in principle that this law may affect individual freedom of expression in any way and to any extent.

Due Process of Law

I shall examine only the general clause affecting due process contained in section 7 of the Charter,[87] and here again my intention is only to emphasize the importance of a broad definition of its scope.

The main issue raised by section 7 is whether its application is substantive or merely procedural. If it is applied only procedurally, it would apply only to acts by which the state individualizes general standards that it has enacted through laws and regulations. Section 7 would therefore apply, essentially, to the manner in which the courts exercise the judicial function and the manner in which the public administration exercises its discretionary powers.

According to this hypothesis, however, section 7 cannot be applied to the substantive content of the state's political acts, or to the acts of individuals. Thus the content of laws, regulations, or purely administrative acts of the state would be exempt from any control under section 7.

However, section 7 sets out the three most fundamental rights found in the Canadian Charter: the right to life, the right to liberty and the right to security of person. Only in the second half of the section, clearly separated by a semi-colon (in the French version), does it add "and the right not to be deprived thereof except in accordance with the principles of fundamental justice."[88]

If these three rights do not apply to the content of laws and regulations, it is tantamount to saying that they are entirely at the mercy of legislatures and governments. The latter could, in fact, set the most outrageous standards concerning the rights while leaving little or no power of discretion to the authorities charged with implementing them. The courts would then have no power in these areas, even from a procedural point of view.

Neither the terms nor the context of the Charter would appear to impose such a narrow scope on section 7. This section sets out three independent and fundamental rights that must be interpreted with the aid of the reasonableness test contained in section 1. Respect for fundamental justice is another requirement imposed by section 7 for cases where legal rules affecting these rights are to be implemented by any discretionary, judicial or administrative power.

It is difficult to imagine that the Charter would leave rights such as the three substantive rights in section 7 entirely at the mercy of a discretionary procedure. In the cruise missile case, the Federal Court of Appeal seems to have ruled that section 7 had only procedural value.[89] It is to be hoped that the Supreme Court will base its decision on a detailed interpretation of the right to security of the person and not on a question of scope[90] as other courts of appeal have sometimes done with respect to the right to liberty.[91]

The second question of this nature raised by section 7 is whether the fundamental justice it prescribes applies only to judicial and quasi-judicial discretion or whether it also applies to administrative discretion. Here again, the wording used does not necessarily restrict the scope of the Charter. The expression "fundamental justice" is used here in a context that does not require, as in the case of section 2(e) of the Bill of Rights, that it be assimilated to the concept of natural justice in administrative law that applies only to judicial functions.[92] The expression "fundamental justice" may include procedural guarantees ranging from the strict formality of a criminal trial to the duty to act fairly in exercising administrative discretion.[93]

Equality

Under the Charter, equality is applicable to "every individual." On the other hand, the French version of section 15, which sets out the right to equality, uses the expression "tous." When it comes down to defining the scope of the Charter, rather than interpreting its rights, the version most generous to the individual should prevail.

Nor should the application of equality under the Charter be restricted to the six types of discrimination described in section 15. This list is preceded by the expression "in particular," which is sufficient grounds for not artificially restricting the scope of equality.

The main issue raised by the equality clause is the effect it is likely to have on the content of laws. It is well known that the Supreme Court has vacillated greatly on this issue with respect to the equality clause in the Canadian Bill of Rights. Its rulings have ranged from "yes" in *R. v. Drybones*,[94] to "no" in *A.G. Canada v. Lavell*,[95] to "it depends" in *Bliss v. A.G. Canada*,[96] while it seems to have introduced a distinction between repressive and distributive legislation, with only the former being subject to the principle of equality. Generally speaking, the Supreme Court has given a literal interpretation to the expression "equality before the law" in the Bill of Rights, concluding that it means equality with respect to consequences of the law and not with respect to the content of a law itself.

The Charter has done everything possible to repudiate this inheritance. This principle of equality is expressed by four phrases, all distinct from each other and all different from those in the Bill of Rights. Unlike the Bill of Rights, the Charter has a formal constitutional character which, moreover, should contribute to encouraging judges to apply the principle of equality to the actual content of the legislation.

Conclusion

The Canadian Charter of Rights and Freedoms is not an instrument of development for Canadian society. Rather, it is the supreme means of defence for individual members of that society. As such, in order to further the well-being of society, it should be broadly applied but narrowly interpreted. This derives from the very concept of fundamental rights and from the specific institutional context in which the Charter is required to function.

In defining the scope of the Charter, content takes second place to framework, form and context, but these peripheral factors should not prevent the Charter from playing a role that may be vital. The ultimate intervention of the Charter should not be impeded by virtue of technical notions that are often artificial. To the extent that words and concepts permit, individuals appealing to the Charter should not receive a preliminary and mechanical response that very often does no more than poorly conceal the desire to avoid having to deal with the merits of the question.

The rights of the Charter should, in fact, be interpreted prudently and extremely seriously. This means essentially an interpretation that tries to get to the root of the matter by weighing values, rights and responsibilities one against another.

An omnipresent charter, if interpreted in absolute and abstract terms, will erode the rights it is supposed to serve. Even worse, it will become a source of growing injustice, of benefit to those who are strongest, most powerful, best organized and most secure, instead of guaranteeing, first and foremost as it should, protection for those who are most vulnerable. Instead of developing a more just, more secure and more gentle society, it will produce a society of confrontation and conflict based on the maximum assertion of rights rather than on fulfilment of responsibilities.

Finally, the Charter should not, as some have predicted it will, become a rich source of livelihood for the lawyers of the future. It should be reiterated that if a charter is significant as a defence mechanism, it can provide nothing more than what a defence mechanism can provide. In the long run, overuse of an immune system produces only self-destructive rejection. The social usefulness of a charter of fundamental human rights does not increase in proportion to the number of times pleas based upon it are accepted.

Notes

This study is a translation of the original French-language text which was completed in April 1984.

1. *Canada Act, United Kingdom, 1982*, c. 11, Schedule B (*Constitution Act, 1982*, ss. 1–34).

2. To date, five major cases have been heard and are under consideration: *Hunter v. Southam* (1983), 147 D.L.R. (3d) 420 (C.A. Alta); *R. v. Big M Drug Mart* (1983), 10 W.C.B. 453 (C.A. Alta); *Operation Dismantle v. The Queen* (1983), 1 F.C. 745; *A.G. of Quebec v. Quebec Association of Protestant School Boards* (1983), C.A. 77; and *Re Skapinker* (1983), 40 O.R. (2d) 481 (C.A.). Since this paper was written, the Supreme Court has handed down a decision in *Skapinker* and in *Q.A.P.S.B.* on May 3 and July 26, 1984, respectively.

3. These figures are intended to show the general situation and not to provide precise statistics. The number of books mentioned includes journals that have devoted an entire issue to the Charter and annotated versions of the Charter; the figure for articles does not include contributions to special issues of journals and to collective works. See the bibliography.

4. R.S.C. 1970, app. III.

5. In addition to considering laws from the point of view of a federal division of powers, the courts can now do this on the basis of substantive principles expressed in very general terms.

6. Corrective justice establishes or re-establishes equality in relationships between people. Distributive justice refers to relationships between society and individuals; it should provide for proportional distribution of the common good.

7. See J. Hersch, *Quelques paradoxes des droits de l'homme* (Zurich: Schultheiss Polygraphischer Verlag, 1979), p. 189:

    A third point: We must not confuse the issue. Improved and increased concern for offering human rights the best chance of concrete realization in the history of mankind must not be permitted to reduce the requirement for massive, basic rights that preserve the individual conscience from the rape of force. . . .
    The major enemy of human rights is the use of force by some who wish to enslave others in order to use them simply as a means of achieving their own goals. However, we must recognize that human rights also have another, more insidious enemy, an enemy which threatens to drown them in a sea of nonsense or unreality: the arrogant and vain rhetoric of the "belle âme" or "schöne Seele." In its lyrical pursuit of an imaginary totality, it is scornful of the distinctions and limits explored by those of more discerning minds. (Trans.)

8. This holds particularly true for the provisions relating to the right to enter, remain in and leave Canada (s. 6); official languages (ss. 16–22); and language rights relating to education (s. 23).

9. The provisions of the Charter that are potentially the most useful for the development of society are its interpretation and exception clauses: s. 6(4), 15(2), 16(3), 25, 27, especially s. 1 and even s. 33.

10. They can ensure that the worst is avoided; for example, a situation in which one or several individuals pay unduly for the happiness and security of all. At the same time, when taken literally, they are a signal of every man for himself which legally sanctions a social status quo.

11. The Quebec *Charter of Human Rights and Freedoms*, R.S.Q., c. C-12, contains a number of provisions of this type: s. 40 for example. See also s. 36 of the *Constitution Act, 1982*, on the equalization of regional disparities. Even relatively detailed provisions like s. 93 and s. 133 of the *Constitution Act, 1867* present serious difficulties for implementation; the application of these provisions in Manitoba is an example. With respect to s. 23 of the Canadian Charter, see D. Proulx, "La précarité des droits linguistiques scolaires ou les singulières difficultés de mise en oeuvre de l'a. 23 de la Charte canadienne des droits et libertés" (1983), 14 *R.G.D.* 335.

12. See H. Brun and G. Tremblay, *Droit constitutionnel* (Montreal: Éditions Yvon Blais,

1982), p. 95 et seq. For example, Article 3 of the French Constitution of October 4, 1958, reads as follows: "National sovereignty belongs to the people who exercise it through their representatives and through the referendum process." (Trans.)

13. *Ibid.*, p. 409.

14. Only once has the Supreme Court given practical recognition to the supremacy of the Bill of Rights over ordinary legislation: *R. v. Drybones* (1970), S.C.R. 282. At other times, it has developed theories that tend to deny such supremacy: *A.G. Can. v. Lavell* (1974), S.C.R. 1349; *R. v. Burnshine* (1975), 1 S.C.R. 693; *A.G. Canada v. Canard* (1976), 1 S.C.R. 170; and *R. v. Miller* (1977), 2 S.C.R. 680. See (1977), 18 *C. de D.* 567 and (1975), 53 *Can. Bar Rev.* 795.

15. The Charter enlarges the traditional role of the courts for three reasons. The first relates to the very general terms used in the Charter. Many of the Charter's provisions use terms that will have to be defined and whose scope will be clarified in each case. The second reason why the role of the courts is enlarged is that the possibility of the Charter's being amended is so slight. The evolution of the Charter is mainly a result of its interpretation by the courts. In practice, it is the courts that will define the real significance of the Charter. The third reason for the greater role of the courts is that only the judicial system has the jurisdiction to interpret and apply the Charter.

16. See, *supra*, note 9.

17. S.C. 1970-71-72, c. 63.

18. See H. Brun, "Le recouvrement de l'impôt et les droits de la personne" (1983), 24 *C. de. D.* 457.

19. R.S.C. 1970, c. C-34.

20. See *Messier v. Delage*, J.E. 83-1082 (S.C.C.): the dissenting opinion of three of the seven judges.

21. See *Pelletier v. Leger*, an unreported decision of the Quebec Superior Court on May 4, 1982, in which a training program especially designed for female public servants was found to be contrary to the equality provisions of the Quebec Charter. See also F.R. Boddendijk, *Minorities and Civil Liberties in Advanced Industrial Societies: A Question of Two Incompatible Values?* Paper presented at the 12th World Congress of the International Political Science Association, Rio de Janeiro, August 1982.

22. See Hersch, *supra*, note 7, at p. 186.
    To implement human rights is to take action in the very context in which there is confrontation between forces and the struggle for life, in order to introduce a new dimension, protection of the rights of the weakest, respect where strength is lacking, something sacred without violence — in other words, in nature itself, a counter-force in human terms. (Trans.)

23. See the remarks of W.S. Tarnopolsky, "The New Canadian Charter of Rights and Freedoms as Compared and Contrasted with the American Bill of Rights" (1983), 5 *Human Rights Quarterly* 227, at p. 272 and "Comparison Between the Canadian Charter of Rights and Freedoms and the International Covenant on Civil and Political Rights" (1982-83), 8 *Queen's L.J.* 211, at p. 230, on the subject of the *Loi assurant la reprise des services dans les collèges et les écoles du secteur public*, L.Q. 1983, c. 1 (Bill 111). The International Labour Organization, in a decision relating to this legislation, gave serious consideration to the prevailing social and economic situation: Decision 1171, November 19, 1983.

24. See W.R. Lederman, "The Power of the Judges and the New Canadian Charter of Rights and Freedoms" (1982), 16 *U.B.C.L. Rev.* 1; Hersch, *supra*, note 7, at p. 185-87:
    Human rights cannot avoid confronting nature, where the prevailing law is the law of the strongest. To say that a requirement is a right is to deny oneself opportunities of an ideal intention, and to carry out concrete implementation in the real and material context of human life.
    In sum, it appears that we may consider most acquired or sought-after rights as giving concrete expression to the conditions of the actual implementation of human rights. (Trans.)

25. See P.H. Russell, "The Political Purposes of the Canadian Charter of Rights and Freedoms" (1983), 61 *Can Bar Rev.* 30.

26. Ss. 6 and 23. These provisions are much more detailed than those dealing with traditional fundamental rights.

27. See, for example, *Reynolds v. A.G. B.C.* (1983), 143 D.L.R. (3d) 365 (S.C. B.C.); *Storey v. Zazelenchuk* (1982), 21 Sask. R. 158 (Q.B.); *Re Ontario Film and Video Appreciation Society and Ontario Board of Censors* (1983), 147 D.L.R. (3d) 58 (D.C. Ont.) on s. 1 of the Charter. See *Shingoose v. Minister of Social Services* (1983), 149 D.L.R. (3d) 400 (Q.B. Sask.) on s. 12.

28. We are not, of course, suggesting that influence can be measured simply by the number or percentage of decisions rendered. It should be noted, however, that the Ontario courts very often have the opportunity to be the first to pronounce on questions of substance relating to the Charter; and the lower courts of the other provinces are often reduced to following what the Ontario Court of Appeal has said on these issues.

29. See, for example, *Quebec Association of Protestant School Boards v. A.G. Quebec,* J.E. 82-903 (1982), 140 D.L.R. (3d) 19 (Q.S.C.), in which the principle of standard interpretation has served to justify the aggressive intervention of the federal government in a matter relating to the constitutionality of a provincial law.

30. See, *supra,* note 7, at p. 37.

31. *Constitution Act, 1867,* R.S.C. 1970, app. II, p. 191, ss. 96 and 101; *Supreme Court Act,* R.S.C. 1970, C. S-19.

32. L. Favoreu, in *Cours constitutionnelles européennes et droits fondamentaux* (Paris: Economica, 1982), p. 29:

> The constitutional judge is different, first because he necessarily has constitutional status, in other words a status that shelters him from the government he is charged with monitoring. His existence, structure and responsibilities are, in principle, set by the Constitution and, in order to change this status, it is necessary to revise the Constitution. . . .
>
> . . . What also sets him apart from the ordinary judge is the fact that, by monitoring the government, even if his actions and methods are judicial in nature, the scope of his decisions is often and inevitably political in nature. (Trans.)

33. See, *supra,* notes 8 and 26.

34. J. Hersch, "Le concept des droits de l'homme, est-il un concept universel?" (Paris: Goethe Institute, unpublished paper, May 1980), pp. 3 and 4.

> From the moment when we develop sciences with their terminologies and their strict methods, techniques with their facilities and limitations, industries with their hierarchies and interdependent and divergent interests, it is no longer enough to recognize the deepest living roots, which we all possess, of human rights. It becomes imperative to conceptualize them and to explain them in detail in terms of legal requirements. It is then that in the name of universal rights, each individual will insist on his right to be himself, and to be different. (Trans.)

35. See R. Décary, "La Cour suprême et la dualité canadienne" (1979), 57 *Can. Bar Rev.* 702, at p. 712.

36. See N. Rouland, "L'acculturation judiciaire chez les Inuits du Canada" (1983), 13 *Recherches amérindiennes* 179, 307, pp. 313–14. See also s. 16(3) of the Canadian Charter as well as art. 22 of the *1948 Universal Declaration of Human Rights* and art. 27 of the *1966 International Covenant on Civil and Political Rights,* whose voluntary protocol Canada signed in 1976. Human beings do not develop their potential just because they have not been killed or because they have not died of starvation. From the point of view of intelligence and human spirituality, the individuals need to be part of a structure, of the culture to which they belong. The necessity of respecting various cultures is an extension of the recognition of the right to intellectual and spiritual development.

37. See, for example, P. Berton, *Why We Act Like Canadians: A Personal Exploration of Our National Character* (Toronto: McClelland and Stewart, 1982).

38. *In Quebec Association of Protestant School Boards, supra,* note 2, at pp. 27 and 30, the Supreme Court made a distinction between derogation and restriction. It was, however, a distinction of degree rather than of kind, and seemed rather obscure:

> Whatever their scope, the limits which s. 1 of the *Charter* allows to be placed on the rights and freedoms set out in it cannot be equated with exceptions such as those

authorized by s. 39(1) and (2) of the *Charter* . . . .

Such limitations cannot be exceptions to the rights and freedoms guaranteed by the *Charter* or amount to amendments of the *Charter*.

39. The Supreme Court considers that federal laws which pursue a "valid federal objective" do not contravene the rights of the Bill of Rights: *Human Rights Commission v. A.G. Canada and Vermette* (1982), 1 S.C.R. 215; *MacKay v. The Queen* (1980), 2 S.C.R. 370; *Bliss v. A.G. Canada* (1979), 1 S.C.R. 183. The expression "valid federal objective" has generally been interpreted as referring to areas of federal competence, which has the effect of depriving the Bill of Rights of any authority over federal laws.

40. *Supra*, notes 8 and 26.

41. The two decisions handed down by the Supreme Court after this paper was written deal with these sections. See, *supra*, note 2. *Skapinker* dealt with s. 6 and *Quebec Association of Protestant School Boards*, with s. 23.

42. Thus, in *Skapinker, supra*, note 2, the Supreme Court at this point came to the conclusion that there was no rapport between s. 6 of the Charter and the Ontario legislation at issue. In our view, this is how we must interpret the case law that established the principle that, initially, Charter rights must be interpreted independently of s. 1. See for example, *R. v. Rauca* (1983), 4 C.R.R. 42 (C.A. Ont.).

43. The Supreme Court decision in *Quebec Association of Protestant School Boards, supra*, note 2, is extremely confusing in this regard. At the beginning and again at pp. 14 and 26 of the reasons, the Court expressly states that it is not dealing with the question of the applicability of s. 1 in the case of a conflict with respect to s. 23 of the Charter. The Court then shows that the Quebec legislation at issue cannot be considered as a reasonable limit upon s. 23 within the meaning of s. 1, since the legislature's precise intention in s. 23 was to override the Quebec legislation (pp. 16–26). This reasoning seems well-founded and, in this case, justified (see, *infra*, note 70). But the Court affirms subsequently that there is a conflict between s. 23 and the Quebec statute that s. 1 cannot mitigate since, in this case, it is a matter of a derogation and not a restriction (pp. 27 and 30). But in so doing, the Court is applying s. 1 in spite of its initial remarks. In any case, it could not have done otherwise without concluding that s. 23 is sufficiently precise to render everything that has a negative effect on it unconstitutional. Otherwise it would require an incompatibility gauge. In this context, the distinction between derogation and limitation seems to make the doubtful distinction between negation and restriction, upon which the Court of Appeal based its decision, even worse: (1983), C.A. 77. In fact, the Supreme Court had a rather difficult time with this case: in the event it had to avoid at any cost the reasonableness of s. 1 and the very strong arguments presented by the Attorney General for Quebec in this regard. The Court should have and could have stood by its initial reasons.

44. As per s. 52 of the *Constitution Act, 1982, supra*, note 1.

45. *Supra*, note 12, at pp. 348–50.

46. A. Tunc, in *Cours constitutionnelles européennes et droits fondamentaux* (Paris: Economica, 1982), p. 8, speaks of the:

. . . mission to ensure the liberty of the citizen or, less abstractly, to attempt to harmonize the necessary exercise of public power with the no less necessary autonomy of the individual. (Trans.)

Mr. Justice D.G. Blair, *The Charter and the Judges: A View From the Bench*, paper delivered at the Canadian Institute for the Administration of Justice symposium in October 1983:

The problem for the courts, is to balance these competing rights and determine which should be paramount in any particular situation.

47. See G. Pépin and Y. Ouellet, *Principes de contentieux administratifs* (Montreal: Éditions Yvon Blais, 1979), p. 94.

48. The Supreme Court has always considered that a law needs only to have a justification for it to be deemed in conformity with the Canadian Bill of Rights: see the *Lavell, Burnshine, Canard, Miller, Bliss, MacKay*, and *Vermette* decisions, *supra*, notes 14 and 39.

49. Almost all the decisions by appeal courts that have, to date, struck down laws in the name of the Charter, could, in my opinion, be justified by applying this test.

50. In ss. 2, and 8-11.

51. Jamaica or Antigua, for example.

52. *A.G. v. Antigua Times* (1976), A.C. 16; *Hinds v. The Queen* (1977), A.C. 195.

53. See, for example, *Quebec Association of Protestant School Boards v. A.G. Quebec* (1982), S.C. 673, pp. 693-94; *Federal Republic of Germany v. Rauca* (1982), 38 O.R. (2d) 705 (H.C. Ont.), p. 716.

54. See A. Morel, "La clause limitative de l'article 1 de la Charte canadienne des droits et libertés: une assurance contre le gouvernement des juges" (1983), 61 *Can. Bar Rev.* 81, at p. 84 et seq.

55. In the following decisions, for example, an exacting proportionality is contrasted to the action of a judge and a director of a prison: *Re Collins and The Queen* (1983), 4 C.R.R. 78 (C.C. Ont.); *Malty v. A.G. Sask.* (1983), 143 D.L.R. (3D) 649.

56. See, *supra*, note 12, at p. 337. In *Skapinker, supra*, note 2, the Supreme Court said as follows in this regard, at p. 39 of the decision:

> The development of the Charter as it takes place in our constitutional law, must necessarily be a careful process. Where issues do not compel a commentary on these new Charter provisions, none should be undertaken. There will be occasions when guidance by *obiter* or anticipation of issues will serve the Canadian community, and particularly the evolving constitutional process. On such occasions, the Court might well enlarge its reasons for judgment beyond that required to dispose of the issues raised.

57. *Ibid.*

58. *Supra*, note 46.

59. The Supreme Court said the following in *Skapinker, supra*, note 2, at p. 12 of the decision:

> It is part of the fabric of Canadian law. Indeed, it 'is the supreme law of Canada,' s. 52, *Constitution Act, 1982*. It cannot be readily amended. The fine and constant adjustment process of these constitutional provisions is left by a tradition of necessity to the judicial branch. Flexibility must be balanced with certainty. The future must, to the extent that it is foreseeable, be accommodated in the present. The Charter was designed and adopted to guide and serve the Canadian community for a long time. Narrow and technical interpretation, if not moderated by a sense of the unknowns of the future, can stunt the growth of the law and hence the community it serves.

60. This provision sought to enable Catholics and Protestants to have public denominational schools. It corresponded to the concept of freedom of religion at the time. Today, it goes against the notion of separation of Church and State, is discriminatory on the basis of religion, and makes it very difficult in Quebec to establish non-denominational schools.

61. The proper interpretation may be one that marries both versions, thus leading logically toward the stricter version rather than the broader version: see *Jones v. Gamache* (1969), S.C.R. 119, p. 126 and s. 8(2)(b) of the *Official Languages Act*, R.S.C. 1970, c. 0-2. However, the context and other interpretation principles might also enter into consideration; see: *R. v. Cie Immobilière BCN* (1979), 1 S.C.R. 865, pp. 871-72. A constitution is not made with a view to obeying rules of interpretation that would operate mechanically.

62. We maintain this position even though a number of appeal court decisions have stated the opposite. See *Re Skapinker* (1983), 40 O.R. (2d) 481 (C.A.), p. 487; *R. v. Rauca* (1983), 4 C.R.R. 42 (C.A. Ont.); *Re Southam v. The Queen (No. 1)* (1983), 146 D.L.R. (3d) 408 (C.A. Ont.). In *Skapinker, supra*, note 2, the Supreme Court did not deal with this issue.

63. *Supra*, note 12, at p. 332.

64. The use of the interpretation clause should not depend upon a particular meaning of the term "limited" or the expression "prescribed by law"; see *A.G. Quebec v. Quebec Association of Protestant School Boards* (1983), C.A. 77 and *Re Ontario Film and Video*

Appreciation Society and Ontario Board of Censors (1983), 147 D.L.R. (3d) 58 (D.C. Ont.). See Morel, *supra*, note 54, p. 89 et seq.

65. *R. v. Burnshine* (1975), 1 S.C.R. 693, pp. 707–708; *R. v. Miller* (1977), 2 S.C.R. 680, pp. 695–96. This, however, does not mean that we are in agreement with the Supreme Court on what this proof should contain: *supra*, note 48.

66. *Supra*, note 12, at p. 332.

67. *Ibid.*, p. 334.

68. *Ibid.*, p. 333.

69. *Ibid.*, p. 344.

70. In *Quebec Association of Protestant School Boards*, Mr. Justice Beauregard of the Court of Appeals based his opinion on "the precise and clear goal" of the legislature in 1982: (1983), C.A. 77, p. 79. It must be said that this case provides only a truncated view of the general value of the Charter. Section 23, which it challenges, is not a fundamental human right either in nature or in form. In fact, this provision of the Charter is a foreign element introduced in order to make certain provisions of the *Charter of the French Language*, R.S.Q., c. C-11, unconstitutional. Thus, it is difficult to criticize the judiciary for taking that well-known fact into account.

Since this paper was written, the Supreme Court has handed down its decision in this case: *supra*, note 2. It confirms that s. 23 does not set forth a fundamental right in the material sense of the term (p. 16 of the decision) and that the purpose of the provision was actually to negate the provisions of the *Charter of the French Language*, which was challenged in that case, at pp. 17–25 of the decision: the basis of its decision, therefore, might have consisted of a confirmation of Mr. Justice Beauregard's opinion, an opinion based on the legislature's intention. Interpreting a Charter right by the intention of its creator is entirely justified in this case. However, this situation should be considered quite exceptional and it should not prevail in the case of Charter rights that are fundamental human rights. It is difficult to see, for example, what the evidence for the opinion expressed on this matter in 1981–82 by the then minister of justice has to do with a legal dispute concerning the right to equality under subsection 15(1) of the Charter. *In Skapinker*, *supra*, note 2, at p. 38 of the decision, the Supreme Court specifically states that it will not rule on the admissibility or the pertinence of such proof. However, it is surprising that the Supreme Court does not make this important distinction with regard to the question of extrinsic proof between evidence under the Charter, the admissibility of which can only freeze the latter in their 1982 state, and proof with respect to the rights in question, the admissibility of which is essential to a just interpretation of the Charter rights.

71. *Supra*, note 8.

72. This question of the application of the Charter does, of course, often centre on the interpretation of the terms of the Charter and even the terms by which rights in the Charter are set forth. But the interpretation in this case is not intended to reveal the material significance of such and such a right, but rather to show whether in certain legal and factual situations this legislation is capable of being invoked. A reply to a challenge based on non-applicability is, by definition, a reply that avoids answering the basic question of whether the fundamental right invoked and guaranteed by the Charter includes the legal rule under attack.

73. S. 32.

74. According to s. 52 of the *Constitution Act, 1982*. See, *supra*, note 12, at p. 627; P.W. Hogg, "Supremacy of the Canadian Charter of Rights and Freedoms" (1983), 61 *Can. Bar Rev.* 69.

75. *Supra*, note 14.

76. S. 32.

77. *Supra*, note 12, at p. 330. See *B.C. Power v. B.C. Electric* (1962), S.C.R. 642. We are thinking especially of the interpretation acts that provide that the government is not bound by a law unless the law makes specific mention of the government. For example, *Interpretation Act*, R.S.C. 1970, c. J-23, s. 16, or *Civil Code of Lower Canada*, art. 9. On the application of the Charter with respect to prerogatives (C.A.) see *R. v. Operation Dismantle* (1983), 1 F.C. 745.

78. Indeed, the immunities we have just mentioned apply to the government only in the organic sense of the term.

79. See K. Swinton, "Application de la Charte canadienne des droits et libertés" in W.S. Tarnopolsky, *Charte canadienne des droits et libertés* (Montreal: Wilson and Lafleur-Sorej, 1982), p. 60; G. Remillard, "Les conditions d'application de la Charte," in *La Charte canadienne des droits et libertés* (Montréal: Barreau du Québec, 1983), p. 72 et seq.; D. Gibson, *Distinguishing the Governors from the Governed: The Meaning of "Government" under the Section 32(1) of the Canadian Charter of Rights and Freedoms*, brief to the Canadian Institute for the Administration of Justice symposium, October 1983.

80. *A.G. Quebec v. Blaikie (No. 2)* (1981), 1 S.C.R. 312.

81. *A.G. Quebec v. Blaikie (No. 1)* (1979), 2 S.C.R. 1016, p. 1027.

82. S. 52 of the *Constitution Act, 1982*.

83. We readily admit that the question of the applicability of the Charter in private law is far from clear. It might well be that for political reasons the courts would close this avenue to the Charter. On the other hand, it is not very clear what legal logic would confine the constitutional Charter to the area of public law. Individuals' acts cannot be sanctioned by the courts unless they are in conformity with the law, which, presumably, primarily includes the Constitution. See J. Rivero, in *Cours constitutionelles européennes et droits fondamentaux* (Paris: Economica, 1982), p. 523.

> I must confess my astonishment and my inability to understand how it can be accepted, for example, since freedom of opinion is a principle entrenched at the constitutional level, that while it is unacceptable for the state to exert pressure on its citizens because of their opinions or to prevent them from expressing themselves, it would be perfectly compatible with this principle for an employer to exert pressure on the freedom of opinion of his employee or to forbid him to express himself. I cannot accept the possibility of a double standard within a society, one applicable to relations between the state and individuals, the other applicable to relations between citizens, and that these two standards would differ in their very essence and in the values they enshrine. Moreover, when a conflict arises between two individuals specifically concerning the exercise of a freedom or fundamental right, the conflict is brought before a judge, i.e., before a state authority. This state authority must necessarily apply to this conflict the rules which bind any state authority, i.e., the fundamental principles of the Constitution. Indeed, this is what, in my opinion, the example of German law reveals, where through the control of decisions made by civil jurisdictions, the Constitutional Court imposes on relations between individuals respect for the fundamental principles of the Constitution. I believe, therefore, that it is essential to specify, to recall, to deepen this idea that fundamental rights must be conceived as a protection of the individual not only against arbitrary public power, but also against the no less formidable threat of private arbitrary power. (Trans.)

If we are correct on this point, that means that the constitutional reform of 1982 had unique consequences for Quebec. Civil law of French origin which has been presented in Quebec thanks to the *Quebec Act of 1774* and s. 92(13) of the *Constitution Act, 1867* would, however, be overwhelmed with respect to the most fundamental principles in the context of pan-Canadian common law. For reasons mentioned above, this situation is appropriate for a very cautious interpretation of Charter rights in Quebec civil law. But we doubt that it could or should go so far as to lead to an absolute refusal by the courts to apply the constitutional Charter to private law in whatever part of the country. Initially, very few thought that the Charter could be applied to private law; *supra*, note 12, at pp. 628–29. We must, however, admit that doctrine now shows a reversal of this tendency: D. Gibson, "The Canadian Charter of Rights and Freedoms, and a New Category of Qualified Privilege" (1983), 61 *Can. Bar Rev.* 124; A. Pratt, "The Charter and How to Approach It: A Guide for the Civil Practitioner" (1983), 4 *Advocate's Quarterly* 425; L. Smith, "Charter Equality Rights" (1984), 18 *U.B.C. L. Rev.* 351. Other authors, while not taking a position, do not in any way close the door to applicability of the Charter to private law: G. Laforest, "The Canadian Charter of Rights and Freedoms: An Overview" (1983), 61 *Can. Bar Rev.* 19; G. Remillard, *supra*, note 79.

84. For a good general overview of this issue, see C.F. Beckton, "Obscenity and Censorship Re-examined under the Charter of Rights" (1983), 13 *Man. L. J.* 351.

85. The following decisions are examples of rulings on this issue based on field of application: *Devine v. A.G. Quebec* (1982), C.S. 355; *Boucher v. C.E.Q.* (1982), C.S.P. 1003; *Roberge v. A.G. Quebec* C.S., Montreal, January 11, 1982.

86. See, for example, *Re Allman and Com'r of Northwest Territory* (1983), 144 D.L.R. (3d) 467 (S.C. N.W.T.).

87. We have here used the expression "due process of law" in a general sense, as we have done from the outset, in order to identify one of the three specific aspects which form the classic field of fundamental human rights, and not with reference to the terminology used by the Charter.

88. The English version of s. 7 seems to us to state this even more clearly.

89. *R. v. Operation Dismantle* (1983), 1 F.C. 745.

90. The difficulty with this case is that a ruling must be made on a preliminary motion to dismiss the action of those challenging. A right to security guaranteed by the Charter rather than the scope of s. 7 could lead to the dismissal of the federal government's preliminary motion and it would, therefore, seem clear that tests could continue to be conducted until a final ruling was handed down. For it to be otherwise, those challenging would have to seek a preliminary injunction which they could not obtain without assuming a burden of proof equivalent, for all intents and purposes, to the one they would have to bear at trial.

91. *Re s. 94(2) of the Motor Vehicle Act* (1983), 147 D.L.R. (3d) 539 (C.A. B.C.); *R. v. Stevens* (1983), 145 D.L.R. (3d) 563 (C.A. Ont.). In *Stevens*, the court simply assumed the substantive application of s. 7 of the Charter without making any ruling on it.

92. *Duke v. The Queen* (1972), S.C.R. 917.

93. *Supra*, note 12, at p. 506.

94. (1970), S.C.R. 282.

95. (1974), S.C.R. 1349.

96. (1979), 1 S.C.R. 183.

Bibliography

References for the Canadian Charter

Arbess, D.J. 1983. "Limitations on Legislative Override Under the Canadian Charter of Rights and Freedoms: A Matter of Balancing Values." 21 Osgoode Hall L.J. 113.

Bala, N.C., and J.D. Redfearn. 1983. "Family Law and the 'Liberty Interest': Section 7 of the Canadian Charter of Rights." 15 Ottawa L. Rev. 274.

Barry, L.D. 1982. "Law, Policy and Statutory Interpretation Under a Constitutionally Entrenched Canadian Charter of Rights and Freedoms." 60 Can. Bar Rev. 237.

Beaudoin, G.A., and W.S. Tarnopolsky. 1982. *Charte canadienne des droits et libertés.* Montreal: Wilson and Lafleur-Sorej.

Beckton, C.F. 1983a. "Obscenity and Censorship Re-examined Under the Charter of Rights." 13 Man. L.J. 351.

———. 1983b. *Freedom of Expression in Canada — How Free?* Brief to the Canadian Institute for the Administration of Justice Symposium in October 1983.

Belobaba, E.P., and E. Gertner. 1982. "The New Constitution and the Charter of Rights." 4 Supreme Court L.R. 1 (Special Issue).

Bender, P. 1983. "The Canadian Charter of Rights and Freedoms and the U.S. Bill of Rights: A Comparison." 28 McGill L.R. 811.

Bilodeau, R. 1983. "La langue, l'éducation et les minorités: avant et depuis la Charte canadienne des droits et libertés." 13 Man. L.J. 371.

Binavince, E. 1982. "The Impact of Mobility Rights." 14 Ottawa L. Rev. 340.

Blair, D.G. 1983. *The Charter and the Judges: A View from the Bench.* Lecture delivered to the Canadian Institute for the Administration of Justice Symposium in October 1983.

Brun, H. 1982. "Quelques notes sur les art. 1, 2, 7 et 15 de la Charte canadienne des droits et libertés." C. de D. 781.

————. 1983. "Le recouvrement de l'impôt et les droits de la personne." 24 C. de D. 457.

Canadian Charter of Rights and Freedoms (1982). 16 U.B.C.L. Rev. 1 (Special Issue).

Canadian Charter of Rights and Freedoms (1982). The Continuing Legal Education Society of B.C., Vancouver.

Canadian Constitution, 1982 (1982). 45 *Law and Contemporary Problems* 1 (Special Issue).

La Charte canadienne des droits et libertés (1983). 61 Can. Bar Rev. 1 (Special Issue).

La Charte canadienne des droits et libertés (1983). Barreau du Québec (joint authorship).

La Charte des droits et libertés. Guide à l'intention des Canadiens (1982). Ottawa: Minister of Supply and Services Canada.

Doherty, A. 1982. "What's Done Is Done: An Argument in Support of a Purely Prospective Application of the Charter of Rights." 26 C.R. (3d) 131.

Driedger, E.A. 1982. "The Canadian Charter of Rights and Freedoms." 14 Ottawa L. Rev. 366.

Duplé, N. 1984. "L'art. 7 de la Charte canadienne des droits et libertés et les principes de justice fondamentale." 25 C. de D. 99.

Ewaschuk, E.G. 1982. "The Charter: An Overview and Remedies." 26 C.R. (3d) 54.

Fitzgerald, P. 1983. "Canadian Rights and Freedoms — First Class or Charter?" 13 Man. L.J. 277.

Friedland, M.L. (1981–1982). "Legal Rights Under the Charter." 24 Crim. Law Quarterly 430.

————. 1983. *Legal Rights Under the Charter.* Brief to the Canadian Institute for the Administration of Justice Symposium in October 1983.

Garant, P. 1983. *L'art. 7 de la Charte demeure énigmatique après 18 mois de jurisprudence.* Brief to the Canadian Institute for the Administration of Justice Symposium in October 1983.

Gautron, A. 1982. "French/English Discrepancies in the Canadian Charter of Rights and Freedoms." 12 Man. L.J. 220.

Gibson, D. 1982. "The Charter of Rights and the Private Sector." 12 Man. L.J. 213.

———— 1983. *Distinguishing the Governors from the Governed: The Meaning of "Government" under s. 32(1) of the C.C.R.F.* Brief to the Canadian Institute for the Administration of Justice Symposium in October 1983.

Hébert, J.-C. 1983. "Le recours de l'article 24(1) de la Charte." 43 R. du B. 951.

Hogg, P. 1982. *Canada Act 1982 Annotated.* Toronto: Carswell.

Hovius, B. 1982. "The Legacy of the Supreme Court of Canada's Approach to the Canadian Bill of Rights: Prospects for the Charter." 28 McGill L.R. 31.

The Impact of the Canadian Charter of Rights and Freedoms on Canadian Business Law. 1983. Toronto: Davies, Ward and Beck.

Laskin, J.B., E.L. Greenspan, G.B. Dunlop, and M. Rosenberg. 1982. *The Canadian Charter of Rights.* Aurora: Canada Law Book.

Low, D.M. 1984. "The Canadian Charter of Rights and Freedoms and the Role of the Courts: An Initial Survey." 18 U.B.C.L. Rev. 69.

MacKay, A.W. 1983. "Judicial Process in the Supreme Court of Canada: The Patriation Reference and Its Implications for the Charter of Rights." 21 Osgoode Hall L.J. 55.

Manning, M. 1983. *Rights, Freedoms and the Courts: A Practical Analysis of the Constitution Act, 1982.* Toronto: Edmond-Montgomery.

McDonald, D.C. 1982. *Legal Rights in the Canadian Charter of Rights and Freedoms.* Toronto: Carswell.

McGinn, F. 1982. "The Canadian Charter of Rights and Freedoms: Its Impact on Law Enforcement." 31 U.N.B.L.J. 177.

McLellan A.A., and B.P. Elman. 1983. "The Enforcement of the Canadian Charter of Rights and Freedoms: An Analysis of S. 24." 21 Alta. L. Rev. 205.

McLeod, R.M., J.D. Takach, H.F. Morton, and M.D. Segal. 1983. *The Canadian Charter of Rights*. Toronto: Carswell.

Montigny, Y. de. 1984. "La Charte des droits et libertés, la prérogative royale et les questions politiques." 44 R. du B. 156.

Moull, W.D. 1984. "Business Law Implications of the Canadian Charter of Rights and Freedoms." 8 Can. Bus. L.J. 449.

The New Constitution and the Charter (1982–1983). 8 Queen's L.J. 1 (Special Issue).

Patenaude, P. 1983. "L'objection éthique et de conscience: impact de la Charte canadienne des droits et libertés." R.D.U.S. 315.

Pépin, G. 1983. "L'absence de pouvoir des organismes administratifs pour des motifs d'ordre constitutionnel: l'article 96 de l'A.A.N.B. et la Charte canadienne des droits et libertés." 43 R. du B. 353.

Pratt, A. 1983. "The Charter and How to Approach It: A Guide for the Civil Practitioner." 4 Advocates' Quarterly 425.

Proulx, D. 1983. "La précarité des droits linguistiques scolaires ou les singulières difficultés de la mise en oeuvre de l'article 23 de la Charte canadienne des droits et libertés." 14 R.G.D. 335.

Richards, J.G., and G.J. Smith. 1983. "Applying the Charter." 4 Advocates' Quarterly 129.

Robinson, R.E., S.C. Coval, and J.-C. Smith. 1983. "The Logic of Rights." 33 U.T.L.J. 267.

Roman, A. 1983. "The Charter of Rights: Renewing the Social Contract?" 8 Queen's L.J. 188.

Russell, P.H. 1982. "The Effect of a Charter Policy-Making Role on Canadian Courts." 25 Can. Pub. Adm. 1.

Ryan, H.R.S. 1983. "The Impact of the Canadian Charter of Rights and Freedoms on the Canadian Correctional System." 1 Ann. can. droits de la personne 99.

Samek, R.A. 1982. "Untrenching Fundamental Rights." 27 McGill L.J. 755.

Smiley, D. 1981. *Canadian Charter of Rights and Freedoms*. Toronto: Ontario Economic Council.

Smith, L. 1984. "Charter Equality Rights." 18 U.B.C.L. Rev. 351.

Tarnopolsky, W.S. 1981. "The Historical and Constitutional Context of the Proposed C.C.R.F." 44 Law and Contemporary Problems 169.

———. 1983. "The New Canadian Charter of Rights and Freedoms as Compared and Contrasted with the American Bill of Rights." 5 Human Rights Quarterly 227.

Tremblay, G. 1982. "La Charte canadienne des droits et libertés et quelques leçons tirées de la Convention européenne des droits de l'homme." 23 C. de D. 795.

Tremblay, L. 1984. "Section 7 of the Charter: Substantive Due Process." 18 U.B.C.L. Rev. 201.

Trudeau, P.E. 1968. *Charte canadienne des droits de l'homme*. Ottawa: Queen's Printer.

Whyte, J.D. 1983. *Legal Rights: The Scope and Application of Section 7 of the Charter*. Brief to the Canadian Institute for the Administration of Justice Symposium in October 1983.

General references in the field of human rights

Anderson, N. 1978. *Liberty, Law and Justice*. London: Stevens and Sons.

André-Vincent, P.-I. 1983. *Les droits de l'homme dans l'enseignement de Jean Paul II*. Paris: Librairie générale de droit et de jurisprudence.

Annuaire canadien des droits de la personne, 1983. 1983. Toronto: Carswell.

Aurenche, G. 1980. *L'aujourd'hui des droits de l'homme*. Paris: Nouvelle Cité.

Becet, J.-M., and D. Colland. 1982. *Les droits de l'homme, dimensions nationales et internationales*. Paris: Economica.

Beckton, C.F. 1982. *The Law and the Media*. Toronto: Carswell.

Berger, T.R. 1981. *Fragile Freedoms*. Toronto: Clarke, Irwin.

Bobbitt, P. 1982. *Constitutional Fate: Theory of the Constitution*: New York: Oxford University Press.

Boddendijk, F.R. 1982. *Minorities and Civil Liberties in Advanced Industrial Societies: A Question of Two Incompatible Values?* Brief to the International Political Science Association Symposium in August 1982.

Brownlie, I. 1981. *Basic Documents on Human Rights*. New York: Oxford University Press.

Brun, H., and G. Tremblay. 1982. *Droit constitutionnel*. Montreal: Éditions Yvon Blais, chap. 12.

Cappelletti, M., and W. Cohen. 1979. *Comparative Constitutional Law*. Indianapolis: Bobbs-Merrill.

Cassin, R. 1969. *Problèmes de protection internationale des droits de l'homme*. Paris: A. Pedone.

———. 1971. *La protection des droits de l'homme dans les rapports entre personnes privées*. Paris: A. Pedone.

———. 1972. *Méthodologie des droits de l'homme*. Paris: A. Pedone.

Cassin, R., R. Modinos, and K. Vasak. 1975. *Revue des droits de l'homme: Human Rights Journal* 8, special issue of *Droit international et Droit comparé*. Paris: A. Pedone.

Colliard, C.A. 1975. *Libertés publiques*. Paris: Dalloz.

Cox, A. 1968. *The Warren Court*. Cambridge: Harvard University Press.

———. 1976. *The Role of the Supreme Court in American Government*. New York: Oxford University Press.

Droits de la personne. 1981. 12 R.G.D. 295 (Special Issue).

Dworkin, R. 1977. *Taking Rights Seriously*. London: Duckworth.

Ely, J. 1980. *Democracy and Distrust*. Cambridge: Harvard University Press.

Falk, R.A. 1981. *Human Rights and State Sovereignty*. New York: Holmes-Meier.

Favoreu, L. 1982. *Cours constitutionnelles européennes et droits fondamentaux*. Paris: Economica; Presses universitaires d'Aix-Marseille.

Gall, G.L. 1982. *Civil Liberties in Canada*. Toronto: Butterworth.

Grenier, B. 1978. *La Déclaration canadienne des droits*. Quebec: Presses de l'université Laval.

Hersch, J. 1979. *Quelques paradoxes des droits de l'homme*. Zurich: Schultheiss Polygraphischer Verlag.

———. 1980. "Le concept des droits de l'homme est-il un concept universel?" Paris: Goethe Institute, unpublished.

Lachance, L. 1959. *Le droit et les droits de l'homme*. Paris: Presses universitaires françaises.

MacDonald, P.J., and J.P. Humphrey. 1979. *The Practice of Freedom*. Toronto: Butterworth.

Machan, T.R. 1975. *Human Rights and Human Liberties*. Chicago: Nelson Hall.

Madiot, Y. 1975. *Droits de l'homme et libertés publiques*. Paris: Masson.

Marie, J.B. 1981. *Glossaire des droits de l'homme: termes fondamentaux dans les instruments universels et régionaux*. Paris: Maison des sciences de l'homme.

Maritain, J. 1947. *Les droits de l'homme et la loi naturelle*. Paris: Paul Hartmann.

Morange, J. 1979. *Libertés publiques*. Paris: Presses universitaires françaises.

Mourgeon, J. 1981. *Les droits de l'homme*. Paris: Presses universitaires françaises.

Mourgeon, J., and J.-P. Theron. 1979. *Les libertés publiques*. Paris: Presses universitaires françaises.

Nelson, J.L., and V.M. Green. 1980. *International Human Rights: Contemporary Issues*. Cruger, N.Y.: E.M. Coleman.

Perry, M.J. 1982. *The Constitution, the Courts, and Human Rights: An Inquiry into the Legitimacy of Policy Making by the Judiciary*. New Haven: Yale University Press.

Pollack, E.H. 1971. *Human Rights*. Buffalo: Jay Stewart.

Pollis, A., and P. Schwab. 1979. *Human Rights: Cultural and Ideological Perspectives*. New York: Praeger.

Ramcharan, B.G. 1979. *Human Rights: Thirty Years After the Universal Declaration*. The Hague: Martinus Nijhoff.

Rivero, J. 1977. *Les libertés publiques*. Paris: Presses universitaires françaises.

Robertson, A.H. 1977. *Human Rights in Europe*. Manchester: Manchester University Press.

Sieghart, P. 1983. *The International Law of Human Rights*. Oxford: Oxford University Press.

Tarnopolsky, W.S. 1975. *The Canadian Bill of Rights*. 2d ed. Toronto: McClelland and Stewart.

UNESCO. 1968. *Le droit d'être un homme*. Paris: R. Laffont.

UNESCO. 1973. *Human Rights: Comments and Interpretations*. Westport: Greenwood Press.

Utz, A. 1967. *Ethique sociale; philosophie du droit*. Fribourg: Éditions universitaires Fribourg.

Vasak, K. 1978. *Les dimensions internationales des droits de l'homme*. Paris: UNESCO.

Wright, J.T. 1979. "Human Rights in the West: Political Liberties and the Rule of Law." In *Human Rights, Cultural and Ideological Perspectives*. New York: Praeger.

2

The Supreme Court of Canada:
Reform Implications for an Emerging National Institution

A. Wayne MacKay and Richard W. Bauman

Introduction: An Emerging Institution

Few Canadian citizens would consider the Supreme Court of Canada to be a national institution, and fewer would expect this group of nine people to have a significant impact on the political, social, and economic life of Canada.[1] Nonetheless, the Supreme Court has been, at least nominally, a national institution since its creation in 1875, and it has had a growing impact on the shape of Canadian society. As umpire of Canadian federalism, the Supreme Court has had an important effect on the exercise of government authority ever since it replaced the Judicial Committee of the Privy Council as the final appellate court.[2] One recent example of the impact of rulings on the distribution of powers is the ruling on ownership of the Newfoundland offshore, which has clearly had a direct economic and political consequence.[3]

The Supreme Court was created in 1875 by a regular federal statute passed pursuant to section 101 of the *Constitution Act, 1867*. Subject to arguments about implicit entrenchment, which will be discussed later, Canada's final appellate court is still a creature of statute.[4] In the early days, the prestige of the Court was not high and there were serious attempts to have it abolished.[5] Even after these turbulent early years, the role of the Supreme Court of Canada as constitutional umpire was not beyond question.

Paul Weiler has been one of the Court's most outspoken critics. In numerous articles and in his book, *In the Last Resort,*[6] he has criticized the performance of the Court on almost every front, including its rulings on matters related to the distribution of powers under the *Constitution Act, 1867*. Weiler went so far as to advocate that the Court should be replaced as final constitutional umpire by a system analogous to compulsory arbitration. Of course the Court has also had its supporters, who argue that its performance in constitutional cases has been quite acceptable.[7] However, even some of the staunch Court supporters, including the late Chief Justice Laskin, have argued that the Court should adopt a bolder and more adventurous role.[8] The tendency of Canadian judges has been to adopt the more restrained and cautious role of the British judge.[9]

Because of this rather restrained British backdrop, it is fashionable to argue that the Supreme Court has not played a policy-making role in Canada. As Chief Justice Brian Dickson observed in an article published in 1982, whether the Supreme Court has played a law-making role is largely a matter of definition.[10] The late Chief Justice Laskin, for one, was clearly of the view that the Supreme Court had a direct impact on the lives of everyday Canadians.

> Such is the character of the cases that come before the Supreme Court that its decisions on them may touch you as husband or wife, as businessman, as corporate executive, as shareholder, as policy holder, as labour union member, as civil servant, as teacher or student, as policeman, as member of an administrative agency, as a member of government, whether municipal, provincial or federal, as a person accused of an offence, and so on. All economic activity and all exercises of governmental authority, whether by legislation or by executive order or regulation, are potentially the stuff or, should I say, the staff of our life.[11]

Only in recent years has the practical impact and the policy-making role of the Supreme Court of Canada come to the attention of the Canadian public. One of the most dramatic examples of this was the 1981 decision on the patriation of the Constitution, in which the late Chief Justice Laskin read the judgment of the Supreme Court on nationwide television.[12] It is generally agreed that this decision helped pave the way for the 1981 November Accord, which made the patriation of the Constitution possible. Included in this patriated package was the *Canadian Charter of Rights and Freedoms*.[13] It is this document which greatly extends the policy function of the Supreme Court of Canada and accentuates the growing public presence of the Court. Evidence of this new public persona is seen in *Maclean's* magazine's extensive and front-page coverage of the appointment of Chief Justice Dickson,[14] and also in the extensive media reference given the Court's role in shaping the Charter of Rights. This media interest continued when the Court handed down its first Charter decision on May 3, 1984 and most newspapers and electronic newscasts commented on *The Law Society of Upper Canada v. Skapinker*.[15] The same kind of headline coverage has been extended to the subsequent two Charter cases.

As a national institution, the Supreme Court of Canada has been relatively free from public scrutiny. Various traditions and customs have grown up around the Court to shield it from the public glare, although these customs are neither expressly articulated nor easily comprehensible to the lay observer. The only time the Court is likely to be the subject of serious scrutiny is when law-related professional bodies meet to discuss the Court's work or when provincial governments lament the untrammelled freedom of the federal cabinet to appoint members to the Court at its discretion. Although suggestions have been made in the past to change various features of the Court, the process of evolution has been slow.

Even before the arrival of the Charter of Rights, the Supreme Court of Canada had begun to emerge from the mists of the Ottawa bureaucracy.[16] The use of the reference mechanism to test such high-profile political measures as the federal anti-inflation program[17] and possible modifications of the Canadian Senate[18] emphasized the political significance of rulings from the Supreme Court of Canada. Rulings under the Charter of Rights will further accentuate the impact of the Court on the social, political and economic life of Canadians. The Supreme Court of Canada has finally been recognized as an important national institution, and with this recognition will come increasing public scrutiny of the Court both as an institution and as a collection of prominent individuals.

Reform of any institution requires the consideration of at least three interrelated variables. First, for us to understand what makes it distinctive, the institution itself must be examined. The values that are implicit in the institutional structure may be so strong that the values of the individual and changing members of the institution are subordinated to the institutional goals. Second, the people who compose the institution must be studied. It is never entirely clear whether the people shape the institution or vice versa. In the judicial context, there are clearly institutional limitations on the individual personalities of the judges.[19] Whether people with more radical views are co-opted by a more conservative institution is an important issue to consider in the context of reform. Finally, the social, political and economic climate will condition the process of reform. The time is ripe for considering reform of the Supreme Court of Canada as it assumes a higher profile and embarks upon a potentially more expansive role in Canadian society.

For purposes of this study, we shall assume that there is something distinctive about the process of judging that distinguishes it from such other political processes as legislating or administering. We shall also assume the continued existence of the Supreme Court of Canada as an appointed legal body at the top of the Canadian judicial hierarchy. Beyond these assumptions, we shall broadly consider reform and go beyond traditional proposals for Supreme Court reform, which have been neither numerous nor particularly original.

Some overarching themes ought to be emphasized at the outset, for they affect all the particular issues that have traditionally been treated by proponents of Supreme Court reform. The Court's work will become more publicized. In the process, it will be liable to be exposed to a widening circle of commentary and responses that will not always be deferential. The perception of the Court's accomplishments and its direction have already become the basis of proposals for reform. Such rough-and-ready labels as "centralist" versus "decentralist," or "liberal" versus "conservative," do not adequately capture the subtle reasoning that goes into a judgment of the Supreme Court. Yet the desire and disposition to apply such convenient labels is a fair indication of a widespread perception that Supreme Court justices carry with them some intellectual or even ideological baggage.

The Court's image — which includes elements of personality, political affiliation, family history, religious background, region of origin, age, gender, and judicial and other professional experience — is at the heart of the discussion over the proper shape of this emerging national institution.[20] In addition to the issues of perception and image, a discussion of reform must also take into account reasonable projections about the type and volume of cases that the Court may be expected to hear in the near and middle-term future. Such circumstances bear directly on the kind of Court that should be sought.

To the authors of this study, seven major themes appear relevant to a consideration of reform in the Supreme Court of Canada.

The first concerns the implications for the Court of its new role as a high-profile national institution. Will the result of the increased publicity and public awareness be a more "politicized" and accessible Court and is this desirable?

The second concerns the impact of the Charter on the role of the Supreme Court of Canada. Will the Charter change the operation of the Court in such basic matters as the leave mechanism, court jurisdiction, the use of extrinsic evidence, form of judgments and judicial style?

The third theme relates to the growing impact of the Supreme Court of Canada on social and economic issues. Although the Court has always had considerable influence by ruling on the distribution of powers, claims based upon a "substantive due process" interpretation of section 7 of the Charter emphasize the potential role in challenging the wisdom of the legislators. Other sections of the Charter, such as those related to language (sections 16–23) and the ones related to mobility (section 6) and equality (section 15), could plunge the Court directly into social and economic policy. Will the Court adopt such a role, and is it ready for it?

Fourth is the importance of perceptions about the Supreme Court and its biases — federal/provincial, liberal/conservative, male/female, English/French, majority/minority. Is there any empirical evidence to support biases on the part of the Court? How should one resolve problems concerning perceptions of bias, even if there is no empirical support of such a view?

Fifth is the need for a more open and representative appointment process. The process of selecting Supreme Court judges is secretive and provides limited input. Is such a system acceptable for selecting a Court with a higher public profile and potentially expansive role?

The sixth point concerns the need for a more varied and representative presence on the Supreme Court itself. What are the socioeconomic and professional profiles of Supreme Court judges? Is there a need for broader representation on the basis of sex, regional affiliation, economic background or ethnic origin?

The seventh concern relates to the proper jurisdiction for the Supreme Court of Canada in the 1980s and beyond. Can the Court continue to be a court of general appellate jurisdiction hearing a wide variety of cases? What will be the impact on the Court's agenda of a flood of Charter cases? What structural changes can be made to accommodate an expanded workload? How should the Court limit its own agenda?

This suggested thematic analysis of Supreme Court reform differs from the more traditional models for reform that have been developed in the past, which have tended to take a more functional line. Many of the same issues, however, would emerge from the above thematic analysis. Since it will be useful to compare our reform proposals with previous ones, we have retained a more functional organization for this paper. However, our broad themes will be considered in the context of each of the functional headings and will be expressly considered in developing specific recommendations for reform. We shall also return to these overarching themes in our conclusion.

Past reform proposals, the structure of similar courts in other western democracies, and statistical information about the Supreme Court of Canada and its judges are presented in tabular or appendix form. As the length of this study suggests, it was an ambitious project. However, it is not an exhaustive study. Where possible, this paper is cross-referenced to other studies done for the Commission. In particular, reference is made to the papers prepared for this volume by Professors Henri Brun and Gilles Pépin, as well as papers in other research sections.

The New Challenges of the Charter

To emphasize the potential significance of the Charter of Rights for Supreme Court reform, we address it first. It is still too early to assert that the Charter will revolutionize the rights of Canadians, but it is reasonably safe to predict that it will significantly alter the operation of courts generally and especially the Supreme Court of Canada.[21] We should emphasize that this will be an additional role for the Court to bear. The Charter opens up new territory for the Court to explore without supplanting some of the traditional functions of the Court (described at length in the section to follow, on jurisdiction). The Court will not cease to be an adjudicator of the distribution of legislative powers under the Canadian Constitution; within our federal structure, it will still be important in determining the limits of provincial and federal statutory and regulatory powers.

Some of the papers prepared for the Commission portray the Charter as a watershed in Canadian political life. Cynthia Williams, in her study, "The Changing Nature of Citizen Rights" (in volume 33), stresses a rights consciousness as an important new ingredient in Canadian constitutionalism. While it is hard to dispute this analysis, it is not so obvious that this phenomenon will produce significant institutional and social change. In the final analysis, it will be the judges, particularly those who sit on the Supreme Court of Canada, who will tell Canadians whether the Charter will have a lasting and significant impact. It is the judges who give concrete form to the abstract phrases.[22]

Predictions about the real impact of the Charter thus require an assessment of judging in Canada. This kind of assessment has led some commentators to conclude that Canadian judges are ill-equipped to deal with the new responsibilities of the Charter of Rights.[23] Others are cautiously optimistic about greater creativity on the Supreme Court of Canada,[24] while Chief Justice Brian Dickson expresses no doubt that the judiciary will meet the challenge of the Charter and will develop a distinctively Canadian jurisprudence.[25] The Chief Justice is judiciously vague as to exactly what role judges should play, but his earlier writings and cases suggest a cautious activism.[26]

Historically, Canadian judges have adopted a restrained, even conservative, judicial style. The precise judicial role may depend upon the context of political events. Canadian judges have been reluctant to second-guess the legislators but have been willing to step in when particular governments become too extreme or radical. One example is the performance of the Supreme Court of Canada with respect to legislation passed by the Social Credit government of Alberta in the 1930s;[27] another is the Court's response to the government practices of Maurice Duplessis in Quebec.[28] Most of the time, however, Canadian judges would likely accept Lord Devlin's description of their role: "I am not one of those who believe that the only function of the law is to preserve the status quo," he said. "Rather I should say that the law is the gatekeeper of the status quo."

As "gatekeepers of the status quo," many judges have demonstrated a very restrictive admissions policy, and it is this that ultimately leads us to recommend a significant change in the appointment process. There have been some judges who staked out a more positive role for judges in protecting basic rights in Canada. Foremost among these was the late Ivan C. Rand.[29] The late Chief Justice Bora Laskin was also vigilant with respect to the protection of the basic rights of the Canadian citizen.[30] Less well-known are the views of former Supreme Court justice Emmett Hall, who advocates a law reform role for judges.[31] The views of Chief Justice Dickson have already been discussed. These judges are the exceptions that prove the rule.

Judicial Review in Canada

In 1867, Canada acquired a constitution that was "similar in principle to that of the United Kingdom." This phrase within the *Constitution Act, 1867*, plus the general acceptance of British practice, has made the supremacy of Parliament one of Canada's foremost constitutional principles. Grafted onto this British parliamentary structure, however, was a written constitution and a federal division of powers. Thus, the doctrine of supremacy of Parliament had to be modified to fit the federal Canadian context.[32] The division of legislative powers implied the need for some umpire of federalism, and it was judicially accepted that the umpire should be the courts.[33]

Canada has had no real equivalent to the U.S. case of *Marbury v. Madison*,[34] and there is an academic debate about the origins of judicial review in Canada. Leading constitutional experts such as William Lederman and Noel Lyon have argued that sections 96 to 101 of the *Constitution Act, 1867* implicitly guarantee a measure of judicial review.[35] Others, in particular Barry Strayer, have argued that judicial review was an extension of colonial practice and that it grew in importance by way of "judicial usurpation."[36]

Political scientist Jennifer Smith offers yet another view on the origins of judicial review in Canada.[37] By looking at the Confederation Debates, she concludes that the unitary court structure generally and the Supreme Court of Canada in particular were intended as tools of centralization. Indeed, judicial review was seen as an alternative to federal disallowance, and a less attractive one from the provincial perspective because it was not open to political debate. Accordingly, the perceptions of the Supreme Court of Canada as a federal rather than national institution do have long historical roots. Whether these perceptions have any validity today is less clear.[38]

What has the arrival of the Charter of Rights done to change the stature of judicial review in Canada? Section 52 of the *Constitution Act, 1982* has asserted, in express form, a kind of judicial supremacy, for the Constitution is to prevail over all conflicting laws. This section, coupled with section 24 which grants a broad judicial remedial discretion, expands the role of courts in Canada. It is significant that these sections were enacted in 1982 with full knowledge of the experiences of judicial review in both Canada and the United States. By contrast, in 1867 the Fathers of Confederation knew little about the nature or scope of courts in a federal parliamentary structure.[39]

This increased judicial role does not necessarily involve a rejection either of democratic principles[40] or the supremacy of Parliament. Section 33 of the Charter of Rights, which allows legislators to override the Charter, is a clear indication that supremacy of Parliament is not dead. Indeed, this section implies a certain mistrust in judges as the final arbiters of fundamental rights and is a classic Canadian compromise between the British and U.S. systems. It was a solution suggested by Paul Weiler even before the Charter was drafted.[41] Legislators also have a role in shaping the Charter by way of anticipating Charter challenges and taking preventive action.[42]

Judicial review is also coloured by the principle of federalism. It has been argued that one of the important goals of the Charter was to provide a symbol of national unity,[43] and in many respects it will be a centralizing force in Canadian political life. However, section 33 of the Charter will still provide a focus for the inevitable forces of decentralization in Canadian society.[44] Even if section 33 itself will not be used frequently, the traditions of deference to Parliament and judicial restraint will be expressed by judges in their interpretation of "reasonable limits" in section 1 of the Charter.

The arrival of the Charter enhances the stature of judicial review in Canada and will change the role of courts in ways that will only become apparent in the fullness of time.[45] Nonetheless, parliamentary supremacy has not been replaced by judicial supremacy. The two principles coexist in the Charter of Rights, and one of the important challenges facing the Supreme Court of Canada is to strike the proper balance between them.

The United States' Model

In responding to the new challenges of the Charter, the Supreme Court will certainly look to the experiences of the United States with its Bill of Rights.[46] In doing that, Canadian judges will be well aware of the different traditions in the two countries. The contrast between the performance of the Canadian and the U.S. Supreme Courts is emphasized by considering the record of the Supreme Court of Canada in interpreting the Canadian Bill of Rights.[47] Chief Justice Dickson, while eager to examine the lessons of U.S. jurisprudence, has repeatedly called for the development of a distinctive Canadian jurisprudence on the Charter of Rights.[48] Academic commentators agree that we should learn from the experiences of the United States, but we should allow Canadian solutions to evolve rather than adopting carbon copies of those developed south of the forty-ninth parallel.[49]

The United States Supreme Court has provided a model for many democratic countries as has the U.S. Constitution generally.[50] U.S. currency carries the motto "In God We Trust," and in matters of fundamental rights, the United States appears to adopt the motto "In Courts We

Trust." Such trust is by no means universal, however, and especially in the heyday of the Earl Warren Court, there were those who were concerned about an imperial judiciary.[51] Furthermore, the performance of the U.S. Supreme Court has been uneven, and in some respects the Warren Court was an aberration.

Even accepting that there has been a recent tradition of activism in the U.S Supreme Court, it does not follow automatically that the Charter will lead the Canadian Court to adopt the same stance. Taking account of the differences between Canada and the United States, even some U.S. commentators have argued that Canadian judges will play a more modest role under the Charter than their equivalents south of the border.[52] Thus the United States offers an example rather than a model. History and proximity suggest that the U.S. example will be more persuasive than others from Europe or the United Nations, but no examples will be determinative.

The Impact of the Charter

Is is impossible to consider properly the impact of the Charter on the role of the Supreme Court of Canada without giving some consideration to the Charter's impact on Canadian society generally. That is also why this discussion has been prefaced by an examination of the Canadian traditions of judicial restraint, in contrast with U.S. models of judicial activism. There has been much academic writing about the potential impact of the Charter of Rights and we make no attempt here to be comprehensive or exhaustive.

Most legal academics have spoken optimistically about the beneficial impact of the Charter of Rights on Canadian society. The list of scholars in this camp is a lengthy one and it would include such names as Walter Tarnopolsky[53] (now a judge on the Ontario Court of Appeal) and Morris Manning, who has written a book on the Charter.[54] There is, however, a shorter list of legal academics who argue that the Charter will produce very little in the way of real change.[55] Their arguments are based upon the process of Charter making, the kinds of rights listed in the document, and the conservative nature of Canadian society. What impact the Charter will have on the rights of Canadians will depend, in large measure, on how it will change the role of courts in Canada.

Peter Russell, one of Canada's foremost court watchers, asserts that the Charter will accentuate the policy-making role of courts in Canada.

> The decisions of Canadian courts interpreting a constitutional charter of rights and freedoms will provide Canadians with a crash course in judicial policy-making.[56]

Russell prefaced the above comment with the assertion that Canadian judges have always been policy makers to some degree, and adopt clearly political roles when they sit on royal commissions, police commissions or human rights inquiries. Chief Justice Dickson also has stressed that judges have never been simple interpreters of the law even in their adjudicative role.[57] The effect of the Charter will emphasize the policy-making role and throw it into the public light. As discussed in the Introduction, this is already apparent in the increased media profile of the Supreme Court of Canada, which has institutional implications.

The essential mandate of the courts, and ultimately of the Supreme Court of Canada, in giving concrete meaning to the abstractions in the Charter of Rights, cannot be overstated. It is not a self-enforcing document and it is through judicial interpretation that it will be given content. Courts are faced with a difficult task of interpretation and policy making. One clear conclusion is that solutions to Charter disputes will depend at least as much on political theory and philosophy as on case precedent.[58]

An important implication of the new Charter role for courts is the need to find mechanisms to inform judges about social, economic and political facts. The Supreme Court has been increasingly receptive to extrinsic evidence in constitutional litigation,[59] and this trend should continue. It may be necessary to follow the U.S. model of the Brandeis brief, but the procedural and administrative aspects of reform will be discussed later. The task of informing judges will be even more important if, as Leo Barry (the recently elected leader of Newfoundland's Liberal Party) suggests, the attitudes and values that these judges should reflect are those of the community and not their own.[60]

Not everyone is convinced that the Charter intended a significant change in Canadian society or in the role of its judges.[61] Even if such change were intended, there are commentators who feel that Canadian judges will not deliver on the promise. Robert Martin and Berend Hovius emphasize that the Court as an institution has been deferential, quite apart from the philosophies of individual members who compose it from time to time.

> We believe that restraint is a principle too deeply imbedded in the thought processes of Canadian lawyers and judges to be abruptly displaced through the adoption of the Charter. Conversely, activism as either an approach to judging or a style of judging does not sit well with Canadian judges.[62]

Peter Russell also questions whether a broader policy-making role for the courts is a good thing.

> However, transferring the policy-making focus from the legislative to the judicial arena also has a negative side. It represents a further flight from politics, a deepening disillusionment with the procedures of representative government and government by discussion as means of resolving fundamental questions of through the judicial process entails the danger, however the courts resolve these issues, of transforming these matters into technical legal questions and of making the answers to these questions hinge on the outcome of a contest between legal adversaries rather than on a political process more likely to yield a social consensus.[63]

Taking account of these kinds of concerns, Henri Brun, in his study on the Charter, which appears in this volume, argues that the Charter should be applied broadly but used sparingly. He asserts that it should be used as a shield rather than as a sword for shaping social policy. Indeed, he argues that the Charter, if used excessively, could be an impediment to the betterment of Canadian society. Brun argues that courts should not become a second legislature but play the more traditional role of shielding citizens from government abuse.

In a different way, William Lederman also makes a plea for a more balanced and traditional role for courts in Canada. He argues that the courts and legislatures must develop a new partnership in the country.

> Nevertheless, independent courts and democratic legislatures are and will remain the two primary legal decision-makers in our constitutional system with essentially coordinate status and complementary functions. We need both and we must continue to rely on both; and, for their part, these two institutions must continuously seek and find reasonable points of equilibrium between themselves in a spirit of partnership as they perform their respective functions.[64]

Only three Charter cases have been decided by the Supreme Court of Canada at the time of this writing.[65] It would be foolish to make any generalizations based upon these cases, but there are hints that the Court intends to take the Charter seriously. If forced to predict the impact of the Charter, we would incline toward the views expressed by Brun and Lederman. It is likely that the Court will take a balanced and cautious approach to the Charter at least in the early decades of its existence. There will still be significant reform implications for the Court, but there will not be the complete judicial revolution that some predict. This may be a chicken and egg problem, because the impact of the Charter on society would be greater if the reforms we propose were adopted.

Reform Implications of the Charter

Whatever the interpretation of the Charter, it does have some important reform implications for the Supreme Court of Canada. As mentioned previously, it will focus attention in an unprecedented fashion on the personalities, values and attitudes of Canadian Supreme Court justices.[66] The flood of Charter cases, even if it does not continue at the same pace, will put real strains on the administrative operations of the Court. There has already been some alteration of the leave process in response to the larger number of leave applications. Furthermore, the workload of the Court is taking on an increasing public law dimension because of the numerous Charter cases.[67] There may be little room left on the Supreme Court docket for private law cases.

The Charter of Rights will also provide a new vehicle by which the Supreme Court can have a direct impact on economic affairs. As will be discussed later, this is already the case with respect to the division of powers under the *Constitution Act, 1867*. In the past, the courts have had little impact on the federal spending power or the shaping of social policy at either the federal or provincial level. Depending upon what approach judges take to the Charter, this could now change.

Section 15 of the Charter, effective from April 1985, will have a wide-ranging potential impact on both social and economic policy. (This section is the focus of a study in this volume prepared by Mary Eberts.) Affirmative action programs or a positive reading of subsection 15(1) of the Charter could require governments to spend money and develop programs to actively promote equality in Canada. It may not be enough that the government itself refrain from discriminatory conduct.

Section 7 of the Charter, which guarantees "life, liberty and security of the person," if interpreted broadly, could mandate a wide range of government expenditures on public housing, medicare, social assistance or even education.[68] In the field of education, minority language education rights, as guaranteed in section 23 of the Charter, would require school boards to spend money on hiring teachers or building schools where numbers warrant such action. Furthermore, the general language guarantees in sections 16–22 of the Charter could also result in courts telling legislators how to spend money.

Section 6 dealing with mobility rights will have a clear economic impact since it will limit provincial legislators in the kind of employment policies that they can pursue. Less obviously, even the legal rights provisions of the Charter (sections 7–14) and the guarantee of fundamental rights in section 2 will plunge the courts into economic affairs. Prisons must not subject inmates to "cruel and unusual punishment," and if a prison is found to be in violation, it may well be required to expend funds to remedy the situation. The imposition of due process hearings on segments of the bureaucracy will also entail public expenditure. Providing equal access to the mentally and physically disabled can be a costly government endeavour.

The examples could be multiplied indefinitely but the point is a simple one: the guarantees under the Charter have a price tag. Thus economics is one of the factors that the courts will have to put into the balance in deciding what are reasonable limits on rights. This squarely raises the question of whether our judges are ready for balancing legal rights against social and economic costs.

These considerations lead us to the heart of our reform proposals: the need for a more open appointment process to the Supreme Court and for greater diversity in the membership of this institution. Paul Weiler argued that we should have a special Constitutional Court that would be composed of poets, social scientists, philosophers and statesmen, in addition to lawyers.[69] We do not go this far in our reform proposals but we do share some of the concerns expressed by Weiler and others[70] about whether the current training for judges is appropriate to their new task. Indeed it is the composition of the Supreme Court that will determine the real impact of the Charter of Rights. We shall return to this point in our reform proposals.

Constitutional Status

The Supreme Court of Canada was created by Parliament in 1875[71] under the legislative power conferred in section 101 of the *Constitution Act, 1867*.[72] That section entitles Parliament to provide for, among other things, "the Constitution, Maintenance, and Organization of a general Court of Appeal for Canada." Its constitutional basis thus distinguishes the Supreme Court from other courts whose members are appointed by the federal government. They are established either by virtue of a different clause contained in section 101,[73] or else by the provisions pursuant to subsection 90(14).[74] In the latter case, the federal government retains the power, under section 96, to appoint superior, district and county court judges in the provinces.

There have been suggestions that the whole judiciary now appointed by federal authorities should be given some constitutional status and protection. Such action would emphasize that Canada is a nation that ranks the rule of law among its highest ideals.[75] Entrenching the existence and essential features of the Supreme Court, in particular, would raise it both symbolically and actually to the status of a national institution with enduring powers capable of counterbalancing those possessed by other instruments of government. We see this as a necessary stage in the continuing development of the distinctive, national role of the Court. It would recognize the significant task of the Court as the final arbiter in crucial economic, political and social disputes that affect the nation as a whole.

It is arguable that the Court already has some degree of constitutional recognition. The situation is not clear-cut. Until 1982, no legal obstacle stood in the way of Parliament's dismantling the Court or altering its composition, jurisdiction or powers. The previous arrangement would have permitted the federal government, acting unilaterally, to abolish the Court by ordinary legislative action.[76] This was changed by the adoption of sections 41 and 42 of the *Constitution Act, 1982*.[77]

Section 41 provides that the "composition" of the Court can be amended only by the unanimous consent of all of the provinces and of Parliament. By section 42, any matters other than composition that relate to the Supreme Court can be altered only by observing the amending procedure provided in subsection 38(1) of that Act. This procedure requires that at least two-thirds of the provinces with at least fifty percent of the total population of all the provinces must agree with Parliament on the changes.

On the surface, these provisions appear to guarantee that some joint action by the federal and provincial governments will be necessary to effect any changes in the Supreme Court. In fact, the issue is controversial. For some writers, sections 41 and 42 effectively entrench the Court in all its material aspects.[78] In the eyes of the other commentators, no such result has yet been achieved.[79]

The two provisions in question deal explicitly only with amendments to the "Constitution of Canada," so far as it relates to the Supreme Court. The documents or sources of law composing the Constitution of Canada are defined by enumeration, pursuant to subsection 52(2) of the Act.[80] Neither the *Supreme Court Act*[81] nor any of its revisions is included in the definition. In the view of Professor Hogg, subsections 41(d) and 42(d) fail to immunize the Court against ordinary legislative measures enacted by Parliament.[82] It would take the express inclusion by reference of the *Supreme Court Act* under the "Constitution of Canada" for those subsections to perform the task of entrenchment.

Second, we must ask what is the proper constitutional interpretation to be placed on the Court's own enabling provision, section 101. That provision has become part of the Constitution of Canada by the operation of subsection 52(2) of the Act.[83] This could be interpreted as an entrenchment of the Court as a general court of appeal for Canada. A better interpretation, however, is that section 101 only guarantees Parliament's right to create a court such as the present Supreme Court of Canada. It does not guarantee the Court's perpetual existence (subject to the special amending procedures requiring unanimity or broad consensus).

Even if it were maintained that changes to the composition and to other matters relating to the Court did require a special constitutional procedure, it is still unclear what would be included in those respective expressions. Does "composition" embrace numbers of judges, their qualifications, and their tenure, as well as simply the number of judges from Quebec? Does it extend so far as to cover possible future amendments dividing the Court into specialized chambers? Similarly, does section 42 require the special amending procedure to be followed when Parliament proposes to change the procedural funding, staffing and day-to-day bureaucratic aspects of the Court's administration? *The Constitution Act, 1982* is not clear about this. The legislative history of that Act makes us no wiser on this point.[84] The limits of federal action in changing the features of a national institution were discussed in a general way in the Senate Reference.[85] The Court there held that certain "fundamental features" or "essential characteristics" of the Senate could not be altered by Parliament's unilateral action.[86] There may be an analogy between the Senate, as a body referred to under the *British North America Act, 1867*, and the Supreme Court, insofar as it is already, or will become, entrenched under the *Constitution Act, 1982*. It would then be up to subsequent courts to define judicially which characteristics of the Supreme Court are "essential" and which of its features are "fundamental" to its purpose and function.

It is, therefore, still possible to argue that the Court has yet to receive entrenched guarantees in the Constitution. Agitation for accomplishing this ordinarily relies upon three arguments. The first concerns the Court's role as an adjudicator of the distribution of legislative powers between the federal and provincial governments. In this role as "umpire,"[87] the Court's status as entirely a creature of one of the adversaries in the contest is inconsistent with the principles of federalism.[88] This is not to say that the Court's past record has shown its partiality toward the actions and aspirations of the federal government; but impartiality is as much a matter of perception and apprehension as of actual performance.

Secondly, with the advent of the Charter,[89] the individual citizen's rights will be measured against decisions and actions taken by all levels of government, including Parliament. It would be unseemly for those rights to be rendered nugatory in the event that Parliament decided to obstruct the enforcement of those rights by removing the judicial power to grant appropriate remedies.

The third argument proceeds on the basis that the Supreme Court has evolved into an institution of great symbolic significance.[90] Its authority is important to governments and private citizens alike, for it is counted on to articulate essential values of Canadian society, especially where these might differ from preponderant values in other legal and political cultures. Canada does not, at least in theory, embrace the doctrine of the separation of governmental powers into the legislative, executive and judicial branches, with all three branches being coordinate[91] and no one among them having an undue concentration of power or dominance over the affairs of the others.[92] More relevant to the Canadian system of government is the doctrine of parliamentary supremacy, in which the court's role is subservient to that of the legislators. In practice, it has evolved that the legislative and executive branches have relinquished "virtually all control over the judiciary."[93] It has also happened that through the review of legislation to determine its constitutional validity and through the judicial review of administrative action, the courts have attained an independent and esteemed place in our governmental structure.[94] Entrenchment of the essential features of the Supreme Court, in particular, would confirm and protect against diminution of the functions it already exercises.

There is little disagreement in the academic literature over the entrenchment of the Supreme Court. Nor is there serious friction about which features should be rendered relatively immutable by such a process. The very existence of the Court might be guaranteed by an appropriately worded clause in the Constitution. This has become especially important since 1949, when the last vestiges of the colonial administration of justice disappeared from the Canadian judicial system.[95] Before that date, if the Supreme Court had been legislated out of existence, the functions of the general appellate court of last resort could have been performed by the Judicial Committee of the Privy Council. In many instances, parties chose to by-pass the Supreme Court and to take their dispute directly to the Privy Council from a provincial court of appeal. Since 1949, the Supreme Court's judgments have been final; they cannot be reviewed by any other tribunal. The Court is no longer just another appellate body in the judicial hierarchy. It sits atop that hierarchy and, as shall be seen in the succeeding sections of this study, occupies an increasingly visible and influential place.

The composition of the Court, as we have discussed above, has also been a prime subject of entrenchment. Currently, it is provided by statute that at least three of the members of the Court shall be appointed from the Quebec bench or bar.[96] There is no statutory direction or limit on the province of origin of the other six judges.[97] In practice, more or less transient patterns have evolved in terms of the regional background of the members at any given time. It would doubtless be difficult for Parliament and the provincial legislatures to reach unanimous agreement on the regional or provincial origin of all of the positions of the Supreme Court. Such origins probably form part of what is meant by "composition," as used in section 41 of the *Constitution Act, 1982*, to which reference has been made above. The provinces and the federal government should at least be able to arrive at some minimum figure for the number of Quebec judges. The province of Quebec would want no less than this, and many of the other provinces would want no more.

The third element that has proved appealing to the advocates of entrenchment has been the jurisdiction of the Supreme Court. The limitations that might be inscribed in the Constitution would partly determine the Court's impact as a national institution. At present, the Court is empowered to hear and decide upon diverse matters, ranging from private disputes on a local level to public law issues of nation-wide impact. Although writers may disagree about the advisability of cutting down this comprehensive jurisdiction, there is little doubt that any changes to the type of work performed by the Court should be subjected to a process of consultation between the federal and the provincial governments. The resulting agreement should then be encased in a constitutional reform, for jurisdiction is a fundamental feature of the Court. The enabling provision in section 101 of the *Constitution Act, 1867* already provides that the Court, if established, shall be a "general court of appeal for Canada." To this extent, the Court's jurisdiction is arguably contained in the Constitution already.[98]

A final candidate for entrenchment is some guarantee of the independence and tenure of the judges on the Supreme Court. Such matters are already provided for in part by statute. The *Judges Act*[99] sets the salaries of the Supreme Court judges, and the *Supreme Court Act* sets forth the conditions under which the judge holds office during good behaviour up to age 75.[100] There is also a significant body of unwritten constitutional restrictions on any interference with the independence of judges and the autonomy of courts.[101] These were built up over centuries of British history and reached Canada before Confederation.[102]

Among the legal rights of an accused person protected by the Charter is that of a "fair and public hearing by an independent and impartial tribunal."[103] Such constitutional language confirms that an independent judiciary is one of the mainstays of the Canadian system of justice. Although some commentators have argued that the drafters of the Constitution of Canada to some degree already achieved this,[104] there is no good reason why this principle should not be made explicit by a constitutional amendment. The independence and tenure of members of the Supreme Court could be entrenched without such a guarantee necessarily being extended to judges at all levels of courts in Canada.

Jurisdiction

The topic of jurisdiction is not the dry-as-dust matter that one might first believe. Within the discussion of what kinds of cases the Court has been permitted to hear are fascinating issues of justiciability, provincial rights and judicial competence. Indeed, many of the questions raised in succeeding sections of this study are foreshadowed in the discussion of jurisdiction. Moreover, although the foregoing sections of this study on the impact of the Charter are liable to create the impression that many of the traditional functions of the Court have been superseded, this is far from the actual situation. The Court, in addition to interpreting and enforcing the Charter, will continue to face other major types of constitutional problems, such as division-of-power issues that have an undoubted impact on economic and social relations within the country.

The following remarks on the Court's jurisdiction will tend to balance those made about the Charter. Issues arising out of the Charter are for the moment more glamorous and perhaps timely, but the whole picture of the Court's work should not be obscured by exclusive emphasis on only one branch of constitutional law. It is useful to recall how the Court has made its mark on the current organization of government control of the economy and affected the political balance between different levels of government. This is discussed in great detail in the studies undertaken for the Commission in the section on Law, Society and the Economy.

Current Jurisdiction

The kernel of the Supreme Court's work is embedded in a descriptive phrase in section 101 of the *Constitution Act, 1867*. In setting up the Court,

Parliament was creating a "general court of appeal for Canada."[105] In spite of these words that specifically express the appellate function of the Court, Parliament over the years has seen fit to endow the Court with some items of "special jurisdiction." This rubric covers matters that are readily classifiable as the subjects of original, not appellate, jurisdiction. Surviving remnants of this special jurisdiction include constitutional questions referred to the Court by the federal cabinet,[106] and private bills or petitions referred by the Senate or by the House of Commons.[107] These matters are manifestly not appeals. (Attempts to rationalize them as falling within the Court's appellate function have been summarized in an interesting way by Peter Russell[108] who shows, in particular, the tenuous validity of the reference device. Since the publication of his article, the constitutional reference has increased in popularity with the federal cabinet.)

The vast majority of the Court's work has historically been devoted to appeals.[109] Immediately before 1975, most of the appeals to the Court were as of right,[110] and these so-called *de plano* appeals outnumbered those brought by leave of one court or another. Appeals as of right existed for both civil and criminal cases, and the *Supreme Court Act* settled which civil appeals could be entertained by the Court. The primary criterion was a monetary limit placed on the "matter in controversy." On the last occasion on which this minimum was increased, it amounted to $10,000.[111] If the amount in dispute exceeded this, the Court was obliged to entertain the appeal from the decision of the provincial appellate court. An appeal could also be brought directly to the Supreme Court, on certain conditions, from the judgment of a court lower in the judicial hierarchy than the court of last resort in the province. These per saltum or "leap-frog" appeals remain possible today.[112] Monetary limits in respect of these have also been abolished.[113] The primary criterion is that they involve a point of law that is of such significance that the Supreme Court grants leave to hear the matter.

Appeals to the Supreme Court in criminal cases are governed by the Criminal Code.[114] Briefly, an accused may appeal as of right a conviction for an indictable offence either where that conviction is upheld by the provincial court of appeal and one of the appellate judges dissented on a question of law, or where an acquittal at trial was set aside on appeal. The Crown can appeal as of right the setting aside of a conviction where a dissent was filed. There are exceptional provisions regarding questions of the sanity of the accused. The Code also provides for criminal appeals by leave of the Supreme Court, with special time limits to apply, but these will not be reviewed in detail here.

Before 1949, the usual mode of access to the Supreme Court was the appeal as of right. Appeals by the Court's leave were possible, but tightly circumscribed. In that year, Parliament augmented the leave-granting mechanism that has since become an important facet of the Court's work.[115] The Supreme Court may itself grant leave to an applicant to have a case heard on its merits.[116] Alternatively, leave may be granted by the highest court of final resort in the province where final judgment was obtained.[117] An applicant may fail to obtain leave from a provincial court of appeal and yet apply thereafter for leave from the Supreme Court itself. The powers and criteria by which such leave can be obtained have been expanded by Parliament since 1949. The most significant changes occurred in 1975, when the following statutory guideline was enacted for the exercise of the Court's discretion in granting leave in a particular case:

> The Supreme Court is of the opinion that any question involved therein is, by reason of its public importance or the importance of any issue of law or any issue of mixed law and fact involved in such question, one that ought to be decided by the Supreme Court or is, for any other reason, of such a nature of significance as to warrant decision by it. . . .[118]

The provision relating to leave granted by a provincial court of appeal is more elliptical than the above. It simply refers to whether the question "is one that ought to be submitted to the Supreme Court for decision."[119]

The civil cases that confront the Supreme Court arise not only out of the provincial judicial systems but, increasingly, from the Federal Court system. The changes wrought in 1971, whereby the Federal Court replaced and enlarged upon the role of the Exchequer Court, have created an important new source of jurisdiction for the Supreme Court.[120] The terms by which leave might be granted to appeal a judgment or determination of the Federal Court of Appeal to the Supreme Court are contained in the *Federal Court Act*.[121] An appeal as of right lies to the Supreme Court from the Federal Court in any case involving a dispute between the federal and a provincial government, or between or among provincial governments.[122]

Finally, there are provisions in other federal legislation that relate to appeals to the Supreme Court. For example, there exists an appeal as of right to the Court on any question of law or of fact arising out of the trial of an election petition under the *Dominion Controverted Elections Act*.[123] There are also appeals by way of the Court's leave on questions relating to bankruptcy;[124] arrangements among creditors of a company;[125] court martial trials;[126] excise taxes;[127] oil and gas decisions or orders in the Territories;[128] provincial comprehensive pension plans;[129] the winding up of businesses;[130] and divorce.[131] The individual statute must be consulted for details as to whether such appeals can be based on questions of law, fact or jurisdiction, or on a combination of these. In some instances the decision or order appealed from is that of an administrative board. In other cases, such as the *Bankruptcy Act*, the appeal is from a decision of a court of appeal.

Although not strictly a matter of the Court's jurisdiction, federal laws also provide for Supreme Court judges or any one of them to be appointed commissioners of inquiry to investigate alleged corrupt or illegal practices in federal general elections.[132]

The importance of the 1975 reforms to the jurisdiction of the Supreme Court can hardly be exaggerated. By removing the monetary jurisdiction from most civil appeals, the changes have enabled the Court to refuse to hear cases that involve no particularly important legal questions. During the intervening decade, the Court has been able to control to a greater extent its own docket. Consequently, it has been able to concentrate its resources on cases that it ranks as the most significant to the nation as a whole. The argument on the motion for leave is heard in a brief session and usually before a three-member panel of Supreme Court judges. The argument will ordinarily not extend beyond 20 minutes in total, and the application will be granted or dismissed immediately upon conclusion of the argument. It will rarely be reserved for decision.[133]

While data on the caseload of the Supreme Court await an assiduous collector and analyst, there have been some attempts to chart the number and types of cases heard by the Court in any given year or term of three sessions.[134] There is as yet no single, authoritative source that one can consult. The data remain for the most part fugitive. This hampers any attempt to draw conclusions about trends in the Court's work. To illustrate the effects of the 1975 changes, Tables 2-1 and 2-2 show the number of different types of cases heard and disposed of by the Court in the years immediately preceding and immediately following the jurisdictional amendments. The data may be supplemented and updated by more recent information.

TABLE 2-1   Origin of Cases Heard

Term	Total Cases Heard	Leave of the Supreme Court	Appeals as of Right	Leave of a Court of Appeal	Others[a]
1970–71	151	15	83	1	1
1971–72	150	21	78	1	1
1972–73	163	21	75	1	2
1973–74	161	22	75	1	2
1974–75	162	29	67	4	1
1975–76	165	28	70	1	1
1976–77	131	60	32	5	3
1977–78	113	72	20	8	0
1978–79	127	75	17	8	1
1979–80	115	79	16	3	2
1980–81	117	74	16	4	6

Source: S.I. Bushnell, "Leave to Appeal Applications to the Supreme Court of Canada: A Matter of Public Importance" (1982), 3 Sup. Ct. Law Rev. 479, at 497.

a. Included in this column are federal and provincial references, rehearings, motions to quash referred, and cases removed from provincial courts for constitutional issues.

TABLE 2-2   Origin of Civil Cases Heard

Term	Total Cases Heard	Leave of the Supreme Court	Appeals as of Right	Leave of a Court of Appeal
1970–71	130	10	88	2
1971–72	124	15	84	1
1972–73	140	20	79	1
1973–74	133	16	83	2
1974–75	136	24	71	4
1975–76	134	23	76	1
1976–77	84	63	29	8
1977–78	79	76	13	11
1978–79	81	84	4	12
1979–80	67	94	0	6
1980–81	67	93	0	7

Source: S.I. Bushnell, "Leave to Appeal Applications to the Supreme Court of Canada: A Matter of Public Importance" (1982), 3 Sup. Ct. Law Rev. 479, at 497.

The figures in Table 2-3 reflect the Court's activity in the 1982 and 1983 calendar years.

TABLE 2-3   Origin of Cases and Motions Heard

	1982	1983
Appeals heard or reheard	129	89
By way of leave of the Supreme Court	115	79
As of right	11	7
By leave of a court of appeal	1	1
As a reference	2	2
Types of appeals heard		
Civil	85	58
Criminal	44	31
Motions for leave heard	419	501
Motions granted	95	117
Civil cases	68	80
Criminal cases	27	37

Source: Based upon statistics compiled and published by the Office of the Registrar of the Supreme Court, *Bulletin of Proceedings Taken in the Supreme Court of Canada*, March 23, 1984, at 330.

A comparison of these figures with those for earlier years reveals that there was a drastic falling off in the total number of appeals heard during 1983. On the other hand, the number of applications for leave to appeal rose sharply over the previous year. Appeals heard only after leave has been obtained continue to form the vast majority of cases heard in the two years of activity described in Table 2-3. Civil cases generally require leave from the Supreme Court or from a court of appeal. References or other matters of special jurisdiction, of course, do not require such leave. Criminal cases continue to account for most of the appeals as of right. Cases arising as of right seem to be growing fewer in each successive year or term, as shown by a comparison of the data in Table 2-3 with those in Table 2-1.

Criticisms of the Jurisdiction

One of the major criticisms of the Court's comprehensive jurisdiction is based on a concept of federalism and the division of judicial as well as legislative power within Confederation. In the federalist view, represented most articulately by Professor Russell, the Court should be confined to questions of law that are important to the nation as a whole and that reflect the distribution of powers made under the Constitution.[135] Instead of letting the Court itself, through the leave-granting mechanism, determine whether a case involves such a question, the "federalization" of the Court would limit its appellate jurisdiction to questions concerning the Constitution and those federal laws validly made under Parliament's legislative powers. It might also be assigned the task of deciding cases involving disputes among the provinces or between the federal government and the provinces.

This proposal would be aimed at remoulding the Court in a modern image. In civil appeals in particular, the further appeal from the decision of the highest provincial court is conceptually inconsistent with the original distribution of powers that reserved to the provinces legislative jurisdiction over "property and civil rights" within the province.[136] All of the provinces now have competent appellate tribunals. Some critics doubt the advisability of allowing an extra level of appeal to a tribunal located possibly thousands of kilometres away from where the trial was held.[137] This argument was advanced before the changes to the largely monetary thresholds that civil cases once had to pass. Those changes have not undermined the federalist argument. As a matter of principle, whether the courts should be organized so that power over the judiciary should be shared at a federal and a provincial level continues to be a vital question.

The argument attributable to Quebec critics of the Supreme Court that it should not be permitted to adjudicate matters of Quebec civil law is different from the federalist thesis. The Quebec complaint is not based on the recognition of a separation of judicial power. Instead it reflects the peculiar nature of the Quebec system of civil law. That system is philosophically and fundamentally unlike the common law system that prevails in the other Canadian provinces. It could plausibly be argued that the Supreme Court's jurisdiction should not embrace civil cases from the Quebec Court of Appeal, while its jurisdiction might continue to include civil appeals from all the other provinces.

The Quebec contentions, based on a theory of cultural and linguistic dualism, or binationalism, have several different aspects. They depend on jurisprudential, historical and federalist premises. It was not long after the abolition of civil appeals to the Privy Council that voices were heard in Quebec decrying the fact that a predominantly anglophone, common law, and federally appointed institution was the highest authority on civil law matters arising out of Quebec.[138] Conceivably, the minority group of members of the Court appointed from Quebec could be overridden by their English Canadian colleagues on such appeals. This could occur even though the judges trained in the common law may not have had any systematic exposure to the Civil Code or training in the proper interpretative skills by which to apply the Code's provisions to a particular case. As well, there have been deep differences between the common law and civilian approaches to such technical legal doctrines as precedent and the relevance or admissibility of academic commentary on the law.[139] Some writers have attempted to demonstrate that elements of the common law have crept into and distorted the Civil Code because of the lack of understanding exhibited by certain Supreme Court judges.[140] This argument, as we shall see, is not limited to the issue of jurisdiction. It arises again in the debate over changing the regional quotas in selecting Supreme Court judges, in setting up separate chambers or panels within the Court's structure, and in determining what type of reasoning should be followed in constitutional cases.

A third argument for altering the Court's present jurisdiction rests on a vision of what the Court's workload is likely to become within the next several years. In general terms, since around 1975 the Court has been able to achieve a fairly consistent balance between civil and criminal appeals. An alternative way of analyzing the caseload is to break it down into private law cases as against public law cases. Examples of private law disputes would be those in the areas of commercial law (including contract, corporations and insurance cases), property, tort, or domestic relations. By contrast, in adjudicating public law issues, the Court might be dealing with anything from a constitutional reference to a problem in administrative, criminal or labour law. This is a rough-and-ready distinction, based on the principal legal issues raised in each case, but it will serve the purpose of showing how public law cases have consistently outnumbered private law cases in recent years. This pattern is the reverse of that which prevailed before 1975. The figures in Table 4 for the 1982 and 1983 calendar years show the approximate ratio between these two kinds of cases.

As an addendum to Table 2-4, it should be noted that 25 of the cases classified in 1983 under motions for leave in public law cases involved

TABLE 2-4 Comparison of Private Law and Public Law Cases

	1982	1983
Private law cases heard	30	21
Public law cases heard	99	68
Motions for leave to appeal in private law cases	138	120
Motions for leave granted in private law cases	24	24
Motions for leave to appeal in public law cases	281	381
Motions for leave granted in public law cases	71	93

Source: *Bulletin of Proceedings Taken in the Supreme Court of Canada*, March 23, 1984, at 329, and additional statistics from the Registrar.

a provision in the Charter as the principal legal issue. In 14 instances, the Court acceded to the request to have the appeal heard on its merits.

The conclusion to which these figures point is that the Court's work is increasingly devoted to public law issues, and various reasons might be offered to account for it. It could be that the gate for private law appealsis less easy to pass through than it once was, even after the 1975 amendments. The cogency of this argument would be difficult to ascertain, because the Court does not make a practice of giving reasons, oral or otherwise, for granting or dismissing motions for leave.[141] Alternatively, a case could be made that as government activities, particularly in the regulatory sphere, have continued to multiply and expand, so the volume of public law cases involving a governmental interest has grown commensurately.[142] Thus, administrative law, immigration and labour law questions are reaching the Court in unprecedented numbers. Also, the volume of criminal cases has not diminished as the Court continues to find issues of public significance in the interpretation of offences and in criminal trial procedure. Possibly the key reason accounting for the volume of public law litigation that is occupying the Court's docket is the way the Court has, in granting leave to appeal, interpreted what is the degree of "public importance" or significance attached to a question.[143] Public law disputes often present on their face the hallmarks of an outcome that will affect the rights of more persons than simply the individuals who were party to the case. For example, questions of public policy are more transparent in an action concerning the availability of judicial review of an administrator's decision than in a lawsuit involving the capacity of a testator or the quantum of damages arising out of an automobile accident. The latter types of cases may present little in the way of novel legal doctrine, while the result of the former kind of dispute can often affect the duties of administrative tribunals all across the country.[144]

As the Court's work in the public law area continues to grow proportionately greater in comparison with private law appeals, the criticism is strengthened that the Court should no longer retain its general jurisdiction. This trend might accelerate as more cases depending on the Charter wind their way up to the Supreme Court level. As the foregoing observations about the Court's load in 1983 indicate, cases that focus on the Charter for the principal legal issue have succeeded at the leave stage at a much higher rate (56 percent of such motions heard in 1983) than for motions generally (20 percent for private law cases and 22.2 percent for non-Charter public law cases in the same calendar year). Proponents of the view that the Court should become a specialized tribunal, confined in its authority to cases raising a significant public law question, will probably gain sustenance for their arguments as Charter litigation swells. Their argument will resemble that favouring the current role of the Supreme Court of the United States. That Court has evolved into an essentially public law tribunal for hearing U.S. constitutional disputes.[145] A corollary to this argument is that experience in the United States has shown how complex public law issues are to adjudicate and how they might require specialized skills on the part of members of the final appellate tribunal.[146] The adoption in Canada of a legislative regime protecting fundamental rights has inspired apprehension that our own court of last resort will trace a similar path.[147] The proposed amendment of the Court's jurisdiction to leave private law disputes to be authoritatively settled by courts of appeal has, in this view, the apparent virtues of being both realistic and conducive to the goal of efficiency.

Critics of the Court's comprehensive authority over all areas of Canadian law have had to contend with the claim that, especially in private civil law cases, the Court has an important function in ensuring that the law is consistent and uniform throughout the country.[148] This argument based on uniformity emphasizes the national character of the Court as an institution, as against its federal role. This function has been called in the past one of the "chief duties" of the Court.[149] Decisions in the early part of this century that spelled out grounds for granting leave to appeal stressed the function that the Court ought to perform in securing uniformity of law in matters concerning the whole of Canada.[150] When the Special Committee of the Canadian Bar Association studying the Court's workload reported prior to the 1975 amendments, it noted that one of the primary criteria of whether a case is of significant public importance is whether it involves a conflict between decisions of the lower courts on a common law principle.[151] This would be applicable also where, in a criminal case, there is conflicting judicial authority on a question of law.

Against this emphasis on the role of the Supreme Court in inducing uniformity, the critic has only to point to the nature of the federal bargain in Canada. Just as provincial legislatures have been granted authority to enact laws relating to their exclusive classes of subject, so the courts in each province ought to be free to interpret and apply laws in accordance with local or provincial circumstances. Provincial legislative power is predicated on the recognition that those legislators understand best what statutory scheme is needed for local conditions. Judicial power should be similarly responsive, even at the cost of making one province's laws on a matter inconsistent with those of another province. Secondly, critics would contend, if uniformity is desirable in an area of provincial jurisdiction, then there are political and practical means for securing this that are more efficient and direct than an appeal to the Supreme Court. The work of uniform law commissioners representing the different provinces is a case in point.[152] They have been especially effective in drafting model insurance statutes and reciprocal enforcement of judgment laws. Or, as in the case of business corporations legislation, the initiative of the federal government or of a reform-minded provincial government may provide the eventual basis for national uniformity. One of the supposed strengths of a federation is diversity. Critics favouring provincial rights may understandably adopt the line that the Supreme Court has no business ironing out legitimate judicial responses to local needs and conditions.

The proposal has even been advanced that the Supreme Court be withdrawn as a forum for hearing division-of-power questions.[153] Professor Weiler has placed great faith in the ability of governments within our federation to negotiate over areas of respective jurisdiction and to reach suitable political compromises. This would remove the Court as a political institution, whose authority could be used by, for example, the federal government in dictating terms of an agreement with a province in a matter significantly affecting the future economic welfare of that province.[154] A recent example is the judgment by the Supreme Court rejecting Newfoundland's claims over control of its offshore Hibernia resources.[155] In Weiler's terms, this is essentially a "political controversy," which is not amenable to resolution in a judicial arena. Adversarial proceedings rely on principles of judicial review which are so vague and unstable that the Court is really making up constitutional standards as it goes along.

A final salvo that may be launched at the Court's general jurisdiction is over its workload. This type of reasoning was especially popular in the ten years preceding the 1975 changes to the *Supreme Court Act*. The contention that the Court is overburdened either by civil cases or by private law appeals carries little conviction today. As Tables 1 to 3 demonstrate, the number of civil cases heard has been substantially reduced since the early 1970s, when a peak was achieved. Through the leave mechanism, the Court has been able to winnow out those relatively few cases it considers worthy of a full review. The same holds true for private law appeals. The Court's workload for the half-dozen years up to 1983 has stabilized at around 125 cases per calendar year or per three consecutive sessions. In 1983, only 89 cases were heard, and an equal number of decisions were rendered, but this was doubtless owing in part to the ailing health of Chief Justice Laskin, one of the most prodigious workers on the Court. By comparison, in 1982, 129 cases were heard and 126 decisions rendered. The 1983 calendar year probably represents an anomaly, and subsequent years will show a climb back toward an annual average of approximately 125 cases.[156] Motions for leave to appeal have shot up in numbers. This increase, if it continues, may eventually press upon the Court's time to hear and determine appeals on their merits. Although the actual procedure for hearing a leave application is brief, and has recently been the subject of technological innovations using satellite transmission, when the number of motions eventually increases to six or seven hundred per year, some procedural amendments or increased research staff for the Court's judges might have to be considered. A contraction of jurisdiction may be one solution, or a partial solution, to such a problem, but the problem itself may be more complex than such thinking recognizes. Further consideration of the leave mechanism is included in the section of our discussions devoted to the procedures surrounding the Court's administration.

Suggestions for Change

The suggestions for reforming the Court's purview are all inspired by some of the arguments recited above, and can be summarized as follows. For federalist reasons, the Court should be restricted to hearing only constitutional cases, or only cases where governments contend with one another. For many of the same reasons, but with the additional considerations affecting Quebec's unique civil law system included, the Court should be structured so that only a select panel chosen from among Supreme Court judges can hear and determine civil law appeals originating from Quebec. The Court's revamped structure is here used to surmount the defect in its general jurisdiction. Instead of limiting the Court to constitutional questions, a legislative reform might limit its jurisdiction to public law questions, which would retain a larger scope for the Court. These would all be fundamental rearrangements of the Court's caseload.

Whichever of the foregoing alternatives might be adopted, the Court would no longer resemble the Judicial Committee of the Privy Council during the era when it heard appeals from Canada. Nor would the Supreme Court's role be akin to that of the House of Lords, which remains the highest court in the United Kingdom. The latter tribunal hears appeals not only in English common law cases, but also in Scottish civil law cases.[157] The case for reform of the House of Lords' jurisdiction in respect of such Scottish cases has never caused the stir that has arisen from the equivalent Quebec complaint.[158]

Response to Criticisms

The argument advanced below is that the Court's general appellate jurisdiction should be kept intact. It should remain the court of last resort on factual and legal issues in all cases, regardless of where they arise in Canada. The judicial system in Canada has traditionally been classified as a unitary system. There is even judicial authority underpinning this description.[159] Attempts to portray the Canadian system as one evolving into a dual court structure do not affect the function of the Supreme Court.[160] It hears appeals both from provincial courts of appeal and from the Federal Court of Appeal. Jurisdictional conflicts between the Federal Court system and the systems of courts in the provinces do not touch the Supreme Court's comprehensive supervision.

The proposals to federalize the Supreme Court run up against many of the deficiencies inherent in a dualistic judicial structure. There is only slight authority for anything but a unitary structure of Canadian courts in general to be found in the *Constitution Act, 1867.*[161] If the Court's jurisdiction were redesigned to reflect only the legislative competence of the federal Parliament, many important national issues would be beyond the purview of the Court. It could not determine many matters relating to commercial law, insurance law, energy and natural resources, and the administration of justice within a province — all areas that exhibit important extraprovincial dimensions. Business firms notoriously do not respect provincial boundaries, and inconsistent or contradictory laws in different provinces may cause unnecessary hardship for the operations of such firms. Actions launched to determine rights of firms with branches in different parts of Canada may require multiple proceedings and hard decisions by courts which must, following conflicts of law rules, determine and apply differing rules of foreign jurisdictions.[162] Actual conflicting verdicts may be reached by courts located in different provinces. This would encourage forum-shopping, delaying tactics, and levering up of costs by the wealthier of the adversaries. Retaining the Supreme Court's general jurisdiction would equalize the litigious battle. The end of the parties' day in court would mean a uniform result, wherever the action originated.

The alleged local sensitivity of judges presiding over provincial courts has an adverse and unpleasant side to it. Just as the Judicial Committee was extolled in the past for its impartiality and distance from the heated passion of conflicting local interests, so the Supreme Court should logically be considered the heir to such epithets. The Court and its individual members have often expressed the view both on and off the Bench that, in performing the appellate function, factual determinations by lower courts will not lightly be upset.[163] The Supreme Court concentrates in the main on legal issues. Those aspects of a case which a lower court can logically best determine are treated as uncontroversial on appeal to the Supreme Court.

The arguments that predate the 1975 amendments have lost much of their force as a result of the changes to the Court's jurisdiction. Gone is the irritant based on monetary limits. A more rational process of determining which cases merit a final appeal to the Supreme Court has been in use. The guidelines by which a panel decides whether a question is of public significance to the nation as a whole are not entirely clear as the judges are discouraged from giving reasons for granting or dismissing leave applications. Nevertheless, this process is eminently preferable as a means for determining which cases shall be heard by a full quorum of the Court.

The argument for drastic change based upon the peculiar circumstances of the province of Quebec is not compelling.[164] Certain institutional structures already present in the Court accommodate the dualistic nature of Canadian civil law. The informal requirement that all civil appeals entered from Quebec shall be heard by a five-judge panel that includes a majority of civilian judges has been largely respected over the years. The further argument that common law judges have occasionally controlled the disposition of these cases is not reflected in the most thorough study yet undertaken of the composition of panels that have adjudicated civil cases out of Quebec.[165] In the words of the author of that study, "the question of common law participation . . . is essentially a non-issue."[166] In general, the common law judges have deferred to their civilian colleagues on such Quebec appeals.

On occasion, much has been made of the obvious opportunity that common law judges and civilian judges have to educate each other in the principles and processes of their respective legal traditions.[167] This is a worthy objective, although the possibility of its occurring depends largely on the scholarly dispositions of the individual judges. Our unusual dual legal heritage has created the situation in which a judge, formally trained in both English-Canadian common law and Quebec civil law, can emerge. This is exemplified in Justice LeDain, who was nominally selected from the province of Ontario but whose interesting experience includes periods of practice and teaching in Quebec as well as in Ontario.[168] Artificial barriers between the common and civil law systems should not be erected by limiting the role of the one court in Canada that is capable of pragmatically transcending the differences in legal culture.

The distinction between private law cases and public law cases is not a useful means for devising a more specialized role for the Court. Although an appeal is classified as raising an issue of public law, that does not necessarily indicate that in some sense it deserves a hearing before the Court while a private law appeal does not. The criterion of "national importance" is not coextensive with, or a subsidiary of, "public law." A case raising an issue of the fiduciary duties of corporate directors in respect of business opportunities that come their way as a result of their role as directors is, to all appearances, a private law dispute. Yet its outcome may affect the standard of business ethics and responsibility that courts across the country will impose on directors generally.[169] This same point is applicable to many legal aspects of business and property law. In the latter instance, construction of laws determining the division of the assets of married or cohabiting partners will be an important part of the Court's recent work, just as it was before many of the principles were put into statutory form.[170] Calling such disputes matters of "private law" tends to underrate the implications of an authoritative holding by the Supreme Court and how it binds lower courts in subsequent cases involving the same legal issues.

Nor is it easy to distinguish between private and public law appeals. This distribution becomes highly artificial given the interrelationships between common law and statutory causes of action arising out of the same conduct. In the words of a distinguished U.S. commentator addressing the issue of jurisdiction: "Only the most arbitrary and dysfunctional distinctions can enable the Supreme Court of Canada, or any other court, to keep out of so-called private law."[171] Cases do not always come before the Court with discretely packaged legal issues. A dispute between a landlord and tenant over the terms of a lease of commercial property may raise important evidentiary issues applicable to the rules of evidence used in the trial of civil actions. Although the style of cause in such a proceeding may indicate that private parties represent the opposing interests, the full resolution of the case can have ramifications far beyond the realm of private law. The area of intersection of the law of trusts and taxation law makes it difficult to determine whether certain types of cases would be subsumable under the head of private law alone.[172] Similar considerations apply to the bifurcation between provincial and federal areas of legislative competence. A suit does not necessarily involve one or the other type of matter. Often these are inextricably mingled in the circumstances of a particular case. To use an example suggested by William Lederman, the facts might give rise to a dispute over the enforceability of a mortgage.[173] The governing law is not just that enacted by the province in relation to real property, but could also involve federal laws regulating interest. Modern business transactions are increasingly subject to duplicative sets of provisions designed to protect consumers or to enforce both local and national standards. A good example is the adoption of building codes and regulations at each of the municipal, provincial and federal levels.

Lederman is also owed a debt for some sage advice about why a court could not reasonably be expected to specialize only in constitutional matters. The threshold step in determining the validity of an impugned existing or proposed law is to characterize the matter that it embraces.[174] This is a subtle process, requiring the Court to take cognizance of other relevant laws passed by the same body and of laws enacted at other levels of jurisdiction. In effect, the Court must have a thorough knowledge of which matters have been legislated upon; how the impugned law fits into an overall legislative scheme; and what are likely to be the effects of the law in operation. These are all criteria for arriving at a proper characterization. After the law is characterized in a certain way — for example, as a matter of intraprovincial trade relating to a specific industry — its matter is assigned to one or other of the classes of subject enumerated in sections 91 and 92 of the *Constitution Act, 1867*. In our example, the characterization would lead to the conclusion that the relevant head of power is the exclusive legislative jurisdiction of the provincial legislature over property and civil rights.[175] A similar point about the inter-dependence of civil law and common law issues in cases originating in Quebec was made by Professor (now Mr. Justice) LeDain.[176]

This process of characterization informs much of the Court's reasoning on division-of-power cases, and in particular those that raise the issue of the applicability of the federal trade and commerce power. This type of case illustrates how the Court's attitude toward commercial arrangements throughout the country is shaped by the individual judge's perception of the distinctive values of business regulation at a local or provincial level as opposed to a national level. Again this area represents an intersection of private and public law. The task of constitutional adjudication here depends on a broad understanding of economic values, the efficient arrangement of private business enterprise, and the role of government regulation in promoting desirable economic goals. The Court has historically had a large, indirect impact on the economic organization of Canadian business. Its views have not always been applauded.[177]

A further argument in favour of retaining the Supreme Court's general appellate jurisdiction is based on the notion of judicial policy making. Despite claims that the Court, after the enactment of the Charter, will finally become a tribunal able to formulate and enforce broad social and economic policies, that capacity has always been present. Anything short of a positivistic view of the Court's function recognizes that even in so-called private law appeals, the Court can exercise its power to change the rules in response to novel circumstances or to changed social conditions. Imposing a duty of care upon classes of individuals in particular factual relationships is one way of implementing a change in the balance between competing social interests.[178] Such a decision also has immediate consequences for business firms and their insurers in calculating risk and obtaining indemnification against loss or injury. Other social and economic policy questions arise in relation to enforceability of contracts in restraint of trade (based on the common law)[179] or agreements that violate federal laws designed to preserve business competition.[180] Such cases raise undisguised questions of "public" policy, even though the cases themselves may be disputes between private parties.

This policy-making function forms part of what Chief Justice Laskin stressed as the "supervisory" role of the Supreme Court.[181] In its capacity as a national, as opposed to federal, institution, the Court is not simply an appellate tribunal. Especially since the changes in 1975 to the Court's jurisdiction, a duty is imposed on the Court to oversee the development of broad legal doctrines in Canada, so long as they affect more than merely local issues. This interpretation of the changes to the Court's jurisdiction is shared in no small degree by Chief Justice Dickson.[182]

Having argued that the Court's general jurisdiction should be left intact, what is to be made of the claim that the Court will become a public law tribunal simply by virtue of the types of cases that will increasingly confront it? We are dealing here with a proposition that is in part a prophecy and in part a prescription. For the foreseeable future, Charter cases will almost surely occupy a growing proportion of the Court's docket, even if they do not amount to the "holocaust" of litigation predicted prior to the adoption of the Charter.[183] Yet private law cases will not be squeezed out. The most workable balance between these types of cases ought not to be frozen by legislative action. The key to the Court's jurisdiction lies in the Court's own discretionary powers to decide which appeals it wants to determine. The real decisions about jurisdiction will be made at the stage of applications for leave; at this point in the progress of a case through the judicial system, hard choices will be made about the relative significance of different types of legal questions. This procedure has not been the result of accident. The 1975 amendments incorporated language giving considerable leeway to the Court to compose its own docket, and only if this discretion were being abused or exercised capriciously would there be grounds for legislative intervention. The available literature does not point to the Court having made flagrant abuses in dismissing motions for leave; nor has the Court frequently had to resort to its power to quash an appeal because a court of appeal erred in granting leave in the first place.[184]

This deserved emphasis on the manner in which leave applications are considered, and on the potential for sifting out the questions most important to the nation as a whole in light of current circumstances and the state of the law, has not received an authoritative exposition from academics. The Court has failed to articulate the grounds for granting or denying leave in a way that provides solid material for an inductive analysis. This situation may change in the future. As Madam Justice Wilson has noted: "The time is ripe for an appraisal of the leave process from a substantive point of view."[185] This will have to be a cooperative effort involving the members of the Court itself, the practising Bar, and legal academics. Questions of the Court's theoretical jurisdiction are generally less urgent at any given moment than are questions about whether the Court has deemed it advisable to settle an inconsistency in the common law based on decisions by courts of appeal. Even if the Court does decide to hear such an appeal on its merits, there is no assurance that it will actually resolve the supposed inconsistency. Decisions may be narrow or broad, and the Court may in effect reserve for another day and possibly a more propitious case the final resolution of a legal dispute.

There have been surprisingly few suggestions that the Court exercise its general jurisdiction through specialized panels made up from within the membership of the Court. In Western European countries, particularly those in which great constitutional changes have been made since World War II, there has been a trend toward having a different court of last resort for different kinds of controversies. There might, for example, be a final administrative court that hears appeals from intermediate appellate tribunals or from boards or agencies at first instance. A separate constitutional panel has been created both in France and in the Federal Republic of Germany (see Appendix B). In the German system, the court is divided into two chambers for the hearing of different sorts of constitutional cases. This kind of arrangement has been proposed in Canada only with respect to the hearing and determination of civil law cases originating in Quebec.[186] In such cases, the Court would have a separate chamber in effect to deal with them. The panel would possibly include ad hoc judges appointed from the Quebec superior courts, to ensure the desired expertise in the canons of the Code-based civil law.

To some extent, the Supreme Court has used panels of judges from within the Court to hear appeals. During the 1983 calendar year, according to the Registrar's statistics, the judgments given by the Court were the result of the Court sitting with various numbers of members, as shown in Table 2-5. As mentioned above, the Court divides into three-member panels for the purpose of hearing leave applications.

TABLE 2-5   Summary of the Number of Judges Participating in Decisions of the Supreme Court of Canada in 1983

Number of Members	Number of decisions
9	6
7	45
5	38
Total number of decisions	89

Source: From *Bulletin of Proceedings Taken in the Supreme Court of Canada*, March 23, 1984, at 328–34, and additional statistics from the Registrar.

There are two key arguments in favour of organizing the Court into a number of specialized chambers. First, the Court would be able to dispose of a greater number of cases. Second, the members could develop and use expertise in certain areas of the law that a judge would have acquired either before being appointed, or would acquire in deciding many cases of the same type. We do not find these arguments compelling, however, and there are better ways to achieve efficiency in managing the docket than by breaking the Court up into separate chambers.

The real problem with the Court's workload exists at the leave stage, and not when cases are heard on their merits. Some suggestions for improvement are made in the subsequent section of this study that deals specifically with the administrative procedures that might be adopted by the Court. As well, the use of specialized chambers leads inevitably to the result that we really have more than one court of final appeal in Canada. This detracts from both the symbolic and authoritative importance of the Court's current role. As has been noted, the Canadian judiciary forms a unitary pattern. Specialized panels would undermine this concept. We might also note that in those countries where different supreme tribunals are used for different types of cases, the judges in each Court often come from quite dissimilar backgrounds. The chief administrative court might be composed of judges trained in a national school of public administration rather than in a law faculty. Finally, the difficulty of distinguishing among several issues in certain cases argues against specializations of panels. A private law issue is not always separable from an issue of public law; nor can an administrative appeal always be separated from a constitutional aspect of the same case, for example. Legal categories are not so discrete, nor do cases fall so neatly into one category or another. Retaining the full jurisdiction of the Supreme Court and leaving it to the judgment of the Chief Justice as to which judges and how many of them should sit on a particular case, allows the flexibility needed for an efficient management of the caseload without sacrificing the role of the Court as a collegial body competent to supervise the growth of the law in Canada as a whole.

The upshot of this discussion of jurisdiction is that the boundaries of the Court's work, its potential for redrawing the lines between the respective legislative powers of federal and provincial governments, its potential for remaking the relationships between individuals or between citizen and government, are not circumscribed in a limited way. Once an action has been initiated, it can usually be pursued as far as the client's interests and resources permit, up to the leave application before the Supreme Court. The Court's members are largely their own gatekeepers. At this point, questions of curial jurisdiction give way to more important questions of judicial process. The vital issue is not whether the Court or a panel within the Court should be allowed to adjudicate a matter. The issue is what kind of judicial minds are deciding whether the matter deserves a full hearing and disposition. Once a general jurisdiction is permitted to the Court, the focus must shift to the questions of who sits on the Court and what background and talents we should reasonably expect those judges to possess.

Composition

The issue of the composition of the Supreme Court is most conveniently broken down into number of members and origins of those judges, particularly by region. As we will see in the discussion that follows, these two topics are intertwined in any consideration of Supreme Court reform.

Number of Judges

The Court currently consists of nine members: one Chief Justice and eight puisne or associate judges. This figure has remained unchanged since 1949, when membership was increased from seven. It had been six during the period of 1875 to 1927.[187] As noted, in accordance with the *Supreme Court Act*, three of the judges must be chosen from the bar or bench of Quebec.[188] There are no other statutory restrictions on the regional qualifications of appointees.

There have been suggestions to increase the size of the Court, and the enlarged Court might comprise from ten to fifteen members. Usually the figure chosen is an odd number, although this has not been invariable. Professor Morin's projected constitutional court would have embraced an equal number of common law and Quebec civil law judges.[189] The number most often proposed is eleven, a figure endorsed by Professor Lederman, [190] the British Columbia government in its 1978 discussion paper,[191] the Pepin-Robarts Report,[192] and the Constitutional Amendment Bill of 1978.[193] It was the preferred number of a majority of the provincial premiers at the First Ministers' Conference on the Constitution,[194] held in September 1980. The proposal by the Alberta government to empanel a court whose members would be chosen from a special constitutional panel of forty to fifty judges for each particular division-of-power case represents the high end of numerical reform.[195]

In general, the appropriate figure is selected by the various proponents according to the regional balance that they think should be reflected on the Court. At present, nine judges of the Supreme Court have been appointed from the following provinces:

TABLE 2-6   Origins of Current Judges

Province	Number of Judges
New Brunswick	1
Quebec	3
Ontario	3
Manitoba	1
British Columbia	1

The backgrounds of judges are not as clear as the above table might lead one to think, however. Justice Estey, although Chief Justice of the Province of Ontario at the time of his selection for the Supreme Court, had early connections and training with the Bar of Saskatchewan. Justice LeDain, the junior member of the present Court, was trained in the Quebec civil law system and taught at McGill University before joining the faculty at the Osgoode Hall Law School and gaining admission to the Law Society of Upper Canada; thereafter, he was appointed to the Federal Court of Appeal and resided in Ottawa.

Efforts to distill some practice or convention out of the past pattern of appointments to the Court have largely produced exceptions. At the time that Professor Russell wrote, he had identified an "unwritten constitutional convention" determining how regions other than Quebec are represented on the Court.[196] In his view, Ontario was guaranteed three positions on the Court; the western provinces and the Atlantic provinces would share the remaining three places. Updating a table prepared in the course of his study, we have, in Table 2-7, a summary of regional representation on the Court since its inception in 1875.

TABLE 2-7   Origin of Judges on the Supreme Court

Year in Which Pattern Altered	Quebec	Ontario	Atlantic Provinces	Western Provinces
1875	2	2	2	0
1888	2	3	1	0
1893	2	2	2	0
1903	2	1	2	1
1905	2	2	2	0
1906	2	2	1	1
1924	2	3	0	1
1927	2	3	0	2
1932	2	2	1	2
1949	3	3	1	2
1979	3	2	1	3
1982	3	3	1	2

Source: Peter H. Russell, *The Supreme Court of Canada as a Bilingual and Bicultural Institution*, Study prepared for the Royal Commission on Bilingualism and Biculturalism (Ottawa: Queen's Printer, 1969), at 64.

Between 1949 and the time of Professor Russell's study, the situation remained stable, despite seven changes in the composition of the Court. For eleven more years and six changes thereafter, the pattern remained the same. It was finally broken when Justice Spence retired from the Court and was replaced by Justice McIntyre from the British Columbia Court of Appeal.[197] This reduced Ontario's places to two. When Justice Martland from Alberta retired in 1982, he was replaced by Justice Wilson from Ontario, and the former distribution was re-established. Upon Chief Justice Laskin's death, his place was filled by Justice LeDain,[198] who is nominally considered an Ontario appointment.

The number eleven is favoured by reformers primarily because some provinces or regions could be given increased representation on the Court. For example, Lederman would permit the Atlantic region and the Western region an added place each.[199] The British Columbia government has naturally favoured an increase in the number of regions to be considered, so that the province of British Columbia would constitute a separate region unto itself rather than being grouped with the Prairie provinces into one

Western region. In some proposals, such as that contained in the Pepin-Robarts Report, Quebec would be given increased proportional representation so that it would contribute five of the eleven judges. The "best efforts" draft that served as the basis for discussion at the 1980 First Ministers' Conference would have adopted this ratio,[200] although in the participants' public discussions during the conference proceedings, eleven was not the preferred number of all the provincial governments, nor was there a consensus on the ratio of Quebec to non-Quebec judges.

The number nine continues to be popular, although that does not mean that the Court would be broken down regionally, as at present. James MacPherson's proposal would conceivably allow a majority of Quebec judges at any given time,[201] and would also reduce Ontario's places to a minimum of one and a maximum of two. The Victoria Charter of 1971,[202] the Molgat-MacGuigan Committee proposals,[203] the Canadian Bar Association Committee that reported in 1979,[204] and the so-called Beige Paper of the Quebec Liberal Party,[205] all would have retained a nine-member Court.

It is worth noting that proponents of an expanded Court do not base their case on the perceived workload of the Court. This differs from the rationale offered by the federal minister of justice in 1949, when the Court was increased in size partly because of an anticipated increase in volume of work after the abolition of appeals to the Privy Council.[206] Today, silence on this point implies that the current number of judges is adequate for the caseload that the Court carries.[207] Of much more concern to critics is the means of ensuring that a truly representative Court will adjudicate "constitutional" issues, that is, in this context, primarily "division-of-power" issues. The Beige Paper echoed a theme originally introduced in the Report of the Tremblay Royal Commission in 1956 by suggesting that a "dualist" bench ought to determine constitutional questions, and that such parity might be achieved by including some ad hoc judges appointed from Quebec superior courts on the panel hearing the case.[208]

For the reasons given in the following section, on the regional selection of judges, there seems little need for increasing the membership of the Court. Perhaps nine members is the maximum number of judges for the optimal combination of collegiality, expertise and efficiency to be attained. It is very difficult to determine the dynamics of a group larger than nine. Having more than nine judges increases the possibility of multiple opinions being filed in cases where the whole Court would sit. This could make it more difficult to discern the determinative principles in such cases, tending to make the law unclear. In the end, regional considerations determine what would be the appropriate size of the Court. The rejection of separate chambers or panels for constitutional and non-constitutional issues, or for private and public law issues, has been discussed. The rationale of constructing a Court on regional lines deserves treatment under a heading of its own.

Regional Representation

The data contained in Table 2-7 above indicate the traditional importance placed upon the region of origin of a Supreme Court appointee. Past experience might excuse Ontarians for thinking that they were "robbed" of a place on the Court when Justice Spence was replaced by a British Columbia appointee in 1979. At any rate, Justice Wilson from Ontario was appointed to succeed Justice Martland from Alberta three years later. What is the principle behind the emphasis on regional origins that makes speculating about filling an opening on the Court a kind of parlour game for lawyers and other Court-watchers? The possible reasons are threefold.

First, it may be argued that by having judges from throughout Canada, the Court's responsiveness to conditions and developments around the country is ensured. A judge's connection with the law of a province or region is presumed to endow that judge with special knowledge of the place. Second, the regional pattern may be said to reflect the federal nature of the Canadian constitution. Although no formal requirement compels the federal government to distribute the six non-Quebec appointments in any particular fashion, the distribution in fact is in accordance with the principle that each of the judges who sits on division-of-power cases can be identified with a particular region. Third, the more or less established pattern may only reflect the pressures and interests within the federal cabinet that regional quotas be respected. This would be a purely political reason for an appointment based on region.

Reform of the Court can begin here. There are no constitutional obstacles and few statutory restrictions in the way of change. The contention that regional variations are important among the judges in order to import local knowledge into the Court is met by the observation that this quality is difficult to discern in the first place and even harder to bring to bear on the Court's decision making. It does not mean that the judge is prone to favour the interests of his or her home region over those of other localities or to weigh local interests more heavily than national interests. The judge is not supposed to be a spokesperson for a certain region or province. Studies into the participation of Court members on appeals that were entered from their home regions or province have confirmed that, in general, participation on those types of appeals will be greater than the participation rate in general.[209] Concurrent findings show the same relation for judgments delivered as for participants. As the Canadian Bar Association Committee has pointed out, the judge on the Supreme Court is not fulfilling an arbitral function, but a judicial function.[210]

If a court is supposed to include in its deliberations an element of knowledge about distinctive local conditions, this function should be performed by a provincially constituted court. The Supreme Court will not, according to the pattern of appointments established for most of the period since 1949, include a representative at any given time from five of the provinces and both territories.[211] It has never included a judge chosen from Newfoundland or Prince Edward Island during that time, and for several decades did not include an appointment from British Columbia. The various suggestions for breaking down appointments by region tend to defy strongly developed provincial feelings about whether one province shares similar conditions with another. British Columbians may legitimately wonder why they are considered, for Supreme Court purposes, as a province in the same region as Alberta, Manitoba and Saskatchewan. Newfoundland does not share the same legislative, political, social or legal history as the Maritime provinces, yet on most proposals it would be lumped together with them for the purpose of selecting a judge from the so-called Atlantic region. Moreover, if geography and special knowledge of local conditions are supposed to be important factors, then the point should be carried to its logical conclusion and the appointments from Quebec and Ontario should purposely be distributed throughout those provinces. Members of the bench and bar who do not reside in Toronto or Ottawa, or Montreal or Quebec City should especially be sought to fill vacancies as they arise.

The regionalist view also ignores the consequences of the concept of judicial independence. When discussions on constitutional change in the past decade touched on the Supreme Court, Chief Justice Laskin was prompted to remark:

> It saddened me that there was so little understanding manifested either about the nature of the Court's work or about the significance of the fidelity of its members to their oaths of office, so little appreciation of the importance of cohesion and collegiality in the dispatch of the Court's work. That work has no regional and, certainly, no political tie-in.[212]

The jurisdiction of the Court, according to the late Chief Justice, involves dealing "with national issues, with matters of general public importance that have no special regional connotation."[213] This is what in part makes the Court a national institution yet in a sense different from the Senate or the federal executive.

The argument in favour of regional criteria as primary determinants of who should be appointed becomes weaker when the Court's role as a division-of-power umpire becomes less prominent in the total picture of the Court's work. Until recently, constitutional cases consisted largely of disputes about the respective areas of federal and provincial legislative jurisdiction. This type of case also included, on occasion, questions of civil liberties under the Canadian Bill of Rights[214] or of the infringement of a province on the federal power to appoint judges under section 96.[215] The rise of Charter litigation, which in terms of successful 1983 motions for leave outnumbered other cases raising constitutional issues, should cause us to re-examine regional qualifications for judges. Whether an appointee is most closely identified with one region or another is largely irrelevant in determining what sort of scope and interpretation that judge will give to the guarantees in the Charter. As will be argued in the section on appointments, there are other, more relevant questions about a potential appointee's background that should be taken into account.

The political rationale for regional selection is not particularly worth perpetuating. Pressures that might be brought to bear upon a federal minister of justice to appoint Supreme Court judges from the backyards of prominent cabinet colleagues — rare though such cases might be — have little to do with fashioning the most talented Court possible. This is not to say that the appointment process should be apolitical and without reference to regions whatsoever. The following section, on appointments, exposes this issue further.

The concept being argued for here is that other considerations should take precedence over those based on region and that there should be no set formula, adopted in statutory form or otherwise, for determining the regional composition of the Court. One proviso to this would be a continuation of a minimum number of appointments from Quebec. This should be entrenched at the time the Court is reformed. This exception does not reflect a need for a regional quota but is, rather, a recognition of the duality of the Canadian legal system and its twin heritage.

Appointment of Judges

Currently the federal government or, more accurately, the cabinet under the aegis of the minister of justice or the prime minister, unilaterally makes appointments to the Supreme Court.[216] There are no statutory requirements for consultation with any judicial officers, provincial attorneys-general, or professional groups before an appointment is made. Some informal patterns of consultation have been established in the past in respect of superior court appointments, but it is unclear how these apply to Supreme Court selections.[217] This situation is likely to change, for in the constitutional negotiations and discussions held since the mid-1970s, the federal government repeatedly has indicated that it would concede some form of provincial input into the appointment process. The nub of the controversy has been over what form this contribution should take.

Previously Suggested Reforms

By now it is recognized that the federal government's position as sole nominator of the Court's membership has interfered with the appearance of the Court as an impartial tribunal, particularly in respect of division-of-power issues. We should stress that this concern was largely confined at the level of appearances only. Despite some apprehension by provinces that the Court might be stocked with appointees favouring a centralist vision of Canadian federalism, this result has not been borne out by studies of the Court's actual judgments during the period since 1949, when it gained a relative degree of autonomy.[218]

The Tremblay Commission Report in 1956 raised the point that provinces should participate in some way in the nomination of Supreme Court judges.[219] The Victoria Charter contained a complex formula for securing the agreement of federal and provincial authorities over any appointment to the Court.[220] The key provision was that the federal minister of justice was bound to consult the attorney-general of the province with which a potential appointee was associated. If they failed to agree on an appointee, the minister of justice would propose the establishment of a nomination council to recommend an appointment. The choice among possible forms of this council rested with the provincial attorney-general, with the body to be composed primarily of the chief federal and provincial law officers or their nominees. The federal minister of justice would submit at least three names to the council, which would make a recommendation from that list. The provincial attorney-general could not propose any names. The initiative thus stayed with the federal minister of justice. The Molgat-MacGuigan Joint Committee generally endorsed the consultative method set forth in the Victoria Charter, but criticized it for failing to allow the provinces to propose names of possible appointees to the nominating council.[221]

Professors Russell and Lederman both have favoured some form of consultation or collaboration. Lederman has envisaged a permanent nominating commission, to be used for all superior court appointments, not just for the Supreme Court of Canada.[222] This commission would be composed of members of Parliament as well as members of provincial legislatures, with bipartisan representation. There would be a requirement for some non-lawyers among them. The commission's function would be limited to maintaining a list of suitable prospective appointees. The appointing authority would have to make a choice from the list presented.

During the past decade, suggested reforms or wholesale replacement of other national institutions have brought in their train interesting possibilities for changing the Court's appointment process. The Constitutional Amendment Bill, proposed in 1978, took the procedure set forth in the Victoria Charter one step further. After the minister of justice and the provincial attorney-general had agreed, or after the nominating council had broken the deadlock over an appointment, the nomination would have had to be submitted for ratification to the House of the Federation.[223] Within a limited time, the House would have had to affirm or reject the nomination. In view of the structure and composition of the House, this would have amounted to a second level of provincial input into the choice of a new judge for the Court.[224]

The necessity of ratification of Supreme Court appointments by a reconstituted Upper House gained adherents during the constitutional debate of the 1970s. The British Columbia government favoured a process of nomination by the federal government (after consultation with the provinces), followed by a reformed Senate's ratification.[225] Other proposals along this line have been made by the Canadian Bar Association Committee (which favoured using a judiciary committee of the Upper House rather than all of the members thereof),[226] the Pepin-Roberts Task Force,[227] the Beige Paper of the Quebec Liberal Party,[228] and James MacPherson.[229] The federal government's views on Senate reform in 1983 did not include specific reference to such a function of a reconstituted Upper House.[230]

The Alberta government was unique, in its proposals of a special constitutional panel, in requiring that only the provincial governments be able to suggest names of possible appointees to the panel.[231] The Pepin-Roberts Report would also have required that the federal cabinet consult with the Quebec attorney-general before filling a vacancy from that province on the Court. If the vacancy were to be filled by an English-Canadian appointee, the task force recommended that the federal cabinet consult all the other nine provincial attorneys-general about possible appointees.[232]

The variety of suggested reforms is large, yet they all rest on the notion that provincial participation should be by way of consultation or negotiation with a provincial attorney-general, or else by means of provincial representation in a reformed national political institution, such as the Upper House. In either event, the proposals go no further than suggesting that the current unilateral process be reformed so as to permit the involvement of a greater number of politicians with provincial interests at heart. These proposals show the marks of the era in which they were put forward. During constitutional conferences of the 1970s and early 1980s, the federal and provincial governments were in nearly constant dispute over the distribution of legislative power within Confederation.[233] It was natural that discussions of Supreme Court reform would take on the colour of the division-of-power disputes being waged at the time. Constitutional law, in the sense of judicial review of the validity of legislative action, is only a small part of the Court's jurisdiction. The entry of appeals arising out of the Charter should cause us to question whether the appointment process ought to reflect something more than federalist concerns. It should be based only in part on finding a mutually agreed-upon method for federal and provincial participation. The concept of regional representation on the Court loses its primacy when the diverse nature of the Court's jurisdiction is taken into account. The same reasoning may be applied to the matter of appointments.

A constant tension in Canadian Supreme Court appointments has been between the principle of merit and reference to such factors as regional origin, political allegiances and religious persuasion. Despite claims that merit has become the overriding consideration,[234] regional patterns of appointment have been generally adhered to. Doubts have arisen during the change in leadership in 1984 of the Liberal Party about the use of judicial appointments as rewards for service to the governing political party. These have led to the establishment of two separate committees of the Canadian Bar Association to study the independence and the appointment of judges.[235] The committee studying the method of selecting judges will take into account the shape of the Court's role in view of the Charter. Although the allegations of political patronage that preceded these studies did not arise out of appointments to the Supreme Court of Canada, the current Chief Justice has recorded his interest in the results of those studies and in the adoption of a method of appointment which ensures that judges be appointed "on the basis of merit and legal excellence alone."[236] In Charter cases and many other areas of adjudication, the regional origins of the judges are largely irrelevant. What becomes preeminently desirable is that the members of the Court be the best possible judicial talent to be found in the country. Merit ought not to give way to political considerations about patronizing each province or region in turn.

A New Appointing Council

The preceding sections of this study have dealt with many of the institutional features of the Supreme Court of Canada. Only relatively uncomplicated changes in the status of the Court, and no change in its jurisdiction, have been proposed. We have argued that the regional and political qualifications of judges are given an undeserved priority. These criteria have little to do with the excellence that appointments ought to recognize. The role of the Court as a panel that adjudicates cultural, economic and social issues, both in constitutional cases and in other disputes involving broad questions of policy and judicial law making, makes it imperative that a method of selection be devised to ensure that all relevant qualities of a potential appointee can be assessed. We must find some way out of the recurrent debate over the role of political and regional patronage in the appointment of federal judges. The model described below is designed to overcome this problem in respect of appointments to the Supreme Court of Canada. It is based upon the unique place that the Court has traditionally occupied as the final arbiter of intergovernmental disputes, as well as on its emerging role as the ultimate referee of the legal relations between government and the governed.

A survey of methods used in other countries, particularly western democratic federations, suggests alternative models for appointments. The procedures followed in the United States, at both the national and state levels, represent a departure from the British tradition that has heavily influenced Canadian, Australian and New Zealand methods. The 50 U.S. states do not follow a uniform plan, but they all hold elections for members of the state judiciary, including those constituting the appellate bench.[237]

For federal appointments, the executive branch performs the task of nominating, while the Senate is responsible for confirming the nomination.[238] Politics play a crucial role at both state and federal levels. Some states have attempted to mitigate this factor by adopting the Missouri plan or one of its variants.[239] This requires significant input from non-elected or professional officials at the nominating stage. Such democratic procedures, relying on direct election, are wholly foreign to the Anglo-Canadian mode of judicial selection. The federal practice of submitting names to the Senate for confirmation, required by the United States Constitution, also reflects a balance of power between the executive and legislative branches that has no parallel in Canada. A leaning toward this type of sharing arrangement is evident, however, in some of the more recent proposals for reforming judicial appointments in Canada.[240]

While we in Canada are conditioned to think of the appointment of judges as one of the prerogatives of the prime minister and the cabinet, in other democracies the executive branch of government plays no role whatsoever. The members of the Constitutional Court of the Federal Republic of Germany are chosen by committees formed within each of the houses of the national parliament.[241] The Canadian experience is patterned after that in the United Kingdom. This method has even there been subjected to significant criticism. It has been seriously proposed that the House of Lords, as a judicial body, be elected by a national vote.[242] In other commonwealth jurisdictions, the influence of political partisanship has given rise to complaints that appointments to the bench be removed from the exclusive powers of the party in power.[243] Although we do not propose anything so drastic as the popular election of Supreme Court judges, we do envision a method of selection that changes the political emphasis of the procedure without totally removing the federal and provincial governments from having a say in the process.

We propose the creation of an Appointing Council that would make both the survey of likely candidates and the final decision on who should be named to the Court when a vacancy occurs. Other proposals for reform have envisaged a nominating council with the power to recommend a name to the appointing authority from a list supplied to the council. In our scheme, the Appointing Council would make the initial list of possible appointees. It would then make the final choice of one name. The power of appointment would be constitutionally assigned to the Appointing Council alone.

The council would be composed of thirteen members. This number has been chosen as an optimum membership for ensuring diversity and collegiality. At least seven members would be women.[244] It is not sufficient, in our view, simply to hope that qualified women would be willing to serve on the council. Women are a numerical majority in Canadian society and should be given an abundant opportunity to be represented on a council that will choose judges, among whose new mandates will be that of settling issues over equality rights. Although not necessarily politicians, the members would be chosen from a pool to which both the federal and provincial governments would nominate individuals. Ideally, the council's membership would be widely diverse in terms of vocational background; age; economic and social status; racial, ethnic, and regional origin; and ideological orientation.[245] Other studies prepared for the Commission, such as the one by Cynthia Williams, attempt to discern the significant cleavages in Canadian society, and this may help in deciding who should be represented on the Council. Service on the council would be paid but would remain strictly a part-time activity. It would in no sense constitute a public office that required the full-time participation that only a politician could devote.[246] If a regional balance were thought to be a significant factor, then this might be sought, although we doubt the wisdom of inscribing regional quotas into the constitutional provisions relating to the council. We purposely refrain from advising the entrenching in the Constitution of any formula for representation. The profile of the council's membership should not be rigidly set out in terms that make further amendment difficult. Over time, the number and balance of interests represented on the council will inevitably shift and the nature of the interests themselves will evolve. As council members come and go, it is appropriate that interests of rising significance be reflected on the council, while those of diminished relevance be superseded.

All members of the council would have to be acceptable to the federal government and to at least four of the provinces. This formula, which is less rigorous than that required for a constitutional amendment, seems to us practicable in the circumstances. It reflects some broad support for the choice of a member, without going so far as to require a degree of acceptability that is appropriate for more significant constitutional matters. The members would not in every case be legally trained. Assessing the professional qualifications of candidates for the Court would, however, be a task involving some sophisticated degree of legal expertise. Therefore, we would advise that at least seven of the members of the council be legally trained. One or two of these might be drawn from such bodies as the Canadian Bar Association's National Committee on the Judiciary or the Canadian Judicial Council. Our proposed scheme would be geared toward ensuring that interests beyond those within the legal profession be represented on the council. The lawyers should reflect various geographical, experiential and income backgrounds. It is critical that the council not be wholly composed of lawyers. There are some aspects of the Court's work that can logically be appraised by a non-lawyer as readily as by a lawyer. The concept of merit that underlies the appointment to the Supreme Court should be broader than suitability in strictly professional terms. The members of the Council would be given staggered terms at the outset. Thereafter, each appointment to the Council would be for a ten-year term. There would be no eligibility for re-appointment at the expiration of a term. The Council would be convened when a vacancy on the Court arose. It would nominate possible appointees and review their credentials. It would be empowered to meet with the candidate in a private session for the purpose of discussing all matters relevant to the candidate's suitability for a place on the Court. This would not be an inquisitorial proceeding, such as occurs in the United States when a nominee is required to appear before the judiciary committee of the Senate and be examined by it in public before being confirmed or rejected by that body. The process that we recommend has the advantage over the current Canadian practice in that some of the mystery and apparent arbitrariness surrounding the selection procedure would be removed. (We hasten to add that the current appointing process has produced some excellent judges — but this may be in spite of the process.)

Of particular concern to the council would be the examination of what "merit" means in the context of being a member of the Supreme Court. Although it is popular to extol merit as the primary basis for appointing a judge, defining merit is still a difficult task. Besides such obvious elements as educational and professional achievements, we might also include those personal qualities and dispositions that are associated with the process of judging. These could be such virtues as integrity, impartiality, articulateness and common sense. Because it is membership on the Supreme Court that is at stake, some issues arise that are larger than mere personal virtue and intelligence, necessary though these may be in a candidate. The candidate's ideological and philosophical convictions might be tested. Such views go beyond simply political opinions, for they could include questions about the nature and role of the law in society, and not just which laws should be adopted or how current laws should be interpreted. The purpose of this questioning would not be the elimination of dissent but rather the promotion of diversity. It has happened in the United States that nominees are often questioned about their opinions on matters that might come before them should they be elevated to the Court.[247]

In view of the unique nature of the Canadian federation, attention might also be paid by the council to the linguistic abilities of candidates. The capacity of a Supreme Court judge to follow an argument in either French or English, without having to resort to simultaneous translation facilities, should be a quality given weighty consideration by the council in selecting judges. (The Court's members in recent years have set a notable example in their ability to use both official languages.)

There is an educative aspect to such scrutiny by the Appointing Council. As long as the process of selection is kept an executive prerogative, there will be little chance for the public to understand what the Court does and what it should be expected to do. Both Chief Justice Dickson and his predecessor have commented on the inadequate image of the Court's work that is conveyed to the citizens of Canada.[248] This is owing in part to the demands and limitations of the media as vehicles for showing what courts do. Brief media profiles of judges that concentrate on individual personalities cannot show which policies the judges of our highest Court tend to follow. Picking out one or another noteworthy facet of an appointee's career as an indication of a judicial trend of thinking is a haphazard way of grasping what sort of qualities and ingrained dispositions will be brought to the Supreme Court. A good example of this is the repeated reference in the Canadian media to Mr. Justice LeDain's chairmanship in the early 1970s of a royal commission of inquiry into the non-medical use of drugs.[249] The resultant report included among its recommendations the removal of the possession of marijuana from the offences covered by Canadian criminal law.[250] The press regarded this finding as noteworthy because it supposedly indicated a liberal temper on the part of the commissioners. Disregarded totally was Mr. Justice LeDain's judicial record while a member of the Federal Court of Appeal, as well as the body of scholarship he published while still an academic. These might or might not so easily have confirmed the "liberal" image that the media evidently were trying to cultivate on his behalf.

The process we have outlined is meant to overcome the limitations inherent in other proposals for reform, which are tied to traditional values and concerns about the need for mystery and a governmental monopoly over the appointing process. They would perpetuate the notion that only executive branches of governments are in a position to evaluate who should hold the highest judicial offices in our federation. If we must have regional and partisan interests included in the selection process, then let them arise in a different context. Instead of choosing judges according to the region from which they come, let the Appointing Council reflect a cross-section of Canada's regions. Instead of allowing political considerations to arise at the stage of choosing the judges, let them arise instead at the time of selecting the members of the Appointing Council.

The key in all these recommendations for revamping the appointment process is to ensure that a body of Canadian jurisprudence will develop in the Supreme Court that is attuned to the broadest aspirations and needs of Canadian society. This means that the judicial policies that inform the Court's judgments should neither be consistently in favour of the interests of a social or economic elite nor be liable to that construction. The arrival of Charter litigation will reveal in stark terms where our judges stand on fundamental issues of political, social and economic liberty. What are the positive duties of the state and what are the negative limits on its powers over the lives of individual citizens? With this in mind, a process that places greater emphasis on ascertaining the policy orientation of prospective appointees should be welcomed. The qualities desirable for responsibly determining such issues in concrete cases should not be made secondary to the principles of regional representation or of political compromise.

This proposal would not preclude the appointment of a majority of Supreme Court judges from one province or region. (Some regional diversity is desirable, or course, so long as it does not interfere with merit appointments.) It would make possible a Court in which the judges show a profile less regular than that seen in the past.[251] Political party affiliations would become less important as policies other than political ones come into focus; not all the judges would be appointed from courts of appeal or from senior government positions, as they have tended to be; economic backgrounds other than that of the elite might be represented on the Court; judges with professional experience outside the large capital cities would perhaps emerge; and the academic, social and professional suitability of the potential appointees would be scrutinized more thoroughly than ever before as the Appointing Council exercised its roving commission to find the best possible judges.

Not to be underestimated is the elimination of some political patronage that this reform would cause. When judicial vacancies arise, the federal government naturally turns to candidates it knows. Our proposal would replace this limited form of knowledge based on the party network with a process more broadly based and less partisan. This is not to say that appointments to the Supreme Court in recent years have been challenged as exercises in pure patronage. Indeed, the Court has been remarkably free from this sort of criticism; the issue has not touched this Court in the way that it has arisen in other federal appointments. There is nothing, however, to prevent Supreme Court appointments from becoming patronage posts in the future, so long as the federal cabinet retains untrammelled discretion.

If the proposed Appointing Council is considered desirable, its duties could be extended to other judicial appointments such as Federal Court judges or those judges referred to in section 96 of the *Constitution Act, 1867*. Indeed, similar bodies could be responsible for all judicial appointments made by the provinces as well as by the federal government. Since many court cases, including those on the Charter, never go beyond the trial level, it is vital to have judges on the front lines who are adequately prepared for the task. The focus of this study, however, is the Supreme Court of Canada. The case for a new appointment process is most compelling with respect to this court of last resort.

The Supreme Court has always been more than just an umpire for disputes between the central government and the provinces. It has a special mandate toward the duality of the Canadian legal system that does not affect any other court in the country. Its jurisdiction and its central items of business continue to change and evolve. The Charter makes this more apparent than ever. The appointment process should emphasize talent, diversity and sensitivity that have social, historical and philosophical dimensions. These transcend narrow regional or political interests. A new procedure for appointing judges of the Supreme Court should boldly recognize these values and how they could provide the basis for what Chief Justice Dickson has called a distinctively Canadian jurisprudence.[252]

Administrative and Bureaucratic Reforms

One of the important effects of the Charter is the substantial increase in the number of cases that should be heard by the Supreme Court of Canada. Depending upon what approach the judges take to the interpretation of the Charter, the flow of cases may even increase in the next few decades. As discussed earlier, the current pressure is at the leave-to-appeal stage, but as leave is granted in a large number of these cases, it will make itself felt at the hearing and judgment-writing stages as well. How the Court should cope with the increasing volume of work and its changing nature is the topic of this section.

Rather than recommending constitutional or statutory changes to deal with the anticipated flood of cases, we have targetted administrative and bureaucratic changes in the institutional operation of the Court. The prime virtue of this solution is that it leaves the problem in the hands of the judges themselves, who are most familiar with the nature and extent of the problem. Earlier in this paper we rejected other reform proposals aimed at a larger workload. Particularly, we rejected a reduction in the jurisdiction of specialized panels. These proposals were rejected, in part, because we felt that the Court as an institution could best cope with such problems and should be given a flexible mandate to do so.

In considering reforms to the bureaucratic structures and operational procedures of the Supreme Court, attention is naturally focussed on the U.S. scene. The volume of work that confronts the United States Supreme Court has been described as a crisis which could lead to the collapse of the whole court structure at the federal level.[253] In Canada, the impact of more cases finding their way into the courts will be felt in the provincial and federal courts as well as in the Supreme Court of Canada. Furthermore, it is not just the increased number of cases emanating from the Charter and elsewhere, but also the new complexity of these cases that requires judges to rethink what kind of information they should receive. On all these issues there is considerable writing in the United States; a selected bibliography including some articles addressing the situation in Canada is presented at the end of the study.

The Growing Workload

Concerns about the workload of the Supreme Court are not new to Canada,[254] but the degree of concern being expressed by both lawyers and judges is quite novel. As explored in the previous section, on jurisdiction, the number of leave applications has grown greatly in recent years and the percentage of Charter cases getting leave is high. When this is coupled with the fact that the number of judgments rendered in 1983 has dropped, it raises serious concerns about delay.

The Court and Chief Justice Dickson in particular are aware of the corrosive effect of delay on justice. In his speech to the 1984 Canadian Bar Association's annual meeting, the Chief Justice said:

> Delay distorts the financial effect of the ultimate verdict on the parties and may impose severe emotional strains. In family law cases involving the custody of children the suffering extends beyond the litigants to innocent third parties. In criminal cases the possibilities for injustice arising from delay are equally obvious. . . .
>
> Much of the delay that litigants encounter is, however, not the result of lawyers' stalling, but of institutional weakness. To some extent I think this aspect of the problem of delay can be ameliorated by a concerted move to minimize inefficiencies in the way courts function and to improve their productivity. We have recently begun to confront this issue at the Supreme Court of Canada.[255]

Chief Justice Dickson went on to describe how the Court had experimented with hearing leave applications by teleconferencing and satellite and how it was in the process of computerizing its caseload. These technological changes are an important advance in an institution that has not been quick to adopt the benefits of the new technological revolution.[256] Furthermore, the Supreme Court is a bureaucracy unto itself, and like many components of the legal establishment, it has been slow to change.

The direction that change should take is far from clear. In the United States, where the Supreme Court receives 4,000 certiorari petitions (their equivalent of the leave application) per year, the problems of altering the judicial bureaucracy to cope with the workload is more acute. Although the members of the United States Supreme Court agree that there is a problem and have spoken extensively on the topic, they do not agree on the solutions. Chief Justice Warren Burger has advocated the creation of another national court to take on some of his Court's workload.[257] Justice John Paul Stevens advocates a separate body to deal with certiorari petitions,[258] while Justice William Brennan Jr., disagrees with both this proposal and that of his Chief.[259] Most of the other sitting justices have also expressed their views on the matter.

The U.S. proposals for change can be broadly classified as either structural or procedural.[260] In the former category is the creation of another court to supplement or complement the work of the Supreme Court. This would be possible under section 101 of the *Constitution Act, 1867*, but we think it would be undesirable and premature for Canada to create another final appellate court or courts for the better administration of the laws of Canada. Even if the Charter is broadly interpreted, the smaller Canadian population and non-litigious tradition will limit the volume of cases. The effect of creating any parallel court would be a reduction in the prestige of the current Supreme Court.[261]

In Canada, the focus of reforms should be procedural and bureaucratic. There are, however, dangers in bureaucraticizing the judicial structure and putting too much emphasis on productivity. Some of these problems have been predicted by U.S. commentators.[262] Nonetheless, some measures must be taken. A frequently made suggestion is the placing of limits on oral arguments at both the leave and hearing levels. As a more flexible alternative to designated time limits, Chief Justice Dickson has suggested pre-hearing conferences to agree on reasonable time allocations.[263] There are many other ways in which the Court can operate more efficiently, but they are best known to judges and will not be discussed here.[264] What follows are brief comments on what we consider major areas of reform.

Law Clerks and Other Support Staff

An obvious way to reduce the workload of the judges is to delegate non-judicial duties to someone in the support staff. There are distinct problems in such delegation, including the definition of which tasks are administrative in nature and the deciding of to whom work should be delegated. Expanding the role of the registrar, creating new administrative positions, and increasing the duties of law clerks are examples of actions that could be taken. We shall focus our comments on enhancing the role of the law clerk because much has been written on law clerking in the United States (see Bibliography) and because one of the authors has direct experience as a Supreme Court law clerk.[265]

Clerking, if it has become an institution at all in Canada, is a recent one. The first law clerk to the Supreme Court of Canada was hired in the late 1960s. In the early years, not all the judges had a law clerk and it says something about the perceived value of these people that most judges now have two of them. There are also law clerks at many of the provincial courts of appeal. In most cases, law clerks are hired directly out of law school; in recent years, they have increasingly been more mature individuals with graduate degrees as well. The tasks of the law clerk vary depending upon the individual judge and clerk relationship. It is fair to say that the clerk plays an important supporting role that falls far short of the Rasputin behind the throne.[266]

Most of the information on law clerks comes from U.S. sources. The image of law clerks that emerges from *The Brethren*[267] has probably coloured most people's perceptions. There is considerable doubt about whether this is an accurate picture of law clerking in the United States, much less in Canada.[268] A more balanced view of clerking in the United States is presented in *Serving Justice*.[269] While American law clerks do have considerable influence, especially with respect to certiorari petitions (leave applications), they are usually not the ghost-writers of judgments that the clerks themselves sometimes claim to be.

Canadian law clerks do not generally write judgments, although they may draft early versions of a judge's opinion. The role of the clerk is to provide research and other support services and to keep the isolated judiciary in touch with current social and legal trends. In this latter respect the one- or two-year term for law clerks is preferable to that of the long-term or career law clerks.[270] While the long-term clerk may be more efficient at the administrative tasks, the short-term clerk is more likely to inject some vital element of innovation. We do not recommend a significant change in the role of the Canadian law clerk, but we suggest that their duties be made more widely known as part of the education about the emerging judicial institution.[271]

There are dangers in delegating duties to law clerks or to any other person in the judicial bureaucracy. These are well articulated by Joseph Vining, who argues that such delegation promotes an unhealthy hierarchy and judgments that are institutional products rather than the work of an identifiable and human judge.[272] The inevitable result of such a development, in Vining's view, is the loss of legitimacy for the Court and its rulings. Others reject Professor Vining's analysis of what is happening in U.S. courts but do not really question that a judge must not relinquish his mandate.[273] Such large-scale delegation has not been a problem in Canada and it should simply be noted as something to guard against.

Another potential danger of delegation is the possible loss of confidentiality. Only in 1979 were law clerks at the Supreme Court of Canada bound by contract to confidentiality. There was, however, a duty and tradition of law clerk confidentiality that developed in the United States[274] and has been practised in Canada. There has been no Canadian equivalent of *The Brethren*,[275] which was largely based upon conversations with law clerks. This may depend less on the stronger moral fibre of Canadian law clerks than on the fact that no one really wants to know what happens behind the scenes. Confidentiality is not a serious problem so long as there is careful hiring and the expectations are clearly communicated. This would apply to other support staff as well.

Duties should be delegated to support staff, such as law clerks, and this has already happened to some degree. Judges must, however, remain firmly in charge of the bureaucracy so that they can exercise the constitutional trust placed in them. The U.S. experiences can offer guidance in these matters.

Reforming the Leave Mechanism

The present operation of the leave mechanism in the Supreme Court of Canada has been described in the earlier Jurisdiction section of this paper. It has also been the subject of both academic[276] and judicial[277] comment. We have discussed also the current experiments with hearing leave applications by satellite. There are still other possible reforms in the leave structure that could help the Court deal with the possible flood of Charter cases.

Some of the U.S. models can be easily dismissed. An increased role for the laws clerks in screening leave applications would not be appropriate.

Law clerks lack the judicial experience necessary for this task. This is a particular problem because there are no written reasons to guide them.[278] One desirable reform might be to give reasons in a few selected cases; such rulings might serve to deter fruitless applications to the Court. Although the writing of reasons would consume some time, it could save more, eventually.

Mr. Justice Stevens of the United States Supreme Court has called for the creation of a separate court just to deal with the numerous certiorari petitions.[279] This solution was based upon the premise that the granting of certiorari petitions was not vital to the jurisdiction of the Supreme Court. Such a view, and the separate court that flowed from it, were flatly rejected by Mr. Justice Brennan[280] of the same Court and by academics.[281] Chief Justice Dickson in Canada shares the Brennan view that leave applications are one of the most vital aspects of the role of a final appellate court.[282]

The need for consistency in leave rulings will be accentuated by the Charter cases where the same kinds of issues arise in many different provinces. Computerizing the Court's caseload, if applicable to both appeals and leave applications, will be a step in the right direction. Giving reasons in selected cases would also help to promote consistency, which is especially important because leave applications are heard by panels of three. The chances of getting leave should not depend on which panel counsel happens to draw, yet the present process is open to such a charge. The work of the three panels needs to be monitored for consistency.

An important way of reducing the time spent on leave applications would be to eliminate or reduce oral arguments at the leave stage. Cases could be pre-screened, at least to decide whether they should be granted an oral hearing or decided on the basis of written submissions. The flood of Charter applications may necessitate a streamlining of the leave process. In the U.S. system, deciding leave on the basis of written submissions is the norm. It is encouraging that the Court is already revamping the leave mechanism. This is a process that should continue.

Extrinsic Evidence: Informing the Court

The Charter and other developments have brought the Supreme Court into growing contact with the political, social and economic life of Canada. It is now common for the cases brought before the Court to raise issues that cannot be resolved on statutory interpretation and case precedent alone.[283] Both the kinds of reference cases that have come before the Court in recent years[284] and the new role implicit in Charter cases suggest that there need to be new ways by which the Court can inform itself. The academic writers have long been calling for an expanded definition of judicial notice, increased admissibility of extrinsic evidence, and the consideration of the Brandeis brief.[285]

The Court has a long way to go on adopting mechanisms that will allow it to consider the wider range of information necessary to determine, for example, who is entitled to an affirmative action program or what are reasonable limits on a guaranteed right under the Charter. When counsel submitted a crude form of a Brandeis brief in *Saumur v. City of Quebec*[286], the Court assessed costs against the lawyer. When it was decided that anthropological research was relevant to deciding whether an Eskimo was an Indian for purposes of the *Constitution Act, 1867*, the registrar of the Court received the written and oral submissions.[287] Times have changed and so has the role of the Court; both these elements require new and more expansive ways for judges to inform themselves.

Public and Media Relations

At the outset of this paper we indicated that the Supreme Court of Canada is emerging as a high-profile national institution. The media, in both print and electronic form, have taken an interest in the work of the Court. This phenomenon is likely to continue as the Court makes important rulings on the Charter of Rights. Traditionally, relations between the Court and the media have been rather strained and marked more by a spirit of confrontation than by one of collaboration. Journalists distrust lawyers and judges as people who speak a foreign language; members of the legal establishment see journalists as more concerned with sensationalism than with accurate legal reporting.[288]

In his address to the Canadian Bar Association, the present Chief Justice made a call for a new approach to the media by lawyers and judges.

> We live in an age of mass communication. Newspapers, television, radio and film can take us virtually everywhere and show us virtually everything. As a result, the public has grown more interested in a wider variety of subjects than ever before. Insofar as this new public interest embraces the law, and the courts, it is potentially an important and beneficial phenomenon. The success of institutions in a democratic society depends on an educated and enlightened citizenry. What is necessary therefore is to ensure that the views of the legal system disseminated by the media constitute education rather than miseducation. To some extent we can ensure this, whether as judges, lawyers or academics by reasonable cooperation with the media. We can give comprehensive answers in response to genuine requests for information and take the time to explain the background that will make sense of a legal issue of current interest.[289]

The same reasoning applies to the Supreme Court itself, which should continue its recent efforts to make hearings and judgments more accessible to the public. Court tours and the installation of simultaneous translation equipment are a start. It may become necessary to have a person, possibly the registrar of the Court, who is responsible for contacts with the press. He or she should not be a public relations agent in the political or propagandist sense of the term, but rather someone who can facilitate contacts between the Court and either the press or the public. Until there are more legally trained journalists, it also may be necessary to produce press summaries of the cases, which would of course have no authoritative value. Our intention is not to suggest detailed solutions but to emphasize that relations with the press and the public are among the problems that should be addressed.

Consistent with our position that the judges themselves should know best what is needed in the way of administrative changes in the judicial process, we will give the final word on the topic to Chief Justice Dickson.

> It seems to me that we are at a critical moment in the evolution of our judicial system. Our legal institutions are the products of centuries of growth and gradual accommodation to changes in society. Recently the tempo of change has accelerated. Society has grown more complex and so have the disputes that require resolution. Canadians, whether as active litigants or as interested observers, are looking to the courts with increasing frequency. I am very optimistic about the capacity of our courts, to meet this challenge. Working together, with the assistance of counsel and academic commentators, I believe we will arrive at correct and equitable solutions to the issues and questions we currently face, even though many of them have never before been the subject of litigation. We are developing a distinctively Canadian jurisprudence, the substance of which is increasingly relevant to a very wide cross-section of Canadians. We must ensure that the fruits of this jurisprudence reach those whom it is intended to serve. On this subject also, I feel strong optimism, and I call upon the members of the Canadian Bar Association, and the legal profession as a whole, to join in our efforts to meet this challenge.[290]

Conclusions and Recommendations

Reform Themes Reconsidered

As the outset of this study we set out seven basic themes that would arise at various points throughout the paper. The proper jurisdiction for the Court, the need for a more open appointment process, and the desirability of a diversity of backgrounds on the Court have been expressly addressed in the body of the paper and will be reiterated in the recommendations that follow. Perceptions about the Court and its role have been the source of many previous reform proposals. We have tended to reject such proposals unless these perceptions had some empirical base.

There are three other related themes — the impact of the Charter on the Court, the growing media profile of Supreme Court judges, and the increasing economic impact of the Court's rulings. All these matters have been addressed, particularly in the first two sections of the paper. The increased profile and the economic impact seem clear; the real impact of the Charter of Rights is more difficult to predict.

Another point raised in the introduction to this paper was the interconnection of the various aspects of Court reform. Changes in jurisdiction would have implications for the number of judges, the principle of regional representation, and the process of appointment. This analysis can be taken one step further to argue that changes in the Supreme Court cannot really be considered in isolation from other judicial reforms. Gilles Pépin, in his study on section 96 of the *Constitution Act, 1867*, which appears in this volume, recommends to the Commission that there be a much larger provincial role in the appointment of section 96 judges. This fortifies us in our conclusion rejecting regional representation on the Supreme Court since that will presumably exist at other levels.

In many respects, judicial reform should be considered as a whole. The kinds of problems and solutions discussed in the context of the Supreme Court could have application to other courts as well. Our task, however, was to consider the Supreme Court of Canada. We have approached this task in a broad way, recognizing that the Commission is looking not simply for present solutions but also into the future. It was our goal to challenge some basic assumptions, such as the one that ties judicial appointments to cabinet. Other sacred cows have been attacked, such as the need for civil law to be interpreted by civilian judges and the need for a regional judiciary in a federal state. We adopt these positions because we believe in them, and with the hope that they will engender some creative debate. Surely one of the roles of a commission such as the present Royal Commission is to question basic assumptions and to propose novel solutions to old problems. That is what we have attempted to do in our recommendations.

Conclusions and Rejected Reform Proposals

A number of past reform proposals were rejected. In these areas, we recommend a maintenance of the status quo as most conducive to the efficient operation of the Supreme Court of Canada. The implicit statement is that the present Court works well in many respects. Reform should not be undertaken for its own sake but only as a means to improving the operation of the Court. Because statistics about the Supreme Court are rare and of recent vintage, it is difficult to assess empirically its performance. Some past reform proposals appear to be based not upon hard data but rather on political desirability, false perceptions and a misunderstanding of the nature of the Court and its work. Rejecting many earlier reform proposals outlined in Appendix A, we make the following recommendations:

- Retain the general appellate jurisdictions of the Court in both public and private law cases. In spite of its growing workload, we suggest that the Court can deal with this problem via its own leave mechanism. We do suggest changes in the present leave mechanism. The maintenance of the broad appellate jurisdiction allows the Court to serve as an important unifying force in Canada's unitary court structure. Even the special case for keeping Quebec civil cases out of the Court is rejected because there is no solid evidence that the current operation of the Court in any way distorts the Civil Code of Quebec.

- Do not create special panels of the Court. At first glance the idea of special panels is appealing as a means for promoting expertise and dealing with the growing workload. However, in practice, most cases cannot be neatly classified as falling within a single subject area. For example, a constitutional issue often arises in the context of a criminal prosecution or a private law suit. Such fragmentation of the Court also would destroy collegiality. The challenges of the Charter of Rights demand judges who are broad generalists and not a collage of varied experts.

- Leave the number of Supreme Court Justices at nine. Here again, increasing the number of judges sounds like a sensible way of coping with a growing caseload. However, nine seems to be an effective number and has worked even in the United States, where the number of cases far exceeds those that come before the Canadian Supreme Court. With nine, it is still quite feasible to sit all the judges and this reduces the problem of getting different or even conflicting rulings from different groupings of a larger court. Those who argue in favour of increasing the number of judges who sit on the Court have not demonstrated that the benefits of such an increase would outweigh the disadvantages.

- Abandon the principles of regional representation as a significant factor in judicial appointments. This is one of our most controversial conclusions. Many previous reform proposals called for increased regional representation rather than its elimination (see Appendix A). Quebec would not be affected by this position since it would be constitutionally guaranteed three seats as a recognition of Canada's dual legal structure. The Appointing Council might consider regional origin as one factor but not as a crucial guideline. It is desirable that there be regional balance, if only as a matter of appearances, but such appearances should not stand in the way of a pure merit appointment. The reason for the rejection of the regional principle is its lack of relevance to the actual operation of the Court. It was a form of window-dressing that simply served to confuse the public about the proper role of the Court.

There is no doubt that having different regional backgrounds represented on the Court is one aspect of the diversity we seek. The perceptions of bias discussed in the Introduction might be reinforced by a Court composed of judges who come largely from one region. In our assessment, regional origin is less significant than some of the other background factors that we hope to inject into the Court by the Appointing Council. Regional representation is a factor, but not a significant one.

Administrative and Bureaucratic Reforms

It is too early to assess properly the real impact of the Charter on the Court, but even in the first few decades it will likely produce more cases for the Court to decide. This may be accompanied by a growing litigious tendency within Canadian society. We advocate administrative and bureaucratic changes as the most flexible way of coping with a growing but uncertain caseload. The revamping of the existing leave mechanism (a process that is already in progress), the hiring of more law clerks and support staff, and the formalizing and streamlining of court procedures are prime examples. The establishment of better procedures for dealing with the media and the general public are also recommended. The advantage of this proposal is that the solution is devised by those most familiar with the problem — the judges themselves.

A useful model to consider in modifying the judicial bureaucracy is that of the United States. The United States Supreme Court has a much larger caseload than does its Canadian counterpart and it has essentially a public law docket with an emphasis on fundamental rights cases. As the numerous American studies reveal, delegating functions to a judicial bureaucracy is not without its dangers. The Court can no longer afford, however, to operate in ignorance of the technological revolution that has engulfed the rest of society. Bureaucratic reforms must be made while care is taken to preserve as many virtues as can be transferred from a smaller and simpler operation to a more complex one.

Constitutional Reform Proposals

The most important proposals for reform of the Supreme Court of Canada require constitutional amendment in accordance with sections 38 to 42 of the *Constitution Act, 1982*. Stephen Scott has prepared a paper for Volume 1 of this research section on the amendment process ("The Canadian Constitutional Amendment Process: Mechanisms and Prospects"), and his conclusions will not be repeated here. It is sufficient to say that any constitutional change in the Court will require the agreement of the federal government and the governments of two-thirds of the provinces comprising at least 50 percent of the population. Certain matters, such as the composition of the Court will require the approval of the federal government and all the provinces. This imposes a practical limit upon the scope of reform, but the barrier diminishes in light of the Commission's mandate to propose long-term solutions to Canadian problems. While there may not be a consensus on certain matters today, it may well emerge in the future.

COURT ENTRENCHMENT

Whether or not the court is implicitly entrenched at the present time, there can be little harm in making such entrenchment explicit. This is a proposal for which it would be easy to muster broad national support at both the federal and provincial levels. A call for entrenchment is consistent with earlier reform recommendations. The real question is, what aspects of the Court should be entrenched?

Most other countries (the United States, for example) have written into their constitutions a guaranteed role for their Supreme Courts. Such a provision in the Canadian Constitution would guarantee the existence of the Court and state its jurisdiction in broad terms. As a recognition of Canada's dual legal system, Quebec's guarantee of three judges on a nine-person Court would be constitutionalized as well. The amending provision could also contain guarantees of independence and tenure, although these may already be implicit in section 7 and subsection 11(d) of the Charter of Rights.

AN APPOINTING COUNCIL

The problem of judicial appointments to the Supreme Court of Canada has generated much discussion and is the subject of a Canadian Bar Association study. We propose the creation of an Appointing Council whose job would be to ensure that judicial appointments be first-rate. It is not new to suggest a nominating Council, and indeed other countries use such a device (see Appendix B). However, the powers and composition of the council proposed here set it apart from prior reform suggestions. This Appointing Council would not be merely advisory but would instead have final appointing power. The council itself would be composed of joint federal and provincial appointees, to avoid the perception of the Supreme Court of Canada as a "federal" court. Both levels of government would nominate people to a pool from which the council members would be drawn.

One of the goals of the proposed appointment system is to escape the secrecy and the political overtones that characterize the current appointment process. We do not wish, however, to embrace the Senate confirmation process in the United States, which is as political as the Canadian system. The hope is that the inevitable political energies would be expended upon the selection of the Appointing Council, rather than on the appointment of the judges. This should remove some barriers to the selection of judges on the basis of pre-defined criteria of merit. One of the council's first tasks would be to devise guidelines for assessing merit. In devising these, it should consult broadly with lawyers, judges, statesmen and others.

In advocating the new Appointing Council as a better road to meritorious appointments, we do not deny that many Supreme Court justices, past and present, deserve their positions on the basis of merit. There have been and continue to be judges who would be selected by the Appointing Council, as well as by the Governor-in-Council. Since new judges will only be appointed as existing ones retire, we recognize that the present justices will continue to play an important role even if an Appointing Council were adopted. Canadians cannot, however, continue to rely on the good faith of our politicians to provide us with a Supreme Court equipped to meet the challenges of the decades ahead.

Representation on the council will not have to conform to any regional guidelines. A different kind of representation will be mandated. The thirteen-person council should include at least seven women. It should represent a range of social, economic, cultural, racial and vocational backgrounds. Guidelines for nominating people to the pool will ensure that there is a sufficiently diverse pool from which to draw. The exact composition of the council should be the subject of a separate in-depth study.

The reason for the diverse composition of the Appointing Council is to promote, without mandating, a diversity of backgrounds on the Supreme Court itself. In making these judicial appointments, the only specified criterion is merit. While it is hard to disagree with the merit principle, the real difficulty is defining the elements of merit in the context of judging at the Supreme Court of Canada. The experiences of other countries and the findings of the Canadian Bar Association study on appointments should provide assistance in defining merit. Some factors that might be considered are gender balance on the court and the regional origin of judges. While not affecting the individual merit of the judge, gender balance and regional representation may affect the collective merit and perceived legitimacy of the Court's decisions.

The Appointing Council is the heart of our reform proposals. With the growing and changing role of judges under the Charter, it has become even more important that judicial appointments be made on the basis of merit. It is also important to have a diversity of backgrounds represented in Canada's highest court — not just in the sense of regional origin but also with respect to gender, race, socioeconomic status and other factors.

Focus on the Appointing Council also emphasizes that an institution is only as good as the people who compose it. While the institution may in turn limit the energies of its members, the creativity and approach of the Court will depend largely upon how it is staffed.

Appendix A

Summary of Past Proposals for Reform of the Supreme Court

	Proposal	Constitutional Status	Jurisdiction	Structural Changes	Membership	Regional Selection	Method of Selection
1.	TREMBLAY COMMISSION (1956)	Existence, jurisdiction and personnel to be entrenched	Quebec civil cases not to be appealable to Supreme Court	If no change in jurisdiction, then Quebec civil cases to be heard by a 5-member panel, 3 of whom had received Quebec legal training. All 3 would have to agree on a decision in order to reverse a decision of the highest Quebec Court For constitutional cases, a court composed of 9 members, including 5 from current Supreme Court, and 4 others chosen from each of the Maritimes, Quebec, Ontario, and Western provinces	No change	Not discussed (except in context of a court of constitutional affairs)	Province to participate in some manner in the naming of members to the Supreme Court
2.	MORIN (1965)	Constitutional entrenchment	All constitutional questions to be sent immediately to the Supreme Court for adjudication	Possibly have separate chambers for civil law and common law judges. Constitutional questions to be heard by a panel composed of an equal number of civil law and common law members	Equal number of judges in separate chambers	No mention of how English Canada's component to be divided up by regional origins.	More precise criteria about scholarship and experience. Choose from civil service and academia as well. If Senate reformed as a binational institution then have it select judges on Supreme Court. If Senate left unreformed, then francophone part of court to be chosen jointly by federal and Quebec governments

Appendix A (cont'd)

	Proposal	Constitutional Status	Jurisdiction	Structural Changes	Membership	Regional Selection	Method of Selection
3.	ABEL (1965)	Not addressed	Court to adjudicate matters only of federal legislative jurisdiction	No need for a bifurcated Court	No change	Not addressed	Not addressed
4.	RUSSELL (1968, 1969)	Eliminate ss. 96 to 101, but retain Parliament's power to create courts for the better administration of justice (though this power would be expressly subject to the power in s. 91(27) regarding criminal courts) Constitutionally guarantee tenure and salaries of Supreme Court judges	Give provinces the power to make highest court in the province the final appellate court on matters of provincial jurisdiction. Supreme Court to deal with: a) constitutional questions; b) matters of law subject to federal legislative competence; and c) conflicts among provinces or between a province and the federal government	Create, if need be, separate civil law and common law chambers. No need for this if all provinces decide to make their highest courts the final authority on some types of matters	Not discussed	Not discussed	Establish a procedure for federal-provincial collaboration in appointment of Supreme Court judges

	Proposal	Constitutional Status	Jurisdiction	Structural Changes	Membership	Regional Selection	Method of Selection
5.	LEDERMAN (1970)	Entrench all essential provisions regarding structure and power of the Supreme Court, including regional quotas	Retain general jurisdiction	Necessity for having judges from both civil and common law traditions sitting on cases together. Quorum of 9 for constitutional questions. Appointment of ad hoc judges from Quebec for civil cases from that province	Increase size to 11 members	Composition to be as follows: a) Atlantic provinces (2); b) Quebec (3); c) Ontario (3); and d) Western provinces (3)	Use nominating commission, with some provincial representatives included, that suggests suitable appointees. Federal government to make final selection
6.	VICTORIA CHARTER (1971)	Entrench basic provisions	To be a general court of appeal, including any constitutional question from any court in Canada. Further appellate jurisdiction to be prescribed by Parliament (including references)	Civil law appeals from Quebec to be heard by 5-member panel, with at least 3 from Quebec. If insufficient Quebec judges, use ad hoc appointees from Quebec superior court of appeal. Parliament to be empowered to establish quorums for particular purposes	No change, except statutory retirement age to be 70 years	At least 3 judges to be appointed from Quebec	Elaborate procedure requiring federal attorney-general to put name before appropriate provincial attorney-general. If no agreement, then a nominating council to be assembled. The council to recommend a choice from among names on a list submitted by federal attorney-general

Appendix A (cont'd)

	Proposal	Constitutional Status	Jurisdiction	Structural Changes	Membership	Regional Selection	Method of Selection
7.	MOLGAT-McGUIGAN PROPOSALS (1972)	Entrench existence, independence, and structure	Province empowered to withdraw matters of strictly provincial law from Court's jurisdiction. Court to retain jurisdiction over: a) matters of federal law; b) constitutional questions; and c) whether a matter is one of strictly provincial law	Not discussed	No change	3 members from Quebec	Supports methods of consultation proposed in Victoria Charter, except that provinces should be able to submit names to the nominating council

Proposal	Constitutional Status	Jurisdiction	Structural Changes	Membership	Regional Selection	Method of Selection
8. CONSTITUTIONAL AMENDMENT BILL C-60 (1978)		To be a general court of appeal. Parliament to assign appellate jurisdiction. Quebec civil law appeals to be decided solely by judges appointed from Quebec. Discretion of Court to refuse to hear an appeal that is not of sufficient public importance		Increase to 11 judges. Retirement age to be 70 years	4 to be chosen from Quebec; 7 from other provinces or territories. Attempt to have members from each of: a) Atlantic provinces; b) Ontario; c) Western provinces; and d) British Columbia	Initial consultation between federal attorney-general and counterpart from particular province concerned. If no agreement on an appointee, then convene a nominating council (composition depending in part on provincial attorney-general's preference). Federal attorney-general to submit names to Council. House of the Federation can then affirm or reject the nomination
9. BRITISH COLUMBIA GOVERNMENT (1978)	Entrench existence, composition, and jurisdiction of the Court	Final court of appeal in all cases (whether of federal or provincial law)		Increase to 11 members	Primary consideration to be merit, but members to be drawn from all five regions of Canada (counting B.C. as a separate and distinct region)	Three stage procedure: a) federal-provincial consultation on proposed nominee; b) nomination by federal government; and c) confirmation by a reformed Senate

Appendix A (cont'd)

Proposal	Constitutional Status	Jurisdiction	Structural Changes	Membership	Regional Selection	Method of Selection
10. ALBERTA GOVERNMENT (1978)		General appellate jurisdiction, with special provisions for constitutional disputes	For constitutional questions, a special constitutional court to be selected and convened, totally separate from the Supreme Court	40- to 50-member panel at any given time eligible to be selected for a 7-member constitutional court, these 7 to be chosen at random. The panel to be composed of experienced superior court judges. The 7 selected would not again be eligible to be part of a constitutional court until all other members of the panel had participated in a constitutional case	Membership in the panel to be based on the current population distribution among the 10 provinces	Each province to submit a list to federal government giving more names than that province entitled to have on the panel. Federal government then to select members of the panel from those lists

Proposal	Constitutional Status	Jurisdiction	Structural Changes	Membership	Regional Selection	Method of Selection
11. CANADIAN BAR ASSOCIATION COMMITTEE (1978)		General appellate jurisdiction. Parliament to prescribe organization, maintenance, and procedure of the Supreme Court. Provinces should not be able to refer questions directly to the court	No special chambers. Quebec civil law appeals to be heard by a 5-member panel, with 3 civilly trained judges	No change	3 judges from Quebec	Provincial input to be achieved through the judiciary committee of a reformed Upper House rather than through a nominating council. The House to hold public hearings on nominees, though deliberations to be in camera. Federal government to have exclusive power to nominate appointees
12. PEPIN-ROBARTS REPORT (1979)	Entrench existence and independence of entire judiciary	General appellate jurisdiction, including power to decide reference. Provinces should be able to refer matters directly to the Supreme Court. Recommends creation of special fund for reimbursing travel costs of litigants	Divide the Court into 3 benches for particular purposes. These include: a) for matters of provincial jurisdiction, separate Quebec civil law and common law sections: b) for matters of federal jurisdiction, a quorum of 7 to 9 judges; and c) for constitutional questions, quorum of the full court	Increase to 11 members	"Broadly regional basis," but including 5 civilly-trained judges, and 6 trained in the common law	Federal cabinet initially to consult with either Quebec attorney-general (on Quebec appointment) or all other attorneys-general on a common law appointment. Nominee to be ratified by an appropriate committee of the Council of the Federation. Chief justice to have a non-renewable term, with alternating appointment between a civil law and common law judge

Appendix A (cont'd)

Proposal	Constitutional Status	Jurisdiction	Structural Changes	Membership	Regional Selection	Method of Selection
13. LEDERMAN (1979)	Entrench provisions regarding structure and functions of the Court	Retain general appellate jurisdiction	Divide the Court into panels to increase productivity and efficiency	Increase to at least 11 members, and possibly up to 15, with 9 as the minimum quorum	Use regional quotas	For all judicial appointments, use official nominating commissions, composed of federal and provincial politicians. These would keep lists of suitable prospective appointees, and submit short lists to the appointing authority. That authority to be obliged to choose from among the names on the lists
14. QUEBEC LIBERAL PARTY (1980)	Entrench existence and jurisdiction of Court, tenure and independence of judges, and government's obligation to support court's needs	General courts of appeal for both federal and provincial matters on any type of question, including Quebec civil law. Questions could be referred by federal or provincial governments or the Federal Council	Litigant could request a "dualist constitutional panel" to hear constitutional matters. This would be composed of the Chief Justice and an equal number of judges from Quebec and the rest of Canada. Some judges from Quebec superior courts could be added ad hoc (based on seniority). Otherwise, the Court itself to determine what panels are appropriate for hearing particular kinds of cases	No change	3 judges from Quebec	Judges to be appointed by federal government after prior ratification of the appointment by the Federal Council. Chief Justice to be chosen alternately from among Quebec and non-Quebec judges

Proposal	Constitutional Status	Jurisdiction	Structural Changes	Membership	Regional Selection	Method of Selection
15. MacPHERSON (1983)	Entrench existence, composition, and jurisdiction of the Court	Retain general appellate jurisdiction, including Quebec civil law appeals	Quebec civil cases to be heard by a panel that includes a majority of civilian judges	No change	a) Atlantic provinces (1); b) Quebec (4); c) Ontario (1); d) Prairie provinces; (1) e) British Columbia (1); and f) one other judge to be appointed from any region	Equal participation by federal and provincial governments. Favours federal government's nominating an appointee and the Senate's ratifying the choice

Sources used in this summary include, in chronological order:

1. Province of Quebec, *Report of the Royal Commission of Inquiry on Constitutional Problems* (Tremblay Commission), 3 vols. (Quebec: Government of Quebec, 1956).
2. Jacques-Yvan Morin, "A Constitutional Court for Canada" (1965), 43 Can. Bar Rev. 545.
3. Albert S. Abel, "The Role of the Supreme Court in Private Law Cases" (1965), 4 Alta. Law Rev. 39.
4a. Peter H. Russell, "The Jurisdiction of the Supreme Court of Canada: Present Policies and a Programme for Reform" (1968), 6 Osgoode Hall L.J. 1.
4b. Peter H. Russell, "Constitutional Reform of the Canadian Judiciary" (1969), 7 Alta. Law Rev. 103.
5. W.R. Lederman, "Thoughts on Reform of the Supreme Court of Canada" (1970), 8 Alta. Law Rev. 1.

(cont'd.)

Appendix A (concluded)

6. "Canadian Constitutional Charter, 1971" (Victoria Charter) contained in Canadian Intergovernmental Conference Secretariat, *The Constitutional Review, 1968–1971* (Ottawa: Information Canada, 1974), 375–96.

7. Government of Canada, *The Final Report to Parliament of the Special Joint Committee of the Senate and the House of Commons on the Constitution of Canada*, Fourth Session of the Twenty-eighth Parliament, 1972 (Ottawa: Queen's Printer, 1972).

8. Bill C-60, The Constitutional Amendment Bill, introduced in the House of Commons in June 1978.

9. Government of British Columbia, *British Columbia's Constitutional Proposals*, Paper No. 4: Reform of the Supreme Court of Canada (Victoria: Province of British Columbia, 1978).

10. Government of Alberta, *Harmony in Diversity: A New Federalism for Canada* (Edmonton: Government of Alberta, 1978).

11. Committee on the Constitution, *Towards a New Canada*, Research Study prepared for the Canadian Bar Foundation (Montreal: Canadian Bar Foundation, 1978).

12. The Task Force on Canadian Unity, *A Future Together* (Ottawa: Minister of Supply and Services Canada, 1979).

13. W.R. Lederman, "Current Proposals for Reform of the Supreme Court of Canada" (1979), 47 Can. Bar Rev. 687.

14. The Constitutional Committee of the Quebec Liberal Party, *A New Canadian Federation* (Montreal: Quebec Liberal Party, 1980).

15. James C. MacPherson, "The Potential Implications of Constitutional Reform for the Supreme Court of Canada" in *Canada and the New Constitution: The Unfinished Agenda*, edited by Stanley M. Beck and Ivan Bernier, 2 vols. (Montreal: Institute for Research on Public Policy, 1983), 1:165

Appendix B

Comparative Survey of Supreme Courts in Selected Western Countries

Country	Supreme Judicial Tribunal	Composition	Constitutional Status	Jurisdiction	Structural Characteristics	Tenure	Selection
UNITED KINGDOM	House of Lords	The Lord Chancellor; 11 Lords of Appeal in Ordinary; and other lords holding high judicial office or eminence as barristers	Originally part of the Curia Regis. Many practices settled by long-standing convention. Some protection afforded by Act of Settlement (1701) and subsequent ordinary statute. Parliament can alter terms of tenure, salary, etc., at will	Predominantly appellate jurisdiction in both private and public law areas. Most of cases arrive on appeal from the English Court of Appeal. Final court of appeal for both criminal and civil cases from Nothern Ireland, and civil cases only from Scotland's Court of Session. Appeal launched by way of petition.	Quorum: 3 Law Lords. Lord Chancellor rarely sits. Can sit as two appellate committees, so up to two cases can be heard simultaneously. Lord Chancellor is also a member of Cabinet and has legislative and political, as well as judicial duties. Leave to appeal must in most cases be granted by an appeals committee of the Law Lords or by the Court of Appeal	Hold Office during good behaviour, subject to removal by joint address of the Houses of Parliament. Appointees become life peers	At least one (or two?) members must come from Scotland. From time to time one is appointed from Northern Ireland. All Law Lords are appointed by the Crown on the advice of the Prime Minister. Must be barristers or advocates of at least 15 years standing, or else have held high judicial office for at least two years. Some informal consultation with Lord Chancellor and other high authorities in administration of justice.

Appendix B (cont'd)

Country	Supreme Judicial Tribunal	Composition	Constitutional Status	Jurisdiction	Structural Characteristics	Tenure	Selection
FRANCE	A. *Conseil d'État* (Council of State)	Professional public administrators	Originally in *ancien régime*, a body of advisers to the monarch. Still technically part of the executive rather than part of the French judiciary	Appellate tribunal for all lower administrative courts. Provides an alternative to judicial review. No intermediate, appellate body. Has some original jurisdiction, e.g., over constitutional status of an administrative act, or over executive legislation. French administrative law, which is not codified, is composed largely of decisions by the *Conseil d'État*			All appointees trained in National School of Administration

Country	Supreme Judicial Tribunal	Composition	Constitutional Status	Jurisdiction	Structural Characteristics	Tenure	Selection
FRANCE	B. *Cour de Cessation* (Court of Cessation)	Approximately 100 judges		Supreme appellate tribunal for all ordinary cases, i.e., civil and criminal matters. Must apply the Code or other legislation; cannot pronounce a general rule as a way of deciding individual cases. Court of Cessation cannot substitute its own decisions for that of the lower court (i.e. not a revision system); but case must be remanded	Sits in 6 specialized chambers; 5 civil and 1 criminal. Will on occasion sit in mixed chambers or plenary assembly (if second appeal rises from lower court in the same case, after the first remanded)		All appointees trained at National School of the Judiciary and must pass competitive examinations during training. Have served practical internship as a judicial apprenticeship. May advance up the judicial hierarchy

Appendix B (cont'd)

Country	Supreme Judicial Tribunal	Composition	Constitutional Status	Jurisdiction	Structural Characteristics	Tenure	Selection
FRANCE	C. Constitutional Council		Created in 1958	Reviews laws (not administrative acts) passed by Parliament. Must be requested to do so by executive or legislature and only before promulgation. Sole purpose for review: to determine whether law conforms to constitutional divisions of power between the executive and parliament. In 1971, however, Council claimed power to review laws for conformity with constitution generally, including unwritten fundamental principles of French republican tradition			
	D. Tribunal of Conflicts	Made up partly of judges and partly of administrators		Not strictly a Supreme Court. It determines whether a case falls within the administrative or ordinary jurisdiction			

Country	Supreme Judicial Tribunal	Composition	Constitutional Status	Jurisdiction	Structural Characteristics	Tenure	Selection
FEDERAL REPUBLIC OF GERMANY	A. Federal Administrative Court (*Bundesverwaltungsgericht*)		Part of the judiciary, rather than of the national executive. Established in 1949 Basic Law (*Grundgesetz*). Judicial independence is protected in the Basic Law	Supreme appellate tribunal for all appeals on administrative matters. Hears appeals only on questions of law. The second level of appeal; immediately lower administrative courts have reviewed the case de novo. Jurisdiction governed generally by Administrative Court Code		Age limit and terms of office may be set by ordinary statute. May be removed for various reasons by order of the Federal Constitutional Court (2/3 majority)	Selected jointly by competent federal ministers and a committee made up equally of competent *Land* (state) ministers and members of the *Bundestag* (lower House of Parliament).
	B. Federal Supreme Court (*Bundesgerichtshof*)			Ordinary civil and criminal jurisdiction; the supreme tribunal on these matters. If it finds reversible error, then it may either reverse or remand, or else modify the decision and enter final judgment itself (a revision system — in common with Austria and Switzerland). Decisions are not binding in future cases		Same provisions as for Federal Administrative Court judges	Same selection procedure as for Federal Administrative Court. All judges trained through post-law school internship and competitive examinations. After a 3-year probationary period, all judges are appointed for life, and can begin to move hierarchy

Appendix B (cont'd)

Country	Supreme Judicial Tribunal	Composition	Constitutional Status	Jurisdiction	Structural Characteristics	Tenure	Selection
FEDERAL REPUBLIC OF GERMANY	C. Federal Constitutional Court (*Bundesverfassungsgericht*)	16 judges divided into two distinct chambers	Jurisdiction, composition, method of selection, independence and tenure of judges are established in the Basic law. Also entrenches the individual's right to bring a constitutional complaint	Hears disputes over public law matters between the Federal government and the *Laender* (states); disputes raised by individuals that basic democratic, political, or procedural rights have been infringed by state action; and disputes over the conformity of any federal of *Land* law with the Basic Law. Federal legislation may assign other duties to it. Decisions are binding in future cases	Made up of two separate panels: the First Senate (headed by the president of the Constitutional Court) and the Second Senate (headed by the vice-president). Each Senate has associate judges. First Senate conducts judiciary review of the legislative and governmental acts that relate to Articles 1-17 of Basic Law. Second Senate handles matters involving certain democratic rights; procedural guarantees; and inter-governmental disputes	Once appointed a judge at any level, the person has the benefit of lifetime tenure and security. 12-year term for Constitutional Court Judge. Cannot be immediately reappointed. Mandatory retirement at age 68	Minimum age = 40 years. Must be eligible for election to *Bundestag* and possess all formal requirements, set out in federal law for judges, including examinations and in-service training. 8 are chosen by *Bundestag* (through its Judicial Selection Committee) the other 8 chosen by 2/3 of the *Bundesrat* (Council of Constituent States). States have informally agreed to share judgeships on proportional basis. *Bundestag* and *Bundesrat* alternate in choos-

Country	Supreme Judicial Tribunal	Composition	Constitutional Status	Jurisdiction	Structural Characteristics	Tenure	Selection
FEDERAL REPUBLIC OF GERMANY					and jurisdictional conflicts. Since 1956, both Senates can use 3-member panels to hear and decide constitutional complaints from individuals and other juristic persons		ing president and vice-president of the Court. Relevant factors: a) party affiliation; b) religious affiliation c) geographic origins; and d) profession (civil servant, judge, professor, legislator)
D. Specialized Courts		(These include supreme tribunals for tax, labour, and social security matters. Each matter has its own separate system of courts for adjudicating cases in that area, with intermediate and final appellate tribunals)					

Appendix B (cont'd)

Country	Supreme Judicial Tribunal	Composition	Constitutional Status	Jurisdiction	Structural Characteristics	Tenure	Selection
UNITED STATES	Supreme Court of the United States	9 members (since 1866), as fixed by Congress	Governed by Article III of the constitution	Original jurisdiction as set forth by Art. III, s. 2, para. 2 (148 cases between 1789 and 1978), including extensive concurrent jurisdiction with state courts and Federal District Court. Appellate jurisdiction has supplied vast majority of cases, particularly as this has involved questions of constitutional law. Cases come from subordinate Federal Courts or from state Supreme Courts. Primary mode of a case reaching the Court is by petition for a writ of certiorari, which Court has discretion to grant. Some cases come by way of writ of appeal (statutory application as of right)	In hearing the merits of an appeal, by whatever mode, the Court sits *en banc*	Lifetime tenure during good behaviour with protection against diminution of salary during term of office	President nominates candidates. Confirmation is by a simple majority vote in the Senate. The Judiciary Committee may conduct public hearings into the suitability of the nominee. President may informally consult the attorney-general, chief justice, ABA standing committee on the Federal judiciary and political leaders. Senate up to 1970s has refused to confirm 26 of the 136 Supreme Court nominees, though only 4 in the current century

Country	Supreme Judicial Tribunal	Composition	Constitutional Status	Jurisdiction	Structural Characteristics	Tenure	Selection
UNITED STATES				or by certification from lower Federal Court. Court has denied over 85% of certiorari applications without reasons. Four justices must vote to hear certiorari application for it to reach a hearing stage			
AUSTRALIA	High Court of Australia	7 members	Chapter III of Constitution sets out the existence and jurisdiction of federal courts, including the High Court	Original jurisdiction (ss. 75 and 76 of Constitution) includes matters arising under a treaty; disputes between states or residents of different states; and writ of mandamus or prohibition against government officer. Additional original jurisdiction can be conferred by federal Cabinet (s. 72). Appellate jurisdiction (s. 73) with some types of appeals being brought	Full Court must sit to hear certain classes of appeals provided under Judiciary Act. Section 79 of constitution permits parliament to prescribe how many judges shall be needed to exercise Court's federal jurisdiction	Life tenure with removal on joint address of both Houses of Parliament on grounds set forth in constitution. But s. 72 may have been effectively amended by 1977 referendum so that judges only hold office for fixed term	Judges appointed by Cabinet (s. 72). Must either be a judge of the Supreme Court or else a practising barrister and solicitor of at least 5 years' standing. Nominally, the attorney-general offers name of candidate to cabinet. Attorney-general must consult with attorneys-general

Appendix B (concluded)

Country	Supreme Judicial Tribunal	Composition	Constitutional Status	Jurisdiction	Structural Characteristics	Tenure	Selection
AUSTRALIA				as of right and others requiring High Court's leave. Some monetary restrictions in civil cases. After 1968 and 1975, little room for appealing a High Court decision to the Privy Council. 1968 legislation abolished such appeals on questions of federal law, including the Interpretation of the constitution. It appears that appeals from state courts to the Privy Council in nonfederal matters are still possible. In 1982 the first ministers of the federal government and the states agreed to abolish these as well.			of the States (s. 6 of High Court of Australia Act)

Sources: Knapp, Viktor, ed., *International Encyclopedia of Comparative Law* (Tubingen: Mohr, 1972).
Merryman, John and Clark, D., *Comparative Law: Western European and Latin American Legal Systems* (Bloomington, Ind.: Bobbs-Merrill, 1978).
Von Mehren, A. and Gordley, J., *The Civil Law System*, 2nd ed. (Boston: Little, Brown, 1977).
Jackson, R.M., *The Machinery of Justice in England*, 7th ed. (Cambridge: Cambridge University Press, 1977).
Kommers, Donald P., *Judicial Politics in West Germany: A Study of the Federal Constitutional Court* (London: Sage, 1976).
Abraham, Henry J., *The Judicial Process: An Introductory Analysis of the Courts of the United States, England and France*, 4th ed. (New York: Oxford University Press, 1980).
Renfree, Harold E., *The Federal Judicial System of Australia* (Sydney: Legal Books Pty. Ltd., 1984).

Notes

This study was completed in December 1984.

1. Peter H. Russell, "The Political Role of the Supreme Court of Canada In its First Century" (1975), 53 Can. Bar Rev. 576. In this study Professor Russell concludes that the Court had little national impact and only gained fleeting prominence in respect to the 1950s civil liberties cases which emerged from Duplessis's Quebec.

2. B. Laskin, "The Supreme Court of Canada: A Final Court of and forCanadians" (1951), 29 Can. Bar Rev. 1038. Professor Laskin (as he then was) argued that the abolition of Privy Council appeals gave the Supreme Court an important new status and role.

3. *Reference Re The Seabed and Subsoil of the Continental Shelf off Newfoundland* (1984), 5 D.L.R. (4th) 385 (S.C.C.).

4. *Supreme Court Act,* R.S.C. 1970, c. S-19.

5. J. McRuer, "The Supreme Court as a National Institution" (1980), 1 Sup. Ct. Law Rev. 467, at 469.

6. P. Weiler, *In the Last Resort* (Toronto: Carswell, 1974).

7. W. Lederman's, "Unity and Diversity in Canadian Federalism" (1975), 53 Can. Bar Rev. 597, is one of many examples.

8. B. Laskin, "The Role and Function of Final Appellate Courts: The Supreme Court of Canada" (1975), 53 Can. Bar Rev. 469.

9. The influence of the British tradition in both the role of the Canadian judge and the substantive content of the law is well illustrated in two monographs by the late Chief Justice Laskin: *The British Tradition in Canadian Law* (London: Stevens and Sons, 1969), and *The English Law in Canadian Courts Since the Abolition of Privy Council Appeals* (London: Stevens and Sons, 1976).

10. B. Dickson, "The Judiciary — Law Interpreters or Law Makers" (1982), 12 Man. Law J. 1.

11. B. Laskin, "What Everyone Should Know About the Supreme Court of Canada," address to the Empire Club, Toronto, March 12, 1981, at 1-2.

12. *Constitutional Amendment References 1981* (1981), 39 N.R. 1 (S.C.C.).

13. Part I of *Constitution Act, 1982,* which is Schedule B of *Canada Act*, 1982 (U.K.), c. 11.

14. "The New Face of the Law" *Maclean's,* April 30, 1984, 14-19 et seq.

15. (1984), 53 N.R. 169 (S.C.C.).

16. W. MacKay, "Judicial Process in the Supreme Court of Canada: The Patriation Reference and Its Implications for the Charter of Rights" (1983), 21 Osgoode Hall L.J. 55, at 60.

17. *Reference Re Anti-Inflation Act* (1976), 68 D.L.R. (3d) 452 (S.C.C.).

18. *Reference Re the Legislative Authority of the Parliament of Canada in Relation to the Upper House,* [1980] 1 S.C.R. 54.

19. B. Laskin, *The Institutional Character of the Judge* (London: Oxford University Press, 1982).

20. For a revealing profile of the 28 people who have sat as Supreme Court judges since 1949 see Robert Martin, "Values, Attitudes, Ideology and Judging: A Study of the Supreme Court of Canada," unpublished background paper submitted to the Royal Commission on the Economic Union and Development Prospects for Canada July 1984.

21. This was the predominant theme developed in W. MacKay et al., eds. *The Canadian Charter of Rights: Law Practice Revolutionized* (Halifax: Dalhousie Continuing Legal Education, 1982).

22. A.D. Gold, "The Legal Rights Provisions: A New Vision or Déjà Vu?" (1982), 4 Sup. Ct. Law Rev. 107, at 129-30; J.E. Magnet, "The Charter's Official Languages Provisions: The Implications of Entrenched Bilingualism" (1982), 4 Sup. Ct. Law Rev. 163, at 170; and W.R. Lederman, "The Power of the Judges and the New Canadian Charter of Rights and Freedoms" (1982), 16 U.B.C. Law Rev. 1 (special Charter edition) are but a few examples of this widely expressed view.

23. D.V. Smiley, "A Dangerous Deed: The Constitution Act, 1982" in *And No One Cheered: Federalism, Democracy and the Constitution*, edited by Keith Banting and Richard Simeon (Toronto: Methuen 1983), at p. 93.

24. *Supra*, note 16. Professor MacKay admits that the *Patriation Reference* was an atypical case and signs of creative judging in that case will not necessarily emerge on a more general front.

25. Chief Justice Dickson has spoken extensively about the new role of the judges under the Charter and the need to fashion a distinctive Canadian jurisprudence on the Charter. A recent example is "The Path to Improving the Accessibility of the Law in Canada," an address to the annual meeting of the Canadian Bar Association, Winnipeg, Manitoba, August 28, 1984.

26. *Supra*, note 10, and B. Dickson, "The Role and Function of Judges" (1980), 14 Law Soc. of Upp. Can. Gaz. 138. His most notable authoritative statement on the role of the judge is in *Harrison v. Carswell* (1975), 5 N.R. 523 (S.C.C.).

27. Alta. Press Bill, [1938] S.C.R. 100.

28. *Roncarelli v. Duplessis*, [1959] S.C.R. 121.

29. I.C. Rand, "The Role of the Independent Judiciary in Preserving Freedom" (1951), 9 U. of T. Law J. l, is a good example as are his well-known cases.

30. B. Laskin, "Our Civil Liberties: The Role of the Supreme Court" (1955), 41 Queen's Quarterly 455. The late Chief Justice made a reasonable effort to practise this role once he became a judge.

31. E.M. Hall, "Law Reform and the Judiciary's Role" (1972), 10 Osgoode Hall L.J. 411.

32. N. Lyon, "The Central Fallacy of Canadian Federalism" (1976), 22 McGill Law J. 40

33. *Valin v. Langlois* (1879), 3 S.C.R. l; aff'd (1879–80), 5 App. Cas. 115 (J.C.P.C.)

34. 5 U.S. 137 (1803).

35. *Supra*, note 32, and W.R. Lederman, "The Independence of the Judiciary" (1956), 34 Can. Bar Rev. 769 and 1139, reprinted in *Continuing Canadian Constitutional Dilemmas* (Toronto: Butterworth, 1981), at 109.

36. B. Strayer, *Judicial Review of Legislation in Canada* (Toronto: University of Toronto Press, 1968), at 3. In a more recent comment, Mr. Justice Strayer has moved closer to the Lederman and Lyon thesis. B. Strayer, "Comment on 'The Origins of Judicial Review in Canada'" (1983), 16 *Can. J. of Pol. Sci.* 593.

37. J. Smith, "The Origins of Judicial Review in Canada" (1983), l6 *Can. J. of Pol. Sci.* 115.

38. Laskin, *supra*, note 11. The late Chief Justice argued forcefully that the Supreme Court of Canada was a national and not a federal institution.

39. Strayer, "Comment on 'The Origins of Judicial Review in Canada'," *supra*, note 36. The general impact of the Charter on judicial review in Canada is explored in B. Strayer, *The Canadian Constitution and the Courts*, 2nd ed. (Toronto: Butterworth, l983).

40. B. Dickson, "The Democratic Character of the Charter of Rights" in *Law, Politics and the Judicial Process in Canada*, edited by F.L. Morton and R. Knopff (1984). This was originally a lecture given at the University of Calgary, September 13, l983.

41. P. Weiler, "Of Judges and Rights or Should Canada Have a Constitutional Bill of Rights" (1980), 60 Dalhousie Rev. 205.

42. This role is particularly apparent with respect to section l5, which was delayed for three years so that legislators could put their houses in order. It has also been judicially articulated in the context of language rights: *Reference Re Ontario Minority Language Rights*, an unreported decision, June 26, l984 (Ont. C.A.).

43. P. Russell, "The Political Purposes of the Canadian Charter of Rights and Freedoms" (1983), 61 Can. Bar Rev. 30.

44. R. Knopff, "Federalism, the Charter and the Court: Comment on Smith's 'The Origins of Judicial Review in Canada'" (1983), l6 *Can. J. of Pol. Sci.* 585.

45. H. Janisch, "Beyond Jurisdiction: Judicial Review and the Charter of Rights" (1983), 43 Rev. du B. 401, argues that the Charter may also change judicial review in the administrative law context.

46. This was demonstrated in the first Charter ruling from the Court: *The Law Society of Upper Canada v. Skapinker, supra*, note 15.

47. B. Hovius, "The Legacy of the Supreme Court of Canada's Approach to the Canadian Bill of Rights: Prospects for the Charter" (1982), 28 McGill Law J. 31.

48. *Supra*, note 25.

49. A. Roman, "The Charter of Rights: Renewing the Social Contract" (1982–83), 8 Queen's L.J. 188, at 198. He argues that we should look to British and Canadian traditions of protecting basic rights at least as much as to those developed in the United States.

50. E. McWhinney, "Federal Supreme Courts and Constitutional Review" (1967), 45 Can. Bar Rev. 578.

51. A. Bickel, "Foreword: The Passive Virtues, The Supreme Court, 1960 Term" (1961), 75 Harv. L. Rev. 40.

52. R. Sedler, "Constitutional Protection of Individual Rights in Canada: The Impact of the New Canadian Charter of Rights and Freedoms" (1984), Notre Dame Law Rev., forthcoming.

53. W. Tarnopolsky and G. Beaudoin, *The Canadian Charter of Rights and Freedoms: Commentary* (Toronto: Carswell, 1982), is only the most publicized expression of his views.

54. M. Manning, *Rights, Freedoms and the Courts* (Toronto: Emond-Montgomery, 1983).

55. R.A. Samek, "Untrenching Fundamental Rights" (1982), 27 McGill Law J. 755; R.A. Macdonald, "Postcript and Prelude: The Jurisprudence of the Charter: Eight Theses" (1982), 4 Sup. Ct. Law Rev. 321; and more cryptically W. MacKay, "Judicial Process in the Supreme Court of Canada" in, *supra*, note 21.

56. P. Russell, "The Effect of a Charter of Rights on the Policy-making Role of Canadian Courts" (1982), 25 *Can. Pub. Admin.* 1, at 33.

57. *Supra*, note 10.

58. N. Lyon, "The Teleological Mandate of the Fundamental Freedoms Guarantee: What to Do with Vague but Meaningful Generalities" (1982), 4 Sup. Ct. Law Rev. 57.

59. *Supra*, notes 12 and 17 and *Reference Re Residential Tenancies Act, 1979*, [1981] 1 S.C.R. 714.

60. L. Barry, "Law, Policy and Statutory Interpretation Under a Constitutionally Entrenched Canadian Charter of Rights and Freedoms" (1982), 60 Can. Bar Rev. 237. One might question whether judges can ever really reflect the values of the community rather than those of their own social class.

61. *Supra*, note 55. *R. v. Altseimer* (1983), 38 O.R. (2d) 783 (Ont. C.A.), at 788. The case directly states that no major transformation was intended.

62. B. Hovius and R. Martin, "The Canadian Charter of Rights and Freedoms in the Supreme Court of Canada" (1983), 61 Can. Bar Rev. 354, at 374.

63. *Supra*, note 56, at 32.

64. Lederman, *supra*, note 22, at 10.

65. *Law Society of Upper Canada v. Skapinker, supra*, note 15; *A.G. Quebec v. Quebec Protestant School Boards* July 26, 1984 (S.C.C.); and *Hunter v. Southam Inc.*, September 17, 1984 (S.C.C.).

66. The Robert Martin study prepared for the Commission is evidence of the growing interest. *Supra*, note 20.

67. A. Chayes, "Foreword: Public Law Litigation and the Burger Court" (1982), 96 Harv. L. Rev. 1, asserts that the tendency in the United States has been for public law to engulf the private sphere.

68. W. MacKay and M. Holgate, "Fairness in the Allocation of Housing: Legal and Economic Perspectives" (1983), 7 Dal. Law J. (no. 3) 383, at 405. The authors conclude that such an interpretation is unlikely.

69. *Supra*, note 41.

70. Macdonald, *supra*, note 55, at 337.

71. *Supreme and Exchequer Courts Act, 1875*, 38 Vict., c. 11 (Can.).

72. Formerly the *British North America Act, 1867*, 30 & 31 Vict., c. 3 (U.K.).

73. Parliament is also given the power to "create additional courts for the better Administration of the Laws of Canada."

74. By subsection 92(14) each province is given exclusive jurisdiction to legislate in respect of:

> The Administration of Justice in the Province, including the Constitution, Maintenance, and Organization of Provincial Courts, both of Civil and of Criminal Jurisdiction, and including Procedure in Civil Matters in those Courts.

75. On the rule of law and its application in this context, see the able discussion in David Phillip Jones, "A Constitutionally Guaranteed Role for the Courts" (1979), 57 Can. Bar Rev. 669.

76. There were moves afoot to abolish the Court within five years after it was founded. The Parliamentary wrangle is described in F.H. MacKinnon, "The Establishment of the Supreme Court of Canada" (1946), 27 *Can. Hist. Rev.* 258.

77. Forming Schedule B to Part II of the *Canada Act*, 1982 (U.K.), c. 11.

78. See Joseph E. Magnet, *Constitutional Law of Canada: Cases, Notes and Materials* (Toronto: Carswell, 1983), at 39; and Ronald I. Cheffins, "The Constitution Act, 1982 and the Amending Formula: Political and Legal Implications" in *The New Constitution and the Charter of Rights*, edited by Edward P. Belobaba and Eric Gertner (Toronto: Butterworth, 1983), at 53.

79. See P.W. Hogg, *Canada Act 1982 Annotated* (Toronto: Carswell, 1982), at 92–94; and Strayer, *The Canadian Constitution and the Courts, supra,* note 39.

80. See the Schedule to the *Constitution Act, 1982* for an itemized list of the constitutive documents.

81. *Supreme Court Act*, R.S.C. 1970, c. S-19, as am. by R.S.C. 1970, c. 44 (lst Supp.), ss. 109, as am. by S.C. 1974–75–76, c. 19, ss. l–8, 10, as am. by S.C. 1974–75–76, c. 19, s. 2, as am. by S.C. 1976–77, c. 25, ss. 19, 20.

82. Hogg, *supra*, note 79, at 13.

83. Professor Russell appears, however, to question whether this has been achieved. See Peter H. Russell, "Constitutional Reform of the Judicial Branch: Symbolic vs. Operational Considerations" (1984), 17 Can. J. of Pol. Sci. 227, at 232.

84. See *Minutes of Proceedings and Evidence of the Special Joint Committee of the Senate and the House of Commons on the Constitution of Canada*, First Session of Thirty-Second Parliament, November 6, l980 to February 13, l981.

85. *Supra*, note 18.

86. Ibid., at 78.

87. A figure of speech discussed at length in Paul A. Freund, *The Supreme Court of the United States* (Cleveland: World Publishing, 1961), at 95–115.

88. See Kenneth C. Wheare, *Federal Government*, 4th ed. (Oxford: Oxford University Press, 1963), at 58.

89. *Supra*, note 13.

90. See the use of this notion of symbolism as an important political aspect of the Court's role in Russell, *supra*, note 83, at 229.

91. Even in the United States, where one of the fundamentals of the federal government structure is the separation of powers, this doctrine has been undergoing reinterpretation by the Supreme Court: see *Nixon v. Administrator of General Services*, 433 U.S. 425 (1977), and Edward S. Corwin, *The Constitution and What It Means Today*, l4th ed., rev. by Harold W. Chase and Craig R. Ducat (Princeton: Princeton University Press, 1978), at 2–3 and 183.

92. Though something very like this doctrine may have been introduced into Canadian constitutional law through judicial reasoning: see John Willis, "Administrative law and the British North America Act" (1939), 53 Harv. L. Rev. 251.

93. See R. MacGregor Dawson, *The Government of Canada*, 5th ed., rev. by Norman Ward (Toronto: University of Toronto Press, 1970), at 74.

94. Strayer, *The Canadian Constitution and the Courts, supra,* note 39.

95. See, *supra*, note 2.

96. *Supreme Court Act*, s. 6, as am. by S.C. 1974–75–76, c. 19, s. 2. By S.C. 1949, c. 37, the Quebec minimum complement was raised from two to three judges. The requirement of at least two Quebec judges can be traced back to the original *Supreme Court Act, 1875, supra*, note 71, s. 4.

97. They must fulfil minimum requirements regarding periods of activity as lawyers or judges in the provinces from which they are chosen: see *Supreme Court Act*, c. 5.

98. See *supra*, note 83 and accompanying text.

99. R.S.C. 1970, c. J-1.

100. *Supreme Court Act*, s. 9. See also *Constitution Act, 1867*, s. 99. It is arguable whether this latter provision applies to judges of the Supreme Court of Canada because of the phrase in s. 101: "notwithstanding anything in this Act . . ."

101. See W.R. Lederman, *supra*, note 35.

102. Ibid., at 808–809.

103. See *supra*, note 13, s. 11(d).

104. E.g., Lederman, *supra*, note 35, at 175–77.

105. Though section 3 of the *Supreme Court Act* states that the Supreme Court is both "a general court of appeal for Canada" and also "an additional court for the better administration of the laws of Canada."

106. *Supreme Court Act*, s. 55.

107. Ibid., s. 56.

108. Peter H. Russell, "The Jurisdiction of the Supreme Court of Canada: Present Policies and a Programme for Reform (1968), 6 Osgoode Hall L.J. 1, at 10.

109. To illustrate, out of 1,031 total cases disposed of by the Supreme Court between 1950 and 1964, only 12, including 7 references, could be classified under the Court's special jurisdiction. See Peter H. Russell, *The Supreme Court of Canada as a Bilingual and Bicultural Institution*, study prepared for the Royal Commission on Bilingualism and Biculturalism (Ottawa: Queen's Printer, 1969), at 116.

110. S.I. Bushnell, "Leave to Appeal Applications to the Supreme Court of Canada: A Matter of Public Importance" (1982), 3 Sup. Ct. Law Rev. 479, at 497.

111. S.C. 1956, c. 48, s. 2.

112. *Supreme Court Act*, s. 39

113. R.S.C. 1970, c. 44 (lst Supp.), s. 2.

114. *Criminal Code*, R.S.C. 1970, c. 34, ss. 618–623, as am. by S.C. 1974–75–76, c. 105, ss. 18, 19.

115. See, *supra*, note 109, at 40.

116. *Supreme Court Act*, s. 41.

117. Ibid., s. 38.

118. Ibid., s. 41(1).

119. Ibid., s. 38.

120. *Federal Court Act*, S.C. 1970–71–72, c.1.

121. Ibid., s. 31(3), as am. by S.C. 1974–75–76, c. 18, ss. 9, 10.

122. Ibid., s. 32.

123. R.S.C. 1970, c. c-28, s. 63.

124. *Bankruptcy Act*, R.S.C. 1970, c. B-3, ss. 164–167, as am. by c. 44 (lst Supp.), s. 10, item 1.

125. *Companies' Creditors Arrangement Act*, R.S.C. 1970, c. c-25, s. 15(1), as am. by c. 44 (lst Supp.), s. 10, item 2.

126. *National Defence Act*, R.S.C. 1970, c. N-4, s. 208(1), as am. by R.S.C. 1970, c. 44 (lst Supp.), s. 10, item 5.

127. *Excise Tax Act*, R.S.C. 1970, c. E-13, s. 60, as am. by R.S.C. 1970, c. 10 (2d Supp.), s. 65, item 14.

128. *Oil and Gas Production and Conservation Act*, R.S.C. 1970, c. 0–4, s. 41(1).

129. *Canada Pension Plan Act*, R.S.C. 1970, c. C-5, s. 30(2).

130. *Winding-up Act*, R.S.C. 1970, c. W-10, s. 108, as am. by R.S.C. 1970, c. 44 (lst Supp.), s. 10, item 8.

131. *Divorce Act*, R.S.C. 1970, c. D-8, s. 18.

132. *Corrupt Practices Inquiries Act*, R.S.C. 1970, c. C-33, s. 3.

133. See Dickson, "The Role and Function of Judges," *supra*, note 26, at 174.

134. See, for the years prior to the mid-1960s, Russell, *supra*, note 109. Since the early 1960s, the Osgoode Hall Law Journal has annually compiled a brief analysis of the cases contained or referred to in volumes of the Supreme Court Review. The best recent quantitative treatment of leave to appeal applications and civil appeals in general since 1970 is Bushnell, *supra*, note 110. The Office of the Registrar of the Supreme Court has recently published data on the Court's caseload in the preceding calendar year. See *Bulletin of Proceedings Taken in the Supreme Court of Canada*, March 23, 1984, at 328–34.

135. *Supra*, note 108, at 31.

136. A class of subject reserved to the exclusive jurisdiction of provincial legislatures by section 92(13) of the *Constitution Act, 1867*.

137. Albert S. Abel, "The Role of the Supreme Court in Private Law Cases" (1965), 4 Alta. Law Rev. 39, at 44.

138. For example, see Province of Quebec, *Report of the Royal Commission of Inquiry on Constitutional Problems*, 3 vols. (Quebec: Government of Quebec, 1956), 3: 287 (hereafter referred to as the Tremblay Commission Report).

139. See Wolfgang Friedmann, "Stare Decisis at Common Law and Under the Civil Code of Quebec" (1953), 31 Can. Bar Rev. 723; Joseph Dainow, "The Civil Law and the Common Law: Some Points of Comparison" (1967), 15 Am. J. Comp. L. 419; and J.H. Merryman, *The Civil Law Tradition* (Stanford: Stanford University Press, 1969).

140. See V. Morin, "L'Anglicisation de notre droit civil" (1937), 40 Rev. du Notariat 145; Pierre Azard, "La Cour suprême du Canada et l'application du droit civil de la Province de Québec" (1965), 43 Can. Bar Rev. 553; J.-L. Baudoin, "The Impact of the Common Law on the Civilian Systems of Louisiana and Quebec" in *The Role of Judicial Decisions and Doctrine in Civil Law and in Mixed Jurisdictions*, edited by Joseph Dainow (Baton Rouge: Louisiana State University Press, 1974), 1; J.-L. Baudoin, "L'interprétation du code civil québécois par la Cour Suprême du Canada" (1975), 53 Can. Bar Rev. 715; Gérald A. Beaudoin, "Du maintien des appels à la Cour Suprême du Canada en matière de droit civil" (1976), 14 Alta. Law Rev. 144; P. Patenaude, "Le Québec et la Cour Suprême" (1976), 14 Alta. Law Rev. 138; and Robert Décary, "La Cour Suprême et la dualité canadienne" (1979), 57 Can. Bar Rev. 702.

141. See Bushnell, *supra*, note 110, at 511; Russell, *supra*, note 108, at 21; P.W. Hogg, "Jurisdiction of the Court — The Supreme Court of Canada" (1980), 3 Canada–U.S. L.J. 39 at 47; and Bertha Wilson, "Leave to Appeal to the Supreme Court of Canada" (1983), 4 Advocates' Q. 1, at 8.

142. See N.E. Simmonds, "The Changing Face of Private Law: Doctrinal Categories and the Regulatory States" (1982), 2 Leg. Stud. 257, at 259–61.

143. Robert G. Richards, "Motions for Leave to Appeal to the Supreme Court of Canada" (1980), 3 Advocates' Q. 460.

144. For example, see the judgments in *Nicholson v. Haldimand-Norfolk Regional Board of Police Commissioners*, [1979] 1 S.C.R. 311; *Martineau v. Matsqui Institution Disciplinary Board*, [1980] 1 S.C.R. 602; and *Harelkin v. The University of Regina*, [1979] 2 S.C.R. 561.

145. Archibald Cox, *The Role of the Supreme Court in American Government* (New York: Oxford University Press, 1976). See also J.W. Hurst, "Functions of Courts in the United States, 1950–1980" (1980–81), 15 L. and Soc. Rev. 401.

146. Abram Chayes, "The Role of the Judge in Public Law Litigation" (1976), 89 Harv. L. Rev. 1281.

147. For example, see Edward McWhinney, "The Canadian Charter of Rights and Freedoms: The Lessons of Comparative Jurisprudence" (1983) 61 Can. Bar Rev. 55, at 65. But see, for a contrary view, Sedler, *supra*, note 52.

148. See John Willis, "Securing Uniformity of Law in a Federal System — Canada" (1944), 5 U. of T. Law J. 352.

149. Ibid., at 354.

150. See, for example, *Doare v. Thomas*, [1922] 3 W.W.R. 117.

151. *Report of the Special Committee on the Caseload of the Supreme Court of Canada* (Ottawa: Canadian Bar Association, 1972), at 15.

152. See Uniform Law Conference of Canada, *Proceedings of the Sixty-Fourth Annual Meeting* (August 1982), Table III, for a cumulative list of uniform acts that have been enacted by some or all of the provinces in Canada.

153. *Supra*, note 6.

154. Ibid., at 172–79.

155. *Supra*, note 3.

156. This is the figure cited by Justice (now Chief Justice) Dickson as the approximate annual average number of cases the Court decides: see Dickson, "The Role and Function of Judges," *supra*, note 26, at 173.

157. See Robert Stevens, *Law and Politics: The House of Lords as a Judicial Body, 1800–1976* (Chapel Hill: University of North Carolina Press, 1978), at 6–15 for a basic review of the historical development of the House of Lords' jurisdiction.

158. See ibid., at 269. For examples of how Scottish law has been "tainted" by the appellate decisions of the House of Lords, see T.B. Smith, *British Justice: The Scottish Contribution* (London: Stevens and Sons, 1961), at 84–89; and David M. Walker, *The Scottish Legal System*, 4th ed. rev. (Edinburgh: W. Green and Son, 1976), at 140–42.

159. *Attorney General of Ontario v. Attorney General of Canada*, [1947] A.C. 127.

160. Peter W. Hogg, "Federalism and the Jurisdiction of Canadian Courts" (1981), 30 U.N.B. L.J. 9.

161. See, *supra*, note 137, at 42.

162. James C. MacPherson, "The Potential Implications of Constitutional Reform for the Supreme Court of Canada" in *Canada and the New Constitution: The Unfinished Agenda*, edited by Stanley M. Beck and Ivan Bernier, 2 vols. (Montreal: Institute for Research on Public Policy, 1983), 1: 165 at 187. Because of the importance of settling whether certain provincial courts can validly apply one set of laws as against another, such conflicts issues have even been classified as "constitutional" and amenable to determinations by the Supreme Court of Canada: see John Swan, "Perspectives of the Conflicts Lawyer" (1982–83), 7 Can. Bus. L.J. 410 at 413–17 (a contribution to a symposium on The Future of the Supreme Court of Canada as the Final Appellate Tribunal in Private Law Litigation).

163. Dickson, "The Role and Function of Judges," *supra*, note 26, at 157.

164. A lucid rebuttal of the traditional Quebec concerns was composed by Professor (now Mr. Justice) LeDain: see Gerald L. LeDain, "Concerning the Proposed Constitutional and Civil Law Specialization at the Supreme Court Level" (1967), 2 Rev. Jur. Thémis 107.

165. David J. Wheat, "Disposition of Civil Law Appeals by the Supreme Court of Canada" (1980), 1 Sup. Ct. Law Rev. 425.

166. Ibid., at 454.

167. W.R. Lederman, "Thoughts on Reform of the Supreme Court of Canada" (1970), 8 Alta. L. Rev. 1, at 10. But see Peter H. Russell, "Constitutional Reform of the Canadian Judiciary" (1969), 7 Alta. L. Rev. 103, at 128: ". . . the appropriate place for the cultivation of this particular legal virtue is in the law-schools of the country, not the Supreme Court."

168. Information obtained from an entry in Kieran Simpson, ed., *Canadian Who's Who 1984*, Vol. 19 (Toronto: University of Toronto Press, 1984), at 687–88.

169. See *Canadian Aero Service Limited v. O'Malley*, [1974] S.C.R. 592; and *Multiple Access Limited v. McCutcheon*, [1982] 2 S.C.R. 181.

170. For example, see *Murdoch v. Murdoch*, [1975] 1 S.C.R. 423; *Rathwell v. Rathwell*, [1978] 2 S.C.R. 436; and *Pettkus v. Becker*, [1980] 2 S.C.R. 834.

171. Ian R. Macneil, "A View from the South" (1982–83), 7 Can. Bus. L.J. 426, at 434.

172. Donovan Waters, "Perspectives of a Property and Trust Lawyer" (1982–83), 7 Can. Bus. L.J. 389, at 400. (This and the immediately preceding article were contributions to the symposium on The Future of the Supreme Court of Canada as the Final Appellate Tribunal in Private Law Litigation).

173. Lederman, *supra*, note 167, at 16.

174. For the two most noteworthy discussions of this step of constitutional analysis, see W.R. Lederman, "Classification of Laws and the British North America Act" in *Continuing Canadian Constitutional Dilemmas* (Toronto: Butterworth, 1981), at 229; and B. Laskin, "Tests for the Validity of Legislation: What's the Matter" (1955), 1 U. of T. Law J. 114.

175. Owing to the strictures established in leading cases on the interpretation of subsection 91(2) of the *Constitution Act, 1867* such as: *Citizens Insurance Co. of Canada v. Parsons*, [1881] 7 App. Cas; and *In Re The Board of Commerce Act, 1919*, [1922] A.C. 191.

176. LeDain, *supra*, note 164, at 112. See also Maurice Tancelin, "Point de Vue Civiliste Québécois" (1982–83), 7 Can. Bus. L.J. 420, at 425–26 (a contribution to the symposium on The Future of the Supreme Court of Canada as the Final Appellate Tribunal in Private Law Litigation).

177. See, for example, the decisions in *Labatt Breweries of Canada v. Attorney General for Canada*, [1980] 1 S.C.R. 914 and *Dominion Stores Limited v. The Queen*, [1980] 1 S.C.R. 844 and the criticisms that these engendered in James C. MacPherson, "Economic Regulation and the British North America Act: Labatt Breweries and Other Constitutional Imbroglios" (1981), 5 Can Bus. L.J. 172. For an overview of how recent Supreme Court judgments have attempted to rationalize the application of the federal trade and commerce power, see Patrick J. Monahan, "The Supreme Court and the Economy" in *The Supreme Court of Canada as an Instrument of Political Change*, vol. 47 of the research studies prepared for the Royal Commission on the Economic Union and Development Prospects for Canada (Toronto: University of Toronto Press, 1985).

178. John Bell, *Policy Arguments in Judicial Decisions* (Oxford: Oxford University Press, 1983), at 43.

179. See, for example, the principles on conspiracy to injure the trade of a competitor set forth in *Canada Cement LaFarge Ltd. v. British Columbia Lightweight Aggregate Ltd.* (1983), 47 N.R. 191 (S.C.C.)

180. On the *Combines Investigation Act*, R.S.C. 1970, c. C-2, see the leading recent cases of *Aetna Insurance Company v. The Queen*, [1978] 1 S.C.R. 731; *Atlantic Sugar Refineries of Canada Co. Ltd. v. Attorney General of Canada*, [1980] 2 S.C.R. 644; and *R. v. K.C. Irving Ltd.*, [1978] 1 S.C.R. 408.

181. *Supra*, note 8, at 474–75.

182. *Supra*, note 25, at 12–13.

183. Russell, *supra*, note 167 at 117.

184. For example, in 1983 only one appeal, which had already been heard by the Supreme Court, was quashed on a motion of the respondent.

185. Wilson, *supra*, note 141, at 8.

186. Jacques-Yvan Morin, "A Constitutional Court for Canada" (1965), 43 Can. Bar Rev. 545.

187. See *supra*, note 109, at 59 *et seq.* for an account of the changes to the composition of the Court during its history.

188. *Supreme Court Act*, s. 6.

189. See *supra*, note 186, at 549.

190. See Lederman, *supra*, note 167, at 11; and W.R. Lederman, "Current Proposals for

Reform of the Supreme Court of Canada'' (1979), 57 Can. Bar Rev. 687, at 695.

191. Government of British Columbia, *British Columbia's Constitutional Proposals*, Paper No. 4: Reform of the Supreme Court of Canada (Victoria: Province of British Columbia, 1978), at 14–15.

192. The Task Force on Canadian Unity, *A Future Together* (Ottawa: Minister of Supply and Services Canada, 1979), at 101.

193. Bill C-60 , *The Constitutional Amendment Bill*, introduced in the House of Commons in June 1978, section 102.

194. See the unofficial transcript of proceedings at the Federal-Provincial Conference of First Ministers on the Constitution, September 1980, compiled by the Canadian Intergovernmental Conference Secretariat, at 229–76.

195. Government of Alberta, *Harmony in Diversity: A New Federalism for Canada* (Edmonton: Government of Alberta, 1978), at 11.

196. *Supra*, note 109, at 63.

197. Justice Spence retired on December 29, 1978 and Justice McIntyre was appointed on January 1, 1979.

198. Justice LeDain was appointed in May 1984.

199. Lederman, *supra*, note 167, at 11.

200. See Documents for the Federal-Provincial Conference of First Ministers on the Constitution, September 1980, compiled by the Canadian Intergovernmental Conference Secretariat, document 800–14/059.

201. MacPherson, *supra*, note 162, at 209.

202. Canadian Constitutional Charter, the product of the Constitutional Conference in Victoria, June 1971, Article 23.

203. *The Final Report to Parliament of the Special Joint Committee of the Senate and the House of Commons on the Constitution of Canada*, Fourth Session of the Twenty-eighth Parliament, 1972 (Ottawa: Queen's Printer, 1972), at 39.

204. Committee on the Constitution, *Towards a New Canada*, Research Study prepared for the Canadian Bar Foundation (Montreal: Canadian Bar Foundation, 1978), at 60–61.

205. The Constitutional Committee of the Quebec Liberal Party, *A New Canadian Federation* (Montreal: Quebec Liberal Party, 1980), at 59.

206. See *supra*, note 109, at 63.

207. The only reference to the Court being "hard-pressed" is in Lederman, "Current Proposals for Reform of the Supreme Court of Canada," *supra*, note 190, at 695.

208. *Supra*, note 205, at 59.

209. See *supra*, note 109, at 65; and *supra*, note 110, at 555–57.

210. *Supra*, note 204, at 60.

211. Of all the proposals for change, only Bill C-60 included a specific reference to the possibility of appointing a judge whose closest connection is with one of the territories rather than with any province: see *supra*, note 193, at s. 103.

212. *Supra*, note 11, at 4.

213. Ibid., at 5.

214. R.S.C. 1970, Appendix III. For an illuminating analysis of the record of the Court in interpreting this federal legislation, see Dale Gibson, "And One Step Backward: The Supreme Court and Constitutional Law in the Sixties" (1975) 53 Can. Bar Rev. 621; and W.S. Tarnopolsky, "A New Bill of Rights in the Light of the Interpretation of the Present One by the Supreme Court of Canada", [1978] L.S.U.C. Lect. 161.

215. This is just as much a topic in administrative law as in constitutional law. For an example of how the dispute is typically raised and resolved, see *Reference Re Residential Tenancies Act, 1979*, [1981] 1 S.C.R. 714.

216. Pursuant to the *Supreme Court Act*, s. 4.

217. See E. Ratushny, "Judicial Appointments: The Lang Legacy" in *The Canadian Judiciary*, edited by Allen M. Linden (Toronto: Osgoode Hall Law School, 1976), at

31. For example, the name of a possible appointee might be submitted to the Canadian Bar Association's National Committee on the Judiciary. Various other sources might be consulted by the minister of justice. The appointment of justices to the Supreme Court of Canada and to the federal judiciary has been the federal cabinet's prerogative and even these channels may not be used in every case.

218. P.W. Hogg, "Is the Supreme Court of Canada Biased in Constitutional Cases?" (1979), 57 Can. Bar Rev. 721.

219. *Supra*, note 138, at 290.

220. *Supra*, note 202, Articles 26–32.

221. *Supra*, note 203, at 39.

222. Lederman, "Current Proposals for Reform of the Supreme Court of Canada," *supra*, note 190, at 699.

223. Bill C-60, *supra*, note 202, s. 107.

224. The House of the Federation would have consisted of 118 members, selected according to a regional formula. Half of the total number of members from the provinces would have been selected by the House of Commons, and the other half by the provincial legislatures: see ibid., ss. 62–63.

225. *Supra*, note 191, at 12–14.

226. *Supra*, note 204, at 60.

227. *Supra*, note 192, at 101.

228. *Supra*, note 205, at 59.

229. MacPherson, *supra*, note 162, at 209.

230. See Mark MacGuigan, *Reform of the Senate: A Discussion Paper* (Ottawa: Government of Canada, 1983).

231. *Supra*, note 195, at 11.

232. *Supra*, note 204, at 60.

233. For an overview of the chronology of events and of the accords reached, see Keith Banting and Richard Simeon, "Federalism, Democracy and the Constitution" in *And No One Cheered*, edited by Keith Banting and Richard Simeon (Toronto: Methuen, 1983), at 2; and Edward McWhinney, *Canada and the Constitution, 1979–1982* (Toronto: University of Toronto Press, 1982).

234. See the statements in Ratushny, *supra*, note 217, at 40–41 about the progress made in promoting the merit principle during the early 1970s.

235. See the *National*, July-August 1984, at 3.

236. *Supra*, note 25, at 7.

237. See L.C. Berkson, "Judicial Selection in the United States: A Special Report" (1980), 64 Judicature 176.

238. John R. Schmidhauser, *Judges and Justices: The Federal Appellate Judiciary* (Boston: Little, Brown, 1979).

239. Richard A. Watson and R.G. Downing, *The Politics of the Bench and Bar: Judicial Selection Under the Missouri Nonpartisan Court Plan* (New York: Wiley, 1969).

240. See Appendix A under the heading of "Selection."

241. See Appendix B.

242. David Pannick, "Election of the Judiciary" (1979), 129 New L.J. 1064.

243. See A.M. Gleeson, "Judging the Judges" (1979), 53 Aust. L.J. 338; Tony Black, "Judicial Appointments: Time for a Change" [1978], N.Z.L.J. 41; and F.M. Neasey, "Comment Upon Proposals for an Australian Judicial System" (1983), 57 Aust. L.J. 335.

244. This minimal female presence is recommended for many of the reasons set forth in Christine Boyle, "Home Rule for Women: Power-Sharing Between Men and Women" (1983), 7 Dal. Law J. 790.

245. For a description of what significant diverse elements compose the Canadian social mosaic, we must turn to social scientists.

246. Such service would illustrate a kind of "representative" democratic activity, as explained in William Mishler, *Political Participation in Canada* (Toronto: Macmillan, 1979), at 155.

247. See Grover Rees III, "Questions for Supreme Court Nominees at Confirmation Hearings: Excluding the Constitution" (1983), 17 Ga. L. Rev. 913.

248. See *supra*, note 11; and *supra*, note 25.

249. For example, see *Maclean's,* April 30, 1984, at 20, and *The Globe and Mail,* May 30, 1984 at 1-2.

250. For the recommendations themselves see the *Final Report of the Commission of Inquiry into the Non-Medical Use of Drugs* (Ottawa: Information Canada, 1973), at 127-40.

251. *Supra,* note 20.

252. *Supra,* note 25.

253. M. Handler, "What to Do With the Supreme Court's Burgeoning Calendars" (1984), 5 Cardozo Law Rev. 249.

254. Canadian Bar Association, *Special Report on the Supreme Court's Caseload,* Report of the Special Committee of the C.B.A. (1970). Such problems were also addressed by Russell, *supra,* note 1.

255. *Supra,* note 25, at 9-10.

256. The law clerks in the Supreme Court of Canada still write their memoranda to the justices or type them themselves, because they are not given access to secretarial service. A computer, even as a research tool, was introduced to the Court only in 1978 and only after some controversy.

257. W. Burger, "Annual Report on the State of the Judiciary" (1983), 69 A.B.A.J. 442.

258. J.P. Stevens, "Some Thoughts on Judicial Restraint" (1982), 66 Judicature 177.

259. W.J. Brennan Jr., "Some Thoughts on the Supreme Court's Workload" (1982), 66 Judicature 230.

260. This is the classification used in a recent article which provides a good overview of the American approaches to a growing agenda: Note, "Of High Designs: A Compendium of Proposals to Reduce the Workload of the Supreme Court" (1983), 97 Harv. L. Rev. 307.

261. This is part of Mr. Justice Brennan's criticism of a National Court of Appeal in the United States, *supra,* note 259. There are also high advocates of such a court: P. Freund, "A National Court of Appeals" (1974), 25 Hast. L.J. 1301.

262. W.H. McCree Jr., "Bureaucratic Justice: An Early Warning" (1981), 129 U. of Pa. Law Rev. 777. He emphasizes that too much delegation can result in the judges' losing control of the process.

263. *Supra,* note 25.

264. Obvious areas of concern are the precise role of the Chief Justice and the process of judgment writing. Both these matters appear to be more formalized in the United States than in Canada. The limits of both space and expertise preclude detailed comments on these issues.

265. Wayne MacKay served as law clerk to the late Chief Justice Bora Laskin for the 1978-79 terms. He is also author of an internal Court memorandum on improving the institution of clerking at the Supreme Court of Canada.

266. There is little written about clerking in Canada but that which has been written confirms that clerks play an important role without usurping the position of the judge: M.J. Herman, "Law Clerking at the Supreme Court of Canada" (1975), 13 Osgoode Hall L.J. 279; and B. Morgan, "A View of Clerking at the Supreme Court of Canada" *Hearsay,* Vol. 3, No. 2 (Autumn, 1978), at 6.

267. B. Woodward and S. Armstrong, *The Brethren* (New York: Simon and Schuster, 1979).

268. P. Bender, "Book Review of *The Brethren*" (1980), 128 U. of Pa. Law Rev. 716; Symposium, "The Brethren: Yea or Nay" (1980), 15 U. of Pa. L. Alumni J. 17; and Fletcher, "Book Review of *The Brethren*" (1980), 68 Calif. Law Rev. 168, are but a few of the many critical book reviews.

269. J.H. Wilkinson, *Serving Justice: A Supreme Court Clerk's View* (New York: Charterhouse, 1974).

270. J.B. Oakley and R.S. Thompson, *Law Clerks and the Judicial Process* (Berkeley: University of California Press, 1980). This book clearly prefers the "traditional" clerk over the "career" one.

271. The space devoted to law clerks in this paper can best be justified as an aspect of educating the public about the Court and its infrastructure.

272. J. Vining, "Justice, Bureaucracy and Legal Method" (1981–82), 80 Mich. Law Rev. 248. This paper was originally delivered at the University of Windsor in Ontario and also appears in the Windsor Y.B. Access to Just., volume 2 (1982).

273. H.T. Edwards, "A Judge's View on Justice, Bureaucracy and Legal Method" (1981–82), 80 Mich. Law Rev. 259.

274. Note, "The Law Clerk's Duty of Confidentiality" (1981), 129 U. of Pa. Law Rev. 1230.

275. *Supra*, note 267.

276. *Supra*, note 108; and B.A. Crane, "Civil Appeals to the Supreme Court of Canada" (1977), 15 Osgoode Hall L.J. 389.

277. Wilson, *supra*, note 141; and W.Z. Estey, "The Role and Operation of the Supreme Court of Canada," an address to the Ontario Advocates' Society, June 23, 1978 are but two examples.

278. Herman, *supra*, note 265, observes that law clerks are least useful with respect to leave applications.

279. *Supra*, note 258.

280. *Supra*, note 259.

281. *Supra*, note 260, at 312–13.

282. *Supra*, note 25, at 12.

283. It can be convincingly argued that cases were never resolved on this narrow a basis but the courts simply refused to acknowledge their broader considerations.

284. *Supra*, note 59.

285. P.W. Hogg, "Proof of Facts in Constitutional Cases" (1976), 26 U. of T. Law J. 386; and Strayer, *The Canadian Constitution and the Courts*, *supra*, note 39, at 239–58.

286. (1953) 2 S.C.R. 299.

287. *Reference re Eskimos*, [1939] S.C.R. 104.

288. W. MacKay, "Courts, Cameras and Fair Trials: Confrontation or Collaboration," a paper delivered to the Canadian Association of Provincial Court Judges during its annual meeting held in St. John's, Newfoundland, September 26, 1984. The debate about cameras in the courtrooms is an excellent example of the mistrust on both sides.

289. *Supra*, note 25, at 5.

290. Ibid., at 18–19.

Selected Bibliography on Judicial Bureaucracy and its Reform

Abramson, J.B. "Should a Law Clerk Ever Reveal Confidential Information?" (1980), 63 Judicature 361.

Acheson, Dean. "Recollection of Service With the Federal Supreme Court" (1957), 18 Ala. L. Rev. 355.

Aldisert, R.J. "Duties of Law Clerks" (1973), 26 Vand. L. Rev. 1251.

American Bar Association. ABA Commission on Standards of Judicial Administration. *Standards Relating to Appellate Courts* (Chicago: American Bar Association, 1977).

Baier, Paul R. "The Law Clerks: Profile of an Institution" (1973) 26 Vand. L. Rev. 1125.

Bender, Paul. "Book Review of *The Brethren*" (1980), 128 U. of Pa. Law Rev. 716.

Bickel, Alexander M. *The Caseload of the Supreme Court — And What, if Anything, We Can Do About It* (Washington, D.C.: American Institute for Public Policy Research, 1973).

Braden, G.D. "The Value of Law Clerks" (1953), 24 Miss. L. J. 295.

Brennan, William J. "Some Thoughts on the Supreme Court's Workload" (1983), 55 N.Y. St. B.J. 14.

Brudney, V., and Wolfson, R. "Mr. Justice Rutledge — Law Clerks' Reflections" (1949), 25 Ind. L.J. 455.

Burger, Warren. "Annual Report on the State of the Judiciary" (1983), 69 A.B.A. B.J. 442.

Cannon, Mark W. "Administrative Change and the Supreme Court" (1974), 57 Judicature 334.

Carrington, Paul D.; Meador, Daniel J.; and Rosenberg, Maurice. *Justice on Appeal* (St. Paul West, 1976).

Casper, Gerhard, and Posner, Richard A. *The Workload of the Supreme Court* (Chicago: American Bar Foundation, 1976).

Clark, Tom C. "Internal Operation of the United States Supreme Court" (1959), 43 J. Am. Jud. Soc. 45.

Coleman, William J., Jr. "The Supreme Court of the United States: Managing Its Caseload to Achieve Its Constitutional Purpose" (1983), 52 Fordham L. Rev. 1.

Crane, Brian. "Law Clerks for Canadian Judges" (1966), 15 Can. B.J. 373.

Darsen, N. "Law Clerks in the Appellate Courts of the United States" (1963), 26 Mod. L. Rev. 265.

Edwards, H.T. "A Judge's View on Justice, Bureaucracy, and Legal Method" (1981), 80 Mich. L. Rev. 259.

Edwards, H.T. "The Rising Work Load and Perceived 'Bureaucracy' of the Federal Courts: A Causation-Based Approach to the Search for Appropriate Remedies" (1983), 68 Iowa L. Rev. 871.

Frank, J.P. "The Supreme Court: The Muckrakers Return" (1980), 66 A.B.A. J. 161.

Fite, Arthur; Potts, Robert L.; and Sweeney, Donald B., Jr. "Law Clerkships: Three Inside Views" (1972), 33 Ala L. 156.

Garcia, "The Role and Experiences of Supreme Court Law Clerks: An Annotated Bibliography" (1977), 70 L. Lib. J. 338.

Gazell, J.A. "Justice Potter Stewart's Philosophy of Federal Judicial Administration" (1982), 32 Case W.L. Rev. 419.

Gressman, E. "Irreverent Questions About Piercing the Red Velour Curtain" (1973), 22 Buff. L. Rev. 825.

Griswold, Erwin N. "Helping the Supreme Court by Reducing the Flow of Cases Into the Courts of Appeals" (1983), 67 Judicature 58.

Hamley, F. "Sample Instructions to Law Clerks" (1973), 26 Vand. L. Rev. 1241.

Handler, Milton. "What To Do With the Supreme Court's Burgeoning Calendars?" (1984), 5 Cardozo L. Rev. 249.

Haworth, Charles R. "Screening and Summary Procedures in the Ninth Circuit Court of Appeals", [1973] Wash. U.L.Q. 257.

Hellman, Arthur D. "The Business of the Supreme Court Under the Judiciary Act of 1925: The Plenary Docket in the 1970's" (1978), 91 Harv. L. Rev. 1709.

Herman, Michael John. "Law Clerking at the Supreme Court of Canada" (1975), 13 Osgoode Hall L.J. 279.

Higginbotham, P.E. "Bureaucracy — The Carcinoma of the Federal Judiciary" (1980), 31 Ala. L. Rev. 261.

Hopkins, James D. "The Winds of Change: New Styles in the Appellate Process" (1975), 3 Hofstra L. Rev. 649.

Johnson, N. "What Do Law Clerks Do?" (1959), 22 Texas B.J. 229.

Jones, Jeffrey J. "Justice Stevens' Proposal to Establish a Sub-Supreme Court" (1983), 20 Harv. J. Legis. 201.

Kaufman, Irving R. "The Pre-Argument Conference: An Appellate Procedural Reform" (1974), 74 Colum. L. Rev. 1094.

Kurland, Philip. "Jerome N. Frank: Some Reflections and Recollections of a Law Clerk" (1957), 24 U. Chi. L. Rev. 661.

Leflar, Robert A. *Internal Operating Procedures of Appellate Courts* (Chicago: American Bar Foundation, 1976).

Lesinski, T.J., and Stockmeyer, N.O. "Prehearing Research and Screening in the Michigan Court of Appeals: One Court's Method for Increasing Judicial Productivity" (1973), 26 Vand. L. Rev. 1211.

Little, Joseph. "The Workload of the United States Supreme Court: Ruling the Pen with the Tongue" (1981), 6 J. Leg. Prof. 51.

McCormack, Alfred. "A Law Clerk's Recollections" (1946), 46 Colum. L. Rev. 710.

McCree, W.H. "Bureaucratic Justice: An Early Warning" (1981), 129 U. of Pa. Law Rev. 777.

Mayne, Wylie E. "No Relief in Sight for a Beleaguered Supreme Court" (1984), 9 Litigation News 3(2).

Meador, Daniel J. *Appellate Courts: Staff and Process in the Crisis of Volume* (St. Paul West, 1974).

Meador, D. "Justice Black and His Law Clerks" (1962), 15 Ala. L. Rev. 57.

Meador, Daniel J. "Professional Assistance for Appellate Judges: A Central Staff of Lawyers" (1974), 63 Fed. Rules Decisions 489.

Millar, Perry S., and Baar, Carl. *Judicial Administration in Canada* (Montreal: McGill-Queen's University Press, 1981).

Miller, A.S., and Sastri, D.S. "Secrecy and the Supreme Court: On the Need for Piercing the Red Velour Curtain" (1973), 22 Buff. L. Rev. 799.

Newland, C.A. "Personal Assistants to Supreme Court Justices: The Law Clerks" (1961), 40 Ore. L. Rev. 299.

Note, "Of High Designs: A Compendium of Proposals to Reduce the Workload of the Supreme Court" (1983), 97 Harv. L. Rev. 307.

Oakley, John B., and Thompson, Robert S. "Law Clerks in Judges' Eyes: Tradition and Innovation in the Use of Legal Staff by American Judges" (1979), 67 Calif. L. Rev. 1286.

Oakley, John B., and Thompson, Robert S. *Law Clerks and the Judicial Process* (Berkeley: University of California Press, 1980).

O'Connell, Kenneth J. "Streamlining Appellate Procedures" (1973), 56 Judicature 23.

Posner, Richard A. "Will the Federal Courts Survive Until 1984? An Essay on Delegation and Specialization of the Judicial Function" (1983), 56 S. Calif. L. Rev. 761.

Resnik, Judith. "Managerial Judges" (1982), 96 Harv. L. Rev. 374.

Shetreet, S. "Remedies for Court Congestion and Delay: The Models and the Recent Trend" (1979), 17 U.W.O.L. Rev. 35.

Smith, George R. "A Primer of Opinion Writing for Law Clerks" (1973), 26 Vand. L. Rev. 1203.

Stockmeyer, N.O. Jr. "Rx for the Certiorari Crisis: A More Professional Staff" (1973), 59 A.B.A.J. 846.

Symposium. "The Brethren: Yea or Nay" (1980), 15 U. Pa. L. Alumni J.

Vining, J. "Justice, Bureaucracy, and Legal Method" (1981), 80 Mich. L. Rev. 248.

Watson, Garry D. "The Judge and Court Administration." In *The Canadian Judiciary*, edited by Allen M. Linden, pp. 163–91 (Toronto: Osgoode Hall Law School, 1976).

Wilkinson, J. Harvie. *Serving Justice: A Supreme Court Clerk's View* (New York: Charterhouse, 1974).

Wilkinson, J. Harvie. Book review of *Law Clerks and the Judicial Process* (1982), 32 J. of L. Ed. 304.

Wilson, Bertha. "Leave to Appeal to the Supreme Court of Canada" (1983), 4 Advocate's Q. 1.

Woodward, B., and Armstrong, S. *The Brethren* (New York: Simon and Schuster, 1979).

Wright, Judge E. "Observations of an Appellate Judge: Use of the Law Clerks" (1973), 26 Vand. L. Rev. 1179.

Wright, Judge E. "Selection, Training and Use of Law Clerks in the United States Courts of Appeal" (1974), 63 Fed. Rules Decisions 464.

3

The Equality Provisions of the Canadian Charter of Rights and Freedoms and Government Institutions

MARY EBERTS

Introduction

This paper considers the impact of the equality sections of the *Canadian Charter of Rights and Freedoms* on government institutions. I focus primarily on the impact of section 15 of the Charter, although I have necessarily considered sections 6, 16 to 22 inclusive, 27, and 28.

The subject matter of this analysis could be extremely broad. When one considers what entities might be included in the term "government institutions," the list is at first awesome: the Governor General, prime minister and cabinet, Parliament, the courts, and a whole host of other bodies. Among this last group, for example, are the military and national police, as well as a large number of bodies charged with policy development or implementation or with providing some crucial service. Examples of this type of body are the Bank of Canada, the Royal Canadian Mint, and the National Library.

There is also a wide variety of councils established for purposes of research, advice, and allocating funding: some examples include the Social Sciences and Humanities Research Council, Canada Council, Science Council of Canada, National Research Council, and the Economic Council of Canada.

There are many regulatory agencies exercising delegated power from Parliament in sectors of the economy. Some, like the Anti-Dumping tribunal, are constituted courts of record; others, like the Canadian Radio-television and Telecommunications Commission, are not.

It is not possible within the confines of this study to analyze in detail the precise implications of the Charter's equality guarantees for each of these institutions. Indeed, the federal government itself is engaged in an extensive and intensive review of how the Charter affects all federal legislation, a review involving many officials and considerable time. Much of that analysis will of course have a bearing on these institutions of government, for one assumes that all bodies constituted by statute or statutory instrument will come to be scrutinized.

Although not having the resources to duplicate the federal statute audit, I wish to avoid being so general as to be redundant. How well I have succeeded in avoiding the two extremes remains to be judged.

This paper is divided into three parts. First, I consider the meaning of the term "government institution." Although for reasons outlined below, I argue that the technical implications of this question should not be of overwhelming interest to bodies assessing their own obligations under the Charter, the question will doubtlessly figure largely in litigation under the Charter. Accordingly, the issue of the meaning of "government institution" is considered in some detail.

The second part considers the interpretation of the equality guarantees of the Charter. The paper includes a survey of how the equality provisions may affect government institutions. In this survey, only a few instances of possible impact of the equality provisions will be identified. I have attempted to address representative questions in enough detail to make the discussion meaningful. The paper concludes with a set of appendices, describing the statutory underpinning for the various entities discussed in the paper.

Before embarking upon the specific analyses of government institutions and the equality provisions, it is useful to set the whole subject in perspective.

The Charter enshrines rights that the citizen may assert against the state. We think of court actions as the way in which citizens seek to put forward their rights, but court actions represent only a small sector of the whole sphere within which the Charter is meant to operate. The Charter is intended to be in large measure a self-enforcing document: the state must abide by the commands of the Charter in its activities, whether or not there is a specific citizen with a specific case to call it to account.

That the Charter is applied by legislatures and governments as well as by courts has very important implications. One can expect, if not desire, that courts will become involved in fairly precise questions of legislative interpretation when considering the application and meaning of the Charter. Although one might hope that a large and remedial interpretation of the Charter will be taken by the courts, these close questions will also arise. Yet there is little reason for governments not to take a large and remedial approach in their assessment of whether the Charter binds them, or one of their emanations, and in assessing the meaning of their obligations under it. Such an approach would resolve any question of whether an entity could be called "governmental" in favour of applying the Charter; it would resolve any dispute about the meaning of the section in favour of implementing the Charter right instead of withholding it.

To understand the importance of the government's attitude toward its constitutional obligations, let us consider the meaning of the "equality" guarantees in the Charter. Section 15, under the heading "Equality Rights," is a clear expression of public policy in favour of equality of treatment, both in the substance and administration of the law. Section 28 affirms the fundamental equality of men and women: if their access to our society's fundamental democratic and legal rights is equal, then it seems difficult to argue that they should not have equal access to other, less constitutionally significant, aspects of citizenship. Section 27 acknowledges and protects the multicultural background of Canadians, and sections 16 to 23 give strong constitutional underpinning to our official languages.

The voice with which the Charter speaks is clear. It is significant that not only the traditional minority interests of race, religion, and ethnic origin are protected, but also that those interests more belatedly recognized as deserving of protection have also attained constitutional recognition. This is surely a sign of the temper of the Canadian public, for there has been an acceleration over the past 40 years in the speed and sensitivity with which Canadians respond to minority interests, and a willingness to offer strong, constitutional guarantees instead of mere legislative protections that are subject to short-term changes in the political environment.

All of these factors should guide governments in applying the equality guarantees. With reference to section 15, it is probably safe to conclude that there is a lack of experience in determining the goal of equality and what measures are most likely to further it. There may well be conflicts in interpreting equality guarantees around such fundamental questions as: does equality mean sameness of treatment, or can special circumstances be recognized? Does the Charter reach only legislative inequalities, or can it be used to force governments to correct factual inequalities in our society? As I outline in this paper, however, I think that section 15 is flexible enough to accommodate not only the individual-oriented equality goals of fair procedure and equal opportunity, but also the more group-oriented goals of furthering equality of condition and equitable distribution of resources.

Governments and government institutions will have a major role to play in determining how the interpretation of section 15 develops. Such a role will come not only because governments retain and instruct the counsel who appear in court on constitutional cases. More importantly, the role arises because governments will have to face the basic equality issues in framing legislation and setting policy. In doing so, they can either behave in accordance with the spirit of the Charter, or they can parse its terms narrowly, so that the governmental obligation in any particular circumstance is circumscribed as tightly as possible.

In my view, the desirable course for governments and government institutions to follow is clear: they, far more readily than the courts and in a greater range of circumstances, can take a large and liberal interpretation of the equality guarantees. They can refuse to shelter in technicalities when considering the scope of the Charter. They can decide in favour of a wide and wise use of the Charter when resolving the questions, many of them complicated, which are outlined below.

What are Government Institutions?

A threshold question in assessing the impact of the equality guarantees on "government institutions" is of course the question of what a government institution is. Although the Charter applies to both federal and provincial governments, I have considered the question of government institutions only in the federal context. The theoretical approach developed here should, however, be equally applicable in the provincial context. I have not explored in detail the question of whether "courts" are subject to the Charter, my assumption for purposes of this paper being that they are.

There is no definition of "institutions of government" used in the Charter. In fact, that particular phrase is used very sparingly, appearing only in sections 16 and 20, which deal with the Official Languages guarantees.

Section 16 provides, inter alia, that English and French have equality of status and equal rights and privileges as to their use in "all institutions of the Parliament and Government of Canada." Subsection 20(1) provides that any member of the public in Canada has the right to communicate with and receive available services from "any head or central office of an institution of the Parliament or Government of Canada" in English or French, as well as, in defined circumstances, "any other office of any such institution." This language does not enlarge our understanding of the concept of "government institutions" all that much.

The principal section of the Charter which deals with its application is section 32. It provides:

32. (1) This Charter applies
   (a) to the Parliament and government of Canada in respect of all matters within the authority of Parliament including all matters relating to the Yukon Territory and Northwest Territories; and
   (b) to the legislature and government of each province in respect of all matters within the authority of the legislature of each province.

The two key words in that section are "Parliament" and "government." Perhaps the least difficult of these terms to define is "Parliament."

Section 17 of the *Constitution Act, 1867* provides that "There shall be one Parliament for Canada, consisting of the Queen, an Upper House styled the Senate, and the House of Commons."

The legislative activities of Parliament are possibly the best known aspect of that institution's identity, and it is clear that the Charter is made applicable to those functions.

Parliament also delegates its legislative power to subordinate legislative bodies, like boards, commissions, or agencies. The cabinet, or a minister of cabinet, will sometimes be the recipient of such delegated power. It is not seriously questioned that the activities of a delegate of Parliament will also be covered by the Charter, by reason of section 32. Such was the holding of the Ontario High Court in *Re McCutcheon and City of Toronto* (1983), 147 D.L.R. (3d) 193. Mr. Justice Linden in that case held that municipal by-laws are subject to the Charter. At p. D.L.R. 203, he reasons that the tenor of subsection 32(1) is to provide "that subordinates (the Governments of Canada and of each province) cannot do that which their principals (Parliament and the legislatures) cannot do. It must be that more junior subordinates, like municipalities, are to be similarly bound by the Charter."

Another important feature of Parliament which must be borne in mind when considering the reach of the Charter is that Parliament is an institution and employer; some of its enactments deal with its own constitution and administration.

For example, the *House of Commons Act*, R.S.C. 1970, c. H-9, and the *Senate and House of Commons Act*, R.S.C. 1970, c. S-8, deal, inter alia, with the eligibility of persons to become Members or Senators, and constraints on their activities once they have so become. The *Public Service Employment Act*, as amended, provides in section 38 that the Governor in Council appoint the Clerk of the Senate and the Clerk of the House of Commons. The *Formal Documents Regulations* list the following "Officers of Parliament": Speaker of the Senate, Clerk of the Senate, Clerk of the House of Commons, Sergeant-at-Arms, Parliamentary Librarian, Associate Parliamentary Librarian, and Gentleman Usher of the Black Rod. Section 2 of the *Financial Administration Act* defines "department" of government as including the staffs of the Senate, the House of Commons, and the Library of Parliament.

The *Library of Parliament Act*, R.S.C. 1970, c. L-7, provides for the administration of the Library, appointment of its officers and staff, and supervision by a joint committee of both Houses.

Quite plainly, Parliament must observe the equality guarantees of the Charter when legislating with respect to its own constitution and administration, and when overseeing that administration through its officers.

The second key word in section 32 is "government." It must be conceded that determining the reach of this term is likely to be one of the most complex exercises in Charter interpretation. In my view, there is probably no one "right" way to approach this analysis. However, it does seem there are certain signs that point the way to some of the boundaries of the term, and these are outlined below.

First of all, one might usefully consider the meaning given to the word "government" in enactments of a constitutional status equivalent to the Charter. Conceivably, this review could encompass all the enactments included in Schedule I to the *Constitution Act, 1982*, as well as the *Constitution Act, 1982* itself. The scope of this paper does not permit such a detailed review to be embarked upon here. Even in the *Constitution Act, 1982*, there are many instances where "government" is used.

Part III of the Act, entitled *Equalization and Regional Disparities*, contains in subsection 36(1) a recital that "Parliament and the legislatures, *together with the government of Canada and the provincial governments*" (emphasis mine), are committed to certain specified principles to reduce regional disparities.

Part IV of the Act provides for the calling of a constitutional conference composed of the Prime Minister of Canada and the first ministers of the provinces within one year of the coming into force of the part to deal with constitutional matters that directly affect the aboriginal peoples of Canada. Subsection 37(3) provides that the Prime Minister of Canada shall invite "elected representatives of the *governments* of the Yukon Territory and the Northwest Territories" (emphasis mine) to participate in discussions of items that directly affect them.

Part V, dealing with the procedure for amending the Constitution of Canada, provides in subsection 38(2) that a constitutional amendment that derogates from "the legislative powers, the proprietary rights, or any other rights or privileges of the legislature or *government* of a province" (emphasis mine) shall require a resolution supported by a majority of the members of each of the Senate, the House of Commons, and the legislative assemblies of at least two-thirds of the provinces that have, in aggregate, according to the latest general census, at least 50 percent of the population of all the provinces.

All these sections seem to use "government" in a broad sense, with the term denoting the civic authority or general governing body in all its aspects, rather than a more specialized part of the whole.

There is one section of the *Constitution Act, 1982* where "government" appears to be used in a much narrower sense. Section 44 provides that, with some restrictions, Parliament may exclusively make laws amending the Constitution of Canada in relation to *the executive government* of Canada or the Senate and House of Commons (emphasis mine).

How, then, can one reconcile the various terms used in the Charter and the *Constitution Act, 1982* and come to some clearer understanding of the scope of the Charter? The terms at issue are "Parliament and government of Canada" (s. 32); "institution of the Parliament or government of Canada" (s. 20); "Parliament . . . together with the government of Canada," "Parliament and government of Canada," and "provincial governments" (s. 36); "elected representatives of the governments of the

Yukon Territory and the Northwest Territories" (s. 37); and "executive government" (s. 44).

There are two decisions of the Supreme Court of Canada which may be of assistance.

In *A.G. of Quebec v. Blaikie (No. 2)* (1981), 123 D.L.R. (3d) 15, the Supreme Court of Canada was dealing with further questions raised by its earlier holding that section 133 of the *Constitution Act, 1867* applies to delegated legislation: [1979] 2 S.C.R. 1016. Section 133 reads:

> 133. Either the English or the French Language may be used by any Person in the Debates of the Houses of the Parliament of Canada and of the Houses of the Legislature of Quebec; and both those Languages shall be used in the respective Records and Journals of those Houses; and either of those Languages may be used by any Person or in any Pleading or Process in or issuing from any Court of Canada established under this Act, and in or from all or any of the Courts of Quebec.
>
> The Acts of the Parliament of Canada and of the Legislature of Quebec shall be printed and published in both those Languages.

In *Blaikie (No. 2)*, the Court deals first, at p. D.L.R. 22, with the concession by the Quebec and Manitoba governments before it that section 133 of the Act applies to "enactments of a legislative nature issued by the Government of the Province, including enactments issued by a group of Ministers being members of the Government, such as the Conseil du Trésor . . . or by a Minister. Stating this to be a proper concession, the Supreme Court observes at p. 22:

> The Government of the Province is not a body of the Legislature's own creation. It has a constitutional status and is not subordinate to the Legislature in the same sense as other provincial legislative agencies established by the Legislature. Indeed, it is the Government which, through its majority, does in practice control the operations of the elected branch of the Legislature on a day-to-day basis, allocates time, gives priority to its own measures and in most cases decides whether or not the legislative power is to be delegated and, if so, whether it is to hold it itself or have it entrusted to some other body.

This description may apply simply to the majority party in the House, or it may be confined more narrowly to the "executive government" described by W. P. M. Kennedy: "The executive government of the dominion is carried on by a cabinet of ministers selected from the political party in power. . . . As soon as a cabinet has taken the oaths of office they act with the governor-general as the executive government of Canada."[1]

The Court in *Blaikie (No. 2)* also finds a way of including the regulation-making activities of certain boards and agencies within the term "government." The following rationale is offered by the Court at p. D.L.R. 28:

> It is because in our constitutional system the enactments of the Government should be assimilated to the enactments of the Legislature that they are

governed by s. 133. Other regulations must, in our opinion, be viewed in the same light when they can also properly be said to be the enactments of the Government.

This happens whenever these other regulations are made subject to the approval of the Government.

The form of words used to subject the regulations to Government approval was regarded as irrelevant. The Court states, at p. D.L.R. 29, that "they can be assimilated to the enactments of the Government and therefore of the Legislature as long as positive action of the Government is required to breathe life into them." Given that the receivers of legislative power derived from Parliament will in any event be fixed with the duty to observe the Charter because Parliament is included in section 32, this type of analysis is perhaps not as significant or necessary in the context of the Charter as it was found to be with reference to section 133 of the *Constitution Act, 1867*.

A useful exposition of the coverage of the mantle of government is found in the decision of the Supreme Court of Canada in *Berardinelli v. Ontario Housing Corporation et al.* (1978), 8 C.P.C. 101. Subsection 6(2) of the *Housing Development Act*, R.S.O. 1970, c. 213, as amended, gave the Ontario Housing Corporation the power to carry out any building development or housing project, including the power to plan, construct, and manage any building development or housing project. The OHC, established by statute as a corporation without share capital, claimed the protection of the *Public Authorities Protection Act*, R.S.O. 1970, c. 374, s. 11 when sued for damages arising from injuries said to be caused by its alleged failure to clear snow and ice from the sidewalk of a building under its direction. Section 11 protects against suits for an act done in pursuance of or execution or intended execution of any statutory or other public duty or authority. . . ."

Mr. Justice Estey states for the majority, at p. 107, that the reference in section 11 to any "statutory or other public duty" applies

> to those aspects of the statutory powers and duties there established which have a public aspect or connotation, and does not comprehend those planning, construction and managerial responsibilities . . . which have a private executive or private administrative application or are subordinate in nature.

The powers of the Corporation are thus divided into two categories:

> [T]he one being those actions which entail a public aspect or are inherently of a public nature and the other being a category of activities, including managerial, which are more of an *internal or operational nature having a predominantly private aspect*. (emphasis in original)

The Court clearly recognizes that drawing these types of distinction will not be easy.

The reasoning in *Berardinelli* suggests that some aspects of an entity's behaviour might be subject to the Charter, while others are not. This approach seems to be more flexible than trying to make a once-and-for-all determination whether an entity is either "in" or "out," although there may well be entities in respect of which the once-and-for-all determination can be made.

The Federal Court of Canada has also offered some useful comments on the reach of section 32.

The Federal Court of Appeal decided in *Operation Dismantle Inc. et al. v. Government of Canada et al.* (1983), 49 N.R. 363 that the Charter could apply to the prerogative power of the Governor in Council. There were two main bases for so holding. First, because Parliament could legislate with respect to the exercise of the prerogative, even if it might not have done so in a particular instance, the prerogative is a matter "within the authority of Parliament" under section 32. Second, the language of section 52 of the Charter, according to Mr. Justice LeDain at p. 375, indicates that "not only statutory provisions and any law made in the exercise of statutory authority, but the common law rules of governmental authority are rendered inoperative to the extent of inconsistency with the Charter."

Some guidance on the outer limits of the Charter's application is also to be found in this case. Mr. Justice Hugesson states at p. 400:

> In my view, s. 32 makes it plain that the rights which the Charter enshrines are protected against direct interference by domestic governments in Canada. Breaches of Charter rights by private citizens acting without official sanction or by foreign powers operating outside the sphere of our domestic law are simply not justifiable under the Charter, although they may, of course, give rise to other remedies."

In *Blaikie (No. 2)*, the Supreme Court included in the reach of section 133 "regulations or orders which constituted delegated legislation properly so-called" and excluded "rules or directives of internal management."

In addition to looking at the constitutional documents and judicial interpretation of the concept "government," it is interesting to observe what Parliament itself has considered "government" for various purposes. Particularly, legislation dealing with the public service of Canada and Crown corporations offers insights into what Parliament considers to be part of "government."

Public Service

The *Financial Administration Act*, R.S.C. 1970, c. F-10, as amended, describes the composition of the Treasury Board and gives the Treasury Board responsibility for general administrative policy in the public service of Canada. In section 7 of the *Financial Administration Act*, "public service" is said to have the meaning assigned to that term in the *Public Service Staff Relations Act*; in essence, this definition encompasses those entities listed in Schedule I to the *Public Service Staff Relations Act*. The *Financial Administration Act* also imports into its organization of personnel the concept of a separate employer, as used in the *Public Service Staff Relations Act*: all those employers listed in Schedule II to the Act. The schedules to all these Acts are attached, and from reviewing them one can derive a good idea of the range of entities that come within the rubric of government for these purposes.

The selection and appointment of persons to fill positions in the public service is done by the Public Service Commission under the *Public Service Employment Act*: R.S.C. 1970, c. P-32, as amended by S.C. 1974–75–76, c. 16, s. 1; S.C. 1974–75–76, c. 66, s. 10; S.C. 1980–81–82–83, c. 143, s. 26. "Public Service" is defined in the *Public Service Employment Act* as having the same meaning as it does in the *Public Service Staff Relations Act*. Furthermore, members of the Royal Canadian Mounted Police and Canadian Forces are deemed in section 2 of the Act to be members of the "Public Service" for purposes of being eligible to compete for positions.

Section 9 of the *Public Service Employment Act* provides that nothing in the Act shall be construed to limit the authority of Her Majesty to appoint ambassadors, ministers, high commissioners or consuls-general of Canada. By section 37, the Act permits a minister, "the person holding the recognized position of Leader of the Opposition in the House of Commons, Leader of the Government in the Senate or Leader of the Opposition in the Senate" to appoint an executive assistant and other persons required in his or her office. By reason of section 38, the Governor in Council may appoint and fix the remuneration of the Clerk of the Privy Council and Secretary to the Cabinet, the Secretary to the Cabinet for Federal-Provincial Relations, the Clerk of the Senate, Clerk of the House of Commons, and the Secretary to the Governor General.

Labour relations in the public service are to a large extent dealt with by the Public Service Staff Relations Board under the *Public Service Staff Relations Act*, the schedules to which have been referred to earlier. These schedules are appended. Similarly, the useful schedules under the *Public Service Superannuation Act*, R.S.C. 1970, c. P-36, as amended, are also appended.

A more general approach to the question of who is a government servant is taken in the *Government Employees Compensation Act*, R.S.C. 1970, c. G-8, as amended by S.C. 1980–81–82–83, c. 47, s. 21. Section 2 of that Act provides that "employee" means, inter alia,

(a) any person in the service of Her Majesty who is paid a direct wage or salary by or on behalf of Her Majesty;
(b) any member, officer or employee of any *department, company, corporation, commission, board or agency established to perform a function or duty on behalf of the Government of Canada* who is declared by the Minister with the approval of the Governor in Council to be an employee

for the purposes of this Act . . . (emphasis mine);

(e) any officer or employee of The Senate, the House of Commons or the Library of Parliament.

Crown Corporations

The descriptions of the various types of Crown corporation are set out in the *Financial Administration Act*, as amended.

Subsection 95(1) of the Act defines "Crown corporation" as a parent Crown corporation or a wholly owned subsidiary. A parent Crown corporation is defined as a corporation that is wholly owned directly by the Crown. Subsection 95(2) of the Act provides that a corporation is wholly owned directly by the Crown if all the issued and outstanding shares of the corporation are held on behalf of or in trust for the Crown, or all the directors of the corporation are appointed by the Governor in Council or by a Minister of the Crown with the approval of the Governor in Council. It is contemplated by subsection 95(2) that shares in a corporation may be held by what the Act describes in subsection 95(1) as an "agent corporation": a Crown corporation that is expressly declared by or pursuant to an Act of Parliament to be an agent of the Crown. Where the shares of another company are held by such a Crown agent corporation, subsection 95(3) of the *Financial Administration Act* provides that these shares are deemed not to be held by or on behalf of the Crown and are not by reason of that fact alone shares held in trust for the Crown. Excluded from the category of parent Crown corporations are "departmental corporations"; these corporations, listed in Schedule B to the Act, are characterized by section 2 of the *Financial Administration Act* as government departments.

A wholly owned subsidiary is defined in subsection 95(1) of the *Financial Administration Act* as a corporation that is wholly owned by one or more parent Crown corporations directly or indirectly through any number of subsidiaries each of which is wholly owned directly or indirectly by one or more parent Crown corporations.

Schedule B to the Act includes the names of departmental corporations. According to subsection 2.1(1), added by S.C. 1984, s. 3, the Governor in Council may add to Schedule B the name of any corporation established by an Act of Parliament that performs administrative, research, supervisory, advisory or regulatory functions of a governmental nature. Schedule C to the Act contains the names of parent Crown corporations. In order to be listed in Part II of Schedule C, a parent Crown corporation must operate in a competitive environment and ordinarily be independent of appropriations for operating purposes: s.-s. 2.1(6), added by S.C. 1984,c. 31, s. 3.

All Crown corporations of whatever type are ultimately accountable through a minister to Parliament for the conduct of their affairs.

There are a number of other general enactments dealing with government corporations or enterprises.

In the *Government Companies Operation Act*, R.S.C. 1980, c. G-7, as amended by S.C. 1974-75-76, c. 33, s. 265 (Item 4), S.C. 1978-79, c. 9, s. 1 "265," and S.C. 1980-81-82-83, c. 47, s. 20, "company" is defined as a company incorporated under Part I of the *Canada Corporations Act*, or a corporation incorporated under the *Canada Business Corporations Act*, all the issued shares of which are owned by or held in trust for Her Majesty in Right of Canada, except, in the case of a company incorporated under Part I of the *Canada Corporations Act*, shares necessary to qualify other persons as directors. Section 6 of the Act provides that the Act applies to a company only from the date of the issue of a proclamation by the Governor General to that effect.

Section 4 of the Act allows each company to employ such officers and servants as it deems necessary to conduct its operations and to determine their conditions of employment and their remuneration. However, a person employed by such a government company who had formerly been with the public service, under section 5, "continues to retain and is eligible for all the benefits, except salary as an employee . . . that he would have been eligible to receive had he remained an employee in the public service, and he is eligible upon retirement from the company for reappointment to the public service."

The *Government Property Traffic Act*, R.S.C. 1970, c. G-10, applies, according to s. 2(1), to "any lands belonging to or occupied by Her Majesty in Right of Canada," permitting traffic regulations for that land to be made.

Similar broad definitions of what is a "government" entity or operation are found in other statutes. The *Canada Shipping Act*, R.S.C. 1970, c. S-9, defines "government ship" in section 1 as "a ship or vessel that is owned by and is in the service of Her Majesty in Right of Canada or of any province thereof or is, while so employed, wholly employed in the service of Her Majesty in such right." The *Government Vessels Discipline Act*, R.S.C. 1970, c. G-12, provides in section 3 that "Every vessel employed by the Government of Canada, either temporarily or permanently, shall be deemed to belong, while so employed, to the Government of Canada for purposes of this Act." The Act, as its title suggests, deals with the maintenance of order on government ships. The *Government Railways Act*, R.S.C. 1970, c. G-11, states in subsection 4(1) that it applies "to all railways that are vested in Her Majesty, and that are under the control and management of the Minister," and the definition of "works" for purposes of the *Government Works Tolls Act*, R.S.C. 1970, c. G-13 "includes the slides, booms, dams, bulk-heads and other works and improvements for facilitating the transmission of timber and lumber down any river or stream that is under the control of the Government of Canada."

One can derive a sort of mosaic-like impression of what the government considers to be government by reviewing a number of legislative enactments. However, moving from a host of particular provisions to the theoretical level is not an easy transition in this area.

Katherine Swinton takes the view that the courts should develop a "governmental function"[2] test to decide which activities and which subordinate agencies and private actors should be subject to the Charter. The courts should focus on whether there is governmental activity, rather than on its form, in deciding whether the Charter applies. The concern with activity rather than form leads her to suggest that government limitations on individual freedoms should be caught by the Charter even when those limitations are in, for example, contract or in what administrative lawyers have called "administrative action."

Unfortunately this "governmental function" test brings with it exactly the same kinds of definition problems as those involved in understanding what "government" means in section 32. Professor Swinton suggests this concept will have to be applied on a case-by-case basis, with the courts emphasizing "the question of whether the action or institution in question carries out a function of the state against which the individual has a need for protection."[3] It is suggested that the concept of Crown agency, and the developments in international law with respect to sovereign immunity, can be of assistance in assessing what functions attract the Charter.

Professor Swinton also suggests that the "state action" doctrine in the United States could be of some assistance in determining what a public function is, although she cautions that the doctrine should be applied on a case-by-case basis and may not be entirely appropriate to Canada.

Two recent decisions of the United States Supreme Court on the subject of state action may be referred to in this connection. In *Rendall-Baker v. Kohn*, 102 S. Ct. 2764 (1982), it was argued that a personnel decision at a privately owned and operated school for hard-to-educate youngsters was "state action" because the school was funded and regulated by the state and engaged in a "public function." In *Blum v. Yaretsky*, 102 S. Ct. 2777 (1982), it was argued that patient transfer decisions in a privately owned and operated nursing home were "state action."

The Court in *Rendall-Baker* quoted its own decision in *Blum* at p. 2786 that a

. . . State can normally be held responsible for a private decision only when it has exercised coercive power or has provided such significant encouragement, either overt or covert, that the choice must in law be deemed to be that of the State.

The Court identified the main issue as whether the alleged infringement of federal rights is "fairly attributable" to the state.

In neither of these cases did the "state action" argument prevail. Receipt of public funds was held to be insufficient to make the decisions acts of the state. On the question of receipt of funding, Chief Justice Burger for the Court drew an analogy with a private contractor doing most or all of his or her work on public contracts, stating at p. 2771, "Acts of such private contractors do not become acts of the government by reason of their significant or even total engagement in performing public contract." Nor does state regulation, even if extensive and detailed, make an entity's actions state actions.

Chief Justice Burger states at p. 2772, with regard to the "public function" argument that

> [O]ur holdings have made it clear that the relevant question is not simply whether a private group is serving a "public function." We have held that the question is whether the function performed has been "traditionally the *exclusive* prerogative of the State."

This recent interpretation of the "state action" doctrine is a restrictive one, and the Court's formulation of the public function test may not be all that useful in the context of determining whether something is "government" within the meaning of section 32, or a "governmental function."

In my view, however, all these various inquiries outlined above do give at least some guidance on how one might use a sort of functional analysis to approach the definition of "government."

An essential starting point is to examine the formal connection between the entity in question and the Parliament or executive or departmental "government." Although the presence or absence of, for example, a power to make regulations or enter contracts subject to regulatory standards may not be dispositive on the question of whether an entity or a particular function is "governmental," such information is an essential first step. Obviously, the more signs of a formal connection between the entity and what we are sure is Parliament or government, the more likely it is that the Charter applies.

Where the ties are attenuated, then some further questions may prove useful. Does, for example, the body in question further government policy or represent Canada officially abroad, even if nominally "private"? Think, in this context, of national sports governing bodies that provide Canada's "official" entries at international competitions, and are heavily funded by government, although "private." More generally, one might borrow the statutory language referred to earlier and ask whether the body had been established "to perform a function or study on behalf of the government of Canada," interpreting that question somewhat more flexibly than the approach to public function taken by the United States Supreme Court (which seems to require that the state has once carried out the function itself). One might also ask whether the body would be claiming, or eligible to claim, Crown privilege. It seems elementary that any body, commercial or otherwise, which aspires to the privileges of "state" status should be subject to the limitations imported by the Charter. Asking this question imports the *Berardinelli* test of whether, on the one hand, the functions entail a public aspect or are inherently of a public nature, or whether, on the other, they are of an internal or operational nature, having a predominantly private aspect.

I agree with Professor Swinton that the Charter would apply to acts that administrative lawyers classify as "administrative" only. Because of the procedural flexibility imparted by sections 52 and 24 of the *Constitution Act, 1982*, our thinking on the application of the Charter does not have to be constrained by the old forms of seeking judicial review of administrative action, or by technical questions posed by judicial interpretation of the *Federal Court Act*. However, where a power would be amenable to judicial review in classical administrative law, it would be hard to argue that it is not also subject to the Charter guarantees.

The possibility that the Charter may be indirectly applied to a particular entity should also be borne in mind. One might wonder, for example, whether Air Canada should per se be subject to the Charter because it is a Crown corporation under Schedule C, Part II to the *Financial Administration Act*, an air carrier like many other air carriers. However, regardless of the status of the corporation, certain of its activities, done pursuant to directives, or with the sanction of decisions, of the Canadian Transport Commission may be reached by the Charter because the Commission is subject to the Charter. The same "flow-through" effect may occur in the telecommunications field (CRTC/CBC) or the human rights field (CHRC/CNR). The Commissions cannot require or sanction activities that would not comport with the Charter because of the Charter's impact on the Commissions themselves, and not necessarily because of any direct impact of the Charter on entities in the regulated industry.

Above all, however, a critical question of perspective should be considered. It is very likely that the types of extremely detailed examination described above may well have to be undertaken in the context of a particular issue being litigated in court, as was the case in *Berardinelli*, for example. Yet as pointed out initially, the courts are not the only arena where questions of the meaning and application of the Charter will be dealt with. Governments and their emanations must apply the Charter to themselves, and so many of the decisions about whether the Charter applies or not will initially be those of the department, agency, or official. In making those decisions, particularly in the context of equality guarantees, it is useful to remember that the guarantees are an expression of public will as well as a code of behaviour. In a close case, such a recollection should incline the agency to follow the commands of the Charter rather than reject them on a technicality about what is "government."

The Equality Guarantees
of the Charter of Rights

The Basic Provisions

The main equality guarantee in the Charter is that in section 15, which provides:

> 15. (1) Every individual is equal before and under the law and has the right to the equal protection and equal benefit of the law without discrimination based on race, national or ethnic origin, colour, religion, sex, age or mental or physical disability.
>
> (2) Subsection (1) does not preclude any law, program or activity that has as its object the amelioration of conditions of disadvantaged individuals or groups including those that are disadvantaged because of race, national or ethnic origin, colour, religion, sex, age or mental or physical disability.

Section 27 of the Charter provides that:

> This Charter shall be interpreted in a manner consistent with the preservation and enhancement of the multicultural heritage of Canadians.

Section 28 states:

> Notwithstanding anything in this Charter, the rights and freedoms referred to in it are guaranteed equally to male and female persons.

The official language guarantees of the Charter found in sections 16 to 22 are also relevant to the present inquiry. Of these, sections 16 to 20 inclusive are particularly relevant to government institutions:

> 16. (1) English and French are the official languages of Canada and have equality of status and equal rights and privileges as to their use in all institutions of the Parliament and government of Canada.
>
> (2) English and French are the official languages of New Brunswick and have equality of status and equal rights and privileges as to their use in all institutions of the legislature and government of New Brunswick.
>
> (3) Nothing in this Charter limits the authority of Parliament or a legislature to advance the equality of status or use of English and French.
>
> 17. (1) Everyone has the right to use English and French in any debates and other proceedings of Parliament.
>
> (2) Everyone has the right to use English or French in any debates and other proceedings of the legislature of New Brunswick.
>
> 18. (1) The statutes, records and journals of Parliament shall be printed and published in English and French and both language versions are equally authoritative.
>
> (2) The statutes, records and journals of the legislature of New Brunswick shall be printed and published in English and French and both language versions are equally authoritative.
>
> 19. (1) Either English or French may be used by any person in, or in any pleading in or process issuing from, any court established by Parliament.

(2) Either English or French may be used by any person in, or in any pleading in or process issuing from, any court of New Brunswick.

20. (1) Any member of the public in Canada has the right to communicate with, and to receive available services from, any head or central office of an institution of the Parliament or government of Canada in English or French, and has the same right with respect to any other office of any such institution where
   (a) there is a significant demand for communications with and services from that office in such language; or
   (b) due to the nature of the office, it is reasonable that communications with and services from that office be available in both English and French.

   (2) Any member of the public in New Brunswick has the right to communicate with, and to receive available services from, any office of an institution of the legislature or government of New Brunswick in English or French.

Section 6 of the Charter, dealing with mobility rights, provides in subsections (2) and (3):

(2) Every citizen of Canada and every person who has the status of a permanent resident of Canada has the right
(a) to move to and take up residence in any province; and
(b) to pursue the gaining of a livelihood in any province.
(3) The rights specified in subsection (2) are subject to
(a) any laws or practices of general application in force in a province other than those that discriminate among persons primarily on the basis of province of present or previous residence;

Section 1 of the Charter provides that:

The *Canadian Charter of Rights and Freedoms* guarantees the rights and freedoms set out in it subject only to such reasonable limits prescribed by law as can be demonstrably justified in a free and democratic society.

There are two main avenues of recourse for Charter violations. The first is suggested by section 52 of the *Constitution Act, 1982*, which provides that ". . . any law that is inconsistent with the provisions of the constitution is, to the extent of the inconsistency, of no force or effect." The issue of consistency with the Charter can be raised, directly or collaterally, in a wide variety of proceedings. Section 24 of the Charter provides an additional method of raising a Charter issue:

(1) Anyone whose rights or freedoms, as guaranteed by this Charter, have been infringed or denied may apply to a court of competent jurisdiction to obtain such remedy as the court considers appropriate and just in the circumstances.

Interpretation

MOBILITY RIGHTS

In *Demaere v. The Queen in Right of Canada Represented by the Treasury Board* (F.C.A. No. A-878-83, February 20, 1984), it was held by the Federal Court of Appeal that subsection 6(2) of the Charter would apply to the federal *Public Service Employment Act*. Mr. Justice Hugesson states at p. 4 of his reasons that the mischief sought to be remedied by section 6 was "not simply interprovincial barriers to the movement of labour but all such barriers within the country, wherever they might be established and by whichever level of government."

The court held that it was a prima facie violation of Demaere's section 6 right to exclude him from a competition for a post in the Pacific Region of the Canadian Air Traffic Administration on the ground that he was at the time of his application stationed in the Western Region of the Administration.

However, the Court also ruled that the exclusion was justified under paragraph 6(3)(a) because of paragraph 13(a) of the *Public Service Employment Act* giving the Public Service Commission the right to "determine the area in which applicants must reside in order to be eligible for employment."

Significantly, the Court ruled that this provision of a federal statute was a law of general application in force in a province within the meaning of paragraph 6(3)(a), and could therefore be relied on to justify the exclusion of Demaere.

The case establishes that the constitutional right to mobility is applicable to the federal sphere, and also permits federal legislation to be used to justify apparent infringements of the right. It thus has considerable significance for federal institutions.

However, the level of analysis of the substantive issue in *Demaere* does leave some questions. Mr. Justice Hugesson held that paragraph 13(a) of the *Public Service Employment Act* did not "discriminate among persons primarily on the basis of province of present or previous residence" (and thus could justify Demaere's exclusion) because

> The applicant was not excluded from the competition because he resides in British Columbia, which is the province of residence of all eligible candidates employed in the Pacific region, but because he resides and is employed in a part of the province which is not in the Pacific region.

The holding is thus to the effect that the federal employer can discriminate on the basis of regions within a province, but not on the basis of provinces. Presumably, the Court's reasoning would mean that a person resident in another province would have a right to bid on the Pacific Region job but a person resident in the "wrong" part of British Columbia would not.

Such a result does, of course, discriminate against Demaere because of his province of residence.

In part, the problem in this case may stem from a wrong focus. The government action complained of was the Commission's decision to draw the boundaries for the competition in a particular way. This action, as the Court found, did infringe Demaere's constitutional rights.

This decision was not subjected to scrutiny in light of section 1 of the Charter. No explanation was given for the choice to exclude section 1. It might be suggested that section 6 is one of the "self-limiting" provisions mentioned by Mr. Justice Ewaschuk in *R. v. Moore* (1983), 10 C.C.C. (2d) 306 (Ont. H.C.J.), where resort to section 1 is unnecessary. However, this does not seem to be the approach taken by the Supreme Court of Canada in *Law Society of Upper Canada v. Skapinker* (1984), 9 D.L.R. (4th) 161. The Court decided that the provision at issue in *Skapinker* did not infringe subsection 6(2), so that its observations about justifying infringements are, strictly speaking, obiter dicta. However, it will be noted that Mr. Justice Estey for the Court contemplates at p. 181 of his reasons that, had an infringement been made out, he might have had to consider "whether the Act is none the less saved by s. 6(3) or s. 1 of the Charter."

If the Court of Appeal had applied the standards of section 1 to the Commission's decision about the competition's boundaries, the Commission would presumably have had to explain why the boundaries were drawn as they were. They could have relied on paragraph 13(a) of the *Public Service Employment Act* for part of that justification, but would still have had to contend with the reality that Parliament could not, by passing paragraph 13(a), give the Commission a totally free hand to draw even arbitrary distinctions, because under the Charter Parliament itself could presumably not draw those sorts of distinctions.

Of course, the decision of the Federal Court finds some support in the holding of the Supreme Court in *Skapinker*. There, Mr. Justice Estey rejects Skapinker's argument that subsection 6(2) confers a separate and distinct right to work (within a province) divorced from the mobility provisions. The rights in subsection 6(2) are held to relate to movement into another province, either for taking up of residence, or to work without establishing residence.

Skapinker deals with provincial legislation having only intraprovincial application. In a national setting, it may well be that intraprovincial mobility may have to be considered guaranteed. Otherwise, as pointed out above, persons in one area of a province denied the right to bid on a job in another area of the same province would be treated differently from persons in other provinces of Canada.

In fact, it may well transpire that the *Demaere* decision has raised more issues than it settled. These will be considered further below.

LANGUAGE RIGHTS

This study does not propose to give a detailed consideration of the official languages guarantees of the Charter. However, one or two points should be noted here.

In *Le Procureur Général du Québec v. Quebec Association of Protestant School Boards et al.* (July 26, 1984), the Supreme Court of Canada held that section 1 of the Charter would be considered in assessing whether provincial legislation was in conflict with the language education rights of section 23 of the Charter. The Court did not exhaustively consider the question of what limits would be authorized by section 1. It did, however, observe, at pp. 22–23 of its reasons:

> Whatever their scope, the limits which s. 1 of the *Charter* allows to be placed on the rights and freedoms set out in it cannot be equated with exceptions such as those authorized by s. 33(1) and (2) of the *Charter*, which in any case do not authorize any exception to s. 23. . . . Neither can such limits be tantamount to amendments to the Constitution of Canada, the procedure for which is prescribed in ss. 38 *et seq.* of the *Constitution Act*, 1982.

Sections 16 to 22 of the Charter are, like section 23, excluded from the operation of the "over-ride" provisions of section 33; these observations of the Court can thus be readily applied to the effect of section 1 on legislation purporting to cut back on the guarantees under sections 16 to 22. Even legislation designed to implement bilingualism in the federal government service would, it seems, be subject to these cautions, so that significant deviations from the constitutional guarantees (which might be considered amendments) are to be avoided.

The constitutional guarantees of official languages have some interesting implications for government. Members of the public who are denied service to which they are entitled under section 20 of the Charter could well bring action under section 24 for damages for violation of those rights, even though there now exists a procedure under the *Official Languages Act* for dealing with complaints that the status of an official language is not being recognized, or the spirit and intent of the Act is not being complied with. That procedure involves a complaint to the Commissioner of Official Languages, and investigation by him or her. The Commissioner is to report his or her findings of a violation of the Act to the Clerk of the Privy Council and to the administrative head of the department or institution concerned. However, the Commissioner may make only recommendations, not binding orders, and the only recourse where the recommendation is not followed is for the Commissioner to report to the cabinet or then to Parliament. The individual who laid the complaint can take no enforcement action independently of the Commissioner.

Given the nature of the remedy under the *Official Languages Act*, it is doubtful in my view that its existence could convince a court to refuse a remedy under section 24 of the Charter. In *Board of Governors of the*

Seneca College of Applied Arts and Technology v. Bhadauria, [1981] 2
S.C.R. 181, the Supreme Court of Canada did hold that a plaintiff could
not bring a civil action for damages for the tort of discrimination where
there was a statutory scheme in existence to deal with discrimination complaints, namely the Ontario Human Rights Code. However, Chief Justice
Laskin found significant that apart from the Code itself, there was no
underpinning for the right or interest alleged by the plaintiff. By contrast,
someone who complains about non-compliance with the official language
provisions of the Charter relies on his or her constitutional rights, not
just the *Official Languages Act*, and so Chief Justice Laskin's concern
on this point is met. Moreover, the Court emphasized in *Bhadauria* that
the scheme of the Human Rights Code was comprehensive, allowing a
wide right of appeal to the courts on both fact and law, and a wide range
of remedial measures, including the availability of damages and full curial
enforcement of Board awards. The scheme under the *Official Languages
Act* is by no means as comprehensive as the one before the Court in
Bhadauria. Hence, it is not likely that it will be held to displace the Charter
remedy for violation of the Charter rights.

The second important ramification of the Charter's official languages
guarantee is that the constitutional rights of these members of the public,
and the government's corresponding obligation to serve them, will
henceforth have to be taken into account in personnel decisions within
the federal civil service. The rights of an individual seeking to complain
(under section 15) of differential treatment on the basis of language, in
hiring or promotion or transfer decisions in the civil service, will have to
be balanced against the public right to service.

EQUALITY RIGHTS

The Four Guarantees

There are, in effect, four guarantees of equality in subsection 15(1): to
equality before the law, equality under the law, the equal protection of
the law, and the equal benefit of the law. Two of these four were added
during the legislative process, namely the guarantees of equality under the
law and to the equal benefit of the law. The genesis of these two addi-
tions is by now familiar to students of the Charter. Equality "under the
law" was sought to make it clear that the Charter applies not only to the
administration of the law but also to its substance. The equal benefit of
the law guarantee was sought in response to the Supreme Court's holding
in *Bliss v. Attorney General of Canada*, [1979] 1 S.C.R. 1983, that it is
not a denial of equality for the unemployment insurance scheme to remove
generally available benefits from women at the time of childbirth and
replace them with special pregnancy benefits for which there is a more
stringent qualifying period.

There have been no judicial decisions interpreting section 15 of the Charter, which will not be in effect until April 1985, some months after the completion date of this paper. Accordingly, one can only speculate about how these four guarantees will be interpreted; some types of speculation are more informed than others.

The guarantee of "equality before the law" is similar to the provision in paragraph 1(b) of the *Canadian Bill of Rights* which was interpreted by Mr. Justice Ritchie in *Attorney General of Canada v. Lavell; Isaac et al. v. Bedard,* [1974] S.C.R. 1349, at p. 1373 to require equality of treatment in the enforcement and application of the laws of Canada by the ordinary courts. It is reasonably certain that the comparable phrase in the Charter will be given at least this interpretation.

Whether the meaning of "equality before the law" could — or should — be extended beyond this guarantee of procedural justice is an open question. In some decisions under the "equality before the law" section of the *Canadian Bill of Rights*, the Supreme Court of Canada did purport to give the phrase an application to the substance of legislation. Speaking for the majority in *R. v. Drybones*, [1970] S.C.R. 282, Mr. Justice Ritchie stated at p. 297:

> [W]ithout attempting any exhaustive definition of "equality before the law" I think that s. 1(b) means at least that no individual or group of individuals is to be treated more harshly than another under that law, and I am therefore of the opinion that an individual is denied equality before the law if it is made an offence punishable at law, on account of his race, for him to do something which his fellow Canadians are free to do without having committed an offence or having been made subject to any penalty.

In *R. v. Burnshine*, [1975] 1 S.C.R. 693, Mr. Justice Martland for the majority seemed to recognize, at least implicitly, that the "equality before the law" guarantee could reach the substance of legislation. However, he states at p. 707 that in order to succeed in such an argument, the person challenging the legislation would have to satisfy the Court that in enacting it, Parliament "was not seeking to achieve a valid federal objective." He offers no general principles for determining what is a valid federal objective; he seems to accept the Crown's statement of the purpose of the legislation at issue in *Burnshine*. Mr. Justice Laskin at p. 717 raises the possibility that, if he could not find a construction of the statute consistent with the Bill of Rights, then it might be necessary to "consider whether the policy alleged to be at its base is consistent with the *Canadian Bill of Rights*" and suggests that this would involve examining "the reality of the policy."

Perhaps the most carefully articulated exposition of the "valid federal objective" test is that of Mr. Justice McIntyre in *MacKay v. The Queen* (1980), 114 D.L.R. (3d) 393. At p. 422, he states:

A valid federal objective, however, must mean something more than an objective which simply falls within the federal legislative competence under the *British North America Act, 1867*. Even in the absence of the *Canadian Bill of Rights*, a federal enactment could not be supported constitutionally if it did not embody such an objective.

He continues at p. 423:

Equality in this context must not be synonymous with mere universality of application. There are many differing circumstances and conditions affecting different groups which will dictate different treatment. The question which must be involved in each case is whether such inequality as may be created by legislation affecting a special class . . . is arbitrary, capricious or unnecessary, or whether it is rationally based and acceptable as a necessary variation from the general principle of universal application of law to meet special conditions and to attain a necessary and desirable social objective.

This analysis contains a number of elements which, it can be predicted, will figure in any application of section 15: an assessment of the validity of the legislative objective (McIntyre, J. asks if it is "necessary and desirable"), and an inquiry into the relation between the legislative objective and the means chosen (McIntyre, J. asks if the variation from universal application of the law is a "necessary one"). These elements have a bearing on whether a departure from the mandated equality is acceptable. In connection with the Charter of Rights one asks, of course, whether this inquiry about acceptability is more properly done within the framework of section 15, or whether it should be done within that of section 1. The analysis was performed within the framework of paragraph 1(b) of the *Canadian Bill of Rights* because there was no counterpart in the Bill to section 1 of the Charter.

Before returning to the question of whether this "acceptability" analysis should proceed within the context of section 15 or section 1, let us finish analyzing the four guarantees in section 15.

The guarantee of equality under the law was intended to make it clear that the substance of legislation could be reached by the command of equality. Because the jurisprudence about "valid federal objective" above was predicated on the assumption that, at least in theory, the Bill could reach the substance of legislation, it might well figure in the analysis of the meaning of "equality under the law." Again, one of the main issues will be whether the assessment of the justification for the departure from "equality" should be done in the framework of section 15 or section 1.

The right to the "equal protection of the law" again echoes the *Canadian Bill of Rights* formulation in paragraph 1(b), guaranteeing the right to "the protection of the law," but the jurisprudence on this branch of paragraph 1(b) is not at all well developed. There is also a parallel with the provision in the Fourteenth Amendment of the United States Constitution that no state shall deny to any person within its jurisdiction the "equal protection of the laws." Indeed, it has been suggested that the phrase "equal protection of the law" will be the window through which U.S. jurisprudence on equality will enter Canadian legal analysis.

The central feature in this U.S. jurisprudence is the three-tiered approach to justifying departures from equality. Where a legislative classification is done on a basis that is "inherently suspect," the Court subjects it to "strict scrutiny" and the state must show a "compelling interest" in maintaining that classification. "Intermediate scrutiny" is accorded to gender-based classifications. To be sustained, this type of classification must bear a "substantial relationship" to "important governmental objectives." The lowest level of scrutiny is "minimal scrutiny"; unless the party complaining of the classification can show that it has no rational basis, it will be upheld. Even if the phrase "equal protection of the law" does import American jurisprudence, the question is, again, whether this sort of justification analysis should take place under section 15 or section 1.

An entirely different way of looking at the equal protection guarantee is to say that it covers statutes that are "protective" in nature, i.e., criminal provisions aimed at "protecting" certain groups, minimum wage and hours of work legislation, provisions giving pregnancy leave and benefits, and so on. The intent of the guarantee, so construed, would be to ensure that the "protection" of such laws is not withheld on an unacceptable basis.

The guarantee of the equal benefit of the law is similar in effect to this latter approach to the equal protection guarantee. Where a statute extends a benefit, the guarantee would ensure that the benefit will be extended even-handedly, not withheld on some arbitrary basis. The potential of this guarantee is wide: much so-called social welfare legislation extends "benefits" to various and different classes of people and is thus potentially subject to this guarantee.

Without Discrimination . . .

Section 15 states that the four guarantees are extended "without discrimination, and in particular without discrimination" on the basis of certain enumerated characteristics.

One issue raised by this language is whether someone challenging a legislative distinction must show that he or she has been adversely affected by it in order to make out a prima facie case of infringement. The suggestion that a showing of adverse impact is required has, in my view, two sources.

One such source is the jurisprudence that has grown up around human rights legislation in Canada, where the idea that differentiation must be accompanied by adverse impact has been widely disseminated. One definition of discrimination often cited by boards of inquiry[4] is that of Lord Reid in the House of Lords' decision in *Post Office v. Union of Post Office Workers*, [1974] 1 All E.R. 229, at p. 238:

Discrimination implies a comparison. Here I think that the meaning could be either that by reason of the discrimination the worker is worse off in some way than he would have been if there had been no discrimination against him, or that by reason of the discrimination he is worse off than someone else in a comparable position against whom there has been no discrimination. It may not make much difference which meaning is taken but I prefer the latter as the more natural meaning of the word, and as most appropriate in the present case.

This element of being "worse off" is echoed in the judgment of the P.E.I. Court of Appeal in *Rocca Group Ltd. v. Muise* (1979), 22 Nfld. & P.E.I. Reports 1, where MacDonald, J. states at p. 10 that, in determining whether discrimination has occurred, it is not enough to find that people have been treated differently. "The next step is to see if the person who has complained has suffered any adverse consequence or has had some affront to his or her dignity before finding there has been discrimination." To the same effect is Professor Ian Hunter's definition of discrimination:

Discrimination means treating people differently because of their race, color, sex, etc. as a result of which the complainant suffers adverse consequences or a serious affront to dignity. . . .[5]

Professor Hunter rejects the definition of discrimination as "treating differently," which had been offered by the board of inquiry in *Simms v. Ford Motor Company*. He states, "Unless the concept of discrimination connotes adverse consequences, many inconsequential and socially harmless practices will run afoul of human rights legislation. . . ."[6]

The second source of this suggested requirement is the passage from Mr. Justice Ritchie's judgment in *Drybones*, quoted above, stating that paragraph 1(b) of the Bill has been violated where one party has been treated "more harshly" than another and made subject to criminal penalties. This reasoning appears again and again in subsequent Supreme Court decisions about equality.

The Oxford English Dictionary meaning of "discrimination" does not carry with it this overlay of "adverse effect"; it means quite simply "distinction" or "differentiation."[7] This seems to be the way in which "discriminate" is used in paragraph 6(3)(a) of the Charter. There, the mobility rights of section 6 are made subject to laws of general application in a province "other than those that discriminate among persons primarily on the basis of province of present or previous residence." The implication of "discriminate" in that context is clearly "differentiation" rather than "adverse impact."

Let us examine the two sources of the "adverse impact" interpretation outlined above to see if they really do require that such an impact be found before a violation of section 15 can be made out.

One of the first points to be noted about human rights jurisprudence is that while there is a body of opinion outlined above that would require a finding of "adverse impact," that opinion is by no means uniform. Mr. Justice Wright of the Manitoba Court of Queens Bench specifically states in *Canada Safeway Limited v. Manitoba Food and Commercial Workers Union et al.*, V CHRR D/2133, at p. D/2135, that the definition of discrimination more consistent with Manitoba Human Rights legislation is as follows: "To discriminate is to make a distinction, to make a difference in treatment or favour." In *Curtis v. Coastal Shipping Limited*, V CHRR D/1998 at p. D/2000, the Board adopted the definition of discrimination given in *Cortner v. The National Cash Register Co.*, 262 N.E. 2nd, 586 (1970), at p. 588:

> "Discriminate" means to make a distinction for or against a person or thing on the basis of the group, class or category to which the person belongs rather than according to actual merit. "Discrimination" means the act of making a distinction in favor of or against a person or thing based on the group, class or category to which that person or thing belongs, rather than on individual merit.

It is reasonably clear that imposing a requirement to show "adverse impact" on someone who complains of a violation of section 15 will narrow the scope of the equality rights guarantee. Because human rights jurisprudence is not uniform on the question of requiring a showing of "adverse impact," it seems particularly restrictive to require "adverse impact" in the Charter context on the basis of human rights jurisprudence. That section 15 was not intended to be limited to a human rights orientation is clear from its title: "Equality Rights." In earlier versions of the Charter, this heading was "Non-Discrimination Rights," and the association was much more clearly with human rights jurisprudence. The title was changed and — arguably — strengthened during the legislative process. Indications are that this sort of legislative history may be favourably received in interpretation of the Charter. The Supreme Court of Canada has, moreover, stated in *Skapinker*, at p. 176, that the headings in the Charter were "systematically and deliberately included as an integral part of the Charter," and therefore the court must take them into consideration when engaged in the process of discerning the meaning and application of the provisions of the Charter.

An egalitarian orientation means more than the mere absence of "adverse impact": it suggests that the inequality itself is the "adverse impact" because it offends the thrust of the guarantee.

Let us turn to the other source of the "adverse impact" theory. In the reasons of Mr. Justice Ritchie, he stated he was attempting no exhaustive definition of equality before the law and gave his definition as a minimum one, saying that paragraph 1(b) means "*at least* that no individual or group of individuals is to be treated more harshly than another under the law. . . ."

Unfortunately, later decisions relying on *Drybones* considered that Mr. Justice Ritchie had laid out in his "at least" statement the *only* situation in which a denial of equality could be found, and the "harshness test" seemed to become the watchword of interpretation. Mr. Justice Ritchie himself, at p. 191 of *Bliss v. Attorney General of Canada*, distinguished the pregnancy leave provisions this way:

> There is a wide difference between legislation which treats one section of the population more harshly than all others by reason of race as in the case of *Regina v. Drybones, supra*, and legislation providing additional benefits. . . . The one case involves the imposition of a penalty on a racial group to which other citizens are not subjected; the other involves a definition of the qualifications required for entitlement to benefits. . . .

The language of section 15 does not accord with the application of a "harshness," "penalty," or adversity analysis. Someone complaining, for example, of denial of a "benefit" may be regarded as trying to become better off, but may not be said to be penalized or treated harshly by not getting the benefit. Nor is it always possible to say that someone complaining of absence of "equal protection" is being treated harshly or penalized by the absence of such protection.

Last, it would be unfortunate if an "adverse impact" requirement had the effect of denying a role to the "public interest" type of lawsuit. Presumably only an individual could show damage, so that organizations would be forestalled from bringing proceedings. This, clearly, is a result that does not occur with respect to other sections of the Charter, as the *Operation Dismantle* and *Citizens' Coalition* cases have shown. Indeed, Joseph Borowski was granted standing to challenge the abortion provisions of the Criminal Code without any showing on his part that they had an adverse impact on him personally.

The Bases of Distinction

Subsection (1) of section 15 of the Charter states that every individual has the rights set out in the section "without discrimination and, in particular without discrimination based on race, national or ethnic origin, colour, religion, sex, age or mental or physical disability."

The specification of some bases in the subsection raises at least two questions. First, will persons be able to complain of a denial of equality based on grounds other than the enumerated ones, and if so, what test will be applied to assess the validity of such distinctions? Second, will distinctions based on one kind of distinction specified in section 15 be evaluated by the same standards and in the same way as distinctions on any other ground so enumerated, or is there in effect a "hierarchy" among the specified grounds? If there is a hierarchy, what is the principle upon which the grounds are ranked?

The jurisprudence under the equality before the law provisions of the *Canadian Bill of Rights* addresses the first of these questions. In *Curr v. The Queen*, [1972] S.C.R. 889, Mr. Justice Laskin states at p. 896 that the existence of one of the prohibited forms of discrimination is not a sine qua non for the operation of the section. Rather "the prohibited discrimination is an additional lever to which federal legislation must respond." Much of the jurisprudence of the Supreme Court dealt with non-enumerated grounds: youth (Burnshine), geographical area (Burnshine, Morgentaler), membership in the military (MacKay), citizenship and domicile (Prata). It is thus extremely unlikely that non-enumerated grounds would be without protection under section 15, particularly in the light of the language of the section. It is clear that the specified grounds are named for emphasis, but the list is not intended to be exhaustive.

In *Bedard* and *Lavell*, Mr. Justice Laskin again addressed the issue of the significance of explicitly mentioning a ground of discrimination. Turning to the question of the applicability of U.S. jurisprudence under the Fifth and Fourteenth Amendments to the constitution, he states at pp. 1386–87:

> Those cases have at best a marginal relevance because the *Canadian Bill of Rights* itself enumerates prohibited classifications which the judiciary is bound to respect; and, moreover, I doubt whether discrimination on account of sex, where as here it has no biological or physiological rationale, could be sustained as a reasonable classification even if the direction against it was not as explicit as it is in the *Canadian Bill of Rights*.

There is support, then, for an argument that the specified grounds may be entitled to more constitutional protection than the non-enumerated grounds, but how is that differentiation going to be made in practice? Bill of Rights jurisprudence is of little help in this sphere because all "equality before the law" arguments, with the exception of *Drybones*, were unsuccessful at the Supreme Court of Canada, whether the basis of distinction being impugned was specified in the Bill or not. It may be suggested, however, that the courts should be less ready to find a justification for distinctions based on enumerated grounds than they are for those based on non-enumerated grounds because the constitutional mandate for equal treatment is stronger in the former case than in the latter. This cannot be an iron-clad rule because some distinctions based on non-enumerated grounds may offend other constitutionally protected values (e.g., denying the right to vote on some ground like region of residence). Obviously, one of the elements that a complainant will have to show when he or she relies on a non-enumerated ground is that the ground is deserving of constitutional protection.

As to whether the enumerated grounds themselves are arranged in any sort of hierarchy, my view is that they are — in a qualified way. The ranking derives from the degree of constitutional protection as a whole accorded to members of that particular group. To take some examples, differentiation on the basis of sex is specifically mentioned in section 15; section 28 arguably strengthens the protection by extending the equality guarantee equally to men and women. Distinctions based on sex would have to be quite rigorously defended in the face of such provisions. The guarantee of religious equality in section 15 may be strengthened by the freedom of religion guarantee in section 2, but the protection for denominational schools in section 29 may, in some cases, cut back or qualify those rights. Similarly, section 15 guarantees equality without discrimination on the basis of age, but the provisions of the *Constitution Act, 1867* themselves include age limitations for public office.

The Role of Section 1

In any analysis focussing on "equality," the inevitable point of departure is that set out by Mr. Justice McIntyre in *MacKay* at pp. 422-23:

> It seems to me that it is incontestable that Parliament has the power to legislate in such a way as to affect one group or class in society as distinct from another without any necessary offence to the *Canadian Bill of Rights*. The problem arises however when we attempt to determine an acceptable basis for the definition of such a separate class, and the nature of the special legislation involved.

The core analysis, then, is determining whether an inequality is acceptable. A central question is whether this analysis is to be done in the context of section 15 of the Charter, section 1, or both.

In *Re Federal Republic of Germany and Rauca* (1983), 41 O.R. (2d) 225, 4 C.C.C. (3d) 385, the Ontario Court of Appeal set out the steps to be followed in a claim of violation of Charter rights. At 4 C.C.C. (3d) 400, the Court states:

> First, it has to be determined whether the guaranteed fundamental right or freedom has been infringed, breached or denied. If the answer to that question is in the affirmative, then it must be determined whether the denial or limit is a reasonable one demonstrably justifiable in a free and democratic society.

In *Re Caddedu and the Queen* (1982), 4 C.C.C. (3d) 97, Mr. Justice Potts of the Ontario High Court has stated that a party alleging that his rights have been violated must establish a prima facie violation of the right. It is open to the party upholding the legislation to resist the establishment of this prima facie case, but if it is established, then the onus shifts to the party relying on the legislation to demonstrate that the limit is a reasonable one imposed by law and demonstrably justifiable in a free and democratic society. According to the Court in *Rauca*, the burden is to establish the reasonableness of the limit on a balance of probabilities.

In *Re Southam and the Queen (No. 1)* (1983), 3 C.C.C. (3d) 515, the Ontario Court of Appeal rejects the Crown's argument that the person who establishes that prima facie his freedom has been infringed or denied must then take the further step and establish on the balance of probabilities that such infringement is unreasonable and cannot be demonstrably justified in a free and democratic society. In *Rauca*, the Court reiterated its rejection of that argument.

In *Skapinker*, the Supreme Court of Canada implicitly followed the two-stage analysis described by the Ontario Court of Appeal in *Rauca*: because the person challenging the legislation did not make out the infringement of the Charter, the respondent was not called on for its justification under section 1 and subsection 6(3).

The two-stage approach to Charter questions outlined by the courts to date has a significant bearing on the issue of where — in section 15 or section 1 — the question of the acceptability of a legislative limit on equality is to be addressed.

Should a person complaining of a violation of the equality guarantees under section 15 have to establish, as part of his or her prima facie case, not only that a distinction exists but also that it is not acceptable? Is it only after the distinction has been shown to be unacceptable that the Crown will be called upon under section 1 to demonstrate that it *is* acceptable — "demonstrably justifiable in a free and democratic society"? To proceed thus would be confusing: What standards would the plaintiff have to meet to show unacceptability under section 15? Would they be the same as those which the Crown would later face under section 1, only reversed? If so, then in effect the Crown has had the burden lifted from its shoulders in the manner explicitly disapproved in *Southam (No. 1)*. If the standards are different, which ones would they be? Would they be the ones developed in the "equality before the law" jurisprudence under the *Canadian Bill of Rights*, or the "equal protection" analysis of the United States Supreme Court? Would the standards to be met by the plaintiff change depending on the type of equality allegedly denied? What standards could, or should, be developed in the case of alleged denial of "equal benefit of the law," to which phrase no body of jurisprudence now attaches?

All these concerns lead to the position that the plaintiff in a section 15 case need not show the unacceptability of the classifications as part of his or her prima facie case. In fact, I have earlier argued against the idea that there must be a showing of adverse impact.

What are the elements of the prima facie case? In some kinds of cases, such as those involving corporations, or foetuses, the threshold issue of whether section 15 even applies will have to be addressed. In all cases, the party complaining of the violation must show that a distinction exists. In some cases, this will be fairly plain, because the difference in treatment of two groups will appear on the face of the legislation. However, this exercise is not always simple, for two reasons. It is sometimes difficult to draw the categories of comparison in a way that will show the court the difference causing the complaint. In *Bliss*, for example, the

Supreme Court approves at pp. 190–91 the statement of Mr. Justice Pratte in the Federal Court of Appeal that "If section 46 treats unemployed pregnant women differently from other unemployed persons, be they male or female, it is, it seems to me, because they are pregnant and not because they are women." This statement not only ignores the obvious fact that only women as a class are liable to get pregnant, so that all distinctions against pregnant people will fall on women, but also fails to recognize that pregnancy itself could have been looked at as a non-enumerated ground of discrimination. The second problem with demonstrating the distinction will be in those cases where the difference is in the impact of an apparently neutral provision. Often it will be necessary to marshall considerable factual evidence to show that a difference does actually exist.

In the case of non-enumerated grounds, it will be necessary to show that there is at least some prima facie reason for taking the ground seriously, although much of the discussion of whether the ground is deserving of protection may fall under the rubric of whether the limit is a "reasonable" one.

Lastly, the prima facie case would include a showing of how or why the distinction complained of offends a particular guarantee. Why, for example, is the statutory item which is withheld or improperly extended to be regarded as a "benefit of the law" or the "protection of the law"?

One can see that even omitting the elements of "adverse impact" and acceptability of the distinction, the applicant for relief under section 15 will not face a mere formality in establishing his or her prima facie case.

One might ask, then, what the implications are of dealing with questions of the acceptability of limits on equality within section 1 instead of section 15. First, requiring that a prima facie case of denial of equality be established under section 15 in the manner outlined above, and proceeding then to assess under section 1 whether the limit on equality is a reasonable and demonstrably justifiable one, means that cases arising under section 15 would be treated in the same way as cases arising under the other sections of the Charter. As there is no explicit indication in the Charter that section 15 should be approached differently from other sections, this consistency of approach is both reasonable and desirable.

Second, performing the analysis of the acceptability of a limit on equality within section 1 rather than section 15 means that the standards chosen by the Charter's framers to guide judicial discretion will have a bearing on the analysis. Section 15 contains no such explicit standards: there is some possibility that a type of American three-tiered or even strict-scrutiny analysis might be grafted onto section 15 because of the presence in the section of the words "equal protection." In my view, it is desirable to use the clear and articulated standards of section 1, which have behind them a substantial Canadian consensus, rather than venture into the uncharted area of judicial discretion by way of section 15. Again, consistency is also a concern; it is not unlikely that judges trying to work out a "justification" analysis within the ambit of section 15 might develop and use different standards from the ones in section 1 and jurisprudence relating to it. There are no clear reasons for preferring unguided judicial experimentation to development within articulated guidelines.

Third, one should bear in mind that section 15 will be guiding legislators as well as courts, and its role in the legislative process adds another dimension to the argument that section 1 should be applied when determining whether a limit on equality is acceptable. Section 1 is very accessible, being part of the text of the Charter; it will simply be easier for legislators to know what is expected of them if section 1 is the touchstone, rather than a body of jurisprudence developed under section 15. Legislators will of course have to resort to the jurisprudence under section 1 to determine the full extent of the checks on their activities, but it is likely that they will readily become reasonably familiar with the evolving standards under section 1, because those standards apply to all sections of the Charter.

The argument in favour of using section 15 alone as the measuring stick for acceptability of limits on equality depends on whether one accepts Mr. Justice Ewaschuk's concept that there are some sections of the Charter that are self-contained, or self-limiting. With regard to such sections, no resort to section 1 is necessary because the whole analysis can be done within the ambit of that particular section. Mr. Justice Ewaschuk advanced this theory of a self-limiting section in connection with the guarantee against "cruel and unusual treatment or punishment" in section 12 of the Charter.[8] The Royal Commission on Equality in Employment states that "section 15 contains its own reasonable limits,"[9] but there is no discussion about why this is so, or what the limits are.

There do not seem to be any reasonable arguments for letting section 15 be free-standing in this way. Although Mr. Justice Ewaschuk's concept may have some appeal where the section itself contains words signifying degree or otherwise indicating social value, like "cruel" or "unusual," it must be remarked that the words in section 15 are clearly not of this type. To let the term "discrimination" govern the interpretation of section 15 would be to encourage courts to regard the section as a form of non-discrimination legislation. This orientation was specifically rejected when a new title was given to the section during the legislative process. Basing jurisprudence on the phrase "equal protection" with its echoes of jurisprudence in the United States may have similar drawbacks, as I have outlined above.

So far I have considered the implications of using section 15 by itself as a measure of the acceptability of a limit on equality. As discussed above, using sections 15 and 1 cumulatively also has its drawbacks. If it is found necessary for the plaintiff to demonstrate that the limit on equality is unreasonable within section 15 in order to make out a prima facie case of violation of the section, proceeding afterwards to section 1 for a further analysis of reasonableness and justifiability, then the plaintiff in a section 15 case in fact faces a hurdle that the plaintiff in any other type of case does not.

If the administration of the Charter is to be even-handed and reasonably predictable, then in my view, for the reasons outlined above, it would be most desirable to require that any analysis of the reasonableness or justifiability of a limit on equality be done within the framework of section 1 of the Charter.

Indirect Inequalities

Reference was made above to the problem of establishing a prima facie case of inequality when the statute or regulation is neutral on its face, and the inequality arises because the statute has a differential impact on members of different groups.

This concept of "impact discrimination" is familiar in the human rights field; in some jurisdictions, like Ontario, it is embodied in legislation. One of the major issues with respect to impact discrimination in the human rights field, where the conduct of "private" parties is under scrutiny, is whether an intent to discriminate must be present before the differential impact can be found wrongful. Two cases raising this issue are scheduled to be heard in the Supreme Court of Canada: *Re CNR and Canadian Human Rights Commission* (1983), 147 D.L.R. (3d) 312, arising under the *Canadian Human Rights Act*, and *Re Ontario Human Rights Commission and Simpsons-Sears* (1982), 38 O.R. (2d) 423, which deals with a provision of the Ontario Human Rights Code. Both involve allegations that apparently neutral employment requirements, Saturday work in *Simpsons* and a hardhat rule in *CNR*, actually contravene the provisions respecting discrimination on the ground of religion because in both cases the employee's religious beliefs precluded compliance with the rule. In both cases, an appeal is before the Supreme Court on the issue of whether the Court of Appeal (of Ontario in *Simpsons* and the F.C.A. in *C.N.R.*) was correct to hold that intent to discriminate is a requisite element.

If the Supreme Court of Canada holds that intent is a necessary element in establishing wrongful discrimination under a human rights statute, then allegations of impact discrimination will be much harder to prove. In almost every case, the alleged discriminator can quite honestly deny a discriminatory intent. The question also arises as to whether a requirement of intent would carry over to analysis of impact inequality in the Charter context.

This issue was addressed by the United States Supreme Court in *Personnel Administrator of Massachusetts v. Feeney*, 99 S. Ct. 2282 (1979), involving a challenge under the Fourteenth Amendment to a veteran's preference for employment in the Massachusetts civil service. The woman employee challenging the preference was able to show that it operates overwhelmingly to the advantage of males.

In reviewing the decisions of the Court in the area of unequal impact, Mr. Justice Stewart points out at pp. 2292–93 that the state must show an "extraordinary justification" to support a classification based on race, and that this rule applies to a classification "that is ostensibly neutral but is an obvious pretext for racial discrimination." However, ". . . even if a neutral law has a disproportionately adverse effect upon a racial minority, it is unconstitutional under the Equal Protection Clause only if that impact can be traced to a discriminatory purpose." This interest in purpose stems from the principle that "the Fourteenth Amendment guarantees equal laws, not equal results."

The Court conducts a two-stage inquiry when a statute gender-neutral on its face is challenged on the ground that its effects on women are disproportionately adverse. First, it tries to discover whether the statute is indeed neutral; as in the case of race, the supposedly neutral term may simply be a pretext for a gender-based classification. If the statute is not based upon gender, then the second question is whether the adverse effect reflects invidious gender-based discrimination.

Mere effect, then, is not enough to invalidate a statute that appears neutral on its face. Only where the neutral classification is an "obvious pretext" for a prohibited classification, or where the purpose of the statute is discriminatory, does the constitution bite.

There have been few decisions in Canadian courts which indicate how the issue might be dealt with under the Charter. In *R. v. Hayden* (1983), 8 C.C.C. (3d) 33, the Manitoba Court of Appeal considered the validity under paragraph 1(b) of the Bill of Rights of paragraph 97(b) of the *Indian Act*, creating the offence of being intoxicated on a reserve. Hall J. A. states at p. 36 that the mere fact that paragraph 97(b) applies to every person does not save it, "for it is obvious that the predominant group on the reservation are Indian people whereas off the reservation the predominant people are of non-native origin." He observes at p. 37 that ". . . place becomes race in terms of where one may not be found intoxicated." In *R. v. Weyallon* (1983), 47 A.R. 360 (N.W.T. S.Ct.), a Dene Indian was convicted of violent rape and accordingly faced a mandatory prohibition against carrying a firearm for five years pursuant to subsection 98(1) of the Criminal Code. Mr. Justice Marshall held that imposition of the mandatory prohibition would be cruel and unusual punishment forbidden by section 12 of the Charter. Weyallon, a hunter and trapper, knew no other skills by which to earn his livelihood, and his crime had not involved a firearm. The judge at p. 362 held that subsection 98(1) "bestows a far greater blow than it would in the case of another — one who does not depend on hunting for his livelihood — clearly those for whom the section was enacted."

In neither *Hayden* nor *Weyallon* did the Court consider the purpose or motive of the provision as discriminatory or invidious. Effect was the primary consideration in each case.

On the other hand, however, consider the position taken in *Morgentaler v. the Queen* (1975), 20 C.C.C. (2d) 449 (S.C.C.). It was argued that section 251 of the Criminal Code involved a denial of equality before the law because differences in geographical location and economic resources meant that not all Canadian women had access to therapeutic abortion committees. Chief Justice Laskin at pp. 463–64 states of this argument:

> It would mean too that the Court would have to come to some conclusion on what distribution would satisfy equality before the law, and that the Court would have to decide how large or small an area must be within in which an acceptable distribution of physicians and hospitals must be found. This is a reach for equality by judicially unmanageable standards, and is posited on the theory that the Court should either give directions for the achievement of relative equality of access to therapeutic abortion committees and approved hospitals to overcome an alleged legislative shortcoming, or should strike down not only s-ss. (4) and (5) of section 251 (which would leave an unqualified prohibition of abortion) but the whole section as being inseverable.
>
> I do not regard s. 1(b) of the *Canadian Bill of Rights* as charging the Courts with supervising the administrative efficiency of legislation or with evaluating the regional or national organization of its administration, in the absence of any touchstone in the legislation itself which would indicate a violation s. 1(b) including the specified prohibitions of discrimination by reason of race, national origin, colour, religion or sex. . . .

This decision is referred to in *R. v. Morgentaler et al.* (1984), 40 O.R. (2d) 353, a decision of Associate Chief Justice Parker of the High Court of Ontario in which he deals with numerous Charter challenges to section 251. The Associate Chief Justice states at p. 392 that evidence of unequal application of the law would not be admissible because the Court must look only at the face of the legislation to determine whether there is an inequality. One questions whether this rationale can really be squared with the holding in *Bedard* and *Lavell* that equality before the law means equality in the administration of the law.

None of these decisions involves application of section 15. There is nothing in section 15 which would require the motive or purpose to be wrongful before a finding of infringement could be made. Obviously, if it were possible to discern a wrongful motive, or use of a neutral ground as a pretext, then the state would have a harder time justifying the distinction.

Affirmative Action

Subsection 15(2) of the Charter provides that:

> Subsection (1) does not preclude any law, program or activity that has as its object the amelioration of conditions of disadvantaged individuals or groups including those that are disadvantaged because of race, national or ethnic origin, colour, religion, sex, age or mental or physical disability.

This subsection was designed to provide an extra safeguard against the possibility that subsection 15(1) on its own might invalidate programs meant to redress historic imbalances in education or employment affecting some groups by using special measures in recruitment, training, and so on. It was feared that such programs, included or sanctioned in law, would constitute a denial of the "equal benefit" of the law or the "equal protection" of the law in respect of those not favoured by them.

In hindsight, one can question this assumption. Even where a prima facie case of denial of equality is made out, it might be relatively painless for the party relying on the program to show it to be a "reasonable limit" and "demonstrably justifiable in a free and democratic society." For example, consider the decision of the Supreme Court in *Re Athabasca Tribal Council and Amoco Petroleum Co. Ltd. et al.* (1981), 124 D.L.R. (3d) 1, dealing with an affirmative action plan which the Tribal Council sought to have made a condition of approval of a tar sands project. When the matter reached the Supreme Court, four of the nine justices hearing the appeal dealt with the issue of whether the plan would contravene clause 6(1)(b) of the Alberta *Individual's Rights Protection Act*, forbidding discrimination in employment. Speaking for the four, Mr. Justice Ritchie states at p. 10:

> In the present case what is involved is a proposal designed to improve the lot of the native peoples with a view to enabling them to compete as nearly as possible on equal terms with other members of the community who are seeking employment in the tar sands plant. With all respect, I can see no reason why the measures proposed by the "affirmative action" programmes proposed for the betterment of the lot of the native peoples in the area in question should be construed as "discriminating against" other inhabitants. The purpose of the plan as I understand it is not to displace non-Indians from their employment, but rather to advance the lot of the Indians so that they may be in a competitive position to obtain employment without regard to the handicaps which their race has inherited.

Had the challenge to the plan come under section 15, this sort of rationale would arguably have provided demonstrable justification for the proposal.

Even so, subsection 15(2) cannot be regarded as mere surplus. It has two possible functions. On the one hand, it may make it difficult for someone to establish even a prima facie case of infringement of the equality rights in subsection 15(1). This is because it might be argued that there is no reachable denial of equal benefit or equal protection where the allegedly offending program falls within the description in subsection 15(2). Thus, one would not even proceed to a section 1 justification analysis. Alternatively, one could suggest that once a prima facie case of violation of subsection 15(1) has been made out, subsection 15(2) is a major factor to be considered in deciding whether the deviation from equality is reasonable and demonstrably justifiable.

What is the impact of section 28 on the status of affirmative action plans under section 15? Does section 28 mean that one is precluded from applying section 1 to assess whether an affirmative action plan is a "limit" on equality demonstrably justifiable in a free and democratic society? This question arises because section 28 declares it is operative "notwithstanding anything in this Charter." The question is important because affirmative action programs could under one mode of analysis constitute a prima facie denial of equality. If this denial cannot be justified in a section 1 analysis, then perhaps it cannot be justified at all. Alternatively, judges barred from using the standard in section 1 may turn to judge-made standards, and such a development could have unpredictable and possibly unfortunate results.

This puzzle requires us to enquire about the equality rights referred to in the Charter which are guaranteed equally to men and women. Are they the rights described in the sections of the Charter prior to the establishment of any valid limitations on them under section 1? Or are they what Whyte calls the "net rights,"[10] derived once the permissible limitations under section 1 have been factored in? If the latter, then men and women are equally entitled to equality rights that recognize the validity of affirmative action plans in favour of the other sex where these can be justified under section 1. If the former, then men and women are equally entitled to the package of section 15 rights, including the possibility that their complaints about affirmative action plans favouring the other sex might be stopped at the first (prima facie) level of analysis by the application of subsection 15(2). In neither case will section 28 preclude the validation of affirmative action plans for women.

The Obligation to Act

Often groups will seek to use the guarantees of section 15 of the Charter to address, not inequality embedded in law, but rather factual inequalities. Their complaint is the lack of legislation to remedy a factual inequality. Can the Charter be used to require legislative or other action?

In the *Operation Dismantle* case, Mr. Justice Pratte observes at p. 368 that ". . . the Charter does not impose on the legislatures and governments in Canada any duty to take positive steps to protect fundamental rights and freedoms; it merely prevents the various legislatures and governmental authorities from adopting legislation or making decisions which would infringe or deny those rights and freedoms."

To the same effect are the observations of Mr. Justice Pennell of the Ontario High Court in *Baxter v. Baxter* (1983), 36 R.F.L. (2d) 186. At p. 189 he observes, ". . . the Charter is written in terms of what the state cannot do to the individual, not in terms of what the individual can exact from the state."

I could not find other observations by courts on this issue. It is conceivable, of course, that a judge might consider it within his or her power to order legislation as remedial action in a successful application under section 24, but such actions depend in the first instance on there having been a violation of a Charter right, presumably because of some shortcoming of existing legislation.

It is in this area of "positive" use of the Charter that the difference between its legislative and judicial applications becomes very significant.

There are two possible ways for the state to respond to the fact that, given present trends in judicial interpretation, a citizen could not force the state through court proceedings to pass legislation aimed at factual inequalities. One possible response is to take refuge in this inability on the part of the citizen, in effect adopting the approach that the state will do only what it is compelled to do. Absent compulsion, it will not act. The other approach is to take its cue from the spirit of the Charter, regarding it as an expression of significant majority will toward the achievement of equality objectives.

Adopting the latter approach will inevitably lead governments to take a large and remedial view toward their legislative and policy-making responsibilities. Such a view is, in my estimation, the more desirable one for governments.

The Relationship of Section 15 and Equality Goals

If one exhorts government institutions to behave in accordance with the spirit of the equality guarantees of the Charter, admittedly one must offer some idea of what that spirit is.

The question is a difficult one, for the meaning of equality is best explored in particular contexts, rather than in the abstract. Moreover, there is a wealth of theoretical work on the meaning of equality, and different groups aspiring to equality advocate different theories.

At this point, given the complexity of the subject, one can offer only a sketch of what might be considered to be the equality goal, or goals. To the extent that section 15 is seen as an instrument for achieving these goals, the goals in turn will colour one's interpretation of the section.

Professor Jill Vickers has developed a most insightful analysis of the types of equality goals that figure in the contemporary debate.[11] While pointing out that in recent Canadian history the question of who ought to enjoy equality, however defined, has proven more significant than the question of what ought to be equalized,[12] she identifies what she calls two major perspectives on what should be equalized. Drawing on the theoretical work of William Ryan, she describes the "fair play" and "fair share" perspectives. "Fair play," according to this analysis, "stresses the racelike quality of human life and the importance of the 'rules of the game' being fair."[13] "Fair share," on the other hand, is based on ". . . the principle that all members of the society obtain a reasonable portion of the goods society produces."[14] Vickers points out that the dichotomy in Canada between these two views may not be so great as would first seem (or as exists in the United States), since most advocates of the fair play position "hold something more than a narrow view of what fair play involves,"[15] allowing them to endorse "the pursuit of policies such as medicare to make real, rather than theoretical, a fair 'race' among competitors. . . ."[16]

Somewhat parallel to the "fair play, fair share" debate is what Vickers describes as the "equal opportunity" and "equality of condition" debate. She describes equality of opportunity as involving the pursuit of paths of action and policies aimed at equality of opportunity for people who will choose to join the competition. Legislation directed against discrimination in hiring is one such policy. Equality of condition goals, however, involve pursuing policies that move toward greater equality of condition for all regardless of their inclination, opportunity, or ability to compete. Such measures include pensions, subsidized housing, and so on.[17]

One might reformulate this debate as "equality of treatment v. equality of results." Both the "fair play" and "equality of opportunity" approaches seem to involve demands that treatment of various groups — established or aspiring — be equal. On the other hand, those who seek a "fair share" or "equality of condition," involving redistribution of available societal goods, are actually calling for "equality of result." The former pair, "fair play" and "equality opportunity," can be viewed as more individualistic; the orientation of the "fair share" and "equality of condition" pair is more toward collective rights.

Added to the tension between these two very broadly defined sets of equality goals is a tension about the best means for achieving them. For example, is "equal treatment" likely to be an effective way of securing any of the equality goals? The Charter of Rights Educational Fund statute audit project refers to this sort of equal treatment as "absolute equality." By this type of analysis, it is forbidden to take into account the differences between one group and another in drawing legislation.[18] Again, Vickers' insights are useful:

> The achievement of more equality for the aspirant groups, however, may require treatment which is *different* from the "norm" to achieve actual equality results. Clearly, treating women or the handicapped the same as men or non-handicapped is unlikely to achieve equal results or even genuine fair play or truly equal opportunity.[19]

At the opposite pole from the "absolute equality" approach is the request that differences should be taken into account in framing legislation. The readily recognizable danger involved in this approach is, however, that so-called differences in capacity, characteristics, and inclinations have long been used as the basis for attempts to exclude members of minority groups from participation in the full range of social and political roles.

How can these various approaches, even in this oversimplified form, be reconciled within the framework of the Charter's equality guarantees? It seems as if the framers of section 15 have actually, whether accidentally or by design, attempted to accommodate all these various ideas within section 15 and section 1.

Clearly the language of section 15, with its frequent repetitions of "equality," seems to suggest a preference for the "equality of treatment" approach, particularly when one remembers that many of the dictionary meanings of "equal" have the connotation of "identical" or "alike."[20] However, section 1 permits departures from the sameness standard where those departures are "reasonable" and "demonstrably justifiable." Legislation reflecting factual differences in target groups may well survive a section 1 analysis; however, the party seeking to uphold the difference in legislative treatment will have to justify it by resort to more than the mere stereotypes that historically have been offered to justify distinctions in law.

Section 15 has a decidedly individualistic cast to it; the equality guarantees are extended to "every individual." Such an orientation does indeed suggest that the "fair play" and "equal opportunity" approaches, with their individualistic orientation, will dominate the section. In fact, the procedural guarantee of equality "before the law" is quite individualistic.

What of the broader and more redistributive goals? Can it be said that section 15 recognizes, requires, or promotes them? In my view, there is some recognition of these goals in section 15, and also an acknowledgment that legislatures will be dealing with them. The guarantee of "the equal benefit of the law" in particular seems to contemplate a role for the Charter in mediating the conflicting claims on social resources if such resources are being distributed under a legislative program. Subsection 15(2) should also be mentioned in this context. The subsection provides a sort of constitutionally protected enclave within which the state may develop or approve programs to promote actively the redressing of historic imbalances in society.

There are many potential interpretation problems in section 15. However, one can say with some confidence that, coupled with section 1, it is a flexible instrument for fostering achievement of varied equality goals. In assessing its own performance in the equality field, the government need not feel that the more far-reaching redistributive equality goals are ruled out by the commands of section 15.

Impact of the Equality Guarantees

Mobility

Some of the implications of the *Demaere* decision are discussed above. That case dealt with the provisions of section 13 of the *Public Service*

Employment Act, R.S.C. 1970, c. P-32, to the effect that before conducting a competition the Public Service Commission shall determine the area in which applicants must reside to be eligible for appointment. The Federal Court of Appeal held that the Commission could draw these boundaries to exclude civil servants employed in one part of a province from applying for a position available in another part.

I find this decision far from satisfactory. Presumably section 6 of the Charter would prohibit the Commission from drawing lines along provincial boundaries, and the overall result may well be that persons in other provinces cannot be excluded from positions without a "demonstrably justifiable" reason, but that persons in other parts of the same province can. It would be preferable in my view to apply the basic guarantee of subsection 6(2) and the justification process mandated by section 1 to the process of drawing boundaries for job competitions. Where there is a constitutionally "good" reason for the boundary, it would survive. In *Demaere*, the Commission might have required applicants from the same region because it was thought that they would be familiar with air traffic patterns there and thus be safer than employees from other regions. This type of rationale should have been advanced.

If *Demaere* is taken at its face value, it may well be that the Commission's activities in drawing boundaries for competitions will go unchanged. However, in view of the criticisms that can be made of the decision, it would be useful to review the Commission's thinking on this process and introduce into it a review for Charter compliance.

Language

Mentioned above are the two possible impacts that I consider useful in this very brief review. First, coordination between the *Official Languages Act* legislation and administration on the one hand, and the Charter guarantees on the other, is necessary to ensure that the *Official Languages Act* is not offensive to the Charter for such reasons as under-inclusiveness. There is a real possibility that the government could face actions for damages under section 24 for failure to provide services.

Second, the constitutional guarantees of access to government services in both official languages may be balanced against the individual rights of civil servants unable to operate in a bilingual environment. Now that the language guarantees have constitutional status, instead of only a statutory form, they presumably will carry more weight when decisions about hiring, transfer, promotion, or training are made.

Equality Rights

EQUALITY BEFORE THE LAW:
CROWN LIABILITY AND OTHER ISSUES

The "equality before the law" guarantee of section 15 may raise important issues concerning Crown privilege. The Crown's position is often different from, and more favourable to, that of the ordinary litigant, and an ordinary litigant suing the Crown is often at a greater disadvantage than he or she would be in an action against another private individual. For example, in the *Crown Liability Act*, R.S.C. 1970, c. C-38, as amended by R.S.C. 1970, (2nd supp.), s. 65, (Item 11); S.C. 1973–74, c. 50, s. 4; S.C. 1974–75–76, c. 93, s. 97, S.C. 1980–81–82–83, c. 47, s. 11, there is a provision imposing a seven-day limitation period in suits against the Crown for damages in tort or for breach of duty attaching to the ownership, occupation, possession, or control of property. Notice in writing of the injury must be served, with a copy to the Deputy Attorney General of Canada, within seven days of the injury. Failure to give notice is not a bar to the action in the case of death, but in all other cases it is a bar that can only be raised with leave of the Court. In section 12 of the Act there is a provision for special notice periods where default judgment is sought against the Crown. These provisions and others like them will be defended on ground that the legislation confers a right of action where none existed at common law, and Parliament is entitled to hedge this right with appropriate limitations.

In *Mulligen v. Saskatchewan Housing Corp. Ltd.* (1983) 2 C.R.D. 252.100–02, Dielschneider, J. of the Saskatchewan Court of Queen's Bench refused to apply the provincial *Proceedings Against the Crown Act* to prevent an injunction application by a Corporation employee trying to stop his transfer to another city which he alleged was being arranged because of a position he took at a Regina city council meeting. The court took the view that Crown immunity would run counter to the right of free speech enshrined in section 2 of the Charter.

Under section 24 of the Charter, it may well be open to a court to relieve against a provision of the *Crown Liability Act* in a proper case.

Another area where the question of equality before the law arises is with regard to diplomatic immunity, which is conferred on a number of representatives of foreign governments or international organizations in Canada pursuant to international and reciprocal arrangements. A person charged with a criminal offence arising out of conduct in which he was engaged with someone with diplomatic immunity could well complain of a denial of equality before the law when his diplomatic accomplice is not charged. A similar situation would be that of a civil litigant denied a full right to sue for a tort or breach of contract because the potential defendant is protected by diplomatic immunity.

The likelihood is that the special position of foreign diplomats in Canada would be regarded as a reasonable limit imposed by law in a free and democratic society, because of the Canadian interests served by reciprocity in these arrangements, and their long tradition and usefulness in smoothing the course of international relations.

A third instance of the possible application of the equality before the law guarantee is in the area of the separate administration of military justice and the internal discipline of the Royal Canadian Mounted Police. Although it may well be possible to argue for the application of the legal rights guarantees of the Charter to these proceedings, it might, in the face of the decision in *MacKay v. The Queen*, be more difficult to dislodge the entire separate system. Nonetheless, the rationales for having a separate structure may not justify, within the structure, the denial of certain basic procedural rights guaranteed by the Charter.

EQUALITY AND PARLIAMENT

Two main avenues of inquiry exist here. First is the question of whether the equality guarantees will affect what Parliament does, and the second will be whether the equality guarantees affect the nature of Parliament.

With regard to the former, it is clear and central to the scheme of the Charter that the legislative activities of Parliament are covered by it. The impact of sections 15 and 52 is to establish that the Charter reaches the substance of law. When Parliament delegates its authority to subordinate bodies, the application of the Charter will go down the "chain" of delegated authority. I have discussed above how far down the chain of delegated authority the reach of the Charter can be expected to go. It is also possible that the "equality before the law" guarantees and the legal rights guarantees may have some impact on Parliament's procedure for dealing with "offences" by its own members.

With respect to the impact of the Charter on the nature of Parliament, let me raise the question of the separate employment status of employees of Parliament and the divergence in benefits and employment safeguards between these employees and those in the public service. I will not document each instance here, but it seems that there is at least a good prima facie case that the employees of Parliament are denied the "equal protection" and "equal benefit" of the statutory rules protecting employees in the regular public service. The existence of a broad category of non-enumerated grounds in section 15 gives these employees an entree into the equality guarantees.

IMPACT ON THE EXECUTIVE

Here let me deal with the Governor General, Governor in Council, prime minister, and cabinet. The cabinet, or a minister, or a group of ministers in the case of Treasury Board have wide regulation-making powers delegated from Parliament in the exercise of which they would in most, if not all, cases be subject to control by the Charter.

In the making of orders-in-council, or other statutory instruments which are not made pursuant to delegated parliamentary power but pursuant to their residual executive or Crown power, they would, as current indicators are showing, also be subject to scrutiny under the Charter.

Another type of power exercised by this executive government is, of course, the appointment power. How this could be made subject to review by the Charter is an interesting question. If, as the few available signs indicate, there is no obligation to take remedial action for underlying factual inequalities, then there would not be much basis for suggesting that the executive could be forced, in making appointments, to redress racial or gender imbalances in the composition of particular bodies. This is not to say, however, that the executive should not have such a policy. Indeed, abiding by the spirit of the Charter as disclosed above would involve such a policy. If the cabinet did have such a policy, it would seem that the language of subsection 15(2) may be broad enough to protect it from challenge under subsection 15(1).

Suppose the executive had a policy of search or consultation which was formalized to an extent but not explicitly aimed at achieving a balance in appointments, like the current policy of consulting the organized Bar about judicial appointments. Could one argue that as long as there was no consultation, and that appointment was a "pure" executive act, the Charter would not require either consultation or striving for racial balance, but that once consultation had begun, the Charter required it be a process the "benefit" of which must be extended equally — i.e., to other organized groups? This is a somewhat conjectural argument, but it, or others like it, may emerge as interested groups seek to penetrate the core of government's discretionary decision making by using the Charter.

Somewhat similar questions arise in connection with the granting powers of government, whether exercised by the cabinet, a particular minister, or a board or council. In traditional administrative law, granting a privilege is a pure "executive" act and not subject to review by any of the prerogative remedies. The grantor is allowed ample leeway to decide whether to give at all and to determine the receiver of his or her largesse.

Many large schemes exist today for the granting of money, whether in the form of grants to citizens' groups, artists, or industries. As most, if not all, such arrangements have some legislative underpinning in statute, regulation, or other statutory instrument, it may well be that they are "laws" the benefit of which much be equally extended. One can envision situations in which, for example, members of one racial or ethnic group protest that a competing group receives more funds pursuant to a multi-cultural grant program. While it may not be possible for people to use the Charter to require that grants be given at all, once the decision is made to give them, the Charter may provide a way of assessing the propriety of administration of such a scheme.

THE PUBLIC SERVICE

Interestingly, it is in the area of personnel administration where the institutions of government may face most of the equality challenges under section 15. Reference has already been made to the differentiation between the staffs of Parliament and the members of the public service and there are many other distinctions in status, rank and benefit which permeate the organization of those who work for government. Because section 15 challenges are not restricted to members of the enumerated groups, there may be many challenges by persons on the "wrong" side of some preference or exclusion in civil service organization. Obviously, a detailed review of massive scope would be necessary to uncover all the possible sources of difficulty. However, a few obvious issues can be raised, chosen from the *Public Service Employment Act*.

Section 11 of the Act provides that appointments in the public service "shall be made from within the Public Service except where, in the opinion of the Commission, it is not in the best interests of the Public Service to do so." The general rule so established is that present public servants have a greater right to apply for positions than do members of the public, who may in some cases be better qualified. The outsiders are clearly denied equal "benefits" of this preference. It may be possible to articulate a rationale for having such a blanket rule favouring insiders; however, I would suggest that the sweeping nature of the preference may fall afoul of these cases that make it clear that the courts will not "read down" a limitation on a right found in a statute in an effort to find a version of it which will comply with the Charter. The adjustments are for Parliament to make.

There are other instances of preference with regard to public service employment which might be said to suffer from the same frailties. In section 37, the staffs of ministers, the Leader of the Opposition, and so forth are given rights to become appointed to the public service in some circumstances without going through a competition. Section 16 permits a sort of veteran's or veteran's widow preference at the discretion of the Public Service Commission.

Section 39 allows the Public Service Commission to exclude from the operation of the Act a position or person or class of positions or persons where the Commission decides that it is not practicable nor in the best interests of the public service to apply the Act; the approval of the Governor in Council is required for the exclusion. One would hope that the merits of such exclusions would henceforth be tested under sections 15 and 1, and that mere administrative convenience or the desire to favour or exclude one particular person would be excluded. The same justification requirement could, in my view, usefully be applied to the provisions of paragraph 13(b) of the Act allowing differentiation in closed competitions.

Section 10 of the *Public Service Employment Act* requires the Commission to choose persons for the public service on the basis of merit, and subsection 12(1) permits the Commission to ". . . prescribe selection standards as to education, knowledge, experience, language, age, residence or any other matters that, in the opinion of the Commission, are necessary or desirable having regard to the nature of the duties to be performed. . . ." The selection standards on the basis of "residence" may be subject to the same scrutiny as those relating to paragraph 13(a) discussed above: a demonstration should be made of a connection between residence and merit.

OTHER INSTITUTIONS

The major question for many institutions is not what effect the Charter will have, but whether the Charter will have any effect at all.

As outlined above, there are two separate means by which the Charter might reach a particular activity or entity. The first depends on the activity or entity being Parliament or an emanation of Parliament, and the second depends on it being government or an emanation of government.

Parliament is, of course, less difficult to identify than "government." Exercises of authority delegated by Parliament, whether the recipients are subordinate in the classical sense of being a creature of Parliament like a board or commission, or are the executive acting pursuant to statute, will be caught by section 32.

The main question in this context is how far down the chain of delegation the Charter descends. Does every entity constituted by or pursuant to an act of Parliament have an obligation to behave in accordance with the Charter? If so, then every corporation set up under the *Canada Business Corporations Act* would have Charter obligations.

It is not possible to give a fully dispositive answer to this question. However, I have set out some touchstones in the commentary above to which I will now return. Those entities exercising delegated authority which would be considered judicial or quasi-judicial (and thus amenable to judicial review) would be caught; already subject to review in administrative law for excess or abuse of power, they are without much strain brought within the Charter net. Arguably, those powers (and bodies) also subject to the dictates of fairness would be caught by the Charter. These bodies, exercising "administrative power" are not only subject to judicial review, but also seem to be contemplated by language such as that in section 6 and subsection 15(2) of the Charter referring to "law, program, or activity." More importantly, it is abundantly clear from the provisions of the legal rights section of the Charter that the document is intended to apply to police powers, which are quite straightforwardly "administrative."

Other touchstones that may be used to distinguish the entities subject to the Charter are useful when we contemplate bodies that are not, apart from the Charter, subject to judicial review. In this connection, one must look at a number of clues: what is the nature and degree of any formal connection between the entity and Parliament or government? How is the entity regarded by Parliament or government? Is it included in statutory descriptions of "institutions of government" found in, for example, the *Privacy Act*, or are its employees regarded as part of the civil service? Is it made a Crown agent? Is it the beneficiary of sovereign immunity? Would it be excluded, or would its activity be included because of the test of private vs. public function set out in *Berardinelli*, or because the organization, while apparently "private" for many purposes, is used for some national purpose or to perform a function or duty on behalf of the government of Canada?

In my view, it is necessary to focus on not only the institution as a whole but also the particular power or function at issue to determine the application of the Charter. The issue must be considered from as many different perspectives as possible to discover whether the Charter applies.

Taking now the "government" rubric of section 32, one must observe that the Charter itself is not entirely clear in its use of the term, and looking outside the Charter to other statutes may help determine in a particular case whether an entity is considered by Parliament to be a part of government. It seems reasonably clear that "government" means at least the executive government in the sense of Governor in Council, cabinet, prime minister or minister, and includes the departments and ministries headed by these ministers. Certainly, the management of the public service is also covered by this expression. As to whether any particular agency or corporation or board may be included in this rubric (if not in the category of Parliament), again the questions to be posed are the same as those above. Not only the degree of formal connection, but the nature of the function performed, and the other elements of government status that may be present should be assessed.

In a study of this scope, it is difficult to be comprehensive or even particular about the precise impact of the Charter on the government institutions that would come into this general category. Such specificity is the undertaking of the statute audit done by the government as a whole to review legislation and practices for compliance with the Charter.

More or Less Equality?

Whatever the institution of government, there is one question arising from the equality guarantees of the Charter it must confront. It is apparent that a major complaint in equality cases is that benefits, or protection, or a certain type of treatment in law is differentially available. A member of Group A sees that members of Group B have something and, perceiving no material difference between Groups A and B, wants the same thing. The most obvious question invariably is whether evenhandedness is achieved by removing the advantage from Group B or by also giving it to Group A?

The question is not an idle one. In times of economic restraint and diminished interest in social programs, governments may be inclined simply to abolish programs when more seek access to them.

The possibility of this reductionist approach has been recognized in Canada's equal pay legislation. Most statutes dealing with equal pay for equal work (or work of equivalent or equal value) provide that a disparity in pay may not be resolved by reducing the pay of the more highly paid individual. This explicit protection is, however, statutory and does not extend across the range of possibly contentious situations that will be brought to light by section 15.

Where this dilemma is faced by a court, the course of action is relatively clear. The offending provision may be declared void in accordance with section 52. The declaration is a signal to the legislature that action on its part is needed. Often, equality problems need the sort of complex solution that a legislature can provide. Revisions to the *Canadian Citizenship Act* made in 1977 after a court challenge to one provision affected by a sex-based inequality show quite well how much better suited than a court a legislature may be to achieve a systematic and comprehensive eradication of inequality.

However, the legislature will inevitably face the dilemma of whether to increase or withhold availability of a right or benefit in order to achieve equality. Some such dilemmas will be posed by judicial decisions; many more may arise in the course of the government's own effort to comply with the Charter.

It is perhaps unfortunate that the framers of the Charter did not include in it a proviso like that in equal pay legislation, forbidding cut-backs of existing benefits in order to achieve equality. Without such a proviso, one must rely to a great extent on political will and political pressure to preserve and extend existing benefits as a way of achieving equality. One hopes that government institutions will take to this task in a manner consistent with the spirit of the Charter.

Conclusion

The government itself has a significant role to play in determining how the equality provisions of the Charter are interpreted. I have argued in this paper that the government should adopt a large and liberal interpretation of the Charter when considering its application to its own institutions and activities, and not take a narrow and technical view. The language of the principal equality guarantee, section 15, is flexible enough to accommodate government efforts to redress historic imbalances by formulating affirmative action programs and otherwise addressing factual inequalities, and governments should take their cue from this flexibility.

It is likely that the Charter's equality guarantees will require review of the government's appointments and granting policies, as well as personnel policies in government employment. The latter seem to be replete with special categories, preferences, and exclusions which may well not survive scrutiny under the Charter.

Overall, it is hoped that the government will choose not to achieve equality by the cynical expedient of removing advantages from those who have them, but rather will aim in each case to abide by the spirit as well as the letter of the Charter.

Appendix A

Privacy Act, as amended, Schedule I

Privacy Act, S.C. 1980–81–82–83, c. 111 (Schedule II), Schedule, as amended by SOR/83-795; S.C. 1980–81–82–83, c. 165, s. 35; S.C. 1980–81–82–83, c. 167, Sched. I, Item 19; S.C. 1980–81–82–83, c. 168, s. 72

Schedule I
(Section 3)

Government Institutions

Departments and Ministries of State

Department of Agriculture
Department of Communications
Department of Consumer and Corporate Affairs
Ministry of State for Economic and Regional Development
Department of Employment and Immigration
Department of Energy, Mines and Resources
Department of the Environment
Department of External Affairs
Department of Finance
Department of Fisheries and Oceans
Department of Indian Affairs and Northern Development
Department of Insurance
Department of Justice
Department of Labour
Department of National Defence (including the Canadian Forces)
Department of National Health and Welfare

Department of National Revenue
Department of Public Works
Department of Regional Industrial Expansion
Ministry of State for Science and Technology
Department of the Secretary of State
Ministry of State for Social Development
Department of the Solicitor General
Department of Supply and Services
Department of Transport
Department of Veterans Affairs

Other Government Institutions

Advisory Council on the Status of Women
Agricultural Products Board
Agricultural Stabilization Board
Anti-Dumping Tribunal
Atlantic Development Council
Atlantic Pilotage Authority
Bank of Canada
Bilingual Districts Advisory Board
Board of Trustees of the Queen Elizabeth II Canadian Fund to Aid in
   Research on the Diseases of Children
Bureau of Pension Advocates
Canada Council
Canada Deposit Insurance Corporation
Canada Employment and Immigration Commission
Canada Labour Relations Board
Canada Mortgage and Housing Corporation
Canada Post Corporation
Canadian Aviation Safety Board
Canadian Centre for Occupational Health and Safety
Canadian Commercial Corporation
Canadian Cultural Property Export Review Board
Canadian Dairy Commission
Canadian Film Development Corporation
Canadian Government Specifications Board
Canadian Grain Commission
Canadian Human Rights Commission
Canadian International Development Agency
Canadian Livestock Feed Board
Canadian Patents and Development Limited
Canadian Penitentiary Service
Canadian Pension Commission
Canadian Radio-television and Telecommunications Commission

Canadian Saltfish Corporation
Canadian Transport Commission
Canadian Unity Information Office
The Canadian Wheat Board
Crown Assets Disposal Corporation
Defence Construction (1951) Limited
The Director of Soldier Settlement
The Director, The Veterans' Land Act
Economic Council of Canada
Energy Supplies Allocation Board
Export Development Corporation
Farm Credit Corporation
Federal Business Development Bank
Federal Mortgage Exchange Corporation
Federal-Provincial Relations Office
Fisheries Prices Support Board
The Fisheries Research Board of Canada
Foreign Investment Review Agency
Freshwater Fish Marketing Corporation
Grain Transportation Agency Administration
Great Lakes Pilotage Authority, Ltd.
Historic Sites and Monuments Board of Canada
Immigration Appeal Board
International Development Research Centre
Jacques Cartier and Champlain Bridges Incorporated
Laurentian Pilotage Authority
Law Reform Commission of Canada
Medical Research Council
Merchant Seamen Compensation Board
Metric Commission
National Arts Centre Corporation
The National Battlefields Commission
National Capital Commission
National Design Council
National Energy Board
National Farm Products Marketing Council
National Film Board
National Harbours Board
National Library
National Museums of Canada
National Parole Board
National Parole Service
Natural Sciences and Engineering Research Council
Northern Canada Power Commission
Northern Pipeline Agency

Northwest Territories Water Board
Office of the Auditor General
Office of the Chief Electoral Officer
Office of the Commissioner of Official Languages
Office of the Comptroller General
Office of the Co-ordinator, Status of Women
Office of the Correctional Investigator
Office of the Custodian of Enemy Property
Pacific Pilotage Authority
Pension Appeals Board
Pension Review Board
Petroleum Compensation Board
Petroleum Monitoring Agency
Prairie Farm Assistance Administration
Prairie Farm Rehabilitation Administration
Privy Council Office
Public Archives
Public Service Commission
Public Service Staff Relations Board
Public Works Land Company Limited
Regional Development Incentives Board
Restrictive Trade Practices Commission
Royal Canadian Mint
Royal Canadian Mounted Police
The St. Lawrence Seaway Authority
Science Council of Canada
The Seaway International Bridge Corporation, Ltd.
Social Sciences and Humanities Research Council
Standards Council of Canada
Statistics Canada
Statute Revision Commission
Tariff Board
Tax Review Board
Textile and Clothing Board
Treasury Board Secretariat
Uranium Canada, Limited
War Veterans Allowance Board
Yukon Territory Water Board

Appendix B

Access to Information Act, as amended, Schedule I

Access to Information Act, S.C. 1980–81–82–83, c. 111, Schedule I, as amended by S.C. 1980–81–82–83, c. 165, s. 34(1); S.C. 1980–81–82–83, c. 167, Schedule I, Item 1; S.C. 1980–81–82–83, c. 168, s. 71

Schedule I
(Section 3)

Government Institutions

Departments and Ministries of State

Department of Agriculture
Department of Communications
Department of Consumer and Corporate Affairs
Ministry of State for Economic and Regional Development
Department of Employment and Immigration
Department of Energy, Mines and Resources
Department of the Environment
Department of External Affairs
Department of Finance
Department of Fisheries and Oceans
Department of Indian Affairs and Northern Development
Department of Insurance
Department of Justice
Department of Labour
Department of National Defence
Department of National Health and Welfare
Department of National Revenue
Department of Public Works
Department of Regional Industrial Expansion
Ministry of State for Science and Technology
Department of the Secretary of State
Ministry of State for Social Development
Department of the Solicitor General
Department of Supply and Services
Department of Transport
Department of Veterans Affairs

Other Government Institutions

Advisory Council on the Status of Women
Agricultural Products Board
Agricultural Stabilization Board
Anti-Dumping Tribunal
Atlantic Development Council
Atlantic Pilotage Authority
Atomic Energy Control Board
Bank of Canada
Bilingual Districts Advisory Board
Board of Trustees of the Queen Elizabeth II Canadian Fund to Aid in
  Research on the Diseases of Children
Bureau of Pension Advocates
Canada Council
Canada Deposit Insurance Corporation
Canada Employment and Immigration Commission
Canada Labour Relations Board
Canada Mortgage and Housing Corporation
Canadian Aviation Safety Board
Canadian Centre for Occupational Health and Safety
Canadian Commercial Corporation
Canadian Cultural Property Export Review Board
Canadian Dairy Commission
Canadian Film Development Corporation
Canadian Forces
Canadian Government Specifications Board
Canadian Grain Commission
Canadian Human Rights Commission
Canadian International Development Agency
Canadian Livestock Feed Board
Canadian Penitentiary Service
Canadian Pension Commission
Canadian Radio-television and Telecommunications Commission
Canadian Saltfish Corporation
Canadian Transport Commission
Canadian Unity Information Office
Crown Assets Disposal Corporation
Defence Construction (1951) Limited
The Director of Soldier Settlement
The Director, The Veterans' Land Act
Economic Council of Canada
Energy Supplies Allocation Board
Farm Credit Corporation
Federal Business Development Bank

Federal Mortgage Exchange Corporation
Federal-Provincial Relations Office
Fisheries Prices Support Board
The Fisheries Research Board of Canada
Foreign Investment Review Agency
Freshwater Fish Marketing Corporation
Grain Transportation Agency Administration
Great Lakes Pilotage Authority, Ltd.
Historic Sites and Monuments Board of Canada
Immigration Appeal Board
International Development Research Centre
Laurentian Pilotage Authority
Law Reform Commission of Canada
Medical Research Council
Merchant Seamen Compensation Board
Metric Commission
The National Battlefields Commission
National Capital Commission
National Design Council
National Energy Board
National Farm Products Marketing Council
National Film Board
National Harbours Board
National Library
National Museums of Canada
National Parole Board
National Parole Service
National Research Council of Canada
Natural Sciences and Engineering Research Council
Northern Canada Power Commission
Northern Pipeline Agency
Northwest Territories Water Board
Office of the Comptroller General
Office of the Co-ordinator, Status of Women
Office of the Correctional Investigator
Office of the Custodian of Enemy Property
Pacific Pilotage Authority
Pension Appeals Board
Pension Review Board
Petroleum Monitoring Agency
Prairie Farm Assistance Administration
Prairie Farm Rehabilitation Administration
Privy Council Office
Public Archives
Public Service Commission

Public Service Staff Relations Board
Public Works Lands Company Limited
Regional Development Incentives Board
Restrictive Trade Practices Commission
Royal Canadian Mint
Royal Canadian Mounted Police
The St. Lawrence Seaway Authority
Science Council of Canada
The Seaway International Bridge Corporation, Ltd.
Social Sciences and Humanities Research Council
Standards Council of Canada
Statistics Canada
Statute Revision Commission
Tariff Board
Tax Review Board
Textile and Clothing Board
Treasury Board Secretariat
Uranium Canada, Limited
War Veterans Allowance Board
Yukon Territory Water Board

Appendix C

Schedules to the Financial Administration Act, as amended

Schedules to The *Financial Administration Act*, R.S.C. 1970, c. F-10, as amended by S.C. 1974-75-76, c. 33, s. 265 (Item 3); S.C. 1976-77, c. 18, s. 1; S.C. 1976-77, c. 34, s. 23; S.C. 1977-78 c. 33, s. 1; S.C. 1978-79, c. 4, ss. 4,5; S.C. 1978-79, c. 9, s. 1 "265"(F); S.C. 1980-81-82-83, c. 40, s. 94.1; S.C. 1980-81-82-83, c. 54, s. 56 (Item 8); S.C. 1980-81-82-83, c. 123, s. 1,2; S.C. 1980-81-82-83, c. 170, ss. 1-23; S.C. 1984, c. 13

Schedules as amended by:

Schedule A

R.S.C. 1970 (2nd supp.), c. 14, s. 31 (Item 1); S.C. 1978-79, c. 13, s. 34 (Item 1); S.C. 1980-81-82-83, c. 54, s. 56 (Item 8); S.C. 1980-81-82-83, c. 167, Sched. I, Item 10

Schedule B

S.C. 1984, c. 31, s. 13, Schedule I

Schedule C

S.C. 1984, c. 31, s. 13, Schedule I

Schedule A
[Departments]

Department of Agriculture
Department of Communications
Department of Consumer and Corporate Affairs
Department of Energy, Mines and Resources
Department of the Environment
Department of Fisheries and Oceans
Department of External Affairs
Department of Finance
Department of Indian Affairs and Northern Development
Department of Insurance
Department of Justice
Department of Labour
Department of Manpower and Immigration
Department of National Defence
Department of National Health and Welfare
Department of National Revenue
Department of Public Works
Department of Regional Industrial Expansion
Department of the Secretary of State of Canada
Department of Supply and Services
Department of the Solicitor General
Department of Transport
Treasury Board
Department of Veterans Affairs

Note: Section 2 of the Act defines "department" to include the staffs of the Senate, the House of Commons and the Library of Parliament.

Schedule B
[Departmental Corporations]

Agricultural Stabilization Board
Atomic Energy Control Board
Canada Employment and Immigration Commission
Canadian Aviation Safety Board
Canadian Centre for Occupational Health and Safety
Crown Assets Disposal Corporation
Director of Soldier Settlement

The Director, The Veterans' Land Act
Economic Council of Canada
Fisheries Prices Support Board
Medical Research Council
The National Battlefields Commission
National Museums of Canada
National Research Council of Canada
Natural Sciences and Engineering Research Council
Science Council of Canada
Social Sciences and Humanities Research Council

Schedule C
Part I

Atlantic Pilotage Authority
Atomic Energy of Canada Limited
Canada Deposit Insurance Corporation
Canada Lands Company Limited
Canada Mortgage and Housing Corporation
Canada Post Corporation
Canadian Arsenals Limited
Canadian Commercial Corporation
Canadian Dairy Commission
Canadian Livestock Feed Board
Canadian National (West Indies) Steamships, Limited
Canadian Patents and Development Limited
Canadian Saltfish Corporation
Canadian Sports Pool Corporation
Canagrex
Cape Breton Development Corporation
Defence Construction (1951) Limited
Export Development Corporation
Farm Credit Corporation
Federal Business Development Bank
Freshwater Fish Marketing Corporation
Great Lakes Pilotage Authority, Ltd.
Harbourfront Corporation
Laurentian Pilotage Authority
Loto Canada Inc.
Mingan Associates, Ltd.
National Capital Commission
Northern Canada Power Commission
Pacific Pilotage Authority
Pêcheries Canada Inc.
Royal Canadian Mint

St. Anthony Fisheries Limited
St. Lawrence Seaway Authority
Societa a responsibilita limitata Immobiliare San Sebastiano
Standards Council of Canada
Uranium Canada Limited
VIA Rail Canada Inc.

Schedule C
Part II

Air Canada
Canada Development Investment Corporation
Canada Ports Corporation
Canadian National Railway Company
Montreal Port Corporation
Northern Transportation Company Limited
Petro-Canada
Teleglobe Canada
Vancouver Post Corporation

Appendix D

Public Service Staff Relations Act, as amended, Schedule I, Parts I and II

Public Service Staff Relations Act, R.S.C. 1970, c. P-35, as amended by S.C. 1972, c. 18, s. 4; S.C. 1973–74, c. 15, ss. 1–5; S.C. 1973–74, c. 36, s. 9; S.C. 1974–75–76, c. 67, ss. 1–31

Schedule I as amended by:

SOR/70-118; SOR/70-477; SOR/71-349; SOR/71-355; SOR/71-360; SOR/71-403; SI/72-78; SI/72-79; SI/72-85; SI/73-18; SI/73-53; SOR/73-594; SOR/73-710; S.C. 1973–74, c. 52, s. 8(2); SOR/74-129; SOR/74-430; SOR/74-501; S.C. 1974–75–76, c. 16, s. 2; S.C. 1974–75–76, c. 49, s. 18, *Schedule* Item 3; S.C. 1974–75–76, c. 67, s. 32; S.C. 1974–75–76, c. 75, ss. 10; SOR/75-183; SOR/76-242; S.C. 1976–77, c. 28, s. 49(F); S.C. 1976–77, c. 33, s. 67; S.C. 1976–77, c. 34, s. 24; SOR/77-618; S.C. 1977–78, c. 20, s. 24; SOR/78-141; SOR/78-283; SOR/78-379; SOR/78-627; S.C. 1978–79, c. 17, s. 8; SOR/79-294; SOR/79-391; SOR/79-695(F); SOR/80-468; SOR/82-112; SOR/82-1100; SOR/83-232; S.C. 1980–81–82–83, c. 165, s. 40

Schedule I, Part I

Departments and other portions of the public service of Canada in respect of which Her Majesty as represented by the Treasury Board is the employer

Departments named in Schedule I to the Financial Administration Act

Agricultural Stabilization Board
Anti-Inflation Board
Anti-Inflation Tribunal
Atlantic Development Board
Board of Grain Commissioners
Bureau of Pensions Advocates, Pension Review Board
Canada Labour Relations Board
Canadian Aviation Safety Board
Canadian Dairy Commission
Canadian Human Rights Commission
Canadian Intergovernmental Conference Secretariat
Canadian Livestock Feed Board
Canadian Penitentiary Service
Canadian Pension Commission
Canadian Radio-television and Telecommunications Commission
Canadian Transport Commission
Defence Research Board
Director of Soldier Settlement
The Director, The Veterans' Land Act
Dominion Bureau of Statistics
Emergency Measures Organization
Energy Supplies Allocation Board
Canadian International Development Agency
Federal-Provincial Relations Office
Fisheries Research Board
Foreign Investment Review Agency
Government Printing Bureau
Immigration Appeal Board
Information Canada
International Joint Commission (Canadian Section)
The Law Reform Commission of Canada
Maritimes Marshland Rehabilitation Administration
Ministry of State for Economic Development
Ministry of State for Science and Technology
Ministry of State for Social Development
Municipal Development and Loan Board
National Capital Commission
National Energy Board

National Library
National Museums of Canada
National Parole Board
Northern Pipeline Agency
Office of the Chief Electoral Officer
Officer of the Commissioner for Federal Judicial Affairs
Officer of the Commissioner of Official Languages
Office of the Co-ordinator, Status of Women
Office of the Governor-General's Secretary
Offices of the Information and Privacy Commissioners of Canada
Office of the Representation Commission
Office of the Superintendent of Bankruptcy
Prairie Farm Assistance Administration
Prairie Farm Rehabilitation Administration
Privy Council Office
Public Service Commission
Restrictive Trade Practices Commission
Royal Canadian Mounted Police
*Staff of the Exchequer Court
Staff of the Supreme Court
Statute Revision Commission
Tariff Board
Tax Appeal Board
Unemployment Insurance Commission
War Veterans Allowance Board

* The Schedule of the Federal Court Act R.S.C. 1970 (2nd supp.) c. 10
  did not change this term.

Schedule I, Part II

Portions of the Public Service of Canada that are Separate
Employers:
Atomic Energy Control Board
Canadian Advisory Council on the Status of Women
Communications Security Establishment, Department of National Defence
Economic Council of Canada
Medical Research Council
National Film Board
National Research Council of Canada
Natural Sciences and Engineering Research Council
Northern Canada Power Commission
Public Service Staff Relations Board
Science Council of Canada
Social Sciences and Humanities Research Council
Staff of the Non-Public Funds, Canadian Forces

Appendix E

Public Service Superannuation Act, as amended, Schedule A, Parts I and II

Public Service Superannuation Act, R.S.C. 1970, c. P-36, as amended by R.S.C. 1970 (1st supp.), c. 32, s. 1, s. 4; R.S.C. 1970 (2nd supp.), c. 14, s. 27; S.C. 1973–74, c. 36, s. 9; S.C. 1974–75–76, c. 81, ss. 2–27; S.C. 1976–77, c. 28, s. 35; S.C. 1980–81–82–83, c. 64, ss. 2–5; S.C. 1980–81–82–83, c. 100, ss. 39, 40

Schedule A as amended by:

SOR/70-367; SOR/70-485; SOR/71-211; SOR/71-212;
SOR/71-312; SOR/71-372; SI/72-12; SI/72-23;
SI/72-36; SI/72-41; SI/73-2; SI/73-90;
SI/74-5; S.C. 1973–74, c. 52, s. 8; SI/74-36;
S.C. 1974–75–76, c. 16, s. 3; S.C. 1974–75–76; c. 75,
ss. 10, 16, 29; S.C. 1974–75–76, c. 77, s. 8;
S.C. 1974–75–76, c. 108, s. 40; SI/75-32;
SI/75-38; SI/75-63; SI/76-47; SI/76-51;
SI/76-88; SI/76-156; S.C. 1976–77, c. 33, s. 67;
SI/77-70; SI/77-188; S.C. 1977–78, c. 20, s. 25;
S.C. 1977–78, c. 29, s. 23; SI/78-2; SI/78-11;
SI/78-27; SI/78-48; SI/78-67; SI/78-78;
S.C. 1978–79, c. 13, s. 15; S.C. 1978–79, c. 17, s. 8;
SI/79-114; SI/79-116; SI/79-139; SI/80-106;
SI/81-6; SI/81-7; S.C. 1980–81–82–83, c. 47,
s. 38; SI/81-38; SI/81-84; SI/82-86;
S.C. 1980–81–82–83, c. 112, s. 20; SOR/83-420;
SI/83-90; S.C. 1980–81–82–83, c. 158, s. 58, Item 5;
S.C. 1980–81–82–83, c. 165, s. 41

Schedule A, Part I

Boards, Commissions and Corporations
Forming Part of the Public Service

Advisory Council on the Status of Women
Agricultural Stabilization Board
Atomic Energy Control Board
Atomic Energy of Canada Limited
Canada Lands Company (Mirabel) Limited
Canadian Arsenals Limited

Canadian Aviation Safety Board
Canadian Dairy Commission
Canadian Film Development Corporation
Canadian Grain Commission
Canadian Human Rights Commission
Canadian Livestock Feed Board
Teleglobe Canada
Canadian Patents and Development Limited
Canadian Pension Commission
Canadian Wheat Board
Cape Breton Development Corporation
Commission of Inquiry on Aviation Safety
Commission Concerning Certain Activities of the Royal Canadian Mounted Police
Commission into Certain Allegations Concerning Commercial Practices of the Canadian Dairy Commission
Commission of Inquiry into Bilingual Air Traffic Services in Quebec
Commission Relating to Public Complaints, Internal Discipline and Grievance Procedure within the Royal Canadian Mounted Police
Crown Assets Disposal Corporation
Defence Construction (1951) Limited
Defence Research Board
Director of Soldier Settlement
Economic Council of Canada
Export Development Corporation
Farm Credit Corporation
Fisheries and Oceans Research Advisory Council
Fisheries Prices Support Board
Fisheries Research Board
Food Prices Review Board
Foreign Claims Commission
Indian Claims Commission
International Joint Commission
The Jacques Cartier and Champlain Bridges Inc.
Loto Canada Inc.
Medical Research Council
Municipal Development and Loan Board
National Battlefields Commission
National Capital Commission
National Commission on Inflation
National Film Board
National Harbours Board
National Museums of Canada
National Research Council of Canada
Natural Sciences and Engineering Research Council

Newfoundland and Labrador Development Corporation
Northern Canada Power Commission
Northern Pipeline Agency
Office of the Correctional Investigator
Petro-Canada
Prices and Incomes Commission (established by Order-in-Council
   P.C. 1969–1249 of 19th June, 1969)
Public Service Commission
Restrictive Trade Practices Commission
Royal Commission on Bilingualism and Biculturalism
Royal Commission on Corporate Concentration
Royal Commission on Farm Machinery
Royal Commission on Financial Management and Accountability
Royal Commission on Newspapers
Royal Commission on the Status of Women in Canada
Royal Commission on Terms and Conditions of Foreign Service
Science Council of Canada
Tariff Board
Task Force on Canadian Unity
Tax Court of Canada
The Director, Veterans' Land Act
The St. Lawrence Seaway Authority
The Seaway International Bridge Corporation Limited
Unemployment Insurance Commission
War Veterans Allowance Board

Schedule A, Part II

Portions of the public service of Canada declared for greater certainty
to be part of the Public Service

A citizenship judge appointed by the Governor in Council pursuant to
   the *Canadian Citizenship Act*
Anti-Inflation Board
Anti-Inflation Tribunal
Atlantic Pilotage Authority
Auditor General of Canada and Office of the Auditor General of Canada
Bureau of Pensions Advocates, Pension Review Board
Canadian Transport Commission
Chief Electoral Officer and Office of the Chief Electoral Officer
Clerk of the Privy Council and Privy Council Office
Communications Security Establishment
Director General of Security and Intelligence
Employees of the Government of the Northwest Territories (which
   Government is deemed for purposes of section 25 to be a Public

Service Corporation)

Employees of the Government of the Yukon Territory (which Government is deemed for purposes of section 25 to be a Public Service Corporation)

Energy Supplies Allocation Board

Governor General's Secretary and Office of the Governor General's Secretary

Great Lakes Pilotage Authority

Immigration Appeal Board

Laurentian Pilotage Board

Members of the staff of the Canadian Council of Resources Ministers

Members of the staff of the Canadian International Grains Institute

Members of the staff of Government House paid by the Governor General from his salary or allowance

Members of the staff of Heritage Canada

Members of the staff of the Parliamentary Centre for Foreign Affairs and Foreign Trade

Office of the Administrator under the *Anti-Inflation Act*

Office of the Commissioner for Federal Judicial Affairs

Office of the Commissioner of Penitentiaries

Office of the Custodian of Enemy Property (which is deemed for purposes of section 25 to be a Public Service Corporation)

Pacific Pilotage Authority

Petroleum Monitoring Agency

Postmasters and Assistant Postmasters in Revenue Post Offices

Public Service Staff Relations Board

Refugee Status Advisory Committee

Secretary to the Cabinet for Federal-Provincial Relations and Federal-Provincial Relations Office

Taxation Division, Department of National Revenue

[Part III Omitted from this Version]

Appendix F

Formal Documents Regulations, as amended

Formal Documents Regulations, C.R.C. 1978, c. 1331, amended SOR/82-400

1. Section 4 provides that Commissions under the Great Seal shall issue to persons appointed to the following offices:
   1. Governor General
   2. Federal Cabinet Ministers and Members of the Queen's Privy Council for Canada not of the Cabinet
   3. Lieutenant-Governors

4. Provincial Administrators
5. Ambassadors and Officers having the rank of Ambassador who are not included in any other category contained in these Regulations
   High Commissioners
   Envoys Extraordinary and
   Ministers Plenipotentiary
6. Federally appointed judges
7. Commissioners under the Judges Act
8. Senators
9. Officers of Parliament:
   (a) Speaker of the Senate
   (b) Clerk of the Senate
       Clerk of the House of Commons
       Sergeant-at-Arms
       Parliamentary Librarian
       Associate Parliamentary Librarian
       Gentleman Usher of the Black Rod
10. Deputy Ministers and Officers having the rank of Deputy Minister who are not included in any other category contained in these Regulations
11. Regular members and officers of permanent federal commissions, boards and corporations
12. Regular members of permanent international commissions
13. Commissioners under the *Inquiries Act*
14. Commissioner and Deputy Commissioner of the Northwest Territories
15. Commissioner and Administrator of the Yukon Territory
16. Chief of the Defence Staff
17. Commissioner and Officers of the Royal Canadian Mounted Police upon their first appointment to the rank of an officer
18. Federally appointed Queen's Counsel
19. Commissioners to administer oaths (whether oaths of allegiance and office, affidavits for use in the Supreme and Exchequer Courts or any other oaths or affidavits)
20. Persons to whom the issuance of a commission under the Great Seal is provided for by law and who are not included in any other category contained in this section

2. Section 5 provides that commissions under the Privy Seal shall issue to persons appointed to the following offices:
   Officers of the Canadian Forces
   Deputies of the Governor General
   Deputies of the Administrator
   Offices of the Canadian Forces when there is an Administrator
3. Section 6 provides that Commissions under the Seal of the Registrar

General shall issue to persons appointed to the following offices:
1. Consuls General, Consuls and Vice Consuls
2. Temporary or *ad hoc* members of permanent federal commissions, boards and corporations
3. Members of temporary federal commissions, boards and corporations
4. Registrars and Marshals in Admiralty
5. Persons in the public service of Canada appointed under an order in council who are not included in any other category contained in section 4, in section 5 or in this section and to whom the Registrar General deems it appropriate that a commission should issue

Appendix G

Departments of Government

Department of Agriculture	R.S.C. 1970, c. A-10
Department of Communications	R.S.C. 1970, c. C-24, as amended by S.C. 1980–81–82–83, c. 54, s. 56 (Item 5)
Department of Consumer and Corporate Affairs	R.S.C. 1970, c. C-27
Department of Employment and Immigration	S.C. 1976–77, c. 54; as amended by S.C. 1980–81–82–83, c. 47, s. 13(F)
Department of Energy, Mines and Resources	R.S.C. 1970, c. E-6; as amended by R.S.C. (2nd supp.), c. 14, s. 8; S.C. 1978–79, c. 13, s. 34; S.C. 1980–81–82–83, c. 106, s. 1
Department of the Environment	R.S.C. 1970 (2nd supp.), c. 14, ss. 2–7, s. 30, Sched. 1; S.C. 1977–78, c. 41, s. 5(2); S.C. 1978–79, c. 13, ss. 13 and 14; SI/78-87
Department of External Affairs	S.C. 1980–81–82–83, c. 167, ss. 2–14.
Department of Fisheries and Oceans	S.C. 1978–79, c. 13, ss. 2–7

Department of Finance	*Financial Administration Act*, R.S.C. 1970, c. F-10, as amended by S.C. 1974–75–76, c. 33, s. 265 (Item 3); S.C. 1976–77, c. 18, s. 1; S.C. 1976–77, c. 34, s. 23, S.C. 1977–78, c. 33, s. 1; S.C. 1978–79, c. 4, ss. 4 and 5; S.C. 1978–79, c. 9, s. 1 "265"(F); S.C. 1980–81–82–83, c. 40 s. 94.1; S.C.1980–81–82–83, c. 123, ss. 1 and 2; S.C. 1980–81–82–83, c. 170, ss. 1–23
Department of Indian Affairs and Northern Development	R.S.C. 1970, c. I-7; as amended by R.S.C. 1970 (2nd. supp.), c. 14, s. 31 (Item 3)
Department of Insurance	R.S.C. 1970, c. 1-17
Department of Justice	R.S.C. 1970, c. J-2
Department of Labour	R.S.C. 1970, c. L-2; as amended by S.C. 1980–81–82–83, c. 60
Department of National Defence	R.S.C. 1970, c. N-4, as amended by R.S.C. 1970 (1st supp.), c. 44, s. 10 (Item 5); R.S.C. 1970 (2nd supp.), c. 10, s. 65 (Item 23); S.C. 1972, c. 13, ss. 73 and 73.1; S.C. 1974–75–76, c. 36, Sch. (DND), vote 1d; S.C. 1974–75–76, c. 66, s. 21; S/I 74-27; S.C. 1976–77, c. 24, s. 62 and s. 63; 1980–81–82–83, c. 17, s. 16; S.C. 1980–81–82–83, c. 125, s. 32
Department of National Health and Welfare	R.S.C. 1970, c. N-9; as amended by R.S.C. 1970 (2nd supp.), c. 14, s. 5(g); SOR 370-517; S.C. 1976–77, c. 28, s. 29

Department of National Revenue	R.S.C. 1970, c. N-15
Department of Public Works	R.S.C. 1970, c. P-38, as amended by S.C. 1976-77, c. 28, s. 36, S.C. 1977-78, c. 22, s. 21
Department of Regional Industrial Expansion	R.S.C. 1970, c. I-11, as amended by S.C. 1974-75-76, c. 59, s. 1; S.C. 1980-81-82-83, c. 167, ss. 15 and 16
Department of the Solicitor General	R.S.C. 1970, c. S-12
Department of State	R.S.C. 1970, c. S-15
Department of Supply and Services	R.S.C. 1970, c. S-18
Department of Transport	R.S.C. 1970, c. T-15
Department of Veterans Affairs	R.S.C. 1970, c. V-1; as amended by S.C. 1972, c. 12, s. 8

Appendix H

Salaries Act, as amended

Salaries Act, R.S.C. 1970, c. S-2, as amended by R.S.C. 1970 (2nd supp.) c. 14, s. 28 and s. 31 (Item 7); S.C. 1974-75-76, c. 44, s. 5; S.C. 1974-75-76, c. 56. s. 1; S.C. 1978-79, c. 13, s. 34 (Item 2); S.C. 1980-81-82-83, c. 54, s. 56 (Item 13); S.C. 1980-81-82-83, c. 77, s. 6; S.C. 1980-81-82-83, c. 149, ss. 1 and 2; S.C. 1980-81-82-83, c. 167, s. 34, Sch. I, Item 22

This Act provides for the salaries of the following public officials:
Lieutenant Governors of the Provinces (s. 3)
Ministers, members of the Queen's Privy Council for Canada, namely (s. 4):
The member of the Queen's Privy Council holding the recognized position of First Minister
The Minister of Justice and Attorney-General

The Minister of National Defence
The Minister of National Revenue
The Minister of Finance
The Minister of Transport
The Minister of Public Works
The President of the Queen's Privy Council for Canada
The Minister of Agriculture
The Secretary of State of Canada
The Minister of Labour
The Secretary of State for External Affairs
The Minister of National Health and Welfare
The Minister of Veterans Affairs
The Associate Minister of National Defence
The Solicitor General of Canada
The Minister of Consumer and Corporate Affairs
The Minister of Employment and Immigration
The Minister of Indian Affairs and Northern Development
The Minister of Energy, Mines and Resources
The President of the Treasury Board
The Minister of the Environment
The Minister of Communications
The Minister of Supply and Services
The Leader of the Government in the Senate
The Minister of Fisheries and Oceans
The Minister of Regional Industrial Expansion
The Minister of International Trade
The Minister for External Relations

Each Minister of State, being a member of the Queen's Privy Council for Canada, who presides over a Ministry of State (s. 5)

Table of Government Institutions

GOVERNMENT DEPARTMENT	Privacy Act (Sch. I)	Access to Information (Sch.I)	P.S.S.R. Part I	P.S.S.R. Part II	P.S.S.A. Sch. A Part I	P.S.S.A. Sch. A Part 2	Financial Admin A	B	C I	C II
Department of Agriculture	x	x	x				x			
Department of Communications	x	x	x				x			
Department of Consumer and Corporate Affairs	x	x	x				x			
Ministry of State for Economic and Regional Development	x	x	x				x			
Department of Employment and Immigration	x	x	x				x			
Department of Energy, Mines and Resources	x	x	x				x			
Department of the Environment	x	x	x				x			
Department of External Affairs	x	x	x				x			
Department of Finance	x	x	x				x			
Department of Fisheries and Oceans	x	x	x				x			
Department of Indian Affairs and Northern Development	x	x	x				x			
Department of Insurance	x	x	x				x			

Appendix I (cont'd)

GOVERNMENT DEPARTMENT	Privacy Act (Sch. I)	Access to Infor- mation (Sch.I)	P.S.S.R.		P.S.S.A.		Financial Admin			
			Part I	Part II	Sch. A Part I	Sch. A Part 2	A	B	C I	C II
Department of Justice	x	x	x				x			
Department of Labour	x	x	x				x			
Department of National Defence (includes the Canadian Forces)	x	x	x				x			
Department of National Health and Welfare	x	x	x				x			
Department of National Revenue	x	x	x				x			
Department of Public Works	x	x	x				x			
Department of Regional Industrial Expansion	x	x	x				x			
Ministry of State for Science and Technology	x	x	x				x			
Department of the Secretary of State	x	x	x				x			
Department of the Solicitor General	x	x	x				x			
Department of Supply and Services	x	x	x				x			

DEPARTMENT / OTHER INSTITUTION	Privacy Act (Sch. I)	Access to Information (Sch.I)	P.S.S.R. Part I	P.S.S.R. Part II	P.S.S.A. Sch. A Part I	P.S.S.A. Sch. A Part 2	Financial Admin A	Financial Admin B	Financial Admin C I	Financial Admin C II
Department of Transport	x	x	x				x			
Treasury Board							x			
Department of Veterans Affairs	x	x	x				x			
Other Government Institutions										
A Citizenship Judge pursuant to Canadian Citizenship Act						x				
Advisory Council on the Status of Women	x	x		x	x					
Agricultural Products Board	x	x								
Agricultural Stabilization Board	x	x	x		x			x		
Air Canada										x
Anti-Dumping Tribunal	x	x								
Anti-Inflation Board			x			x				
Anti-Inflation Tribunal			x			x				
Atlantic Development Board			x							

Appendix I (cont'd)

GOVERNMENT INSTITUTION	Privacy Act (Sch. I)	Access to Information (Sch.I)	P.S.S.R. Part I	P.S.S.R. Part II	P.S.S.A. Sch. A Part 1	P.S.S.A. Sch. A Part 2	Financial Admin A	Financial Admin B	Financial Admin C I	Financial Admin C II
Atlantic Development Council	x	x								
Atlantic Pilotage Authority	x	x							x	
Atomic Energy of Canada		x		x	x				x	
Atomic Energy Control Board					x			x		
Auditor General of Canada and Office of Auditor General of Canada						x				
Bank of Canada	x	x								
Bilingual Districts Advisory Board	x	x								
Board of Grain Commissioners			x							
Board of Trustees of the Queen Elizabeth II Canadian Fund to Aid in Research on the Diseases of Children	x	x								
Bureau of Pension Advocates	x	x	x			x				
Canada Council	x	x								
Canada Deposit Insurance Corporation	x	x							x	

GOVERNMENT INSTITUTION	Privacy Act (Sch. I)	Access to Information (Sch.I)	P.S.S.R. Part I	P.S.S.R. Part II	P.S.S.A. Sch. A Part 1	P.S.S.A. Sch. A Part 2	Financial Admin A	Financial Admin B	Financial Admin C I	Financial Admin C II
Canada Development Investment Corporation										x
Canada Employment and Immigration Commission	x	x	x		x			x		
Canada Labour Relations Board	x	x								
Canada Lands Company Limited					x				x	
Canada Mortgage and Housing Corporation	x	x							x	
Canada Ports Corporation										x
Canada Post Corporation	x								x	
Canadian Arsenals Limited					x				x	
Canadian Aviation Safety Board	x	x	x		x			x		
Canadian Broadcasting Corporation										
Canadian Centre for Occupational Health and Safety	x	x						x		
Canadian Commercial Corporation	x	x							x	
Canadian Cultural Property Export Review Board	x	x								

Appendix I (cont'd)

GOVERNMENT INSTITUTION	Privacy Act (Sch. I)	Access to Information (Sch.I)	P.S.S.R. Part I	P.S.S.R. Part II	P.S.S.A. Sch. A Part I	P.S.S.A. Sch. A Part 2	Financial Admin A	B	C I	C II
Canadian Dairy Commission	x	x	x		x				x	
Canadian Film Development Corporation	x	x			x					
Canadian Forces		x								
Canadian Government Specifications Board	x	x								
Canadian Grain Commission	x	x			x					
Canadian Human Rights Commission	x	x	x		x					
Canadian Intergovernmental Conference Secretariat	x	x	x							
Canadian International Development Agency			x							
Canadian Livestock Feed Board	x	x	x		x					
Canadian National Railway										x
Canadian National (West Indies) Steamships, Limited									x	

GOVERNMENT INSTITUTION	Privacy Act (Sch. I)	Access to Information (Sch.I)	P.S.S.R. Part I	P.S.S.R. Part II	P.S.S.A. Sch. A Part I	P.S.S.A. Sch. A Part 2	Financial Admin A	B	C I	C II
Canadian Patents and Development Limited	X				X				X	
Canadian Penitentiary Service	X	X	X							
Canadian Pension Commission	X	X	X		X					
Canadian Radio-television and Telecommunications Commission	X	X	X							
Canadian Saltfish Corporation	X	X							X	
Canadian Sports Pool Corporation									X	
Canadian Transport Commission	X	X	X			X				
Canadian Unity Information Office	X	X								
The Canadian Wheat Board	X				X					
Canagrex									X	
Cape Breton Development Corporation					X				X	
Centennial Commission										

Appendix I (cont'd)

GOVERNMENT INSTITUTION	Privacy Act (Sch. I)	Access to Information (Sch.I)	P.S.S.R. Part I	P.S.S.R. Part II	P.S.S.A. Sch. A Part I	P.S.S.A. Sch. A Part 2	Financial Admin A	Financial Admin B	Financial Admin C I	Financial Admin C II
Central Mortgage and Housing Corporation										
Chief Electoral Officer and Office of Chief Electoral Officer						x				
Clerk of the Privy Council and Privy Council Office						x				
Communications Security Establishment, Department of National Defence			x			x				
Crown Assets Disposal Corporation	x	x			x			x		
Defence Construction (1951) Limited	x	x			x				x	
Defence Research Board			x		x					
The Director of Soldier Settlement	x	x	x		x			x		
The Director, The Veterans' Land Act	x	x	x		x			x		
Director-General Security and Intelligence						x				
Economic Council of Canada	x	x		x	x			x		
Eldorado Aviation Limited										

GOVERNMENT INSTITUTION	Privacy Act (Sch. I)	Access to Information (Sch.I)	P.S.S.R. Part I	P.S.S.R. Part II	P.S.S.A. Sch. A Part 1	P.S.S.A. Sch. A Part 2	Financial Admin A	Financial Admin B	Financial Admin C I	Financial Admin C II
Eldorado Nuclear Limited										
Emergency Measures Organization			X							
Energy Supplies Allocation Board	X	X	X			X				
Export Development Corporation	X				X				X	
Farm Credit Corporation	X	X			X				X	
Federal Business Development Bank	X	X								
Federal Mortgage Exchange Corporation	X	X							X	
Federal–Provincial Relations Office	X	X	X							
Fisheries Prices Support Board	X	X			X			X		
Fisheries and Oceans Research Advisory Board	X	X	X	X						
Fisheries Research Board of Canada	X	X	X		X					
Food Prices Review Board					X					
Foreign Claims Commission					X					
Foreign Investment Review Agency	X	X	X							

Appendix I (cont'd)

GOVERNMENT INSTITUTION	Privacy Act (Sch. I)	Access to Information (Sch.I)	P.S.S.R. Part I	P.S.S.R. Part II	P.S.S.A. Sch. A Part 1	P.S.S.A. Sch. A Part 2	Financial Admin A	Financial Admin B	Financial Admin C I	Financial Admin C II
Freshwater Fish Marketing Corporation	x	x							x	
Government Printing Bureau			x							
Governor General's Secretary						x				
Grain Transportation Agency Administration	x	x								
Great Lakes Pilotage Authority, Ltd	x	x				x			x	
Harbourfront Corporation									x	
Historic Sites and Monuments Board of Canada	x	x								
Immigration Appeal Board	x	x	x							
Indian Claims Commission					x					
Information Canada			x							
International Development Research Centre	x	x								
International Joint Commission (Canadian Section)			x		x					

GOVERNMENT INSTITUTION	Privacy Act (Sch. I)	Access to Information (Sch.I)	P.S.S.R. Part I	P.S.S.R. Part II	P.S.S.A. Sch. A Part 1	P.S.S.A. Sch. A Part 2	Financial Admin A	B	C I	C II
Jacques Cartier and Champlain Bridges Incorporated	x				x					
Laurentian Pilotage Authority	x	x				x			x	
Law Reform Commission of Canada	x	x	x							
Loto Canada Inc.					x				x	
Maritimes Marshland Rehabilitation Administration			x							
Medical Research Council	x	x		x	x			x		
Members of the staff of the Canadian Council of Resource Ministers						x				
Members of the staff of the Canadian International Grains Institute						x				
Members of the staff of Government House paid by the Governor General						x				
Members of the staff of Heritage Canada						x				
Merchant Seamen Compensation Board	x	x								

Appendix I (cont'd)

GOVERNMENT INSTITUTION	Privacy Act (Sch. I)	Access to Information (Sch.I)	P.S.S.R. Part I	P.S.S.R. Part II	P.S.S.A. Sch. A Part I	P.S.S.A. Sch. A Part 2	Financial Admin A	Financial Admin B	Financial Admin C I	Financial Admin C II
Metric Commission	x	x								
Mingan Associates Ltd.									x	
Montreal Port Corporation										x
Municipal Development and Loan Board			x		x					
National Arts Centre Corporation	x									
The National Battlefields Commission	x	x	x		x			x		
National Capital Commission	x	x	x		x				x	
National Design Council	x	x								
National Energy Board	x	x	x							
National Farm Products Marketing Council	x	x								
National Film Board	x	x		x	x					

GOVERNMENT INSTITUTION	Privacy Act (Sch. I)	Access to Information (Sch.I)	P.S.S.R. Part I	P.S.S.R. Part II	P.S.S.A. Sch. A Part 1	P.S.S.A. Sch. A Part 2	Financial Admin A	Financial Admin B	Financial Admin C I	Financial Admin C II
National Gallery of Canada										
National Harbours Board	x	x								
National Library	x	x	x							
National Museums of Canada	x	x	x		x			x		
National Parole Board	x	x	x							
National Parole Service	x	x								
National Research Council of Canada	x	x		x	x			x		
Natural Sciences and Engineering Research Council	x	x		x	x			x		
Newfoundland and Labrador Development Corporation					x					
Northern Canada Power Commission	x	x		x	x				x	
Northern Pipeline Agency	x	x	x		x					
Northern Transportation Company Limited										x
Northwest Territories Water Board	x	x								

Appendix I (cont'd)

GOVERNMENT INSTITUTION	Privacy Act (Sch. I)	Access to Information (Sch.I)	P.S.S.R. Part I	P.S.S.R. Part II	P.S.S.A. Sch. A Part 1	P.S.S.A. Sch. A Part 2	Financial Admin A	B	C I	C II
Office of the Administrator under the Anti-Inflation Board						x				
Office of the Auditor General	x									
Office of the Chief Electoral Officer	x		x							
Office of the Commissioner for Federal Judicial Affairs			x			x				
Office of the Commissioner of Official Languages	x		x							
Office of the Commissioner of Penitentiaries						x				
Office of the Comptroller General	x	x								
Office of the Co-ordinator, Status of Women	x		x							
Office of the Correctional Investigator	x	x			x					
Office of the Custodian of Enemy Property	x	x				x				
Office of the Governor General's Secretary			x			x				
Office of the Information and Privacy Commissioners of Canada			x							

GOVERNMENT INSTITUTION	Privacy Act (Sch. I)	Access to Information (Sch.I)	P.S.S.R. Part I	P.S.S.R. Part II	P.S.S.A. Sch. A Part I	P.S.S.A. Sch. A Part 2	Financial Admin A	Financial Admin B	Financial Admin C I	Financial Admin C II
Office of the Representation Commission			x							
Office of the Superintendent of Bankruptcy			x							
Pacific Pilotage Authority	x	x				x			x	
Pêcheries Canada Inc.									x	
Pension Appeals Board	x	x								
Pension Review Board	x	x								
Petro-Canada					x					x
Petroleum Compensation Board	x	x								
Petroleum Monitoring Agency	x	x								
Port of Quebec Corporation									x	
Prairie Farm Assistance Administration	x	x	x							
Prairie Farm Rehabilitation Administration	x	x	x							

Appendix I (cont'd)

GOVERNMENT INSTITUTION	Privacy Act (Sch. I)	Access to Information (Sch.I)	P.S.S.R. Part I	P.S.S.R. Part II	P.S.S.A. Sch. A Part I	P.S.S.A. Sch. A Part 2	Financial Admin A	B	C I	C II
Privy Council Office	x	x	x							
Public Archives	x	x	x							
Public Service Commission	x	x	x		x					
Public Service Staff Relations Board	x	x		x		x				
Public Works Lands Company Limited	x	x							x	
Refugee Status Advisory Committee						x				
Regional Development Incentives Board	x	x								
Restrictive Trade Practices Commission	x	x	x		x					
Royal Canadian Mint	x	x							x	
Royal Canadian Mounted Police	x	x	x							
St. Anthony Fisheries Limited									x	
The St. Lawrence Seaway Authority	x	x			x				x	

GOVERNMENT INSTITUTION	Privacy Act (Sch. I)	Access to Information (Sch.I)	P.S.S.R.		P.S.S.A.		Financial Admin			
			Part I	Part II	Sch. A Part I	Sch. A Part 2	A	B	C I	C II
Science Council of Canada	x	x		x		x		x		
The Seaway International Bridge Corporation, Ltd.	x	x				x				x
Secretary to the Cabinet for Federal–Provincial Relations and Federal–Provincial Relations Office						x				
Social Sciences and Humanities Research Council	x	x		x				x		
Societa a responsibilita limitata Immobiliare San Sebastiano									x	
Staff of the Exchequer Court			x							
Staff of the Non-Public Funds, Canadian Forces				x						
Staff of the Supreme Court			x							
Standards Council of Canada	x	x								
Statistics Canada	x	x	x							
Statute Revision Commission	x	x	x							
Task Force on Canadian Unity					x					

GOVERNMENT INSTITUTION	Privacy Act (Sch. I)	Access to Information (Sch.I)	P.S.S.R. Part I	P.S.S.R. Part II	P.S.S.A. Sch. A Part 1	P.S.S.A. Sch. A Part 2	Financial Admin A	Financial Admin B	Financial Admin C I	Financial Admin C II
Tariff Board	x	x	x		x					
Tax Appeal Board			x							
Tax Court of Canada					x					
Tax Review Board	x	x	x							
Teleglobe Canada					x					x
Textile and Clothing Board	x	x								
Treasury Board Secretariat	x	x								
Uranium Canada, Limited	x	x							x	
Vancouver Port Authority										x
Via Rail Canada Inc.									x	
War Veterans Allowance Board	x	x	x		x					
Yukon Territory Water Board	x	x								

Notes

This study was completed in December 1984.

I would like to thank my partner J.C. Baillie, Q.C., for his valuable comments on a draft of this paper, and Debra Walker for all her assistance in preparing the manuscript and doing the tables.

1. W.P.M. Kennedy, *The Constitution of Canada 1534-1937*, 2d ed. (Toronto: Oxford University Press, 1938).

2. Katherine Swinton, "Application of the Canadian Charter of Rights and Freedoms" in *The Canadian Charter of Rights and Freedoms: Commentary*, edited by W.S. Tarnopolsky and G.A. Beaudoin (Toronto: Carswell, 1982), p. 49.

3. Ibid., at p. 59.

4. See *Jorgensen v. B.C. Ice and Cold Storage Ltd. and United Fishermen & Allied Workers Union*, II C.H.R.R. D/289 (Smith, p. D/298-299); *Bhinder v. C.N.R.*, II C.H.R.R. D/546 (Cumming et al., p. D/558); *Carson et al. v. Air Canada*, V C.H.R.R. D1857 (Kerr et al., p. D/1862), *Nelson & Atco Lumber Ltd. v. Borho* (1976), 1 B.C.L.R. 207 (B.C.S.C.) p. 214.

5. I.A. Hunter, "Human Rights Legislation in Canada" (1976), 15 U.W.O. L.Rev. 21, p. 33.

6. Ibid., at p. 30.

7. *The Shorter Oxford English Dictionary*, 3d ed. (Oxford: Clarendon Press, 1973), p. 564. The text of the definition of "discriminate" given there is: 1. To make or constitute a difference in or between; to differentiate. 2. To perceive or note the difference in or between; to distinguish. 3. To make a distinction. In the examples following the definition the phrase "To discriminate against" is defined as "to make an adverse distinction with regard to." By contrast, Walter Tarnopolsky has pointed out that the term "discrimination" as used in Canadian human rights legislation is intended to have the third of the three meanings suggested in Webster's *New World Dictionary of the American Language*, namely "A showing of partiality or prejudice in treatment; specific action or policies directed against the welfare of minority groups": Walter S. Tarnopolsky, *Discrimination and the Law* (Toronto: Richard De Boo, 1982), p. 85.

8. In the case of *R. v. Moore* (1983), 10 C.C.C. (3d) 306 (Ont. H.C.J.).

9. *Report of the Commission on Equality in Employment* (Ottawa: Minister of Supply and Services Canada, 1984), p. 12.

10. John D. Whyte, "The Effect of the Charter of Rights on Non-Criminal Law and Administration" (1982), III C.H.R.R. c/82-7 at p. c./82-10 and 11.

11. Jill McCalla Vickers, "Major Equality Issues of the Eighties" in *Canadian Human Rights Yearbook 1983* (Toronto: Carswell, 1983), pp. 47ff.

12. Ibid., p. 56.

13. Ibid., p. 55.

14. Ibid., p. 55.

15. Ibid., p. 56.

16. Ibid.

17. Ibid., p. 57.

18. Information obtained from CREF.

19. *Supra*, note 11, p. 57.

20. *The Shorter Oxford English Dictionary*, supra, note 7, p. 673. The meanings given are: 1. Identical in amount, magnitude, number value, intensity, etc; neither less nor greater. 2. Possessing a like degree of a quality or attribute; on the same level in dignity, power, excellence, etc.; having the same rights or privileges. 3. Adequate or fit in quantity or degree; adequately fit or qualified. Of persons: Having competent strength, endurance, or ability. 4. Evenly proportioned; uniform in effect or operation. 5. Fair, equitable, impartial. . . .

4

The Problem of Section 96 of the Constitution Act, 1867

GILLES PÉPIN

Introduction

Section 92(14) of the *Constitution Act, 1867* gives the legislatures, within their respective provinces, "exclusive" jurisdiction over the "administration of justice," specifically for organizing "Provincial Courts, both of Civil and of Criminal Jurisdiction" and providing for their maintenance.

Each province now has a system of courts of justice, not necessarily identical to each other, but in their essence conforming to the following model: *lower courts* of first instance, often of mixed jurisdiction (civil and criminal); a *superior court* with initial jurisdiction over any action not expressly assigned to the lower courts, and specifically empowered with a supervisory power over the latter in order to restrain them, where necessary, from exceeding the limits of their jurisdiction; a collegial *appeal court*, charged, where required, with correcting decisions of judges of the lower courts or the superior court, and with assuring uniformity in the various decisions of the many judges of first instance who sit in the different judicial districts of the province[1].

However, the actual text of the *Constitution Act, 1867* makes some important exceptions to this so-called exclusive power of the provinces with regard to judicial organization. These appear in sections 96 to 101 in a chapter entitled "Judicature."

Sections 96 to 100 give the federal authorities important responsibilities in the organization of the courts of justice created by the legislatures. Judges of the main provincial courts, that is "the Superior, District and County Courts," are appointed pursuant to section 96[2] by the Governor General of Canada. In fact, this is the decision of the federal Cabinet, based on the recommendation of the federal minister of justice, who will at the very least have consulted a committee of the Canadian Bar Association.[3] Sections 97 and 98 require the Governor General to appoint judges from among the members of the bar in the province concerned. Section 100 gives Parliament the responsibility for fixing the salaries, pensions and allowances of the superior, district and county court judges, and for providing the sums necessary for this purpose.[4] Section 99, amended in 1960, and dealing with judges of the superior courts — there is no mention of county or district courts — requires them to retire at the age of 75 and states that until that time they hold office during good behaviour, but that they be removed by the Governor General on the request of the Senate and House of Commons.[5]

It is already clear from these provisions that the courts established by a legislature do not come within the exclusive jurisdiction of the legislature, and that their maintenance requires the participation of federal authorities (Parliament and the Government). Furthermore, section 96 is one in a series of sections of the Constitution that deal with the same kind of concern: the status of judges of the major provincial courts (i.e. their appointment, removal, allowances and benefits); the *Constitution Act, 1867* makes no reference to members of the other courts of justice.[6] Mr. Justice Pigeon's remarks about the provincial superior courts are easy to understand:

> While it is usual to refer to these courts as provincial, they are so only in a limited sense. Under s. 96 the federal government plays the most important role in their establishment: the appointment of the judges and, under s. 100, their salaries are fixed and provided by Parliament.[7]

The federal authorities also have other powers in matters of judicial organization, as can be seen in section 101.[8] However, that is not a case of responsibilities directly related to the maintenance of provincial courts established by the legislatures.

According to section 101, Parliament has exclusive jurisdiction — and this is without restriction — to establish a general court of appeal for all of Canada, and to define its composition and powers. Pursuant to this section, the Supreme Court of Canada was established in 1875. The source of this supreme jurisdiction is therefore a federal statute, not the Canadian Constitution;[9] its judges are appointed, paid and may be removed from office by the federal authorities alone, and they have what is undoubtedly an important right of control over decisions of the provincial courts.[10] The provincial legislatures and executives play no role either in the composition or the powers of this supreme and federal court which ultimately "states the law" ("*jus dicere*") in force in Canada, be it federal or provincial, public or private.

Section 101 also allows Parliament to establish additional courts, parallel to the provincial courts, that are responsible, either exclusively or concurrently with the provincial courts, for better enforcement of federal law. However, in principle, it is the provincial courts that have the task in the first instance and at the first level of appeal, of settling disputes arising from the application of both provincial and federal legislation, subject to a final appeal to the Supreme Court of Canada.[11] Mention may be made here of the establishment of the Exchequer Court of Canada in 1875 and its replacement in 1971 by the present Federal Court, with a considerably enlarged jurisdiction.

The Federal Court is exclusively federal in nature; an act of the Canadian Parliament[12] defines the status of its judges (at least partially) as well as their jurisdiction, which must be limited to the application of existing federal law.[13] The judges of the Federal Court are appointed, paid and may be removed by the federal authorities.[14] According to P.W. Hogg:

> The establishment of the Federal Court, with its broader jurisdiction and more elaborate structure (it has a trial division and an appeal division), is a step in the direction of the dual court system in the United States, a system which leads to multiple litigation and complex jurisdictional disputes.[15]

It should be clear that, although the organization of the federal courts is within the exclusive jurisdiction of the Parliament of Canada, notwithstanding the "national" role and ultimate position of the Supreme Court of Canada, the same cannot be said of the jurisdiction of the legislatures with respect to the provincial courts. The latter are organized and maintained according to the tenet of cooperative federalism, under provisions contained in the Constitution. Hence, judges of the principal courts of justice in Canada, be they federal or provincial, are appointed, paid and removed by federal authorities (Parliament or the Government) and the definition of the responsibilities of the Supreme Court, in federal and provincial matters, is also the exclusive responsibility of Parliament.

Aside from the recent dispute raised by the definition of the Federal Court's jurisdiction,[16] it is section 96 of the *Constitution Act, 1867* that has been the main source of litigation and political dispute since 1867. Yet its wording seems clear enough: the Governor General shall appoint the judges of the superior, district and county courts in each province. Nevertheless, there are more than 200 reported cases dealing with the section. Over the 1975–83 period, the Supreme Court of Canada addressed the scope of section 96 on 12 occasions;[17] this figure does not include decisions dismissing petitions for leave to appeal to the court.

This plethora of trials (or references) is particularly due to the broad interpretation that the judges themselves have given to the text of section 96. In fact, this section has been construed so as to assure judges of the superior, district and county courts of a kind of monopoly in the exercise of several important judicial functions in provincial matters, thereby also assuring the effectiveness of the Governor General's power of appointment. Thus, the judges whose task it has been to interpret the Constitution have given section 96 the following meaning: the Governor General appoints the judges of the superior, district and county courts and, notwithstanding section 92(14), the provincial legislatures are not allowed, in provincial matters, to assign certain judicial functions to anyone other than these judges. Consequently, the provinces have been prevented from granting specific responsibilities either to courts presided over by judges named by the Lieutenant Governor in Council, or to institutions other than courts of justice: officers of the court, administrative tribunals, ministers, etc.

An exclusive executive power of appointment (s. 96), presented as an exception to an exclusive legislative competence over organization (s. 92(14)), has been viewed as a rule restricting the power of the provinces to provide for their own judicial and administrative organization and to assign among various provincial institutions, as they deem fit, the numerous judicial functions relating to subjects within their legislative power. Thus, for example, in 1972 the Supreme Court of Canada decided that Quebec Provincial Court judges appointed by the Lieutenant Governor in Council were, in the light of section 96, unable to exercise jurisdiction that they had been given in 1949 by the National Assembly: to quash, on grounds of illegality, a regulation enacted by a municipal corporation.[18] In 1959 this same Court also decided that the Ontario Legislature did not have the power to delegate certain powers with respect to liens to a "master," although these special powers had been granted in 1916, and notwithstanding the fact that the statute in question provided that at the request of one of the parties the dispute had to be settled by a judge of the "High Court."[19]

This broad interpretation of the scope of section 96 explains the quantity of controversies already referred to, for, rightly or wrongly, a large number of such devolutions of powers by the provinces to institutions other than the superior, district and county courts have as a result been subject to challenge. The line of demarcation between the powers within the "block" of jurisdictions that is guaranteed to "section 96 judges" and between the other judicial functions has never been precisely drawn.

There has consequently been a remarkable degree of uncertainty in the provincial administration of justice, an uncertainty that compromises the usefulness and effectiveness of the provincial courts of justice and administrative bodies. Section 96 is at the root of several judicial battles based on challenges to the jurisdiction of judges or others appointed by the provincial authorities and empowered by provincial legislation to settle disputes in matters that are constitutionally within the jurisdiction of the legislatures. The imprecision of the rules that set out the scope of section 96 has been an open invitation to lawyers who seek to buy time or annoy their opponents. As Professor Le Dain has remarked:

> The general issue in this area of the constitution is the extent to which the exclusive federal power under section 96 of the B.N.A. Act to appoint the judges of the superior, district and county courts in the provinces is to inhibit the provincial power to redistribute judicial business among the provincial courts in the interest of a more efficient administration of justice (for which

the provinces have the primary responsibility under the constitution) or to assign it to specialized tribunals for particular regulatory purposes.[20]

Until the summer of 1983, it was generally believed that the restrictions imposed on the legislative powers of the provinces by section 96 (and sections 97 to 100), and above all by the abundant case law that these sections had generated, did not apply to Parliament. The latter appeared, in federal matters, to have complete freedom to delegate judicial powers as it saw fit. This double standard did nothing to mitigate provincial complaints about section 96. However, in a unanimous, unsigned and highly enigmatic decision, the Supreme Court of Canada has formulated some propositions that are likely to open the way for more procedural battles based on section 96. In *McEvoy*, the Supreme Court declared, without, however, being particularly specific, that:

> Section 96 bars Parliament from altering the constitutional scheme envisaged by the judicature sections of the *Constitution Act, 1867* just as it does the provinces from doing so [. . .] The judicature sections of the *Constitution Act, 1867* guarantee the independence of the superior courts; they apply to Parliament as well as to the provincial Legislatures.[21]

As a source of serious problems for the provinces and soon for Parliament, section 96 must be called into question. However, its repeal or amendment cannot be considered without taking into consideration the fact that it is not an isolated provision but rather one linked closely with section 97 to 100 of the *Constitution Act, 1867*, sections that belong to the chapter entitled "Judicature."

This study endeavours to present as concisely as possible the "problem" of a section that Chief Justice Laskin, in 1982, described as a constitutional "anomaly."[22] The principal problems raised by this provision will be addressed under the following headings:

- the raisons d'être of section 96;
- the scope of section 96 in provincial matters;
- the amendment to section 96 currently proposed by federal and provincial authorities; and
- application of section 96 to the Parliament of Canada.

The Raisons d'être of Section 96

It is certainly legitimate to consider why section 96 appears in the *Constitution Act, 1867*; the importance that it should be given, its construction and the approach to a possible amendment to it may obviously depend on the reasons it was originally enacted.

It should be noted that this involvement of federal authorities in the organization of the provincial courts of justice is not consistent with the traditional rules of federalism;[23] all the more so because, as has already been pointed out, the provinces have no analogous power with respect to the establishment of federal courts, particularly the Supreme Court of Canada.

A study of the parliamentary debates of the 1867 Act indicates that section 96 as well as the related sections 97 to 100 attracted little attention from the Fathers of Confederation. Today it is of more importance to consider the reasons that the Supreme Court of Canada, in its research of legislative intent, has itself declared to be at the root of section 96.

According to the Fathers of Confederation

The equivalent of sections 96 to 100 can be found in the Quebec Resolutions (1864), numbers 31 to 37.[24] It follows from the very wording of Resolution no. 33 that the question of the appointment of judges was specifically linked to the payment of their salaries:

> The General Government shall appoint and pay the Judges of the Superior Courts in each Province, and of the County Courts in Upper Canada, and Parliament shall fix their salaries.

The financial side of sections 96 to 100 was noted during discussions of the United Canada Assembly, a point to which Professor Bora Laskin attached considerable importance.[25] Although a Member of the assembly may have considered that Resolution no. 33 guaranteed the independence of judges from provincial authorities,[26] the best-known position is that of Attorney General Langevin. He clearly stated the objectives that some have attributed to the resolution in question: to give the central authorities the political power to select the candidates, and from the point of view of the provinces, to make the federal treasury assume a major expense associated with the administration of justice.[27]

The Supreme Court of Canada was to find much more in sections 96 to 100.

According to the Supreme Court of Canada

The country's highest court has explained the presence of section 96 in two different ways in two unanimous decisions, neither of which takes the other into consideration. This fact can be explained by chronology in the case of the first decision, but it is hard to account for in the case of the second.

Existence of an Integrated Judicial System

In the Ontario Residential Tenancies Commission reference (May 1981), Mr. Justice Dickson (*per curiam*) maintained that sections 96 to 100 were the results of a "compromise" among the Fathers of Confederation, who were anxious to establish an integrated ("unitary") judicial system, that is to say, a system of provincial courts of justice empowered to settle disputes arising from both federal and provincial legislation; whence the decision to share responsibilities for the organization of the principal courts of justice. According to Mr. Justice Dickson:

> Under s. 92(14) of the B.N.A. Act the provincial legislatures have the legislative power in relation to the administration of justice in the province. This is a wide power but subject to subtraction of ss. 96 to 100 in favour of the federal authority. [. . .] Section 92(14) and ss. 96 to 100 represent one of the important compromises of the Fathers of Confederation. It is plain that what was sought to be achieved through this compromise, and the intended effect of s. 96, would be destroyed if a province could pass legislation creating a tribunal, appoint members thereto, and then confer on the tribunal the jurisdiction of the superior Courts. What was conceived as a strong constitutional base for national unity, through a unitary judicial system, would be gravely undermined.[28]

The role of the provincial courts to apply federal and provincial legislation was stressed by Mr. Justice Pigeon in 1979, speaking for a majority of his brethren on the Supreme Court. With respect to the role of the Superior Courts, Mr. Justice Pigeon noted:

> It must be considered that the basic principle governing the Canadian system of judicature is the jurisdiction of the superior courts of the provinces in all matters federal and provincial. The federal Parliament is empowered to derogate from this principle by establishing additional courts only for the better administration of the laws of Canada. Such establishment is not therefore necessary for the administration of these laws.[29]

Some judges of the Supreme Court had in fact already invoked this reasoning in 1879 in a well-known case.[30]

It is appropriate, however, to add the following to Mr. Justice Dickson's statements. If the provinces cannot undermine the compromise of 1867 by substantially withdrawing jurisdiction from the judges of the superior, county and district courts and transferring it to judges appointed by the Lieutenant Governor in Council, the federal authorities ought also to respect the same compromise. The unitary judicial system is undermined if the Parliament of Canada makes significant use of its exclusive power to establish additional federal courts. The federal authorities cannot have it both ways: on the one hand, considerable supervisory power over the organization of the principal provincial courts (ss. 96 to 100), thereby limiting the exclusive legislative competence of the provinces (s. 92(14)); and on the other hand, the establishment, free from all legal constraints, of a significant federal judiciary and, specifically, of the Supreme Court of the country (s. 101). Otherwise there is no compromise, only a virtually paramount federal power in matters of judicial organization; the theme of joint use of the provincial courts as the raison d'être of the division of powers accomplished by sections 92(14) and 96 to 100 no longer makes sense if the federal authorities act as if there were no compromise. From this standpoint, it is easy to understand the efforts of the Supreme Court in recent years to restrict the jurisdiction of the Federal Court.[31]

INDEPENDENCE OF SUPERIOR COURT JUDGES

During the 1930s the members of the Judicial Committee of the Privy Council noted on several occasions that section 96, as linked with sections 99 and 100, is intended to ensure the independence of judges of the major provincial courts. In 1932 Lord Blanesburgh observed:

> It cannot be doubted that the exclusive power of that section [96] conferred upon the Governor-General to appoint the judges of the superior, district and county courts in each Province is a cardinal provision of the statute. Supplemented by s. 100, which lays upon the Parliament of Canada the duty of fixing and providing the salaries, allowances and pensions of these judges, and also by s. 99 which provides that the judges of the Superior Courts shall hold office during good behaviour, being removable only by the Governor-General on address of the Senate and House of Commons, the section is shown to lie at the root of the means adopted by the framers of the statute to secure the impartiality and the independence of the Provincial Judiciary. A court of construction would accordingly fail in its duty if it were to permit these provisions and the principle therein enshrined to be impinged upon in any way by Provincial Legislation.[32]

And in 1938 Lord Atkin formulated his famous dictum: sections 96, 99 and 100 are

> three principal pillars in the temple of justice and they are not to be undermined.[33]

At every attempt to present section 96 as a provision whose purpose is to secure the independence of the judges of the principal provincial courts, critics have had a field day pointing out the unique nature of this proposition: federal appointment as opposed to provincial appointment is in itself no guarantee of independence. If appointment by a government distinct from the one that is responsible for the court's establishment is essential to the independence of the judges, must one conclude that justices of the Supreme and federal courts of Canada are not independent? In 1938, after the two decisions of the Judicial Committee of the Privy Council previously cited, Chief Justice Duff, speaking for the Supreme Court of Canada, expressed his skepticism about this theory in his reasons in *Re Adoption Act*.[34]

In January 1982, Mr. Justice Estey, speaking for the majority of the Supreme Court, indicated that such a justification for section 96 did exist, but hesitated to endorse it.

Behind that simple provision [s. 96] lie many real as well as fanciful theories as to its role and purpose in our Constitution. The generally accepted theory has been that the national appointment of superior, county and district court judges was designed to ensure a quality of independence and impartiality in the courtroom where the more serious claims and issues in the community arise; and an aura of detachment said to be analogous to that of the royal justices on circuit from Westminster is thought to be the aim of the authors of s. 96. See *O. Martineau and Sons, Ltd. v. City of Montreal*, [1932] A.C. 113, where Lord Blanesburgh, at p. 121, stated ". . . the section is shown to lie at the root of the means adopted by the framers of the statute to secure the impartiality and independence of the Provincial judiciary." Duff C.J. reviewed the same argument in the Adoption Reference, at pp. 415–16, but evidently did not find it compelling [. . .]. Whatever its purpose, [s. 96] has raised difficulties of application since Confederation.[35]

But Mr. Justice Estey said nothing about the opinion cited above and pronounced by his brother Dickson *per curiam* eight months earlier in the Ontario *Residential Tenancies* reference.

In June 1983, in the *McEvoy* case,[36] the Supreme Court of Canada stated its opinion that the presence of sections 96 to 100 in the 1867 Act was explained by the need for the judges of the provincial superior courts to be independent. Its unanimous and highly enigmatic opinion nevertheless made no mention, on this point, either of the other view held by Dickson, J. in *Re Residential Tenancies Act, 1979* (May 1981), or of the similar but highly reserved view of the majority,[37] given by Estey, J. in *Re B.C. Family Relations Act* (January 1982).

The Court affirmed *ex cathedra* that:

The traditional independence of English superior court judges has been raised to the level of a fundamental principle of our federal system by the *Constitution Act, 1982* [sic] and cannot have less importance and force in the administration of criminal law than in the case of civil matters. Under the Canadian Constitution the superior courts are independent of both levels of government.

The provinces constitute, maintain and organize the superior courts; the federal authority appoints the judges. The judicature sections of the *Constitution Act, 1867* guarantee the independence of the superior courts; they apply to Parliament as well as to the provincial Legislatures.[38]

The Court seems to accord considerable importance to the simple fact that superior court judges are appointed by the federal authorities. This attitude raises the old question: do judges of the Supreme Court and the Federal Court lack independence because they are not appointed by the provincial authorities? Undoubtedly attention must be brought to bear on *all the sections* on the judicature that protect the independence of superior court judges. Incidentally, would the Supreme Court be prepared to put the same proposition for county and district court judges who are not, it will be remembered, subject to section 99? In any event, the Supreme Court will soon have the chance to clarify its thinking on the independence of the Canadian judiciary.[39]

This second justification is far from irrelevant, provided that sections 99 and 100 are considered, rather than section 96 alone. By giving Parliament, and not the Governor General alone, the responsibility for assuring the tenure and salaries of provincial superior court judges, the Constitution certainly guarantees these judges a minimum of functional independence.[40] But the degree of guaranteed independence is not the same for judges of provincial county and district courts, who are also appointed by the Governor General. Incidentally, sections 96 to 100 are silent as to the status of judges of other provincial and federal courts, particularly those of the Supreme Court of Canada.

In 1867, however, there was no certainty that such a supreme court would ever exist, not to mention any additional federal courts. Consequently, the silence of the Fathers of Confederation concerning the status of judges of these federal courts is not surprising. It is also understandable that they had no intention of including in the *Constitution Act, 1867* provisions relative to the status of judges in every provincial lower court (e.g. justices of the peace) that would be in existence following enactment of the statute.

The two reasons adopted by the Supreme Court of Canada to explain the presence of sections 96 to 100 would seem, after some reflection, to complement each other. The provincial courts had the task of settling disputes arising from federal and provincial statutes. Therefore the Fathers of Confederation planned to give the federal authorities certain responsibilities in the organization of the principal courts. They also found it advisable to guarantee the judges of the principal courts a minimum of functional independence. The two unanimous and different views of the Supreme Court of Canada in *Re Residential Tenancies Act, 1979* and *McEvoy* are therefore not incompatible. Moreover, both show that section 96 cannot be isolated from the other provisions of the 1867 Act that deal with the judicature.

The Scope of Section 96 in Provincial Matters

It is unnecessary at this time to show that since 1867 the application of section 96 in specific cases has led to numerous, varied and sometimes contradictory judgments.[41] We need only point out that in May 1981, in the leading case of *Re Residential Tenancies*,[42] Mr. Justice Dickson reviewed the precedents in a decision endorsed by his brethren of the Supreme Court. Undoubtedly Mr. Justice Dickson did not deem it necessary to discuss every judgment rendered on the subject since 1867; had he tried, he might have been unable to formulate his own list of rules for the interpretation of section 96. His set of rules is not particularly precise; his opinion, however, permits us to avoid a long detour into the past when trying to appreciate the current scope of section 96.

Before discussing the reasons for decision of Mr. Justice Dickson, it is appropriate to examine briefly two trends in the case law that are now no longer followed. They do, however, reveal a certain set of attitudes that have influenced the construction of section 96.

Two Trends in the Case Law — Ultimately Abandoned

It should be noted that in the past some judges have not hesitated to use section 96 to limit as much as possible the exclusive jurisdiction of the provinces in the administration of justice (s. 92, para. 14). In 1976, a majority of the Supreme Court, in the famous *Di Orio* case,[43] recognized a broadened scope of this jurisdiction with respect to the provincial power to set up inquiries into organized crime.

WANT OF JURISDICTION OF PROVINCIAL AUTHORITIES TO APPOINT JUDGES TO ANY COURT WHATEVER

From 1867 to 1892 there were judges, as well as federal justice ministers, who completely denied the existence of a provincial authority to appoint judges. They claimed that the power to appoint was a manifestation of the royal prerogative and could only be exercised by the Governor General, who was the Queen's sole representative in Canada.[44] The judgment of the Judicial Committee of the Privy Council in *Liquidators of Maritime Bank* put an end to this centralist thesis.[45] In 1921 the Saskatchewan Court of Appeal correctly stated:

> Were it not for sec. 96 of the B.N.A. Act, the power to appoint or to provide for the appointment of the judges of all Provincial Courts would exist in the Provincial Legislature, under heading 14 of sec. 92.[46]

And yet in a 1923 decision of the Judicial Committee of the Privy Council we find:

> The power of appointing Judges to any Courts the Province of Alberta might establish was, under sec. 96 of the same Act of 1867, vested in the Governor General.[47]

That is probably why in 1938 Chief Justice Duff found it necessary in *Re Adoption Act* [48] to condemn once again (*per curiam*) such a school of thought, this time with considerable vigour.

The second set of cases to be examined is not unrelated to the first. In the famous but vague 1938 decision, *Toronto Corporation v. York Corporation*,[49] the Judicial Committee of the Privy Council implied that owing to section 96, a legislature had no authority to delegate a judicial function to an institution (i.e. a court of justice, an administrative body) that was not subject to the legal provisions of sections 96 to 100 of the *Constitution Act, 1867*.

That was the source in Canadian public law of a degree of separation of powers in provincial matters. In the same year, the theory was severely criticized by the Supreme Court of Canada in *Re Adoption Act*,[50] and in 1948 the Privy Council politely and indirectly repudiated the theory in the equally well-known case of *John East Iron Works Ltd*.[51] However, many Canadian decisions between roughly 1938 and 1960 were affected by *Toronto Corporation*, which was cited as precedent.[52]

This explains why in 1981 Mr. Justice Dickson, in the *Residential Tenancies* case, found it useful to address the issue. Specifically, he wrote:

> As Professor Hogg has noted in his work on *Constitutional Law of Canada* (1977), p. 129, there is no general "separation of powers" in the *British North America Act, 1867*. Our Constitution does not separate the legislative, executive, and judicial functions and insists that each branch of government exercise only its own function. Thus it is clear that the Legislature of Ontario may confer non-judicial functions on the courts of Ontario and, subject to s. 96 of the *B.N.A. Act*, which lies at the heart of the present appeal, confer judicial functions on a body which is not a court.[53]

In 1978 Chief Justice Laskin expressed a similar view in *A.G. of Quebec v. Farrah*:

> The time has long gone when s. 96 [. . .] could be properly interposed against a provincial administrative agency merely because it empowered to exercise judicial functions. *Toronto v. York*, which raised a ban on this ground against provincial administrative tribunals, was severely restricted in *Labour Relations Board of Saskatchewan v. John East Iron Works Ltd*.[54]

It is therefore well established that the exercise of provincial judicial functions is not in itself an exclusive attribute of courts of justice, and specifically of superior, district and county courts. Curiously enough, the opposite view is completely inconsistent with the practice followed before and after 1867.

Only the devolution of judicial functions that are "protected" by section 96 has raised constitutional difficulties. What are these functions, or more specifically, how are they identified? That is the question!

Current Rules of Interpretation of Section 96

The apparently clear wording of section 96 (and of sections 99 and 100) constitutes an important exception to the powers of the legislatures in the functioning of courts of justice. However the case law has considerably extended the scope of this constitutional provision. At the beginning of the 1960s Professor Bora Laskin wrote that section 96 had given rise to a "relentless pursuit to excise original sin in provincial lawmaking."[55]

In 1975 in *Tomko*, Chief Justice Laskin summarized, on behalf of a strong majority of his brethren, the general scope of section 96:

> Section 96 [. . .], in terms an appointing power [. . .], is now regarded as a limitation not only on provincial power to provide for the appointment of Judges of the status of those mentioned in s. 96 but also on their power to invest agencies of their creation and members thereof appointed under their authority with jurisdiction or powers that (to use the formula adopted by the Privy Council and by this Court in a succession of cases) are broadly conformable or analogous to jurisdiction or powers exercised and exercisable by Courts which are within s. 96.[56]

Judges faced with interpreting the *Constitution Act, 1867* have therefore refused to bring under section 96 only those courts therein enumerated[57] and courts or bodies which, given their overall judicial responsibilities, could be considered to be institutions of equivalent importance. In order to protect most of the powers or similar judicial responsibilities of the superior, district and county courts, judges have preferred to give section 96 a "functional" rather than an "institutional" scope. Particularly since 1975, however, the "institutional setting" has been important in determining whether an administrative body[58] is contemplated by section 96. Chief Justice Laskin, in the *Family Relations Act* reference, wrote in 1982:

> It is not for this Court, by deploring the presence in the Canadian Constitution of such an anomalous provision as s. 96, to reduce it to an absurdity through an interpretation which takes it literally as an appointing power without functional implications.[59]

Ever since the Supreme Court of Canada declared that section 96, together with sections 99 and 100, has as its purpose a guarantee of a unitary Canadian judicial system and the independence of provincial superior court judges, the "functional" interpretation seems to be more justified than it was previously. On the one hand, this leaves the federal authorities with a significant right to participate in the organization and maintenance of the major provincial courts, which as a rule, are called upon to ensure respect for both federal and provincial legislation; the provinces are not empowered to deprive these courts of their nature as "principal" judicial institutions by freely reducing their jurisdictions.[60] On the other hand, this construction also tends, in the interest of the citizen, to ensure that constitutional guarantees of independence apply to courts with major areas of jurisdiction; it is impossible to deprive them unilaterally of these jurisdictions in favour of institutions that do not provide the same constitutional guarantees.

However, beyond the fact that the independence of the judiciary has a solid foundation in statute and tradition, as is the case for the judges of the Supreme Court of Canada, the value of "functional" objectives is diminished if the application of this method of interpretation becomes the source of considerable uncertainty and of major problems for the administration of justice. It is generally agreed that section 96 had led to a serious malaise in the functioning of courts and provincial administrative bodies, given that the case law has been unable to identify precisely the jurisdiction reserved for "section 96 judges." As P.W. Hogg noted in 1977:

> [. . .] the difficulty lies in the definition of those functions which ought properly to belong to a superior, district or county court. The courts have attempted to fashion a judicially enforceable rule which would separate "s. 96 functions" from other adjudicatory functions. The attempt has not been successful, and it is difficult to predict with confidence how the courts will characterize particular adjudicatory functions. The uncertainty of the law, with its risk of nullification, could be a serious deterrent to the conferral of new adjudicatory functions on inferior courts or administrative tribunals (. . .).[61]

The proposal for a federal-provincial amendment to section 96 is at least partially explained by this uncertainty.[62]

Mr. Justice Dickson's theory in Re Residential Tenancies Act remains extremely useful, because it sets out the approach of the Supreme Court of Canada bench in determining whether a function may be exercised only by a judge of superior, district or county court.[63] A three-stage reasoning is proposed. But Mr. Justice Dickson's notes actually suggest a four-stage approach.

- Does the function delegated by the legislature to an institution other than a "section 96 court" have a judicial character? This first requirement is not one of the three stages proposed by Mr. Justice Dickson, but it is qualified elsewhere in his opinion as being the "initial question."[64]
- In the affirmative, does this function correspond to a jurisdiction exercised by the superior, district or county courts at the time of Confederation? This is the "1867 Statute Book Test."
- In the affirmative, does this function preserve its judicial character when analyzed in its institutional setting (or in its legislative setting)?
- In the affirmative, does the institutional setting indicate that the exercise of this function is ancillary to the accomplishment of a general

administrative role or is indispensable to the fulfilment of the entire legislative scheme?

If the answer to any of the first three questions is negative, there is no need to proceed further; section 96 is not encroached upon. A positive answer to the fourth question has the same effect. In practice, given the uncertainty of the answers to each, judges take care to examine more than one of these questions.

We shall now review the different stages of the "Dickson Test," noting that the simplicity of their wording is equalled only by the vagueness of their actual content.

JUDICIAL NATURE OF THE FUNCTION

In administrative law, the concept of judicial function is interpreted very broadly,[65] mainly with a view to providing citizens with certain procedural guarantees in their relations with the public administration and providing access to certain remedies before courts when citizens feel they have been wronged by the administration's activities; thus, the expression "quasi-judicial" function has been generally used. For the purposes of applying section 96, a far more restrictive construction has been retained by the Supreme Court, as some excerpts from Mr. Justice Dickson's opinion reveal:

> If the answer to the initial question as to "judicial power" is in the negative, then that concludes the matter in favour of the provincial board [. . .] [T]he question of whether any particular function is "judicial" is not determined simply on the basis of procedural trappings. The primary issue is the nature of the question which the tribunal is called upon to decide [. . .] [T]he hall-mark of a judicial power is a *lis* between parties in which a tribunal is called upon to apply a recognized body of rules in a manner consistent with fairness and impartiality. The adjudication deals primarily with the rights of the parties to the dispute, rather than considerations of the collective good of the community as a whole.[66]

This restrictive view of judicial power, which makes reference to both procedural and material identification criteria, while apparently favouring the latter, is perfectly legitimate, given the constitutional context of section 96.[67] This section is an exception to the legislative competence of the provinces (s. 92(14)) and should not be construed too liberally. The characteristic activities of "section 96 courts" in 1867 were above all judicial. The courts of justice and, more specifically, the superior, district and county courts, had the task (as they do today) of settling disputes according to pre-existing legal standards and following adversarial rules of procedure serving to expose the truth in fact and in law. The two grounds used to justify the presence of section 96 in the *Constitution Act,*

1867 are based on judicial function in its classic and restricted meaning.

For example, a judge of the Quebec Superior Court recently concluded that the *Occupational Health and Safety Act* did not violate section 96 by delegating to an inspector the authority to order an offending firm to respect the Act or its regulations. In this case, the inspector had required the employer to provide his employees with safety footwear at no charge, as required by regulation, or else face penal proceedings. The Court rejected the argument that the inspector's duty was unconstitutional, specifically on the grounds that this was not a judicial function because his role was not principally to settle disputes but to ensure that the Act and its regulations were respected.[68]

The problem with this form of qualification is shown in the Supreme Court of Canada's finding that certain powers of the Quebec Rental Board were constitutional. In a sort of preface to his opinion, Mr. Justice Chouinard (*per curiam*) succinctly dismissed from the debate the question of the jurisdiction of the tribunal to fix rents, on the grounds that this was not a judicial function, even in the event of a disagreement between landlord and tenant. He endorsed the view of counsel for the Quebec government:

> In this area, the Board does not proceed in the manner of a court. What it really does is to implement an administrative policy of supervising the housing market, based primarily on the good of the community as a whole. Thus, the rights of parties are closely associated with the implementation of a common policy regarding the supervision of rental levels[69] (translation).

The Court therefore subscribed to the view that disputes of this kind are settled with reference to economic and social considerations. It would have been interesting if the Supreme Court had gone into greater detail, because the Act is silent on this subject.[70] The Quebec Court of Appeal made no declaration as to the non-judicial nature of this aspect of the tribunal's jurisdiction.[71]

A JUDICIAL FUNCTION BROADLY ANALOGOUS TO A JURISDICTION EXERCISED BY A "SECTION 96 COURT" IN 1867

A legislature may not confer on judges other than those of superior, district and county courts judicial duties that in 1867 formed part of their jurisdiction, or any broadly analogous function. On this subject, Mr. Justice Dickson wrote in the *Residential Tenancies* reference:

> If [. . .] the power is in fact a judicial power, then it becomes necessary to ask a second question: in the exercise of that power, is the tribunal analogous to a superior, district or county court? . . . [This step] involves consideration, in the light of the historical conditions existing in 1867, of the particular power or jurisdiction conferred upon the tribunal. The question here is

whether the power or jurisdiction conforms to the power or jurisdiction exercised by superior, district or county courts at the time of Confederation [. . .] If the historical inquiry leads to the conclusion that the power or jurisdiction is not broadly conformable to jurisdiction formerly exercised by s. 96 courts, that is the end of the matter.[72]

We can see the flexibility of a rule of application that gives such importance to laws in force in 1867, even if subsequently repealed, rather than to the contemporary needs of the administration of justice. This rule also forces judges to speculate, frequently with considerable variations, on the similarities and dissimilarities of jurisdictions of "section 96 courts" in 1867 and of judicial functions conferred more than a century later on institutions made up of individuals appointed by provincial authorities, who are often neither judges nor even jurists. Just as it is always possible to say that one person resembles another "slightly, considerably or a lot," even when the two people are not twins, it is likewise easy for judges to conclude, with good grounds, that a judicial function is or is not generally analogous to one exercised in 1867 by a "section 96 court." Legal historians may also play a decisive role in settling such controversies.

Three elements need to be added to this historical criterion of construction, even though Mr. Justice Dickson does not mention them in his comments.

A judicial function is contemplated by section 96 only if it was the exclusive jurisdiction of a "section 96 court" in 1867. The Supreme Court decided in 1983 that judicial powers delegated to the Quebec Rental Board do not offend section 96, since in Lower Canada in 1867 the Recorder's Court (not listed in section 96) had jurisdiction in similar matters concurrently with that of the Superior Court and the Circuit Court, two courts contemplated by section 96.[73] In the same vein, Mr. Justice Estey noted, in *Re B.C. Family Relations Act*:

> [. . .] the proponents of the superior courts cannot demonstrate the historic existence of an exclusive jurisdiction in the field of guardianship or custody analogous to that proposed in the legislation now before this Court.[74]

This requirement of exclusivity is fully appropriate, but it sometimes adds to the difficulty of historical research because the statutes of 1867 were not drafted with section 96 in mind.

A legislature may not, however, circumvent section 96 by assigning to a body made up of provincial government appointees a judicial function "protected" by the said section while at the same time guaranteeing "section 96 courts" concurrent jurisdiction, or providing the latter with the possibility of intervening in appeal; in both cases the legislature is still assigning a jurisdiction historically contemplated by section 96 to someone other than a judge of a superior, district or county court. On this subject Chief Justice Laskin made the following observation in the *Family Relations Act (B.C.)* reference:

> Neither the fact of certain concurrency of jurisdiction with the British
> Columbia Supreme Court nor its subjection to review or appeal provide any
> basis for entitling the Provincial Court to absorb s. 96 court functions on
> the ground that it has not been transformed into a superior, district or county
> court.[75]

Finally, although other jurists might disagree with this author, the application of the historical test does not require a study of the law in force only in the province concerned. When the Quebec Court of Appeal in 1964 ruled unanimously that the magistrate's Court of the province had become a court of the same importance as a section 96 court, it partly based its opinion on a comparison with the 1867 jurisdiction of county and district courts in Upper Canada.[76] The Appeal Courts of Alberta and British Columbia have recently adopted a similar position.[77] In the *B.C. Family Relations Act* reference, the Supreme Court judges of the majority (Estey) and the minority (Laskin) found it appropriate to consider the state of the law in force in other Canadian provinces, and even, as the Supreme Court had done in 1938 in its famous reference in *Re Adoption Act*, to look at British legislation in force in 1867.[78] If the study of British legislation is relevant,[79] there can be no reason to treat the law in force in other Canadian provinces any differently. The idea that restrictions on provincial legislative jurisdiction may vary from province to province holds little appeal.

From this standpoint, one might wonder about the different decisions of the Supreme Court of Canada in the case of the Ontario Residential Tenancies Commission (in 1981) and the Quebec Rental Board (in 1983), when the principal activities of the former were held to be unconstitutional while those of the latter, though similar, were held to be constitutional. It is legitimate to ask whether the Supreme Court would have emasculated the Ontario commission had counsel for the provincial government mentioned the legislation in force in Lower Canada, under which Recorder's Courts in 1867 dealt with landlord and tenant disputes; it was this historical argument that enabled the Quebec Rental Board to avoid the shadow of section 96.[80] Logically, how can the Quebec Rental Board terminate a lease if the granting of this power to an Ontario rental commission or even a judge named by the Lieutenant Governor of this province is forbidden by section 96? How can this peculiar situation be justified in the light of the different reasons explaining the presence of section 96 in the *Constitution Act, 1867*?

Among the many judgments and references occasioned by section 96, there are few in which the "1867 statute book test" is not applied, although often with different results. The lengthy and complex opinion of the Supreme Court of Canada in the 1982 *Family Relations Act* reference is typical.[81] A majority of the judges partly set aside a unanimous decision of the British Columbia Court of Appeal declaring unconstitutional a provincial statute that assigned duties with respect to guardianship, custody, and occupancy or use of family residences to judges appointed by the Lieutenant Governor.

Reference to the historical test has in particular led the Supreme Court of Canada to declare unconstitutional the strong privative clauses adopted by the legislatures in order to block the traditional supervisory power of the superior courts over the lower courts and provincial administrative bodies. In *Crevier v. A.-G. of Quebec*, Chief Justice Laskin concluded (*per curiam*) that the fact of totally excluding an institution from the scope of this supervisory authority actually allowed the institution itself to determine the extent of its own jurisdiction. In so doing, the institution was implicitly exercising a type of jurisdiction that was part of the traditional supervisory power belonging to the superior courts in 1867. According to the Chief Justice:

> [. . .] given that s. 96 is in the *British North America Act* and that it would make a mockery of it to treat it in non-functional formal terms as a mere appointing power, I can think of nothing that is more the hallmark of a superior court than the vesting of power in a provincial statutory tribunal to determine the limits of its jurisdiction without appeal or other review.[82]

This was an unusual case of applying section 96 and the historical test. Not being subjected to the supervisory power of the superior courts was deemed to be a transfer of the supervisory power which, in itself, is a jurisdiction protected by section 96 and the institution in question could not then exercise any duty whatever because its very creation was incompatible with section 96.[83]

In another case of the application of the historic test,[84] the British Columbia Court of Appeal considered the constitutionality of the jurisdiction of the province's Employment Standards Board, a body empowered to rule on claims for unpaid wages against employers. In differing with the trial judge, the Court of Appeal held the jurisdiction to be one that before 1867 belonged to magistrates not enumerated in section 96.[85] The Supreme Court of Canada will also have to decide whether the Quebec Court of Appeal was correct in declaring unconstitutional a section of the *Securities Act* that gives the minister of financial institutions the power in certain circumstances to suspend temporarily members of the board of directors of a firm that trades in securities, following a recommendation to this effect by the Securities Commission. In applying the method proposed by Mr. Justice Dickson, the Court of Appeal concluded that the minister was exercising over the corporation concerned a judicial function analogous to the supervisory power of the superior courts.[86]

The application of the historical test to provincial institutions with an appellate jurisdiction is at the root of an extensive debate, especially in Quebec,[87] and the judgments show how, without an intensive analysis of the judicial reality governing the versatile concept of appeal, judges have tended to be too hasty in concluding that this type of responsibility is part of the traditional supervisory power of the superior courts.[88] Undoubtedly it would be a mistake to have blind confidence in the 1978 opinion of Chief Justice Laskin in the *Farrah* case:

[. . .] it is also open to a Province to establish an administrative tribunal of appeal as part of a valid regulatory statute and to invest such a tribunal with power to make decisions on questions of law in the course of exercising an appellate authority over decisions of the primary agency [. . .] the fact that a right of appeal is given as part of and within the administrative organization cannot have any significant bearing on the issue.[89]

Not only did the Chief Justice refuse to apply this principle to the appeal tribunal being impugned — the Quebec Transport Tribunal — but in 1981 he went so far as to state (per curiam) something considerably different in declaring that the Quebec Professions Tribunal was unconstitutional. This was a body with the duty to hear appeals from decisions taken by disciplinary committees of various professional corporations. After pointing out principally that the institution was protected by a strict privative clause, Laskin C.J. added:

Even if it were otherwise and the supervisory authority of the Superior Court on questions of jurisdiction was expressly preserved, it would still not be a complete answer to a contention that the Professions Tribunal is exercising powers more conformable to those belonging to a s. 96 court than those properly exercisable by a provincial administrative or quasi-judicial tribunal or even a provincial judicial tribunal.[90]

The Supreme Court of Canada was not at its best when it gave its reasons for subjecting the Quebec Transport Tribunal and the Professions Tribunal to section 96. D. J. Mullan notes with respect to the second case:

To be as cryptic as the [Supreme] Court was in Crevier is irresponsible and conducive to more litigation as various refinements are tested against a will o' the wisp judicial standard of invalidity. In the meantime, this lack of clear direction means administrative appeal tribunals across the country are placed in a position of considerable uncertainty while the core has been removed from a progressive and innovative Quebec attempt at professional regulation.[91]

Even though the Supreme Court, in the more recent *Capital Regional District v. Concerned Citizens of British Columbia*,[92] showed that it was not disposed to seek out violations of section 96 in every provincial body with an appellate jurisdiction, this judgment still fails to provide a satisfactory analysis of the notion of appeal in public law, a notion that has no predetermined judicial content in principle. In this case, the Supreme Court reversed a unanimous ruling of the British Columbia Court of Appeal that section 96 did not authorize the legislature to give the provincial cabinet responsibility for settling appeals from decisions of the Pollution Control Board. The Court of Appeal had believed, however, that it was following

Supreme Court of Canada precedents. Chief Justice Laskin, who delivered the Court's judgment, was in favour of the provincial statute's validity, referring to the institutional test (*infra*) without paying much attention to historical considerations.

Appeal is neither historically nor fundamentally a form of legal action contemplated by section 96. It is hard to see how such a responsibility assigned to provincial government appointees should not be submitted to the various tests formulated by Mr. Justice Dickson in the *Residential Tenancies* reference. It should be necessary to ensure that a body with an appellate jurisdiction is exercising a judicial function within the meaning of section 96, something which should not be the case when decisions are made legally in light of economic and social considerations.[93] Incidentally, recourse to the historical test could reveal that a court not enumerated in section 96 had, in 1867, an analogous jurisdiction. A careful study of the legislation might also reveal that the impugned appellate jurisdiction gives the provincial body powers that are substantially different from those of "section 96 courts" before 1867; for example, the appellate body might be enabled to make the decision that the first trier of fact ought to have made.[94]

It is inappropriate to make a further study of this difficult question; such a study would require us to consider the various types of appeal provided for by the legislator (appeal on the record, appeal "de novo," appeal on questions of law, appeals to courts of justice or to administrative bodies) and could not ignore the fact that it may be difficult to analyze the nature of a right of appeal without knowing the nature of the decision taken by the first authority. The case law is not particularly forthcoming on this subject. However, it seems that granting a body an appellate jurisdiction limited to questions of law is likely to unleash section 96 attacks, above all if the body concerned does not have other responsibilities. In such a case, and without making the appropriate qualifications, some judges tend to consider that the legislature assigned the body a responsibility analogous to the traditional supervisory power of the superior courts. Such is the apparent consequence of Mr. Justice Dickson's summary of *Farrah* in his opinion in the *Residential Tenancies* reference:

> In *Farrah*, a Transport Tribunal was given appellate jurisdiction over the Quebec Transport Commission. The Tribunal performed no function other than deciding questions of law. Since this function was normally performed by s. 96 courts and divorced from the broader institutional framework of the Act, the impugned sections were held to be unconstitutional.[95]

I shall conclude with some observations on the historical test in relation to two *obiter dicta* of justices of the Supreme Court of Canada. The first in particular could lead to some flexibility in decisions concerning the application of section 96, while the second is above all likely to add to the existing confusion in the state of the law.

Mr. Justice Estey, in the reference on the *B.C. Family Relations Act*, speaking for a majority of his brethren said that the court should not remain indifferent to the fact that certain judicial functions are more adequately exercised by courts of summary procedure than by "section 96 courts." After noting that the institutional test has relaxed the application of section 96 with respect to administrative tribunals, he added:

> But [the permissive view] has almost equal importance and value when the program outlined in the enabling statute lends itself to interpretation and application in the quick and relatively less expensive summary procedures of the so-called inferior tribunals. The rights and duties created by such statutes frequently are of a kind or are directed to a sector of the community so as to be better and more expeditiously realized and interpreted by the less formal and less demanding procedures of the provincial court. It is not to denigrate the role of the superior court or its efficacy in the modern community. It is only to say that the highly refined techniques evolved over centuries for the determination of serious and frequently profound difficulties arising in the community are unnecessary for the disposition of much of the traffic directed to the magisterial courts by contemporary provincial legislation. That traffic can sometimes bear neither the cost nor the time which sometimes inevitably must be borne or devoted by the parties to causes in the courts of general jurisdiction (the descendants of the royal courts of justice) and the county courts.[96]

Thus, practical considerations should permit judges to allow some encroachments on those jurisdictions historically protected by section 96.

On the other hand, in the same reference on family law, Chief Justice Laskin, dissenting, with the support of Ritchie J., observed rather mysteriously that a study of the law in force in 1867 was insufficient to determine if a judicial function was exercised by a "section 96 court." In addition, it was necessary to verify whether a jurisdiction had not been incorrectly assigned to a court not enumerated in that section. According to Laskin C.J.:

> The caution sounded by counsel for the Attorney General of Canada against accepting what he called an anomalous jurisdiction vested in an inferior court before 1867 as a ground for justifying an escape from s. 96 has merit. It is not as if jurisdiction vested in an inferior court before 1867 was so vested in contemplation of an eventual federal constitution containing a provision like s. 96.[97]

If such a thesis is upheld, the case law on the application of section 96 becomes even more kaleidoscopic.

A FUNCTION OF A "SECTION 96 COURT" UNCHANGED BY ITS INSTITUTIONAL SETTING

The final two elements in the "Dickson Test" refer to similar considerations as is shown by this important excerpt from Mr. Justice Dickson's notes:

> Step two involves consideration of the function within its institutional setting to determine whether the function itself is different when viewed in that setting. In particular, can the function still be considered to be a "judicial" function? [. . .] If, after examining the institutional context, it becomes apparent that the power is not being exercised as a "judicial power" then the inquiry need go no further for the power, within its institutional context, no longer conforms to a power or jurisdiction exercisable by a s. 96 court and the provincial scheme is valid. On the other hand, if the power or jurisdiction is exercised in a judicial manner, then it becomes necessary to proceed to the third and final step in the analysis and review the tribunal's function as a whole in order to appraise the impugned function in its entire institutional context. The phrase — "it is not the detached jurisdiction or power alone that is to be considered but rather its setting in the institutional arrangements in which it appears" — is the central core of the judgment in *Tomko*. It is no longer sufficient simply to examine the particular power or function of a tribunal and ask whether this power or function was once exercised by s. 96 courts. This would be examining the power or function in a "detached" manner, contrary to the reasoning in *Tomko*. What must be considered is the "context" in which this power is exercised. *Tomko* leads to the following result: it is possible for administrative tribunals to exercise powers and jurisdiction which once were exercised by the s. 96 courts. It will all depend on the context of the exercise of the power. It may be that the impugned "judicial powers" are merely subsidiary or ancillary to general administrative functions assigned to the tribunal (*John East, Tomko*) or the powers may be necessarily incidental to the achievement of a broader policy goal of the legislature (*Mississauga*). In such a situation, the grant of judicial power to provincial appointees is valid. The scheme is only invalid when the adjudicative function is a sole or central function of the tribunal (*Farrah*) so that the tribunal can be said to be operating "like a s. 96 court."[98]

We can see that institutional considerations, based on an analysis of the institutional setting of the judicial function being impugned, may justify an exception to the rule that a provincial government appointee may not exercise a jurisdiction "historically" protected by section 96. The nature of jurisdiction being contested has been changed by its context.

This type of consideration may primarily indicate the non-judicial nature of the jurisdiction being attacked.

In practice, this step in Mr. Justice Dickson's reasoning overlaps that which he himself refers to as the "initial question," which he did not deem necessary to include in his three-stage reasoning: is the function in question judicial?[99] To determine the nature of power assigned to a body, it is necessary to examine the various formal and material indications that appear in the legislative text; therefore it is necessary to look at the institutional context. I believe that there is no need to determine if a function is judicial in order subsequently to see if the function remains judicial once placed in its institutional context; an analysis of the context is necessary for the initial qualification. Step two in Mr. Justice Dickson's reasoning in fact recalls the "initial question"; section 96 contemplates judicial functions only, in the strict sense of the term, and in order to conclude that a function is indeed judicial, the entire legislation by which the legislature has delegated this power must be studied.

If at the inception it becomes clear that a certain power is not strictly judicial, especially because of its institutional setting, there is no need to undertake lengthy research and produce detailed politico-socio-juridical studies concerning the possible analogies with jurisdictions exercised before 1867 by "section 96 courts."

In my opinion, when Mr. Justice Dickson concluded in *Residential Tenancies* that the impugned powers, "when viewed in their institutional setting, remain essentially 'judicial powers',"[100] he was merely convincing himself that the powers in question were judicial, within the meaning of section 96. Incidentally, Chief Justice Laskin in *Concerned Citizens* ought to have concluded that the appellate jurisdiction given the provincial Cabinet was non-judicial (within the meaning of section 96) when he noted (*per curiam*) that it was able to make decisions in light of public policy.[101]

For that reason I shall dwell no further on this aspect of the "Dickson test."

More fundamental is the proposition that a truly judicial function that is historically within the scope of section 96 may actually escape its grasp because of its institutional context.

To say the least, it is far from easy to explain satisfactorily the operation of the "institutional setting" theory, as an exception to the rigour of the historical test. Mr. Justice Dickson himself recognized (*per curiam*) in *Residential Tenancies* that this theory has no particularly specific context:

> The teaching of *John East, Tomko*, and *Mississauga* is that one must look to the "institutional setting" in order to determine whether a particular power or jurisdiction can validly be conferred on a provincial body. [. . .] As the British Columbia Court of Appeal noted in its consideration of s. 96 in *Re Pepita and Doukas*, at p. 582: ". . . it is notable that no general tests are offered or established in the *Tomko* judgment for the characterization of the function, the characterization of the institutional arrangements, and the examination of their interrelationship. Instead the judgment continues with a consideration of the particular function in its context. . . ."[102]

In short, an element of subjectivity is involved, and it is not unreasonable to suggest that the theory has given rise to a degree of judicial impressionism. Relaxation of the rigours of the historical test — which also has left room for a large degree of interpretation that is far from immune to subjectivity — is not undesirable, but it does add to the shifting sands of section 96 case law.

In practice, it would seem that the rule can only benefit an institution with principally administrative responsibilities; the delegation to such an institution of a judicial function protected by section 96 would be allowed when such delegation is necessarily accessory to the accomplishment of greater administrative responsibilities, and does not have the effect of transforming the administrative body into a court of justice. The administrative context acts as a catalyst in transforming the judicial function in question. This statement is based on the following.

In the *B.C. Family Law* reference Chief Justice Laskin, who in *Tomko* (1975), marked the Canadian birth of the "institutional setting" theory, noted that "court cases" and "administrative law cases" should not be confused.[103] Furthermore, Mr. Justice Estey, speaking for the majority, pointed out that it is easier to hold the "permissive view" of construction of section 96 when the dispute deals with an administrative tribunal rather than a court of justice.[104] And Mr. Justice Dickson (*per curiam*), in the *Residential Tenancies* reference, observed:

> I do not think it can be doubted that the courts have applied an increasingly broad test of constitutional validity in upholding the establishment of administrative tribunals within provincial jurisdiction. In general terms it may be said that it is now open to the provinces to invest administrative bodies with "judicial functions" as part of a broader policy scheme. [. . .] *Tomko* added a further dimension. An administrative tribunal may be clothed with power formerly exercised by s. 96 courts, so long as that power is merely an adjunct of, or ancillary to, a broader administrative or regulatory scheme.[105]

Recently, in *Concerned Citizens of B.C.*, Chief Justice Laskin relied mainly on the institutional setting theory to uphold (*per curiam*) the validity of an appellate jurisdiction delegated to the provincial Cabinet. In particular, he wrote:

> I would add this as a summary. Of the four functions that are reposed in the Lieutenant-Governor in Council, only one relates to its appellate authority. The other three concern its administrative authority and include its appointing power, its regulation-making power and its directory and supervisory power. Its appellate authority, in the circumstances, does not stand as a detached power turning it into a purely judicial tribunal.[106]

Similarly, in *Mississauga* Chief Justice Laskin upheld (*per curiam*) the constitutionality of the Ontario Municipal Commission's power in the case of amalgamation to settle certain disputes between municipalities; he stressed the fact that this ancillary judicial function of the Commission cannot be dissociated from its total administrative duties in the overall scheme of municipal reorganization.[107] From the same standpoint, the Quebec Court of Appeal ruled in *Théroux* (the Supreme Court of Canada denied leave to appeal) that the Superintendent of Insurance did not violate section 96 in exercising an appellate jurisdiction with respect to disciplinary decisions made by the board of directors of the Insurance Brokers Association. Mr. Justice Nolan observed:

The Superintendent of Insurance is the key official in the "service des assurances" established by the Act respecting Insurance. Section 5 of this Act states that he "shall have supervision of the insurance business in Quebec and exercise the duties and powers assigned to or vested in him by law" [. . .] As the government official responsible for the supervision of the insurance business in Quebec and having the right under the Act Respecting Insurance to grant certificates to insurance agents and the power to suspend or cancel such certificates it seems that the right to sit in appeal which s. 25 par. 11 granted to the Superintendent is clearly ancillary to his other rights and duties and an integral, albeit subsidiary, part of competent provincial legislation dealing with the administration of insurance industry in Quebec.[108]

On the other hand, in 1980 the Nova Scotia Court of Appeal held as unconstitutional certain judicial functions contemplated by section 96 and delegated by the *Lands and Forests Act* to a Commissioner empowered to settle disputes relating to property rights. According to Mr. Justice MacKeigan (*per curiam*), the Commissioner did not exercise any administrative responsibilities and his judicial role could not be integrated with other provisions of the Act:

> The Commissioner's function is purely judicial, unalloyed by any administrative duties, and separate from any broad legislative scheme.[109]

With reference to these examples from the case law, the fact that in declaring that the Quebec Transport Tribunal, the Quebec Professions Tribunal and the Ontario Residential Tenancies Commission were unconstitutional, the Supreme Court of Canada scarcely considered the important contemporary legislation creating these bodies can be explained on the grounds that these institutions were called upon to exercise a role that was solely or principally judicial; the "institutional setting" rule, in the absence of administrative arguments, was of no help to them. This point was emphasized by Mr. Justice Dickson (*per curiam*) in the *Residential Tenancies* reference:

> It appears upon reading the Act as a whole that the central function of the Commission is that of resolving disputes [. . .] Here the chief role of the Commission is not to administer a policy or to carry out an administrative function. Its primary role is to adjudicate. The administrative features of the legislation can be characterized as ancillary to the main adjudicative function."[110]

If the foregoing analysis is an accurate reflection of a body of case law that has not always been well articulated,[111] two important teachings result.

On the one hand, considering that the legislatures will often assign a variety of responsibilities to a specific body, there will certainly be cases where it is difficult to determine if an institution is principally judicial with an ancillary administrative function, or principally administrative with an ancillary judicial function.

On the other hand, the courts of justice or comparable bodies cannot profit from the relaxation offered by the "institutional setting" rule.[112] There can be no metamorphosis of the judicial function protected by section 96 because there is no administrative catalyst. The more a body exercises administrative duties, the greater are the chances that legislatures will be justified in expecting courts to authorize one or more functions historically protected by section 96 to be delegated to that body. It would seem easier for the provinces to delegate important judicial functions to members of the administration (e.g., a minister or a commission) than to judges (e.g., of the Quebec Provincial Court). This result hardly seems compatible with one of the raisons d'être of section 96: to ensure that judicial powers of a certain degree of importance are exercised by individuals whose independence and impartiality are guaranteed.

At the very least, we can hope that the courts will welcome the words of Mr. Justice Estey who, in the *Family Law* reference, noted that there should be greater sensitivity to the fact that some judicial functions are better carried out by courts of summary jurisdiction.[113] Once again, considerations of public policy would bring a desirable flexibility to the case law while, unfortunately, adding to the existing confusion.

The inability of the courts of justice to profit from the "institutional setting" rule may carry over to their auxiliaries. An article published in Quebec suggests that the special protonotary, one of the main auxiliaries of the Superior Court, is exercising several judicial duties illegally.[114]

The Amendment to Section 96 Currently Proposed by Federal and Provincial Authorities

After a short examination of the objective and substance of the proposed amendment to the *Constitution Act, 1867*, which incidentally will be subject to the new rules for constitutional amendment in the Constitution, we shall see why the proposed text is unacceptable.

The Objective and Substance of the Amendment

The case law briefly described above shows that section 96 has engendered byzantine precedents allowing judges a large degree of discretion, not devoid of subjectivity, when they are called upon to decide whether a provincial statute violates this section of the *Constitution Act, 1867*. These decisions are usually made after the provincial legislation has come into force, and sometimes many years after the institution in question has been granted the impugned function. The administration of civil, criminal and administrative justice is inconsistent with such uncertainty concerning the devolution of so-called judicial responsibilities to courts of justice and to administrative bodies that are not made up of persons with the status of judges who are appointed, named and recalled by federal authorities (sections 96 to 100). Particularly in Quebec, where there are no county or district courts, it is not appropriate that frequently overworked superior courts hold such a substantial historic monopoly on the exercise of several judicial functions. This is especially true since the Supreme Court ruled in *Crevier* that all so-called lower provincial courts and provincial administrative bodies are subjected by the Constitution, pursuant to section 96, to the supervision of superior courts empowered to intervene in cases of want or excess of jurisdiction.

The political authorities have decided to make a constitutional correction to what Chief Justice Laskin called a "constitutional anomaly": whence the proposed amendment to section 96. The text of the amendment was published in August 1983 in a "discussion paper" prepared by the federal Department of Justice.[115]

The notes accompanying the proposed amendment, and its title, show that the object of this proposal, which has been submitted to the scrutiny of public opinion, is to give legislatures greater freedom of action in the organization of their administrative tribunals. I say "greater freedom" given that, as already pointed out, the "institutional setting" rule, although undoubtedly vague, already allows the provinces to endow administrative bodies with judicial functions protected by section 96.

The following passage appears in the explanatory notes:

> Yet some provinces remain critical of Section 96 for a number of reasons. They are concerned about the uncertainty it creates concerning the ability of the provinces to confer effective powers upon provincially appointed tribunals. Some find it an annoying anachronism to use in any way the pre-1867 powers of the Section 96-type courts as a criterion for establishing a valid tribunal. Others would wish their legislatures to be completely free to determine the forum in which, and based on which, the decisions of their administrative tribunals will be reviewed.[116]

The proposed amendment reads as follows:

> 96B. (1) Notwithstanding section 96, the Legislature of each Province may confer on any tribunal, board, commission or authority, other than a court, established pursuant to the laws of the Province, concurrent or exclusive jurisdiction in respect of any matter within the legislative authority of the Province.
>
> (2) Any decision of a tribunal, board, commission or authority on which any jurisdiction of a superior court is conferred under subsection (1) is subject to review by a superior court of the Province for want or excess of jurisdiction.

> ———
>
> 96B. (1) Par dérogation à l'article 96, la législature d'une province peut, dans les domaines ressortissants à son pouvoir législatif, attribuer compétence concurrente ou exclusive à tout tribunal, organisme ou autre autorité non judiciaire constituée en vertu d'une loi de la province.

(2) Les décisions des autorités à qui a été attribuée compétence de cour supérieure en vertu du paragraphe (1) sont susceptibles de révision par une cour supérieure de la province pour défaut ou excès de pouvoir.

There are several reasons why this proposed amendment should not be adopted.[117]

Why the Amendment is Unacceptable

THE IRRATIONAL EXCLUSION OF PROVINCIAL COURTS AS BENEFICIARIES OF THE INTENDED FLEXIBILITY

By virtue of section 96B, the legislatures would be henceforth authorized to delegate directly a judicial function that has historically been protected by section 96 to administrative bodies that are "other than a court," in a field that falls within their legislative competence. The "institutional setting" rule would no longer have much practical importance, as appears to be the case, if it is true that it only benefits bodies with principally administrative duties.

Nevertheless, the actual case law would continue to apply to judicial authorities ("courts") composed of provincially appointed judges; it remains the "status quo ante" as far as the latter are concerned. If section 96B were adopted, it would be easier to assign important judicial functions to administrative bodies, but it would still be illegal to assign a judicial function exercised in 1867 by a "section 96 court," or a function of the same type, to a provincially appointed judge. For example, it appears that the Quebec National Assembly could delegate to the minister of municipal affairs the power to quash municipal by-laws, which was withdrawn from Provincial Court judges following *Séminaire de Chicoutimi*;[118] the ban would continue to apply to Provincial Court judges. The Ontario legislature would be empowered to delegate to its Residential Tenancies Commission the judicial functions ruled unconstitutional by the Supreme Court in 1981, after having ensured that the commission was distinct from a court of justice, for example by assigning to it — not necessarily in the public interest — a series of discretionary powers. The Ontario legislature would still be forbidden to have these judicial duties assumed by a court composed of judges appointed by the Lieutenant Governor.

An unusual situation: it would be easier than it is today for the legislatures to delegate important judicial powers to provincial administrators than to provincial judges, who benefit from guarantees of independence recognized either by provincial statutes or by tradition.

Section 96B minimizes the importance of courts made up of provincially appointed judges and for no reason, it widens the distinction between superior and inferior courts.

As "courts" would be unable to benefit from the official liberalization of the scope of section 96, the proposed amendment might make it impossible to apply Mr. Justice Estey's opinion, in the *Family Relations Act* reference, favouring the granting of certain judicial functions contemplated by section 96 to the lower courts when the effective exercise of these functions requires a summary procedure.[119] Section 96B could thereby prevent courts consisting of provincially appointed judges from benefiting from this possible additional flexibility in the case law, which is based on convenience, logic or necessity.

A PANDORA'S BOX: THE CONCEPT OF "AUTHORITY OTHER THAN A COURT"

The possible enactment of subsection 96B(1) would open a new front in our courtroom battles. Judges interpreting the Constitution would be required to define what is meant by "authority other than a court," because a judicial function protected by section 96 could not be assigned to a provincial "court."

The legal concept of "court" is like a chameleon; a "court" is defined differently in different contexts. For example, in interpreting its own jurisdiction, the Supreme Court of Canada has considered itself without jurisdiction to hear appeals from decisions made by quasi-judicial bodies rather than by courts, because the *Supreme Court Act* authorizes appeals only from judgments of "courts" or their "judges."[120] Yet this highest court held that the bilingualism rules provided for in section 133 of the *Constitution Act, 1867* apply not only to Quebec "courts," as the text specifies, but also to "non-curial adjudicative agencies."[121] Speculating on the meaning of "court," the judges of the House of Lords in 1980 said that two questions must be asked: "When is a court a court?" and "When is a court not a court?" One of their Lordships noted without equivocation:

> At the end of the day it has unfortunately to be said that there emerges no sure guide, no unmistakable hallmark by which a "court" or "inferior court" may unerringly be identified. It is largely a matter of impression.[122]

Of course in a future lawsuit or reference, the Supreme Court of Canada would ultimately settle, possibly with some imprecision, this problem of the interpretation of section 96B by adding in some way certain clarifications to the text. It might adopt the following line of thought: for the purposes of section 96B, those bodies having the status of a "court" pursuant to provincial legislation as well as any authority that solely or principally exercises judicial functions would be qualified as a "court." The result is evident. It would no longer be necessary, as it is now, to apply the "institutional setting" theory in order to authorize delegation of judicial functions protected by section 96 to administrative bodies; but to ensure that the body to which powers are delegated is not really a court disguised by some provincial legislative subterfuge, it would be necessary to check that the judicial functions are only ancillary to the performance of a task that is principally administrative.

Whatever the case, the explanatory notes accompanying the draft section 96B make a form of admission:

> The above draft of a proposed Section 96B assumes that our courts would be able to devise a useful distinction between "courts" and "tribunals."[123]

THE POSSIBILITY OF INCREASING LIMITATIONS ON THE JURISDICTIONS OF PROVINCIAL COURTS AND THE PROBLEM OF BALANCE OF POWERS

If the proposed amendment were adopted, the legislatures would be empowered to assign any judicial function, old or new, to an institution other than a "court" of justice. Especially, the provinces would be free to remove any part of the current jurisdiction from "section 96 courts" and *a fortiori* from other provincial courts; however, administrative bodies or inferior courts would still be subject to the supervisory power of the superior courts for want or excess of jurisdiction (*infra*).

Therefore, under the Constitution the provinces would be completely free to increase the judicial role of their public administration (government, ministries, commissions, boards, municipal corporations, civil servants, judicial auxiliaries, etc.), although we should not forget that in the present state of the case law, the "institutional setting" theory already gives them considerable latitude. An increase in the judicial functions of the public administration often entails a reduction in the responsibilities of judges, who normally exercise "judicial power" within a state. Even though the administration of justice is a concern of the public as a whole, the public as a whole is not called upon to render justice.

The proposed amendment to the Constitution leads to a major philosophical-political-legal debate, one that cannot be avoided simply by claiming that the legislatures would not make inordinate use of the freedom of action given them by section 96B or that judges could always correct any abuses by interpreting and reinterpreting the concept of "authority other than a court" with respect to the cases put before them.

How is it possible to propose a constitutional amendment that would open the door officially, and perhaps quite wide, to the delegation of important judicial powers to provincial administrative bodies, without first considering carefully the various rationales for the devolution of judicial functions to institutions other than courts of justice? How can such a proposal be made without a preliminary attempt to analyze the possible consequences on the operation of the judicial (i.e., the provincial courts and Supreme Court of Canada) and the administrative branches? How can a possible reduction in the responsibilities of "section 96 courts" be reconciled with the two grounds invoked to justify the presence of sections 96 to 100 in the Constitution Act, 1867: to guarantee the participation of the federal authorities in the organization and maintenance of provincial courts having important judicial responsibilities in federal and provincial matters, and to ensure that the principal judicial functions are exercised by judges with a minimum of functional constitutional independence? How can the delegation of important judicial functions to administrators be accepted when circumspection must be exercised in doing the same to lower court judges who, however, can offer certain guarantees of independence pursuant to provincial legislation and tradition?

In fact, it appears that the authors of the draft section 96B understood that the proposed amendment was directly linked to the larger question of the administration of justice in Canada. The explanatory notes contain the following passage:

> Certain principles were suggested in the course of these discussions which appeared to command considerable provincial support. They were to the effect that the Constitution should:
> (1) guarantee the existence of a superior court of general jurisdiction in each province;
> (2) guarantee the independence of the judiciary;
> (3) enable a province to establish bodies to administer the application of its laws;
> (4) enshrine the power of judicial review in the superior court of general jurisdiction; and
> (5) provide that there not be a dual system of courts.[124]

In light of all of these goals, strict attention should be given to the amendment of section 96, a provision that is part of a series of sections devoted to the Canadian judicature (96 to 101).

The proposed amendment affords an excellent opportunity for greater reflection on two fundamental issues: the adequacy of our judicial system given the current needs of society; and the different facets of the phenomenon of "administrative justice." It is certainly appropriate to correct the worst of the problems caused by section 96, but only after reflecting seriously on the whole of the problem areas underlying this section and the decisions based on it. Such reflection must precede any amendment, not follow it.

THE AMBIGUITY INHERENT IN THE FORMAL RECOGNITION OF THE SUPERVISORY POWERS OF SUPERIOR COURTS

Subsection 96B(2) serves to narrow the scope of the exception provided for in subsection 96B(1): the provincial superior courts will exercise their supervisory jurisdiction in the event of want or excess of jurisdiction by the authorities covered by the exception in subsection 96B(1).

This is neither the time nor the place to analyze the highly controversial and complex object of the supervisory role of superior courts over lower courts and administrative bodies that is exercised pursuant to their traditional review power which, incidentally, should not be confused with their appellate jurisdiction. This object is referred to in a very general way by the expression "want or excess of jurisdiction" or by the concept of "jurisdictional error" and even that of "ultra vires." Nevertheless, the supervisory role of the superior courts may in exceptional cases extend to "intrajurisdictional errors of law" (sometimes simply referred to as "errors of law") unless the legislature has forbidden superior judges to intervene on these grounds, by enacting a "privative clause." An intrajurisdictional error, that is, one committed by a lower court judge or by an administrator within his jurisdiction, is not a case of want or excess of jurisdiction. Even if, in the absence of a privative clause, superior court judges are authorized to correct this type of error, they tend not to do so, especially if the intrajurisdictional error is made by a body specializing in that particular field of law.[125]

As we have already seen, in provincial matters the right to exercise judicial review is already recognized to the superior courts by section 96. Let us not forget that in the important *Crevier* case, Chief Justice Laskin wrote (*per curiam*):

> It is true that this is the first time that this Court has declared unequivocally that a provincially-constituted statutory tribunal cannot constitutionally be immunized from review of decisions on questions of jurisdiction. In my opinion, this limitation, arising by virtue of s. 96, stands on the same footing as the well-accepted limitation on the power of provincial statutory tribunals to make unreviewable determinations of constitutionality. There may be differences of opinion as to what are questions of jurisdiction but, in my lexicon, they rise above and are different from errors of law, whether involving statutory construction or evidentiary matters or other matters. It is now unquestioned that privative clauses may, when properly framed, effectively oust judicial review on questions of law and, indeed, on other issues not touching jurisdiction. However, given that s. 96 is in the British North America Act and that it would make a mockery of it to treat it in non-functional formal terms as a mere appointing power, I can think of nothing that is more the hallmark of a superior court than the vesting of power in a provincial statutory tribunal to determine the limits of its jurisdiction without appeal or other review.[126]

That is the context within which the purpose of subsection 96B(2) must be examined.

Subsection 96B(1), which declares an exception to the application of section 96, undoubtedly represents the intention to maintain constitutionally the superior courts' right of control over those judicial functions that historically were protected by section 96 and that would henceforth be delegated under subsection (1) to provincial bodies other than courts.

However, the scope of subsection 96B(2) is not as broad as what was stated in *Crevier*, and its application might give rise to particular problems.

First of all, simple intrajurisdictional errors are not subject to judicial review. This is probably because in *Crevier* Chief Justice Laskin recognized that the legislatures now have the ability to remove this type of error from the scope of judicial review by the superior courts. It is difficult to see how an amendment to section 96 alone could be used to increase the constitutional guarantees pertaining to judicial review by adding to it a controversial area while at the same time reducing the legislative competence that *Crevier* recognized to the provinces in this field. The notes accompanying the draft amendment contain the following passage:

> [. . .] the draft presently suggests that judicial review be granted on the basis of want or excess of jurisdiction. These grounds seem broad enough to ensure the observance of the rule of law as developed by the courts. The expressions appear to allow some considerable scope for developing in order to meet changing circumstances.[127]

Superior court judges would still have the power to define the scope of the expression "want or excess of jurisdiction" (or "jurisdictional error"), and history tells us that, when they consider it necessary, they are able to transform an error within jurisdiction into a case of want or excess of jurisdiction.

Besides, subsection 96B(2) does not deal with the supervisory power of the superior courts as a whole, but only with respect to "a tribunal, board, commission or authority on which any jurisdiction of a superior court is conferred under subsection (1)."

Subsection 96B(2) takes no account of the operation of judicial review over lower "courts" (which are not covered by the liberalization in subsection (1)) and administrative bodies when the latter exercise functions that are not within the jurisdiction "of a superior court conferred under subsection (1)." Under these circumstances, it would seem that the supervisory power will continue to be guaranteed constitutionally by virtue of section 96 and *Crevier* and that, in principle, in the absence of a privative clause, it will apply to errors within jurisdiction.

In order to decide if the exercise of the supervisory power would no longer be governed by *Crevier* but rather by subsection 96B(2), it is necessary to ask if the institution in question is "other than a court" (*supra*) and if the jurisdiction exercised is in fact a "jurisdiction of a superior court." How can this second question be answered without once more adopting the reasoning formulated in the second section of this paper (The Scope of Section 96 in Provincial Matters), raising as an additional difficulty the need to distinguish historically between the activity of superior courts in 1867 (subsection 96B(2) applies) and the authority of county and district courts (subsection (2) does not apply). County and district courts are not superior courts, as can be seen from sections 96 to 100 of the *Constitution Act, 1867*; section 99 deals only with superior court judges.

It is possible that the authors of the draft amendment had the impression that "jurisdiction of a superior court" was in some way synonymous with "jurisdiction of a section 96 court."

Whatever the case, it seems that in the absence of a privative clause in the provincial enactment, the supervisory power exercised pursuant to section 96B cannot in principle cover errors within jurisdiction, unlike the supervisory power guaranteed by section 96 and *Crevier*. The logic of this distinction is not clear. Why should the supervisory role of superior courts in provincial matters be guaranteed by two sections of the Constitution (96 and 96B), each contemplating different subjects and, in principle, having a different field of action?

THE AMENDMENT'S SILENCE
ABOUT FEDERAL INSTITUTIONS

The draft amendment to section 96 has been available for public criticism since August 1983. Probably the authors of the discussion paper published by the federal Department of Justice did not have time to change their explanatory notes and draft to take account of the very important opinion of the Supreme Court of Canada, in June of the same year, in *McEvoy v. Attorney-General of New Brunswick*.[128]

In this reference, the Supreme Court surprised many observers by ruling that section 96 restricted the freedom of action of Parliament with respect to the devolution of judicial functions relating to subjects under its legislative competence; the following section of this paper will examine that question.

It is already evident that, henceforth, any amendment to section 96 must take this new element into consideration in the process of interpreting the well-known section of the *Constitution Act, 1867*. It would be inappropriate to adapt section 96 to the needs of Parliament with another amendment; the process of constitutional amendment is too complicated. In addition, it is fitting that the powers of Parliament and the legislatures relative to the administration of justice be considered from a comparative point of view during debate on section 96B.

For the above reasons, the draft constitutional amendment (s. 96B) is unacceptable in its present form; moreover, it has not been preceded by a detailed study of its administrative and judicial context. This is not a case of amending a regulation or even a statute, but rather the Canadian Constitution. The proposed amendment must be able to apply for many years in the future, and should not become an obstacle to the necessary transformations of the judicial or administrative systems.

Application of Section 96 to the Parliament of Canada

After noting that before the summer of 1983 it was generally held that section 96 did not apply to the Parliament of Canada, I shall endeavour to draw certain conclusions from a recent opinion of the Supreme Court declaring the opposite to be the case, though in terms that leave many questions unanswered and which will certainly contribute to much litigation.

A Generally Held Opinion: Section 96 Cannot Be Set Up Against Parliament's Legislative Activity

It was generally held that section 96 — as well as sections 97 to 100 — did not restrict Parliament's authority and discretion to delegate the responsibility for settling disputes that originated from the application of valid federal legislation; the legislator had the choice of a federal court (s. 101), a provincial superior court,[129] a provincial inferior court, a federal or provincial administrative body, etc. "Section 96 does not inhibit the Federal Parliament," was the standard view, based especially on the opinion of Chief Justice Laskin.[130]

This reasoning was used to justify Parliament's assigning, pursuant to certain sections of the *Criminal Code*, important legal authority to provincially appointed judges. It also explains why the Supreme Court of Canada found no constitutional obstacle to Parliament's decision in 1970 to withdraw from the provincial superior courts their traditional supervisory power over federal administrative bodies and to give it to the Federal Court. Recently Mr. Justice Estey, with the agreement of his brethren of the Supreme Court of Canada, wrote:

> That the federal Parliament can direct the review of the actions of a federal board to the Federal Court is no longer in doubt in our law.[131]

It also appears quite proper that Parliament considered it necessary to enact legislative measures dealing with the appointment, tenure, retirement age, remuneration and pension of the justices of the Supreme Court of Canada and the Federal Court, because textually sections 96 to 100 of the *Constitution Act, 1867* only contemplate the provinces' courts and could not therefore apply to federal courts established pursuant to section 101.[132]

Some jurists, and in particular Professor Lederman, did not share this point of view, but their more qualified opinion did not appear to have been adopted by the courts.[133] That explains why most observers were not in the least surprised when the New Brunswick Court of Appeal declared in 1981, in the reasons of Chief Justice Hughes:

In my view of the jurisprudence which has come to my attention, s. 96 of the B.N.A. Act, 1867 has been interpreted as a limiting provision respecting the legislative power of the Legislatures but provides no fetter upon Parliament.[134]

In that case, the Court of Appeal was asked to rule on the constitutionality of a scheme proposing the creation in New Brunswick of a unified court of criminal jurisdiction, made up of judges appointed by the Lieutenant Governor in Council; this court would be called upon to hear cases dealing with infractions of federal criminal law and provincial penal law; in provincial matters its jurisdiction would be created by a provincial enactment, and in federal matters by federal legislation. The two governments concerned had apparently already agreed upon the proposal and both pleaded its constitutionality before the Court of Appeal. The questions presented to the Court dealt correctly not only with the jurisdiction of the Legislature to carry out its part of the scheme[135] but also with that of Parliament to withdraw from the province's superior court of criminal jurisdiction all (or a large part — the project was not too specific on this point) of the powers it had exercised in 1867 in the field of criminal law. The Court of Appeal concluded that section 96 was no obstacle, because it did not restrict the freedom of action of Parliament in federal matters.

In June 1983, the Supreme Court of Canada expressed a contrary view.[136]

A HORNET'S NEST:
THE CONTRARY BUT IMPRECISE OPINION
OF THE SUPREME COURT OF CANADA

The Supreme Court's opinion is so brief, laconic and even obscure that it is impossible to grasp its exact scope.[137] In the Court's defence, however, it should be noted that the proposed scheme contained very serious ambiguities, specifically on the question of whether the Superior Court would or would not continue to exercise its supervisory power over the new unified court; unfortunately, the proposal submitted for judicial examination did not take the form of a legislative text. Some general observations may, however, be drawn from the Supreme Court's opinion, though they may give rise to more questions than they answer.

There can be no doubt that sections 96 to 100 restrict Parliament's freedom of action:

> The Judicature sections of the *Constitution Act, 1867* [. . .] apply to Parliament as well as to the provincial Legislatures.[138]

Why? Because the purpose of these sections is to guarantee the independence of superior court judges — the Supreme Court does not refer to county or district court judges — a purpose that is not confined to the provinces.[139] However, the Court posits another ground: Parliament is not allowed to hamper the exercise of the power (and duty) of appointment expressly granted to the Governor General by the Constitution by substantially reducing the judicial responsibilities of the superior courts.[140] If Parliament limits the jurisdiction of the provincial superior courts in favour of judges appointed by the Lieutenant Governor in Council, the importance of the Governor General's power of appointment is accordingly reduced.

Certain passages suggest that the restrictions upon the legislative power of Parliament in federal matters are identical to those imposed upon the provinces in provincial matters. As the Court stated:

> Section 96 bars Parliament from altering the constitutional scheme envisaged by the judicature sections of the *Constitution Act, 1867* just as it does the provinces from doing so.[141]

Elsewhere in its opinion the Court also appears to hold the view that under the circumstances it is appropriate to apply the principles set forth in *Residential Tenancies*.[142]

But other parts of the judgment suggest at least some hesitancy in applying the same ground rules. The Supreme Court points out that if the new unified court of criminal jurisdiction were not subject to the supervisory power of the superior court of criminal jurisdiction, *Crevier might* apply.[143] The rationale for the opinion appears to be that the Supreme Court considers that section 96 would be violated because Parliament would effectively be withdrawing from the superior court virtually its entire jurisdiction in criminal matters, and not simply some of its responsibilities:

> What is being contemplated here is not one or a few transfers of criminal law power, such as has already been accomplished under the *Criminal Code*, but a complete obliteration of superior court criminal law jurisdiction [. . .] There is, in our view, a cardinal difference between mere alteration or diminution of criminal jurisdiction and complete exclusion of such jurisdiction.[144]

The same quantitative consideration does not apply when section 96 is being applied to provincial legislation. Perhaps the Supreme Court wishes to invite lawyers not to impugn legislative provisions currently included in the *Criminal Code* when they assign to provincial courts made up of judges appointed by the provinces (e.g., in Quebec, the Court of Sessions of the Peace) important jurisdiction in criminal matters.[145] Hence, the Court seems to recognize a special status for Parliament, after stating that it is subject to section 96 as are the provinces. At no time does the Court examine whether the jurisdiction of county and district courts is also protected from federal initiatives.

It is also important to note that nowhere does the Supreme Court of Canada refer to the decisions in which it has recognized that, without violating the *Constitution Act, 1867*, Parliament has withdrawn the traditional power of supervision by provincial superior courts over federal administrative bodies and given it to the Federal Court.[146] The unified court of criminal jurisdiction was to be created by the province of New Brunswick pursuant to section 92(14), and not by Parliament, possibly pursuant to section 101. Consequently in *McEvoy* the Supreme Court was not strictly required to, and indeed took considerable care not to, deal with the problem of the coexistence of sections 96 to 100 with section 101, which grants Parliament the power to create "additional courts" for the better administration of federal laws, and this "notwithstanding anything" in the 1867 Act. Although the Court maintained that sections 96 to 100 limited Parliament's jurisdiction as much as that of the provinces, it did not also hold that these constitutional provisions applied to Parliament when it created additional federal "courts" and delegated judicial powers to them. It did not say a word about this important question, notwithstanding . . . the generality of some of its affirmations.

This is obviously a hornet's nest. Section 96 would not apply to Parliament in all circumstances; and when it could be invoked, there would be no guarantee of a complete application of the same "ground rules" as apply to provincial legislation.

Up to a certain point section 96 would limit the freedom of action of Parliament in cases where it granted judicial functions to provincial institutions, be they courts of justice or administrative bodies.

But it is still unclear whether section 96 applies to "courts" created pursuant to section 101 and if, therefore, a distinction should be drawn between courts presided over, on the one hand, by judges who, pursuant to federal legislation, have a status equivalent to that of "section 96 judges," as is more or less the case with the Federal Court, and, on the other hand, those who do not (regarding appointment, tenure, etc.).[147]

Section 96 would very probably render invalid any bestowal by Parliament of judicial functions historically protected by section 96 on federal bodies that are not "courts," subject perhaps to the liberalization that apparently results from *McEvoy*. These bodies cannot benefit from the protection of section 101, raising therefore the fundamental question asked in the preceding section of this paper: how can one determine whether or not a federal body is a court?[148]

The grounds used to justify the presence of sections 96 to 100 in the 1867 Act speak in favour of the application of these sections to the legislative jurisdiction of Parliament. For example, how can Parliament decree that a lower federal court or administrative body should not be subject to the traditional review by superior courts (i.e. for want or excess of jurisdiction)? It is apparent that because of the wording of sections 96 to 101 and the Supreme Court decision in *McEvoy*, there is no easy way, given the current state of the law, to establish a balance between the limitations on provincial legislative jurisdiction and those that should also be imposed upon the legislative powers of Parliament. Much litigation looms on the horizon.

Conclusion

The hundreds of decisions and references since 1867, including a dozen from the Supreme Court of Canada since 1975, are evidence that section 96 is the source of serious restrictions on the exclusive jurisdiction of the legislatures from using their discretion in assigning judicial functions to their provincial institutions (i.e., courts of justice, administrative bodies) in order to apply legislation that they otherwise have the power to enact. Moreover, the Supreme Court of Canada has just opened a new front in the unending "battle of 96" that has raged for more than a century by ruling that the same section also restricts, though perhaps to a lesser degree, the discretion of Parliament to delegate judicial duties in federal matters to provincial institutions. This decision also appears to suggest that the freedom of Parliament would also be limited when it wishes to call upon the services of federal administrative bodies. Nevertheless, the same may not be the case when Parliament grants judicial functions to additional federal "courts" created under the "notwithstanding" power of section 101, although it is perhaps necessary here to make some distinctions depending upon the legal status of those persons presiding over such courts: section 96 might perhaps be an obstacle to parliamentary sovereignty if the judges of these additional courts do not have a status comparable to that of judges of "section 96 courts."

The law as defined in these cases permits the identification of the restrictions on provincial legislative jurisdiction, and gives judges who are responsible for its application a considerable margin of interpretation from which para-legal considerations are not absent. This partially explains the divergent views expressed in many of the decisions. The legislatures are actually prevented from assigning to any person or body other than a "section 96 judge" a *judicial function* that is part of a *type of jurisdiction* exercised *exclusively in 1867* by the superior, district or county courts, unless the *institutional setting* in which this function is found serves as a catalyst and renders it *ancillary to a broader administrative function.* The future will tell if perhaps the ground rules of the interpretation of section 96 are different when Parliament is involved. Even with the explanation that judges have been drawn into defining the scope of section 96 in a "functional" way, they have taken upon themselves an impossible task: to establish relatively clear, manageable, and realistic criteria that would allow the identification of judicial functions that must be ascribed solely to "section 96 courts" in today's state with its all-encompassing legislation.

The problems raised by section 96 limit the freedom of the legislatures and Parliament to assign judicial functions to institutions that they believe to be better equipped to exercise them (in 1984, and not in 1867), considering the specificity of the function, the nature of the particular institution chosen and, let it be hoped, the needs of the citizen as well as the administration of justice in general (e.g., overloading of various courts of justice). Even more, the "institutional setting" rule of interpretation, officially proclaimed by the Supreme Court of Canada in 1975 in order to avoid emasculating many provincial administrative tribunals, is a genuine invitation to delegate judicial functions to bodies distinct from courts (i.e., in their structure, procedures and discretionary powers) and to escape in that way from the grasp of section 96, even if such delegation is not always rational or in the best interests of the public.

In Quebec, the rationalization of the judicial system has sometimes been considered by proposing the creation of a unified court of first instance, made up of judges whose status (i.e., appointment, remuneration, independence, etc.) is already defined by an existing provincial statute. This court would be divided into specialized divisions (civil, family, criminal, administrative, etc.). Given the current state of the law, such a reform could only be partial, even assuming that Parliament does not attempt to obstruct matters by withdrawing from the new court its responsibilities in federal matters, because the National Assembly is not empowered to remove from Superior Court judges the numerous judicial functions that are historically protected by section 96. It is no secret that some judicial functions currently assigned to Quebec provincial institutions are very vulnerable to a section 96 challenge, and their transfer to the new unified court composed of provincially appointed judges would not remove this sword of Damocles.

This situation is unacceptable, and one can only regret that judges are led to make observations, relevant as they may be, such as those made by Mr. Justice Dickson on behalf of the Supreme Court of Canada in the *Residential Tenancies* reference:

I am neither unaware of, nor unsympathetic to, the arguments advanced in support of a view that s. 96 should not be interpreted so as to thwart or unduly restrict the future growth of provincial administrative tribunals. Yet, however worthy the policy objectives, it must be recognized that we, as a Court, are not given the freedom to choose whether the problem is such that provincial, rather than federal, authority should deal with it. We must seek to give effect to the Constitution as we understand it and with due regard for the manner in which it has been judicially interpreted in the past. If the impugned power is violative of s. 96 it must be struck down.[149]

The uncertainty created by the case law on section 96 is incompatible with the importance of the exercise of judicial functions in our society. It is unacceptable that the powers bestowed upon courts of justice and bodies not made up of "section 96 judges" can be so easily impugned, rightly or wrongly, by lawyers who often are simply seeking to paralyze an institution and buy time; the utility and effectiveness of the institutions in question are sapped by these legal challenges, which are a goldmine for lawyers but which do nothing to enhance the reputation of our judicial system. It may be inevitable that the legislation dealing with social relations is complex but it is unacceptable that citizens seeking a rapid and economical determination of their rights are exposed to the judicial jousting occasioned by the rules of interpretation of section 96, rules whose purpose is to allow judges to determine, often many years after enactment of a statute, if the authority chosen by the legislator to settle disputes is legally able to do so. What a bizarre spectacle the Supreme Court judges present us with when, mired in the shifting sands of section 96, they hold, for example, that a Quebec civil servant has jurisdiction to cancel a lease but an Ontario civil servant has not. As Professors Brun and Tremblay have pointed out:

> In the current state of affairs, there are almost as many "constitutional" cases dealing with jurisdictional squabbles between federal, superior and provincial courts as there are substantive constitutional cases. This situation provokes a politico-judicial emulation that inhibits the effective independence of judges and tribunals.[150]　　　　　　　　　　　　　　　(translation)

Is it necessary to pay such a high social price in order to preserve for federal authorities the power to appoint judges to the principal provincial courts ("section 96 courts"), a power above and beyond that to appoint judges to the federal courts, and notably to the Supreme Court of Canada, and this at a time when the number of cases inspired by section 96 is likely to increase? Indeed, the governments are now trying to amend legislation in many traditional areas of law (including property law, contracts, civil liability, etc.) with a view to adapting them to new social requirements (environmental protection, protection of specific social groups like workers, etc.), and they regularly create specialized institutions to oversee the application of this new legislation. These reforms are often threatened by the spectre of section 96.

At this stage of the discussion, other considerations come into play. Section 96 should not be viewed as a provision whose effect is simply to give the right to patronage to federal rather than provincial authorities. It is an integral part of a group of sections (96 to 101), that are grouped in the *Constitution Act, 1867* as a chapter entitled "Judicature"; this chapter completes section 92(14), which accords the legislatures a broad jurisdiction in the area of the "administration of justice."

Section 101, a colossal exception to section 92(14), gives federal authorities important and exclusive powers in the creation of federal courts, particularly with respect to organizing and circumscribing the responsibilities of the Supreme Court of Canada; the exclusive nature of these powers is at the least annoying, given that sections 96 to 100 together with section 92(14) indicate that the organization and maintenance of the principal provincial courts depend on the co-operation of both federal and provincial authorities.

Nevertheless, the chapter entitled "Judicature" is the institutional framework with which section 96 is interwoven. The Supreme Court of Canada has, indeed, declared that sections 96 to 100 appear in the 1867 Act for the following reasons: to ensure federal participation in the organization and maintenance of the courts of justice that are called upon in principle to settle disputes arising from the application of both federal and provincial legislation; and to ensure the independence of judges of the provincial superior courts (it would be more correct to speak of a "minimum" of independence). In addition, the Supreme Court has recently discovered in section 96 a guarantee of the existence in provincial matters of the traditional task of superior court judges, to review at the very least jurisdictional errors (i.e., want or excess of jurisdiction) committed by lower courts and administrative bodies. It is possible that this guarantee, which is in principle distinct from the earlier guarantee dealing with the review of the constitutionality of legislation and executive action, may extend to federal matters; my hesitation on this subject is related to the new issue arising from questions about the scope of section 96 in federal matters.

From the moment that section 96 — combined with sections 97 to 100 — is officially given such constitutional purposes by the Supreme Court of Canada, it can no longer be viewed in the same way by anyone who is legitimately disturbed by the numerous controversies and kaleidoscopic case law that it engenders, and it is easier to accept that the legislators cannot easily limit the judicial responsibilities of superior, district and county courts. One can no longer approach the issue of the possible repeal or amendment of section 96 from the same standpoint; fundamental issues are at stake in the current constitutional context. Section 101 is also a part of this key group of provisions because it deals, on the one hand, with the organization and the role of the court that heads the entire Canadian judicial system and, on the other hand, with the additional federal courts that Parliament may create in order to bestow upon them very limited responsibilities because one explanation for the existence of sections 96 to 100 is that provincial courts ought, in principle, to be empowered to settle disputes arising from the application of federal statutes. One's view of the substance of section 101 and the use that has been made of it is closely linked to one's opinion of both the existence and the scope of sections 96 to 100. (For example, is the jurisdiction of the Federal Court too extensive?)

It is impossible for this paper to deal satisfactorily (and briefly) with possible solutions to the very serious and therefore unacceptable difficulties engendered by the section 96 law. Any solution is in reality interwoven in a vast constitutional framework (sections 92(14), 96 to 101 and even 91(27)), whose scope is not the purpose of this paper. Nor may such a solution be considered while ignoring another fundamental problem inherent in the issue of section 96: under what circumstances does the public interest require that judicial functions be assigned to bodies that are not courts of justice, under what rules of procedure should these functions be exercised and to what degree of judicial review (and by which courts) and to which remedies available should these judicial functions be subjected? And how can these issues be addressed acceptably without at the same time raising questions about the ability of our current judicial machinery to meet the needs it must satisfy?

The extent of the difficulties raised by the necessity to amend section 96 explains why I consider the amendment currently proposed by the federal and provincial authorities (section 96B) unacceptable. Its wording is technically deficient; in addition, it fails to consider the general legislative environment of section 96, and it is so casual as to suggest including within the chapter of the Constitution devoted to the "Judicature" a provision authorizing legislatures to delegate important judicial functions to members of the administration but not to provincially appointed judges.

I can only subscribe to a recommendation of the Canadian Bar Association:

> Be it hereby resolved that the Canadian Bar Association recommend to the Minister of Justice and the Attorneys General of the provinces that the suggested amendment to Section 96 of the Constitution Act, 1867, be deferred until a thorough study has been made of the need to reform all of the judicature provisions of the Constitution Act, 1867, including the jurisdiction of the courts, tenure and appointment of judges, the independence of the judiciary and the constitution and appointment of members to the Supreme Court of Canada.[151]

In this respect, the notes accompanying the draft section 96B already suggest some of the possible guides for this fundamental reform. It is said therein that the provinces — the opinion of the federal authorities on this subject is not known — subscribe to the following goals: the Constitution should guarantee the existence of a superior court of general jurisdiction in each province and should state that a dual system of provincial and federal courts has no place in Canada;[152] the Constitution should also officially recognize that it is the responsibility of the superior courts to supervise the lower courts and administrative bodies; the independence of the judiciary must be guaranteed by the Constitution; the Constitution should not prevent the provinces from creating bodies with responsibility for applying their legislation. Of course these principles were adopted at a time when it was probably believed that sections 96 to 100 would not restrict the legislative jurisdiction of Parliament; but this new development does not change the value of these goals which, nevertheless, in no way address the role and the composition of the Supreme Court of Canada.

In light of the foregoing comments, it would be presumptuous to attempt to provide, in the conclusions of this paper, a definitive list of amendments that should be made to the *Constitution Act, 1867* to solve the problems raised by section 96, while at the same time taking into consideration all constitutional provisions relating to the administration of justice. At best, we can outline some general approaches that have not yet been clarified by the detailed studies suggested above and which are inspired by the basic principles proposed by the provinces as a group — a consensus that cannot be ignored.[153]

In the first place, the status of the Supreme Court of Canada must be settled. For example, it appears unthinkable that the provincial authorities should not at the very least participate in the appointment of members of this court, especially at a time when their politico-legal role continues to grow. The following remark applies to all members of the judiciary, but in particular to justices of Canada's highest court:

> All legislation has to be applied to specific situations, and such application requires interpretation. As Bishop Hoadley warned King George I, "Whosoever hath an absolute authority to interpret any written or spoken laws, it is he who is truly the Law-giver to all intents and purposes, and not the person who first wrote and spoke them."[154]

The Constitution should also confirm the principle of unitary jurisdiction that has applied to judicial organization in Canada since 1867, and by which it is normally the provincial courts that administer justice, subject ultimately to the appellate jurisdiction of the Supreme Court of Canada. This principle permits not only an explanation of the presence of sections 96 to 100 but also justifies certain restrictions made by the Supreme Court, although a source of practical difficulties, to the jurisdiction of the Federal Court. The Fathers of Confederation were clearly in favour of the principle of unitary jurisdiction. In 1867 it was the provincial courts that administered justice, both federal and provincial; section 129 of the *Constitution Act* declares so specifically. If the authors of this statute had wished to establish a dualist system of federal and provincial courts, they would not have limited themselves, in section 101, to providing for possible additional federal courts; they would not have expressly refused, in two specific places (ss. 92(14) and 91(27)), to give Parliament the power to create courts of criminal jurisdiction; they would not have used the general expression "administration of justice" in section 92(14) alone. The judicial system of a country must endeavour to be as simple as possible, in the interest of the citizen, and the principle of unitary jurisdiction favours such an objective. What a medieval and discouraging spectacle to see a citizen searching for a judge legally empowered to hear his or her case.

The existence of a provincial superior court and its basic jurisdiction should probably be guaranteed by the Constitution. This court should be called upon to settle all disputes not expressly assigned by the appropriate legislator to other federal or provincial institutions; the Constitution should specify that other institutions could be either courts or administrative bodies (or something else). Furthermore, such a court would have the unquestionable right to exercise the traditional supervisory power over lower courts and administrative bodies on grounds that should be considered further but which would certainly include constitutional questions; even after reflection, it is conceivable that one might find no better expression than "want or excess of jurisdiction." If it appears necessary to give to a federal court — as is currently the case with the Federal Court — certain powers of supervision in federal matters, the Constitution should so provide expressly because this is such an important exception to the principle of unified jurisdiction.

The necessary independence of all judges of provincial and federal courts (including the Supreme Court) should be guaranteed by the Constitution. In this respect, there is no distinction between lower and superior courts: all are called upon to dispense justice. The guarantees could certainly go beyond the subjects actually mentioned in sections 97 to 100 of the Constitution, dealing for example with the process of choosing judges, their immunities, their income guarantees, etc. The pertinent sections should be drafted so as to indicate clearly that they do not apply to members of the administrative bodies to whom the legislators might have delegated judicial functions. This does not exclude the possibility that elsewhere (e.g., the *Canadian Charter of Rights and Freedoms*, a federal or provincial statute or the common law) there might be certain provisions recognizing the rights of citizens when they are dealing with administrative bodies empowered to exercise judicial powers. The right to an apparently impartial decision is an example of such a right.

The existence of a provincial court of appeal would be provided for, but further questions would have to be asked about the responsibilities granted it by the Constitution. This issue is linked to the problem of defining the role of the Supreme Court of Canada.

With the independence of the judiciary guaranteed, provincial authorities would appoint, remunerate and remove judges of the provincial courts, pursuant to provisions of the Constitution; the federal authorities would do likewise with federal court judges. The executive power to appoint judges would then lie, as is the general rule, with the authorities that have the legislative jurisdiction to create the courts and ensure their operation. Given that the judges of the superior courts and provincial appeal courts would have important responsibilities in both federal and provincial matters, their appointment would be subject to a mandatory process of consultation with the federal authorities. This is not a new suggestion; it appears for example in the report of the Task Force on Canadian Unity:

> The current practice under section 96 of the BNA Act whereby judges to higher provincial courts are appointed by the governor general on the advice of the central cabinet is a questionable remnant of federal centralization. We suggest that consideration be given to a procedure whereby all provincial judges would be appointed by the provincial governments, but in the case of higher court judges only after consultation with the central government,

since they interpret central laws as well. Federal Court judges would, of course, continue to be appointed by the central government.[155]

This consultation procedure would best be modelled on the one that would likely be set up for the appointment of judges to the Supreme Court of Canada. The distribution of the appointing power among provincial authorities would probably facilitate the access by jurists from different milieux to the major provincial courts.

If the more elaborate studies suggested above confirm the relevance of the preceding proposals, the legislatures would finally have the power to delegate judicial functions to any provincial institution of their choice: superior or lower courts of justice, administrative (or other) bodies. Parliament could do the same with respect to federal and provincial institutions. The choice of an administrative authority would be by legislation; the exercise of judicial powers by such an authority (or a lower court) would be undeniably subject to review by the superior courts if an aggrieved citizen so demanded; the same would apply, incidentally, to the non-judicial functions of the authority.

Thus, the legislatures would have the jurisdiction to create a modern system of courts of justice to which they themselves would name the members. It is possible that they would be less likely to delegate judicial responsibilities to institutions other than courts of law. A detailed study of the rationale for "administrative justice" would certainly help the governments make enlightened decisions on this subject.

Notes

This study is a translation of the original French-language text which was completed in July 1984.

1. For an example of a provincial statute providing for the establishment of a judicial system, see, in Quebec, the *Courts of Justice Act*, R.S.Q., c. T-16.
2. "The Governor General shall appoint the judges of the Superior, District, and County Courts in each Province except those of the Courts of Probate in Nova Scotia and New Brunswick."
3. See particularly, A.L. Linden (ed.), *The Canadian Judiciary*, 1976.
4. "The Salaries, Allowances, and Pensions of the Judges of the Superior, District, and County Courts (except the Courts of Probate in Nova Scotia and New Brunswick), and of the Admiralty Courts in Cases where the Judges thereof are for the Time being paid by Salary, shall be fixed and provided by the Parliament of Canada." On this subject, see the *Judges Act*, R.S.C. 1970, c. J-1.
5. "(1) Subject to subsection two of this section, the Judges of the Superior Courts shall hold office during good behaviour, but shall be removable by the Governor General on Address of the Senate and House of Commons.

   "(2) A Judge of a Superior Court, whether appointed before or after the coming into force of this section, shall cease to hold office upon attaining the age of seventy-five years, or upon the coming into force of this section if at that time he has already attained that age."
6. See, however, infra, n. 10. The transitional provisions of section 129 of the *Constitution Act, 1867* are not here taken into account.
7. *R. v. Thomas Fuller Construction Ltd.*, [1980] 1 S.C.R. 695, 706 (for the majority).

8. "The Parliament of Canada may, notwithstanding anything in this Act, from Time to Time provide for the Constitution, Maintenance, and Organization of a General Court of Appeal for Canada, and for the Establishment of any additional Courts for the better Administration of the Laws of Canada."

9. It is not appropriate at this point to consider the special problem of including in the Constitution of Canada all sections (or a part) of the *Supreme Court Act*. On this issue, see: S.A. Scott, "Pussycat, Pussycat or Patriation and the New Constitutional Amendment Processes" (1982), *Univ. of Western Ont. L.R.* 247, pp. 269–75; H. Brun and G. Tremblay, *Droit constitutionnel*, 1982, pp. 366–70. This inclusion has intentionally or unintentionally been accomplished by certain provisions of the *Constitution Act, 1982* relative to the amendment process (ss. 41 and 42).

10. *Supreme Court Act*, R.S.C. 1970, c. S-19. Section 35 states: "The Supreme Court shall have, hold and exercise an appellate, civil and criminal jurisdiction within and throughout Canada." See also the *Judges Act*, R.S.C. 1970, c. J-1. Consult W.R. Lederman, "The Supreme Court of Canada and the Canadian Judicial System" (1975), 13 *Transactions of the Royal Society of Canada* 209.

11. *R. v. Thomas Fuller Construction Ltd.*, [1980] 1 S.C.R. 695.

12. *Federal Court Act*, R.S.C. 1970, c. 10 (2nd Supp.). See also *the Judges Act*, R.S.C. 1970, c. J-1.

13. *Quebec North Shore Paper Co. v. Canadian Pacific Ltd.*, [1977] 2 S.C.R. 1054.

14. *Supra*, n. 12.

15. P.W. Hogg, *Constitutional Law of Canada*, 1977, p. 125.

16. On this subject see in particular J.M. Evans, "Federal Jurisdiction — A Lamentable Situation" (1981), 59 *Can. Bar Rev.* 124.

17. *Tomko v. Labour Relations Board (N.S.)*, [1977] 1 S.C.R. 112; *Jones v. Edmonton Catholic School District no. 7*, [1977] 2 S.C.R. 872; *A.G. Quebec v. Farrah*, [1978] 2 S.C.R. 638; *Corporation of the City of Mississauga v. Regional Municipality of Peel*, [1979] 2 S.C.R. 244; *Canadian Broadcasting Corp. v. Quebec Police Commission*, [1979] 2 S.C.R. 618; *Re Residential Tenancies Act, 1979*, [1981] 1 S.C.R. 714; *Crevier v. A.G. Quebec*, [1981] 2 S.C.R. 220; *Massey Ferguson Industries Ltd. v. Government of Saskatchewan*, [1981] 2 S.C.R. 413; *Re B.C. Family Relations Act*, [1982] 1 S.C.R. 62; *Capital Regional District v. Concerned Citizens of British Columbia*, [1982] 2 S.C.R. 842; *McEvoy v. A.G. of New Brunswick* (1983), 148 D.L.R. (3d) 25 (S.C.C.); *Re Attorney-General of Quebec and Grondin* (1984), 4 D.L.R. (4th) 605 (S.C.C.). See also *Abel Skiver Farm v. Town of Sainte-Foy*, [1983] 1 S.C.R. 403.

18. *Séminaire de Chicoutimi v. City of Chicoutimi*, [1973] S.C.R. 681.

19. *Attorney General for Ontario v. Victoria Medical Building Ltd.*, [1960] S.C.R. 32.

20. "Sir Lyman Duff and the Constitution" (1974), 12 *Osgoode Hall L.J.* 261, p. 325. See also P.S. Millar and C. Baar, *Judicial Administration in Canada*, 1981, pp. 75–106.

21. *McEvoy v. A.G. of New Brunswick* (1983), 148 D.L.R. (3d) 25, 38 (S.C.C.).

22. *Re B.C. Family Relations Act*, [1982] 1 S.C.R. 62, 72.

23. K.C. Wheare, *Federal Government*, 4th ed., 1963, p. 68; W.J. Wagner, *Federal States and Their Judiciary*, 1959, pp. 119 and 325.

24. For the text of these resolutions, see *Parliamentary Debates on the Confederation of British North American Provinces*, 1865, p. 3.

25. "It is not an unreasonable reading of the 'Judicature' sections of the B.N.A. Act that section 96 was far from being the pivotal provision to which the others were subordinate. Rather it appears that section 96 was a projection of section 100 or, at least, to be read in conjunction with it. If the Parliament of Canada was to fix and provide the salaries of provincial judges, it might properly appoint them. [. . .] The separation of the provisions for appointment and for payment as they appeared in the B.N.A. Act was, so far as there is any evidence at all, the draftman's work." "Municipal Tax Assessment and Section 96 of the British North American Act: The Olympia Bowling Alleys Case" (1955), 33 *Can. Bar Rev.* 993, pp. 997–98.

26. Burwell, M.P. in *Parliamentary Debates*, *supra*, n. 24, pp. 580–81.

27. *Parliamentary Debates*, *supra*, n. 24, p. 394.

28. *Re Residential Tenancies Act, 1979*, [1981] 1 S.C.R. 714, 728.

29. *R. v. Thomas Fuller Construction Ltd.*, [1980] 1 S.C.R. 695, 713. On the jurisdiction of provincial courts in federal matters, see F. Chevrette and H. Marx, *Droit constitutionnel*, 1982, pp. 833-40. Recently, in a unanimous decision of the Supreme Court of Canada, Mr. Justice Estey noted that, when in doubt, the jurisdiction of provincial courts in disputes arising from the application of federal statutes must be presumed: *Northern Pipeline Agency v. Perehinec* (1984), 4 D.L.R. (4th) 1, 8.

30. *Valin v. Langlois* (1879), 3 S.C.R. 1. Having noted that provincial courts had the duty to apply both federal and provincial statutes, Mr. Justice Fournier pointed out that this arrangement could undoubtedly explain the origin of ss. 96 to 100 and that if the courts "were to have been exclusively at the service of local governments then the latter would have been left to choose and remunerate the officers upon whom the federal government could impose no duties" (translation), p. 46. See also Mr. Justice Ritchie's opinion.

31. *Quebec North Shore Paper Co. v. Canadian Pacific Ltd.*, [1977] 2 S.C.R. 1054; *McNamara Construction (Western) Ltd. v. The Queen*, [1977] 2 S.C.R. 654; *R. v. Thomas Fuller Construction Ltd.*, [1980] 1 S.C.R. 695. But the Supreme Court appears to be more indulgent toward the Federal Court; see *Rhine v. The Queen*, [1980] 2 S.C.R. 442. For a criticism of the position that the Supreme Court has taken with respect to jurisdiction of the Federal Court, see J.M. Evans, *supra*, n. 16. In my view, the author does not accord sufficient importance to the constitutional aspect of this controversy. The Supreme Court has liberalized its position in recognizing a jurisdiction in constitutional matters for the Federal Court: *Northern Telecom Canada Ltd. v. Communications Workers of Canada* (1983), 147 D.L.R. (3d) 1 (S.C.C.).

32. *Martineau and Sons Ltd. v. City of Montreal*, [1932] A.C. 113, 121.

33. *Toronto Corporation v. York Corporation*, [1938] A.C. 415, 426.

34. *In re Adoption Act*, [1938] S.C.R. 398, 415 and 416.

35. *Re B.C. Family Relations Act*, [1982] 1 S.C.R. 62, 93 and 94.

36. *McEvoy v. A.G. of New Brunswick* (1983), 148 D.L.R. (3d) 25 (S.C.C.).

37. This justification is presented as "not compelling"; *supra*, n. 35.

38. *McEvoy v. A.G. of New Brunswick* (1983), 148 D.L.R. (3d) 25, 38 (S.C.C.). In *Dupont v. Inglis*, [1958] S.C.R. 535, which was not cited by the Court, Mr. Justice Rand stressed on behalf of the Supreme Court that sections 96ff. were "provisions vital to the Judicature of Canada" (p. 542).

39. The Court has granted leave to appeal from two judgments where this question is raised: *R. v. Valente* (1983), 145 D.L.R. (3d) 452 (Ont. C.A.); *Beauregard v. Government of Canada* (1983), 148 D.L.R. (3d) 205 (F.C.A.). In 1960, when section 99 of the *Constitution Act, 1867* was amended, with respect to the retirement age of judges, the federal government attempted within this section to put judges of county and district courts on the same footing as superior court judges; see G. Pépin, *Les tribunaux administratifs et la Constitution — Études des articles 96 à 101 de l'A.A.N.B.*, 1969, pp. 125-29.

40. The issue of independence of the Canadian judiciary is far from clear. On the one hand, the content of this notion is difficult to express with precision (appointment, remuneration, tenure, immunity, extra-judicial work, obligation of reserve, etc.) and, on the other hand, it is often difficult to determine its origin, based on a plurality of foundations that have not the same legal authority (constitution, statute, constitutional convention, tradition, public opinion, etc.). See specifically on this subject: W.R. Lederman, "The Independence of the Judiciary" (1956), 34 *Can. Bar Rev.* 769 and 1139; S. Shetreet, *Judges on Trial: A Study of the Appointment and Accountability of the English Judiciary*, 1976; H. Brun and D. Lemieux, "Politisation du pouvoir judiciaire et judiciarisation du pouvoir politique: la séparation traditionnelle des pouvoirs a-t-elle vécu?" (1977), 18 *Cahiers de D.* 265; *Beauregard v. Government of Canada* (1983), 148 D.L.R. (3d) 205 (F.C.A.); *R. v. Valente*.

41. See, in particular, G. Pépin, *supra*, n. 39; P.W. Hogg, *supra*, n. 15, pp. 115-21 and 129-39; H. Marx and F. Chevrette, *supra*, n. 29, pp. 870 and 903-14; J.F. Jobin, *L'article 96 de la Loi constitutionnelle de 1867 et les organismes inférieurs d'appel*, 1984.

42. [1981] 1 S.C.R. 714.

43. *Di Orio v. The Warden of the Common Jail of the City of Montreal*, [1978] 1 S.C.R. 152.

44. See G. Pépin, *supra*, n. 39, pp. 93–104.

45. *Liquidators of Maritime Bank v. The Receiver General of New Brunswick*, [1892] A.C. 437. It was decided that the Lieutenant Governor was also a representative of the Queen and that he was enabled to exercise the royal prerogatives dealing with subjects under the legislative jurisdiction of the provinces.

46. *Rimmer v. Hannon* (1921), 60 D.L.R. 637.

47. *Scott v. Attorney General of Canada* (1923), 3 W.W.R. 929, 932 (Lord Atkinson).

48. *In re Adoption Act*, [1938] S.C.R. 398, 404ff.

49. [1938] A.C. 415. It was in this judgment that Lord Atkin advanced his theory of the "three principal pillars in the temple of justice."

50. *In re Adoption Act*, [1938] S.C.R. 398, 409ff. (Chief Justice Duff, *per curiam*).

51. *Labour Relations Board of Saskatchewan v. John East Iron Works Ltd.*, [1949] A.C. 134, 151–53.

52. See specifically on this subject G. Pépin, *supra*, n. 39, pp. 213–31.

53. *Re Residential Tenancies Act, 1979*, [1981] S.C.R. 714, 728. See also pp. 729–30.

54. [1978] 2 S.C.R. 638, 642 (Spence, Dickson and Estey, J.J., concurring).

55. "Provincial Administrative Tribunals and Judicial Power — The Exaggeration of Section 96 of the British North American Act" (1963), 41 *Can. Bar Rev.* 446, p. 446.

56. *Tomko v. Labour Relations Board (N.S.)*, [1977] 1 S.C.R. 112, 120.

57. In Quebec it is necessary to add to the list in question the old "circuit courts" presided by a judge of the Superior Court: *Séminaire de Chicoutimi v. City of Chicoutimi*, [1973] S.C.R. 681, 689 (Fauteux, J., *per curiam*).

58. For a rare example of application of the institutional method to a court of justice, see *Renvoi touchant la constitutionnalité de la Loi concernant la juridiction de la Cour de magistrat*, [1965] Que. Q.B. 1, reversed on technical grounds by the Supreme Court of Canada, [1965] S.C.R. 772. The Quebec Magistrate's Court is now called the Provincial Court.

59. *Re B.C. Family Relations Act*, [1982] 1 S.C.R. 62, 72 (Ritchie, J., concurring). Along the same lines, see Chief Justice Laskin's comments, *per curiam*, in *Crevier v. A.G. Quebec*, [1981] 2 S.C.R. 220, 237. On this subject, consult P.W. Hogg, *supra*, n. 15, 1977, pp. 130 and 131; N. Duplé, "Nouvelles récentes de l'article 96" (1977), 18 *Cahiers de D.* 315.

60. Note once again that this federal participation is nevertheless based on the assumption that Parliament will use its power to create additional federal courts (s. 101) with circumspection.

61. *Supra*, n. 15, p. 131.

62. *The Constitution of Canada — A Suggested Amendment Relating to Provincial Administrative Tribunals*, Discussion Paper, Federal Department of Justice, 1983. We will deal with this proposed amendment at length later in this paper.

63. It appears that, without violating section 96, a legislature may withdraw certain functions from superior court judges and give them to district or county court judges. The fact that all of these judges are within the ambit of sections 96 to 100 of the *Constitution Act, 1867* might explain why the provinces have such legislative discretion; see *Attorney-General of British Columbia v. McKenzie*, [1965] S.C.R. 490; *Reference Constitutional Validity of Section 11 of the Judicature Amendment Act*, [1971] 2 O.R. 521 (Ont. C.A.). Nevertheless, it must be pointed out that the status of these judges is not identical, because section 99 of the 1867 Act does not apply to members of county and district courts. On this subject and some other aspects of problems of interpretation of section 96 not dealt with in this study, see: *Report on Administration of Ontario Courts*, Ontario Law Reform Commission, 1973, vol. 1, pp. 69–88; P.W. Hogg, *supra*, n. 15, pp. 119 and 133–34.

64. *Re Residential Tenancies Act, 1979*, [1981] 1 S.C.R. 714, 734–36 for the three-stage reasoning, and at p. 730 on the initial question of the judicial nature. Chief Justice Laskin has summarized, *per curiam*, the three-stage reasoning in *Massey Ferguson Indus-*

tries Ltd. v. Government of Saskatchewan, [1981] 2 S.C.R. 413, 429. Mr. Justice Chouinard repeated the summary, *per curiam*, in *Re Attorney-General of Quebec and Grondin* (1984), 4 D.L.R. (4th) 605 (S.C.C.).

65. See, in particular, *Minister of National Revenue v. Coopers and Lybrand*, [1979] 1 S.C.R. 495.

66. *Re Residential Tenancies Act, 1979*, [1981] 1 S.C.R. 714, 730, 735 and 743.

67. Nevertheless, in *A.G. of Quebec v. Blaikie*, [1979] 2 S.C.R. 1016 the Supreme Court ruled that the linguistic guarantees of section 133 of the *Constitution Act, 1867* contemplated not only courts of justice but also "non curial adjudicative agencies." It will be interesting to see which interpretation this expression receives in this different but still constitutional context. See also section 19 of the *Canadian Charter of Rights and Freedoms*, which partially repeats the text of section 133.

68. *Stelco Inc. v. Comn ission de la santé et de la sécurité au travail*, Juris-Express 84–441 (Que. S.C.).

69. *Re Attorney-General of Quebec and Grondin* (1984), 4 D.L.R. (4th) 605, 616 (S.C.C.).

70. The two decisions cited by Mr. Justice Chouinard as authorities on this point do not offer any reasons.

71. *L'Atelier 7 Inc. v. Babin et le Procureur général du Québec*, [1982] Que. C.A. 325. See also *Re S.B.I. Management Ltd.* (1982), 128 D.L.R. (3d) 89 (Alta. C.A.), under appeal to the Supreme Court of Canada; *Re Aamco Automatic Transmission Inc. and Simpson* (1981), 113 D.L.R. (3d) 650 (Ont. Div. Ct.).

72. *Re Residential Tenancies Act, 1979*, [1981] 1 S.C.R. 714, 730-34.

73. *Re Attorney-General of Quebec and Grondin* (1984), 4 D.L.R. (4th) 605 (S.C.C.).

74. *Re B.C. Family Relations Act*, [1982] 1 S.C.R. 62, 110 (Martland, Beetz, McIntyre and Chouinard, J.J. concurring). See also p. 109 as well as *Dupont v. Inglis*, [1958] S.C.R. 535, 542; *Canadian Broadcasting Corp. v. Quebec Police Commission*, [1979] 2 S.C.R. 618, 639-40; *Re Residential Tenancies Act, 1979*, [1981] 1 S.C.R. 714, 738.

75. *Re B.C. Family Relations Act*, [1982] 1 S.C.R. 62, 71 (Mr. Justice Ritchie, concurring). See also: *Séminaire de Chicoutimi v. City of Chicoutimi*, [1973] S.C.R. 681; *Attorney General for Ontario v. Victoria Medical Building Ltd.*, [1960] S.C.R. 32; *Re Residential Tenancies Act, 1979*, [1981] 1 S.C.R. 714, 745. Consult also *McEvoy v. A.G. of New Brunswick* (1983), 148 D.L.R. (3d) 25, 38 (S.C.C.).

76. *Renvoi touchant la constitutionnalité de la Loi concernant la juridiction de la Cour de magistrat*, [1965] Que. Q.B. 1 (Que. C.A.), reversed on technical grounds by the Supreme Court of Canada, [1965] S.C.R. 772.

77. *Reference re Proposed Legislation Concerning Leased Premises* [. . .] (1979), 89 D.L.R. (3d) 460, 466 (Alta. C.A.); *Re Pepita and Doukas* (1980), 101 D.L.R. (3d) 577, 585–87 (B.C.C.A.).

78. *Re B.C. Family Relations Act*, [1982] 1 S.C.R. 62, 72, 84–87, 104, 109–10. See also *Stelco Inc. v. Commission de la santé et de la sécurité au travail*, Juris-Express 84–441 (Que. S.-C.).

79. In *Residential Tenancies*, Mr. Justice Dickson noted, *per curiam*: "in the *Adoption Reference*, Duff C.J. looked to the historical practice in England and concluded that the jurisdiction conferred on magistrates under the legislation before the Court in the *Reference* was analogous to the jurisdiction under the English *Poor Law*, a jurisdiction which had belonged to courts of summary nature rather than to Superior Courts. On this basis, the legislation was upheld." *Re Residential Tenancies Act, 1979*, [1981] 1 S.C.R. 714, 729-30.

80. *Re Attorney-General of Quebec and Grondin* (1984), 4 D.L.R. (4th) 605 (S.C.C.). We may ask also if the Supreme Court would have refused leave to appeal from a judgment of the Nova Scotia Court of Appeal dealing with the unconstitutionality of certain judicial powers of the province's Residential Tenancies Board: *Re Burke and Arab* (1982), 130 D.L.R. (3d) 38 (N.S.C.A.) and *Attorney-General of Nova Scotia v. Burke*, [1983] 1 S.C.R. 55. On rentals commissions, see also *Re Pepita and Doukas* (1980), 101 D.L.R. (3d) 577, 585–87 (B.C.C.A.).

81. *Re: B.C. Family Relations Act*, [1982] 1 S.C.R. 62.

82. *Crevier v. A.G. Quebec*, [1981] 2 S.C.R. 220, 237. For the differences that existed previously both in case law and doctrine, see P.W. Hogg, "Is Judicial Review of Administrative Action Guaranteed by the British North America Act?" (1976), 54 *Can. Bar Rev.* 716. See also the very different opinion of Professor Bora Laskin: "Certiorari to Labour Board: The Apparent Futility of Privative Clauses" (1952), 30 *Can. Bar Rev.* 986, pp. 989–91. Refer also to: H. Arthurs, "Protection Against Judicial Review" (1983), 43 *R. du B.* 277; D.J. Mullan, "The Constitutional Position of Canada's Administrative Appeal Tribunals" (1982), 14 *Ottawa L.R.* 239; R. Dussault and M. Patenaude, "Le contrôle judiciaire de l'administration: vers une meilleure synthèse des valeurs de liberté individuelle et de justice sociale" (1983), 43 *R. du B.* 163, pp. 174–80; R.A. Macdonald, "Constitutional Law — Validity of Legislation — Privative Clause Ousting Judicial Review — Crevier v. Attorney General for Quebec" (1983), 17 *U.B.C.L.R.* 111; B.L. Strayer, *The Canadian Constitution and the Courts*, 2nd ed., 1983, pp. 76–86.

83. A privative clause that is not watertight is not unconstitutional: see *Re Attorney-General of Quebec and Grondin* (1984), 4 D.L.R. (4th) 605 (S.C.C.); *Théroux v. Brosseau*, [1983] Que. C.A. 350. See also *Capital Regional District v. Concerned Citizens of British Columbia*, [1982] 2 S.C.R. 842. In *Crevier*, [1981] 2 S.C.R. 220, Chief Justice Laskin recognized that a privative clause may prevent superior courts from exercising judicial review relative to errors committed by lower courts and administrative bodies within their jurisdiction, that is errors that do not go to the jurisdiction of the institution contemplated by the privative clause. Nevertheless the Chief Justice candidly admitted that: "There may be differences of opinion as to what are questions of jurisdiction" (p. 236).

84. See also *Séminaire de Chicoutimi v. City of Chicoutimi*, [1973] S.C.R. 681, and *Attorney General for Ontario v. Victoria Medical Building Ltd.*, [1960] S.C.R. 32.

85. *Re Evans and Employment Standards Board* (1983), 149 D.L.R. (3d) 1.

86. *Desmeules v. Le prêt hypothécaire*, [1983] Que. C.A. 43. Leave to appeal granted by the Supreme Court of Canada.

87. The Quebec National Assembly has given a number of appellate jurisdictions to bodies other than "section 96 courts," for example, the Provincial Court, the Labour Court, the Social Affairs Commission, the Real Estate Evaluation Revision Board, the Professions Tribunal, the Public Service Board, the Municipal Commission, the Police Commission, etc.

88. Consult more particularly J.F. Jobin, *supra*, n. 41; D.J. Mullan, *supra*, n. 82.

89. *A.G. Quebec v. Farrah*, [1978] 2 S.C.R. 638, 642–43 (Spence, Dickson and Estey, J.J. concurring). See also *Dupont v. Inglis*, [1958] S.C.R. 535, reversing (1957), 8 D.L.R. (2d) 26 (Ont. C.A.).

90. *Crevier v. A.G. Quebec*, [1981] 2 S.C.R. 220, 230.

91. Mullan, *supra*, n. 82, p. 259.

92. [1982] 2 S.C.R. 842.

93. On this subject, see certain passages from a decision of the Quebec Court of Appeal: *Commission municipale du Québec v. Ville de Lévis*, [1979] Que. C.A. 28, leave to appeal refused by the Supreme Court of Canada (see original French). In the judgment dealing with the constitutionality of the Quebec Transport Tribunal, Chief Justice Laskin quickly eliminated some appellate responsibilities of this tribunal in stating simply that: "Neither s. 58(b) nor s. 56 involves a function which can be designated as 'judicial' for the purposes of s. 96": *A.G. Quebec v. Farrah*, [1978] 2 S.C.R. 638, 644. See also *Re Gray Line of Victoria and Chabot* (1981), 125 D.L.R. (3d) 197 (B.C.S.C.). In *Concerned Citizens* Chief Justice Laskin made the following laconic observation: "There are no express directions in s. 12(5) that compel the Lieutenant-Governor in Council to yield to a purely judicial assessment of an appeal [. . .] Policy remains open to a body which is a policy-making tribunal." [1982] 2 S.C.R. 842, 851.

94. The Quebec Court of Appeal has demonstrated a certain sensitivity to this type of preoccupation in concluding, unlike the Supreme Court, that the Professions Tribunal does not violate section 96: *Procureur général du Québec v. Crevier*, [1979] Que. C.A. 333. See also *Re Evans and Employment Standards Board* (1983), 149 D.L.R. (3d) 1. (B.C.C.A.).

95. *Re Residential Tenancies Act, 1979,* [1981] 1 S.C.R. 714, 733. Chief Justice Laskin summarizes *Farrah* differently in *Re B.C. Family Relations Act,* [1982] 1 S.C.R. 62, 69.

96. *Re B.C. Family Relations Act,* [1982] 1 S.C.R. 62, 106 and 107. Nevertheless, it should be added that this generous viewpoint hardly appears compatible with certain parts of Mr. Justice Dickson's opinion (*per curiam*) in *Re Residential Tenancies Act, 1979,* [1981] 1 S.C.R. 714, 749.

97. *Re B.C. Family Relations Act,* [1982] 1 S.C.R. 62, 72.

98. *Re Residential Tenancies Act, 1979,* [1981] 1 S.C.R. 714, 735-36.

99. See our observations on this subject in the section on the judicial nature of the function in question.

100. *Re Residential Tenancies Act, 1979,* [1981] 1 S.C.R. 714, 745.

101. *Capital Regional District v. Concerned Citizens of British Columbia,* [1982] 2 S.C.R. 842, 851.

102. *Re Residential Tenancies Act, 1979,* [1981] 1 S.C.R. 714, 733.

103. *Re: B.C. Family Relations Act,* [1982] 1 S.C.R. 62, 68.

104. Ibid., p. 106.

105. *Re Residential Tenancies Act, 1979,* [1981] 1 S.C.R. 714, 732-33.

106. *Capital Regional District v. Concerned Citizens of British Columbia,* [1982] 2 S.C.R. 842, 851. See also p. 854. As we have already indicated, Chief Justice Laskin is open to criticism for not having gone into greater detail whether or not, under the circumstances, the appeal was effectively a devolution of judicial functions.

107. *Corporation of the City of Mississauga v. Regional Municipality of Peel,* [1979] 2 S.C.R. 244.

108. *Théroux v. Brosseau,* [1983] Que. C.A. 350, 361-62. See also *Re Inman and Ivor* (1982), 134 D.L.R. (3d) 717 (Ont. Div. Ct.).

109. *Re Attorney-General of Nova Scotia and Gillis* (1980), 111 D.L.R. 349, 359.

110. *Re Residential Tenancies Act, 1979,* [1981] 1 S.C.R. 714, 746-47. See also Chief Justice Laskin's notes in *Crevier,* [1981] 2 S.C.R. 220, 233-34. In *McEvoy v. A.G. of New Brunswick* the Supreme Court of Canada ruled that the criminal court in question violated 96 in particular on the following grounds: "nor will the court exercise administrative powers to which its adjudicative functions are incidental" (1983), 148 D.L.R. (3d) 25, 36 (S.C.C.).

111. See, for example, the application of the institutional setting theory in *Re Scowby and Glendenning* (1983), 148 D.L.R. (3d) 55 (Sask. C.A.). The question was whether the Human Rights Commission was contemplated by section 96. Leave to appeal granted by the Supreme Court of Canada.

112. *Contra: Re Murdy and City of Toronto* (1981), 118 D.L.R. (3d) 304 (Ont. Div. Ct.).

113. See *Re B.C. Family Relations Act,* [1982] 1 S.C.R. 62, 106-7.

114. S. Bouchard, M.-M. Lavigne, and P. Renaud, "L'inconstitutionnalité des pouvoirs du protonotaire spécial" (1981), 22 *Cahiers de D.* 429.

115. *The Constitution of Canada, supra,* n. 62.

116. Ibid., p. 7.

117. See also: *Rapport du Comité conjoint de l'Association du Barreau canadien (Section Québec) et du Barreau du Québec sur l'avant-projet de modification relative aux tribunaux administratifs provinciaux,* January 1984; Canadian Bar Association, *A Response to the Minister of Justice and Attorney-General of Canada on the Discussion Paper: The Constitution of Canada, A Suggested Amendment Relating to Provincial Administrative Tribunals,* February 1984; Laval University, *Colloque sur la réforme des institutions fédérales,* March 1984, summary of communications presented on *La réforme de l'article 96 de la Loi constitutionnelle de 1867.*

118. *Séminaire de Chicoutimi v. City of Chicoutimi,* [1973] S.C.R. 681.

119. See *Re B.C. Family Relations Act,* [1982] 1 S.C.R. 62, 106-7.

120. *Théberge Limitée v. Le Syndicat national des employés de l'aluminium d'Arvida,* [1966] S.C.R. 378.

121. *A.G. Quebec v. Blaikie*, [1979] 2 S.C.R. 1016.

122. *Attorney-General v. British Broadcasting Corporation*, [1980] 3 A11 E.R. 161, 175 (Lord Edmund-Davies). Also, for example, the Quebec Police Commission was considered as a "court" for the purposes of a particular statute: S*nyder v. Montreal Gazette Ltd.*, [1978] Que. S.C. 32.

123. *Supra*, n. 62, p. 12.

124. Ibid., p. 8.

125. See, for example, *Teamsters Union v. Massicotte*, [1982] 1 S.C.R. 710.

126. *Crevier v. A.G. of Quebec*, [1981] 2 S.C.R. 220, 236-37.

127. *Supra*, n. 62, p. 14.

128. (1983), 148 D.L.R. (3d) 25 (S.C.C.).

129. On the jurisdiction of the Canadian Parliament to assign judicial functions to provincial institutions, see the subsection on the existence of an integrated judicial system.

130. See, for example, *Re: B.C. Family Relations Act*, [1982] 1 S.C.R. 62, 76. See, specifically, P.W. Hogg, *supra*, n. 82.

131. *Northern Telecom Canada Ltd. v. Communication Workers of Canada* (1983), 147 D.L.R. (3d) 1, 17 (S.C.C.). See also *Commonwealth of Puerto Rico v. Hernandez*, [1975] 1 S.C.R. 228; *Solicitor General of Canada v. Law Society of British Columbia and Jabour*, [1982] 2 S.C.R. 307; *Canadian Labour Relations Board v. Paul L'Anglais Inc.*, [1983] 1 S.C.R. 147. Nevertheless, *Jabour* and *Paul L'Anglais Inc.* establish that the Canadian Parliament may not withdraw from the provincial superior courts their traditional responsibility in the judicial review of the constitutionality of federal statutes and of decisions made by federal administrative bodies. But section 96 was not cited to support this limit on the jurisdiction of Parliament. As for the concurrent jurisdiction of the Federal Court in similar matters, now made extremely complicated following precedents limiting the Court's jurisdiction to the application of existing federal law, see *Northern Telecom Canada Ltd. v. Communications Workers of Canada* (1983), 147 D.L.R. (3d) 1. The transfer of judicial review from the provincial superior courts to the Federal Court was accomplished with section 18 of the *Federal Court Act*, R.S.C. 1970, c. 10 (2nd supp.); there is no need here to consider the exceptions to this jurisdiction of the Federal Court. On the specific problem of judicial review of the constitutionality of statutes, see B.L. Strayer, *supra*, n. 82, pp. 63-104. The exercise of judicial review by the provincial superior courts over federal administrative bodies is quite unique testimony of the existence, before 1970, of an integrated judicial system in Canada.

132. *Supreme Court of Canada Act*, R.S.C. 1970, c. S-19; *Federal Court Act*, R.S.C. 1970, c. 10 (2nd supp.). See also the *Judges Act*, R.S.C. 1970, c. J-1. Pursuant to the statutes cited above, Federal Court judges have a status comparable to that of the judges of the superior provincial courts; one noteworthy difference is that the retirement age of Federal Court judges is 70 and not 75. Consult P.W. Hogg, *supra*, n. 15, pp. 126-27.

133. W.R. Lederman, *supra*, n. 40, pp. 1175-76; R. Elliott, "Constitutional Law — Judicature — Is Section 96 Binding on Parliament?" (1982), 16 *U.B.C.L.R.* 314; D.J. Mullan, *supra*, n. 82, pp. 260-69.

134. *Reference Re Establishment of a Unified Criminal Court of New Brunswick* (1982), 127 D.L.R. (3d) 214, 222.

135. Under sections 92(14) and 91(27) of the *Constitution Act, 1867*, the legislatures are responsible for the creation of courts of criminal jurisdiction. As to whether or not section 101 may authorize Parliament to do otherwise on the grounds that it is empowered to create additional federal courts of criminal jurisdiction "notwithstanding anything in this Act," see P.W. Hogg, *supra*, n. 15, 1977, p. 124, n. 43. Note in passing that the Federal Court exercises some criminal jurisdictions; section 3 of the *Federal Court Act* specifies that the Court "shall continue to be a superior court of record having civil and criminal jurisdiction."

136. *McEvoy v. A.G. of New Brunswick* (1983), 148 D.L.R. (3d) 25 (S.C.C.).

137. See G. Lehoux, "McEvoy c. P.G. du N.B. et P.G. du Can: une autre pièce au temple de la justice canadienne" (1983), 14 *Revue générale de droit* 169; R. Elliott, "New Brunswick Unified Criminal Court Reference" (1984), 18 *U.B.C.L.R.* 127.

138. *McEvoy v. A.G. of New Brunswick* (1983), 148 D.L.R. (3d) 25, 38 (S.C.C.).

139. Ibid.

140. Ibid., pp. 37 and 38.

141. Ibid., p. 38.

142. Ibid., p. 36.

143. "Unreviewable authority might put the provincially-established court and its provincially-appointed judges in a s. 96 position notwithstanding that its jurisdiction comes from Parliament. *Crevier v. A.G. Que et al.* [. . .] might be considered as apt." Ibid.

144. Ibid., pp. 37–39.

145. I believe that given, for example, the important responsibilities in criminal matters exercised by justices of the peace before 1867, there is no certainty that every federal legislative provision assigning an important criminal jurisdiction to provincially appointed judges violates section 96. On this question, however, it is necessary to take into consideration the following passage from the Supreme Court decision: "There is no doubt that jurisdiction to try indictable offences was part of the superior court's jurisdiction in 1867; none of the parties suggests otherwise. Nor does anyone argue that lower courts had concurrent jurisdiction to try indictable offences in 1867." *McEvoy v. A.G. New Brunswick* (1983), 148 D.L.R. (3d) 25, 36. (S.C.C.)

146. See *Northern Telecom Canada Ltd. v. Communications Workers of Canada*, (1983), 147 D.L.R. (3d) 1 (S.C.C.).

147. To summarize briefly the thesis of Professor Lederman, sections 96 to 100 apply to the Canadian Parliament but are respected if the governments delegate federal judicial functions to federal courts presided over by judges with a comparable legal status pursuant to federal legislation. See W.R. Lederman's article, *supra*, n. 40, and also his article, *supra*, n. 10, pp. 221–24. Though he offers different grounds, Professor Elliott expresses a similar view in his article "Constitutional Law — Judicature — Is Section 96 Binding on Parliament?" (1982), 16 *U.B.C.L.R.* 314.

148. See the subsection entitled, "A Pandora's Box: The Concept of Authority Other than a Court."

149. *Re Residential Tenancies Act, 1979*, [1981] 1 S.C.R. 714, 749–50. See also Chief Justice Laskin's opinion, *supra*, n. 59; the Chief Justice appears to invite the political authorities to correct the constitutional "anomaly" that section 96 represents.

150. Brun and Tremblay, *supra*, n. 9, p. 531. Here the authors allude not only to problems raised by section 96 but also to the dispute over delimitation of the Federal Court's jurisdiction.

151. Canadian Bar Association, *supra*, n. 117.

152. Note that in a document published in August 1983 by the federal Department of Justice and entitled *Proposals to Amend the Federal Court Act* we find the following passage: "While as a matter of general principle, it is neither practical nor desirable to have two judicial systems, one dealing with subject matters under section 91 of the *Constitution Act, 1867* and the other with those falling within section 92, it is useful to have throughout Canada a specialized Federal Court that exercises jurisdiction in certain well-defined areas" (p. 2).

153. See also N. Duplé, "La réforme constitutionnelle de l'article 96 de l'Acte de l'Amérique du Nord britannique, 1867," in S. Beck and I. Bernier (eds.), *Canada and the New Constitution: The Unfinished Agenda*, 1983, vol. 1, p. 129.

154. W. Murphy and C.H. Prickett, *Courts, Judges and Politics*, 1961, p. 156.

155. *A Future Together: Observations and Recommendations*, 1979, p. 109. Of course provincial lower courts are also required to apply federal laws.

Richard W. Bauman is Assistant Professor in the Faculty of Law, Dalhousie University, Halifax.

Henri Brun is Professor in the Faculty of Law, Université Laval, Quebec.

Mary Eberts is a barrister with the law firm of Tory, Tory, DesLauriers and Binnington, Toronto.

A. Wayne MacKay is Professor in the Faculty of Law, Dalhousie University, Halifax, and is also Assistant Research Coordinator for the Institutional and Constitutional Arrangements section of the Legal and Constitutional Research Area, Royal Commission on the Economic Union and Development Prospects for Canada.

Gilles Pépin is Professor in the Faculty of Law, University of Montreal.

THE COLLECTED RESEARCH STUDIES

Royal Commission on the Economic Union and Development Prospects for Canada

ECONOMICS

Income Distribution and Economic Security in Canada (Vol.1), *François Vaillancourt, Research Coordinator*

Vol. 1   Income Distribution and Economic Security in Canada, *F. Vaillancourt* (C)*

Industrial Structure (Vols. 2-8), *Donald G. McFetridge, Research Coordinator*

Vol. 2   Canadian Industry in Transition, *D.G. McFetridge* (C)
Vol. 3   Technological Change in Canadian Industry, *D.G. McFetridge* (C)
Vol. 4   Canadian Industrial Policy in Action, *D.G. McFetridge* (C)
Vol. 5   Economics of Industrial Policy and Strategy, *D.G. McFetridge* (C)
Vol. 6   The Role of Scale in Canada–US Productivity Differences, *J.R. Baldwin and P.K. Gorecki* (M)
Vol. 7   Competition Policy and Vertical Exchange, *F. Mathewson and R. Winter* (M)
Vol. 8   The Political Economy of Economic Adjustment, *M. Trebilcock* (M)

International Trade (Vols. 9-14), *John Whalley, Research Coordinator*

Vol. 9   Canadian Trade Policies and the World Economy, *J. Whalley with C. Hamilton and R. Hill* (M)
Vol. 10 Canada and the Multilateral Trading System, *J. Whalley* (M)
Vol. 11 Canada–United States Free Trade, *J. Whalley* (C)
Vol. 12 Domestic Policies and the International Economic Environment, *J. Whalley* (C)
Vol. 13 Trade, Industrial Policy and International Competition, *R. Harris* (M)
Vol. 14 Canada's Resource Industries and Water Export Policy, *J. Whalley* (C)

Labour Markets and Labour Relations (Vols. 15-18), *Craig Riddell, Research Coordinator*

Vol. 15 Labour-Management Cooperation in Canada, *C. Riddell* (C)
Vol. 16 Canadian Labour Relations, *C. Riddell* (C)
Vol. 17 Work and Pay: The Canadian Labour Market, *C. Riddell* (C)
Vol. 18 Adapting to Change: Labour Market Adjustment in Canada, *C. Riddell* (C)

Macroeconomics (Vols. 19-25), *John Sargent, Research Coordinator*

Vol. 19 Macroeconomic Performance and Policy Issues: Overviews, *J. Sargent* (M)
Vol. 20 Post-War Macroeconomic Developments, *J. Sargent* (C)
Vol. 21 Fiscal and Monetary Policy, *J. Sargent* (C)
Vol. 22 Economic Growth: Prospects and Determinants, *J. Sargent* (C)
Vol. 23 Long-Term Economic Prospects for Canada: A Symposium, *J. Sargent* (C)
Vol. 24 Foreign Macroeconomic Experience: A Symposium, *J. Sargent* (C)
Vol. 25 Dealing with Inflation and Unemployment in Canada, *C. Riddell* (M)

Economic Ideas and Social Issues (Vols. 26 and 27), *David Laidler, Research Coordinator*

Vol. 26 Approaches to Economic Well-Being, *D. Laidler* (C)
Vol. 27 Responses to Economic Change, *D. Laidler* (C)

---

* (C) denotes a Collection of studies by various authors coordinated by the person named.
(M) denotes a Monograph.

POLITICS AND INSTITUTIONS OF GOVERNMENT

Canada and the International Political Economy (Vols. 28-30), *Denis Stairs and Gilbert R. Winham, Research Coordinators*

Vol. 28 Canada and the International Political/Economic Environment, *D. Stairs and G.R. Winham* (C)
Vol. 29 The Politics of Canada's Economic Relationship with the United States, *D. Stairs and G.R. Winham* (C)
Vol. 30 Selected Problems in Formulating Foreign Economic Policy, *D. Stairs and G.R. Winham* (C)

State and Society in the Modern Era (Vols. 31 and 32), *Keith Banting, Research Coordinator*

Vol. 31 State and Society: Canada in Comparative Perspective, *K. Banting* (C)
Vol. 32 The State and Economic Interests, *K. Banting* (C)

Constitutionalism, Citizenship and Society (Vols. 33-35), *Alan Cairns and Cynthia Williams, Research Coordinators*

Vol. 33 Constitutionalism, Citizenship and Society in Canada, *A. Cairns and C. Williams* (C)
Vol. 34 The Politics of Gender, Ethnicity and Language in Canada, *A. Cairns and C. Williams* (C)
Vol. 35 Public Opinion and Public Policy in Canada, *R. Johnston* (M)

Representative Institutions (Vols. 36-39), *Peter Aucoin, Research Coordinator*

Vol. 36 Party Government and Regional Representation in Canada, *P. Aucoin* (C)
Vol. 37 Regional Responsiveness and the National Administrative State, *P. Aucoin* (C)
Vol. 38 Institutional Reforms for Representative Government, *P. Aucoin* (C)
Vol. 39 Intrastate Federalism in Canada, *D.V. Smiley and R.L. Watts* (M)

The Politics of Economic Policy (Vols. 40-43), *G. Bruce Doern, Research Coordinator*

Vol. 40 The Politics of Economic Policy, *G.B. Doern* (C)
Vol. 41 Federal and Provincial Budgeting, *A.M. Maslove, M.J. Prince and G.B. Doern* (M)
Vol. 42 Economic Regulation and the Federal System, *R. Schultz and A. Alexandroff* (M)
Vol. 43 Bureaucracy in Canada: Control and Reform, *S.L. Sutherland and G.B. Doern* (M)

Industrial Policy (Vols. 44 and 45), *André Blais, Research Coordinator*

Vol. 44 Canadian Industrial Policy, *A. Blais* (C)
Vol. 45 The Political Sociology of Industrial Policy, *A. Blais* (M)

LAW AND CONSTITUTIONAL ISSUES

Law, Society and the Economy (Vols. 46-51), *Ivan Bernier and Andrée Lajoie, Research Coordinators*

Vol. 46 Law, Society and the Economy, *I. Bernier and A. Lajoie* (C)
Vol. 47 The Supreme Court of Canada as an Instrument of Political Change, *I. Bernier and A. Lajoie* (C)
Vol. 48 Regulations, Crown Corporations and Administrative Tribunals, *I. Bernier and A. Lajoie* (C)
Vol. 49 Family Law and Social Welfare Legislation in Canada, *I. Bernier and A. Lajoie* (C)
Vol. 50 Consumer Protection, Environmental Law and Corporate Power, *I. Bernier and A. Lajoie* (C)
Vol. 51 Labour Law and Urban Law in Canada, *I. Bernier and A. Lajoie* (C)

The International Legal Environment (Vols. 52-54), *John Quinn, Research Coordinator*

Vol. 52 The International Legal Environment, *J. Quinn* (C)
Vol. 53 Canadian Economic Development and the International Trading System, *M.M. Hart* (M)
Vol. 54 Canada and the New International Law of the Sea, *D.M. Johnston* (M)

Harmonization of Laws in Canada (Vols. 55 and 56), *Ronald C.C. Cuming, Research Coordinator*

Vol. 55 Perspectives on the Harmonization of Law in Canada, *R. Cuming* (C)
Vol. 56 Harmonization of Business Law in Canada, *R. Cuming* (C)

Institutional and Constitutional Arrangements (Vols. 57 and 58), *Clare F. Beckton and A. Wayne MacKay, Research Coordinators*

Vol. 57 Recurring Issues in Canadian Federalism, *C.F. Beckton and A.W. MacKay* (C)
Vol. 58 The Courts and The Charter, *C.F. Beckton and A.W. MacKay* (C)

FEDERALISM AND THE ECONOMIC UNION

Federalism and The Economic Union (Vols. 58-72), *Mark Krasnick, Kenneth Norrie and Richard Simeon, Research Coordinators*

Vol. 59 Federalism and Economic Union in Canada, *K. Norrie, R. Simeon and M. Krasnick* (M)
Vol. 60 Perspectives on the Canadian Economic Union, *M. Krasnick* (C)
Vol. 61 Division of Powers and Public Policy, *R. Simeon* (C)
Vol. 62 Case Studies in the Division of Powers, *M. Krasnick* (C)
Vol. 63 Intergovernmental Relations, *R. Simeon* (C)
Vol. 64 Disparities and Interregional Adjustment, *K. Norrie* (C)
Vol. 65 Fiscal Federalism, *M. Krasnick* (C)
Vol. 66 Mobility of Capital in the Canadian Economic Union, *N. Roy* (M)
Vol. 67 Economic Management and the Division of Powers, *T.J. Courchene* (M)
Vol. 68 Regional Aspects of Confederation, *J. Whalley* (M)
Vol. 69 Interest Groups in the Canadian Federal System, *H.G. Thorburn* (M)
Vol. 70 Canada and Quebec, Past and Future: An Essay, *D. Latouche* (M)
Vol. 71 The Political Economy of Canadian Federalism: 1940–1984, *R. Simeon* (M)

THE NORTH

Vol. 72 The North, *Michael S. Whittington, Coordinator* (C)

COMMISSION ORGANIZATION

Chairman

Donald S. Macdonald

Commissioners

Clarence L. Barber	William M. Hamilton	Daryl K. Seaman
Albert Breton	John R. Messer	Thomas K. Shoyama
M. Angela Cantwell Peters	Laurent Picard	Jean Casselman-Wadds
E. Gérard Docquier	Michel Robert	Catherine T. Wallace

Senior Officers

Executive Director
J. Gerald Godsoe

Director of Policy	*Senior Advisors*	*Directors of Research*
Alan Nymark	David Ablett	Ivan Bernier
	Victor Clarke	Alan Cairns
Secretary	Carl Goldenberg	David C. Smith
Michel Rochon	Harry Stewart	
Director of Administration	*Director of Publishing*	*Co-Directors of Research*
Sheila-Marie Cook	Ed Matheson	Kenneth Norrie
		John Sargent

Research Program Organization

Economics	Politics and the Institutions of Government	Law and Constitutional Issues
Research Director	*Research Director*	*Research Director*
David C. Smith	Alan Cairns	Ivan Bernier
Executive Assistant & Assistant Director (Research Services)	*Executive Assistant*	*Executive Assistant & Research Program Administrator*
I. Lilla Connidis	Karen Jackson	Jacques J.M. Shore
Coordinators	*Coordinators*	*Coordinators*
David Laidler	Peter Aucoin	Clare F. Beckton
Donald G. McFetridge	Keith Banting	Ronald C.C. Cuming
Kenneth Norrie*	André Blais	Mark Krasnick
Craig Riddell	Bruce Doern	Andrée Lajoie
John Sargent*	Richard Simeon	A. Wayne MacKay
François Vaillancourt	Denis Stairs	John J. Quinn
John Whalley	Cynthia Williams	
	Gilbert R. Winham	
Research Analysts	*Research Analysts*	*Administrative and Research Assistant*
Caroline Digby	Claude Desranleau	Nicolas Roy
Mireille Ethier	Ian Robinson	
Judith Gold		*Research Analyst*
Douglas S. Green	*Office Administration*	Nola Silzer
Colleen Hamilton	Donna Stebbing	
Roderick Hill		
Joyce Martin		

*Kenneth Norrie and John Sargent co-directed the final phase of Economics Research with David Smith